# HEIGHTS OF
# WEALTH

## JANET DIANE MOURGLIA-SWERDLOW

Expansions Publishing Company, Inc.
Saint Joseph, Michigan
USA

Copyright © 2021 Expansions Publishing Company, Inc.

Published by:    Expansions Publishing Company, Inc.
P.O. Box 12
Saint Joseph Michigan 49085 USA
269-519-8036
Skype: eventsatexpansions
customersupport@expansions.com
www.expansions.com

ISBN: 978-1-7349281-3-6

Cover Photo by Jonathan J. Swerdlow
www.jonathanswerdlow.com

# Books by Stewart A. Swerdlow & Janet Diane Mourglia-Swerdlow

*13-Cubed: Case Studies in Mind-Control & Programming*
*13-Cubed Squared: More Case Studies in Mind-Control & Programming*

*1099 Daily Affirmations for Self-Change*

*Alternative Medical Apocrypha: Body-Mind Correlations*

*Blue Blood, True Blood: Conflict & Creation*

*Decoding Your Life: An Experiential Course in Self-Reintegration*

*Healer's Handbook: A Journey Into Hyperspace*

*Healing Archetypes and Symbols*

*Heights of Deprogramming*
*Heights of Health*
*Heights of Relationships*
*Heights of Spirituality*
*Heights of Wealth*

*Hyperspace Helper*

*Hyperspace Plus*

*King Bee, Queen Bee*

*Little Fluffs Children's Series*

*Montauk: Alien Connection*
*Revelations of Time & Space, History and God*

*Stewart Says…*

*Template of God-Mind*

*True Reality of Sexuality*

*True World History: Humanity's Saga*

*White Owl Legends: An Archetypal Story of Creation*

# Dedication

To
Robert Austin Mourglia
Born 1926
The Father of My Earth Body
Guardian of My  Soul-Personality in this Lifeline
Who Taught Me to Respect the Universal Spiritual Laws of Life
and Gave Me the Priceless
Gift of Time.

# Contents

# Introduction

My father tells stories of his childhood growing up in a small rural town in Southwestern Missouri. In those days, most people had a garden and raised a good share of their food because this was their only option. At 12 years old his father put him to work in a filling station. My dad was resentful that he had to pay for everything from that day forward. So, he joined the military at 17 years old and went to war. My dad said when he moved away from his home town, he thought the Stock Market was a place where cattle were bought and sold. My mother told stories of her family loading up the pickup truck at night, her mother driving, and her father standing on the running board with his rifle, searching for wild game. She was proud that during the Depression her family always had food because they also raised a garden and most of their food.

Living in Seattle, far from their families was actually very brave. Considering their upbringing, it was amazing how they were able to raise a family and handle their finances. Making ends meet was a challenge for my parents. As a young child, I never thought too much about money because I trusted my parents to provide. When I didn't get the things I wanted, it did not cross my mind that I had any control over this until I reached my early teen years. Then, I found that by hard work I could get what I wanted. I learned to sew so I had clothes that I liked; I babysat to get my first set of contact lenses and my beloved Norwegian Elkhound as well as extras like fancy shoes and make-up. Being able to purchase what I wanted made me feel independent and powerful like I could accomplish whatever I set my mind to do.

Like the majority of people, I always wanted more money to get more things. The world was my oyster and all I had to do was work hard. When I published my first book in my mid-twenties I knew it would be a best seller and make millions of dollars. Well, when that didn't happen my world came crashing down. Thus I really began my study of Wealth. What surprised me the most was that I needed more than hard work and that Wealth was much more than money. This forced me to delve into my mind-pattern and appreciate absolutely everything in my life, both positive and negative. My dad told me how he learned to carry a $100 bill in his pocket to give him the feeling of Wealth. He said at one time he didn't have more than a few cents in his pocket, so this gave his mind-pattern a boost. I have used this trick for many years. I loved the feeling of having $100 with me at all times. Thankfully and gratefully, my dad worked on his mind-pattern and is financially independent, even coming to my financial rescue several times when my business was viciously attacked.

I would love to tell you that I know everything there is about Wealth, but like any subject, there is always something to learn. I have definitely come a long way. But, it is a long and arduous journey out of mind-patterns of low Self-Worth/Value and suffering, all of which are inherent in my genetics. Add in a dash of Poverty Programming and you have quite a soup to sort through. In this book, you will find my journey which I have shared over the years in my Expansions' study blogs. Self-observation and contemplation have helped me as well as thousands of others from around the world who have participated in these blogs.

*Take your time.*

*Don't rush.*

*Ask a lot of questions.*

*Build a sturdy foundational mind-pattern that will bring you True Wealth in the way that is most correct and beneficial for you.*

*Wishing You Blessings in All That You Do!*

# Beyond Lies of Limitations

You are well-positioned to break out of the Lies of Limitations that you have allowed others to place on you. You are going to find the limitations that you didn't even know you had so that you can increase your forward movement. You only think that you are beyond limitations, so by identifying them, you stretch your thinking even further.

I remember feeling the bottom drop out of my world when I realized that Santa Claus wasn't real. I trusted that lie. When I realized it was a fake story, I tried to keep on going like nothing was wrong but inside I think it set the stage for glossing over the truth. It is a challenge when you realize that those who you are supposed to trust set up a lie for you to live and love and believe in.

Another example, in school we were taught that you could be President of the US if you wanted to be—that everyone has an equal chance. Not that I wanted to be President, but it never crossed my mind that I "couldn't be" with the way the system is set up. All the Presidents are related, which has been proved numerous times, but this wasn't taught in school, or anywhere else in my world. So, I still was living within the "lie".

Accepting one lie opens the frequency for a multitude of lies to invade your personal space. You don't know the lies from the Truth.

- What were the first lies that you remember that limited how you viewed your Self and or the World?
- What lie did you live that expanded your belief of who you are or could be, that never materialized for you?
- How did this affect your attitude and life?

Some lies don't appear to be Self-limiting, but they clearly define your path in a way that makes you feel unlimited. But when the path doesn't take you the way you think it should, then you feel like a failure.

When I published my first book in 1990, I felt totally free and unlimited; the world was my oyster. I had dreams of being on Oprah and my book floating to the top of the bestseller charts. There was not a doubt in my mind that this would easily happen. Of course, I've certainly learned through the years, why it wouldn't, but at the time, I tried and tried and tried. Then, when I went the "I don't know anybody" route, such as famous people who could put me where I wanted to be, my Oversoul said I have it which is way better than famous people.

In the meantime, I watched myriads of other authors rapidly rise into the public eye, selling more books in one year than I have sold in the decades I have had my books out. I have really had to learn how to break through my own lies of limitations as well as those that I accepted from the outside world. And, sometimes, I realize, I broke through one set of lies to replace them with another set of lies.

## Replacing Lies with Lies

I was raised on sugar. I ate toast with sugar-sweetened jam or sugar-coated cereals or coffee cake with sugar-sweetened fruit juice for breakfast every day. I had cookies for lunch, dessert after dinner, and sometimes a sugar-filled bedtime snack. My mother even put sugar in the vegetables "to bring out their natural sweetness".

As I became more nutritionally aware in my early twenties, I stopped eating so much sugar, or so I thought.

I ate fruit instead, including fruit-juice sweetened jams. Tons and tons of fruit. Instead of white sugar, I changed to honey, fruit syrups, and maple syrup. I didn't know that I was exchanging one sugar for another sugar. I did start cutting down my use of all commonly-labeled sugars, but other sugars took their place.

Carbohydrates are another word for sugar. One of my favorite snacks was corn chips with salsa. I didn't realize that corn chips are sugar. I made desserts using flour for crust and fruit-juice sweetened jams and thought I was making a sugar-free dessert. I ate whole-grain toast with butter. More sugar.

As much as I knew, as many years as I studied and read, I still was eating too much sugar. All the women's magazines and diet ads; even health food magazines do not address all the sugars that you eat. Sugar-free is not sugar-free. When I read these articles I think about all the people who religiously follow the advice contained in the articles without a clue that they are still consuming sugar.

Lies, lies, lies. I exchanged one lie for another. I ask my Self if I had known, would I have done things differently. I would like to answer yes, but then I have to ask if I was ready to hear the Truth.

- Are there times when you exchanged one lie for another because you weren't ready for the Truth?
- Have you fallen into a nutritional lie?

**Money Lies**

One of the best lies out there is that you should not have money. I can't tell you how many people have tried to discredit Stewart and I and our work because we charge money. Yet, people do not think twice about giving to their church. Organized religion is amazingly wealthy, yet organized religion often talks about the evil of money. Every society has some form of energy exchange.

- How have you fallen into the money-is-evil lie that holds you back from receiving the limitless Wealth of the universe?
- How about the lie that you don't deserve?
- Or the lies that others deserve, but not you?
- When is your first memory of not deserving?
- Or feeling guilty for material possessions?

Resentment is one of the biggest blocks to growth. You Lie to your Self all the time about having it within you. You may not think you have resentment, but when you trace what is going on in your life, you are going to find it. I have had an ongoing battle within my Self recognizing resentment. The outer world lays the traps and I realize I fall into them more than I realize. I observe more and more this happening.

For example, I had some money with which I planned to pay bills. Then my accountant phoned me with my Federal Income Tax that was due. Then she told me about my state income tax that was due. Then she told me about my quarterly report taxes that were due. Then my credit card company automatically took my merchant fees out of my account. That cost me a $99 overdraft fee! Which also meant I had bills sitting on my desk that were due. So what's my Lie?

My Lie is that I don't feel resentment. I realized that the bills waiting on my desk were ones that I resented. Focusing on the bills that are due instead of the income stream. Focusing on debt instead of on income. This closes everything off and I find my Self resentful instead of appreciative; I want to blame the system instead of looking at me.

I have learned to send out via the Oversoul level Pale Pink Unconditional Love into the money system, credit card system, banking system, whoever and whatever was connected with receiving my hard-earned funds.

- Why do funds have to be "hard-earned"?
- Do you resent the money system?
- Is the system set up for you to resent?
- Does resentment cause your income stream to shrink while the money system's income stream grows?
- Do 99% of the masses fall into this money trap of resentment?
- Is it purposely designed for you to dislike, resent, blame, and hate?
- Is it designed to fragment you and turn you against the system?
- Are you contributing to this system that cannot exist without your mind-pattern?
- Have you been set-up, manipulated, and lied to?
- Does what you give out come back to you?

Then, I found a bill on my desk that was 1 day late. This 1 day means a $35 late fee plus the possibility that my interest rate on the credit card will be doubled. When I realized how much resentment I still held onto and where it was coming from, I got physically ill. Headache, stomachache, and then spent the night with everything coming out of both ends of me.

As I released the nonphysical mind-pattern of resentment everything that physically held it into my physical body virtually let go. It took me a few days to recover from this incident. I learned that if you resent your bills, you subconsciously sabotage your ability to bring in the money to pay your bills, thus proving that your resentment is justified. Self-sabotage in a major way as well as a Self-fulfilling prophecy. Money is simply energy.

- Do you resent your own energy?

## Charities

When I was younger I was so upset about all the hungry children in the world while I had enough food to fill my stomach. It was common at the time to show photos of starving children all over the world. Guilt, guilt, guilt.

I really had to work through "If I could do something I would be able to. There is a lesson that they need that I cannot take away."

When I started my nutrition work I learned that most Black people are lactose and gluten-intolerant. This made me think about the boat-loads of dried milk and wheat that the US sent to Africa and about all the people who gave their $5 and $10 to help feed a starving child.

If I couldn't help the children, then I thought I should help animals. I joined PETA and gave them my hard-earned money on a regular basis. Until I came to know that they really were just in place to stir up trouble. I eventually learned that PETA is lobbying against dog breeders and dog shows, going so far as to turn show dogs out onto highways so that they wouldn't have to be locked up and abused.

You know that the billionaires could end poverty in a second without losing any sleep. The lie is that if you give a few dollars here and there you are doing something. A lot of good people give their hard-earned funds to charities that will never make a difference where the masses want them to make a difference.

One night while eating dinner there was a knock on my front door. Through the glass, I saw a boy about 7-8 standing there so I was prepared for the "selling boy scout this or that" speech and ready with my usual answer of "I already gave".

I opened the door, he started with the usual speech which I politely acknowledged. But, when he told me that he was collecting for Juvenile Diabetes Type I, it was all I could do not to break down in tears. I gave him $5. Not enough to make any difference anywhere except I was hoping that it would give him hope and make him feel good about him Self. And I sent silent prayers of encouragement to him via the Oversoul level. I knew exactly why I gave and what the money was for.

• Have you ever been caught up in the lies of charity?

## Independence

Everyone is taught to be independent. Don't be dependent because if you are, then shame on you. I was listening to the radio the other day as the host was talking about a 25 year old still living at home, sponging off his parents. I've heard many entertainment icons talk about how they want to make it on their own. This is a lie that feeds Isolation Programming.

Instead of being Interdependent, where we all help each other, we are striving, as a society to be Independent, Isolated and Alone.

The military, corporations and governments break up families all the time. Sending them here or there or anywhere away from familiar support structures. The goal is to break the support structure. Then, put you under stress where you have to form new support structures that are chosen for you. I've been in situations where I have sought out others as support, not because I necessarily wanted that person, but because under the stresses these people were my seemingly only options.

You are not taught to be interdependent. Established, old money families keep their children close. They usually all run the family businesses together. They live together and play together. Their focus is not on breaking up the family, but making it stronger. Marriages still mean strategic alliances to them while the masses are encouraged to marry for love, even though most people do not understand what love means.

• How have you fallen into the dependent/independent lie?
• Is Interdependence a more correct and beneficial goal for all people?

One of the biggest lies I fell into easily as a younger woman was Women's Lib. I truly believed that men and women were exactly the same except for their genitalia. I was all about equal rights and got extremely upset whenever my then husband received preferential treatment over me, a female.

As farmers, all the checks came into my husband's name. I was upset because even though I worked as hard as he did all the money went to him. I felt like I had no money and no power in the world. Thus, I worked even harder to be even more belligerent and intolerant toward anyone that I felt put me down as a woman.

As the son of a single mother, he did work with me to elevate my status in the outside world. Of course, he had his own issues, and privately I was just his property. In fact, in the throes of divorce, he made the comment about "losing his most precious possession".

Then, one day I read how that the bones in women's arms and legs were positioned differently than a male. This caught my attention. For the first time, I realized that maybe there were more male/female differences than I had been led to believe. This really stayed with me as I began to energetically explore female/feminine energy vs. male/masculine energy. This led me to realize how big of a lie I had fallen into. I began to understand that females were being taught to emulate males rather than how to be females.

As the family falls apart, you have fewer clues to your own identity. Who you are; where you come from; a sense of belonging somewhere and to someone. Even people with dysfunctional families have a place. The lie that is told is that if you don't like it, you leave it.

We are created to be All One, not A-Lone, so you always look to connect with other people. When you fail to connect it usually isn't because you don't want to; instead, this is usually a result of not knowing how. The trap is laid for you to move further and further from your own identity.

## Food Lies

When I read health magazines, I am always amazed at the missing factor of the mind. This is so rarely addressed it is no wonder that people are not healthy. In addition to ignoring the mind, the plan is for people to be afraid to eat anything except for what the government gives them.

As a former farmer, one of the biggest lies that I hear is that if we stopped eating cattle, there would be more farmable ground. This is just another emotional lie told so people stop eating meat. As my dad would say, "Horsefeathers!" Cattle graze on the ground that is generally not farmable, or they clean up cropland when the crops are done for the season, adding their own special fertilizer to be tilled into the ground later for added soil nutrients.

You have your choice of many eating lifestyles, all designed to see which ones catch on so they can be further manipulated into your nutritional downfall. Pescatarian, a person who eats fish as their only flesh food, is one path you can choose. Vegetarians are now working on becoming vegans, indicating they are moral, disciplined, and better than those who are not.

People say they are giving up red meat to be healthy or to (gag me with a spoon) save the planet. The energy fields of these people always show that they are iron-deficient, low in amino acids and their internal systems are failing. Even without looking at their energy fields, you can tell who they are because after a length of time on a red meatless diet, their iron-deficient bodies are as pale as ghosts. In addition, demonic energies are repelled by iron, so with anemia on the rise, these people are virtually open doors for astral attachment and other demonic forces to enter. You have to take a look at the mind-pattern of these people.

- What food lies have you bought into?
- What did it do to your body?

- How did you find out it was a lie and what did you do about it?
- Can you choose the food that your body needs in a world that is trying to force you into a cookie-cutter-one-pill-feeds-all kind of diet?

When I read about vitamins and supplements, I think about how people used to get these same vitamins and supplements by digging in their own backyards. I do use them, but I consider them a boost to the mind-pattern, not the answer. I also know that I will survive without them.

Losing access to supplements is a fear that is has been instilled in many people. There is too much money in supplements for the global handlers to remove them from the shelves. Observe how there is always a new supplement, vitamin, or combination for you to take, depending upon your ailment or personal need.

- Do you take supplements on a regular basis?
- Are you dependent on them?
- What would you do if they were no longer available?

You are lied to all the time about what you can or cannot do. You are told you can't sell your home because there is not a market. You can't get a job or change jobs because there are no jobs. You are sick because the pharmaceutical companies keep you enslaved. You do not have medical options because the system is corrupt.

- What lies are you told that keep you feeling that you can't go anywhere in your life?
- Lies that keep you feeling hopeless, depressed, and downtrodden?
- Do you feel like someone else is dictating your life which then keeps you in a box?

**Travel Lies**

I know a lot of people with a fear of travel. After 9/11 travel became even more daunting and intimidating, purposefully designed this way so you travel in fear. Or better yet, you don't travel at all. With the Coronavirus Plannedemic of 2020, another layer of fear has been added. You are basically told that if you travel, you will get sick, infect others and you all may die. Many countries will not even let you in or if they do you have to quarantine for 14 days. This is even happening here in the US. If you travel from state to state, you must quarantine for 14 days upon arrival.

I have also read that some people who have picked up rocks here and there are searched at airports and then arrested, saying that the rocks are ancient archeological artifacts that are being stolen. I have been searched, patted down, luggage opened and rifled through, clothes on and off through every checkpoint, hands in the air as you go through their x-ray machines, glared at, stared at, pulled out of lines to say I have too much carry-on, interrogated, accosted, and everything else in between.

The lie is that you can travel but the global handlers are going to do their best to make sure you don't really want to go. Add this to what you hear in the news about all the horrors that go on in each country. Fake or not, this can feed your travel fears.

I was a little bit nervous the first time we went to Bosnia because of recent war. I was nervous when we went to Antarctica, sailing back and forth on the Drake Passage, one of the roughest seas in the world. I was nervous the very first time I flew in my 20s. I was nervous the first time I went from the West Coast to the East Coast.

I know people who are fine traveling as long as they are in their own bed every night. I know people who are from this area and have never been to Chicago. I have known people who are afraid to fly. You have to know that you are okay wherever you are. If something is going to happen, it is going to happen. For example, every now and then I read about someone sitting in their own living room when a plane crashes through the roof of their home.

Travel opens up your own inner world, including DNA. And, it can activate programming, which is another reason to always do your inner work wherever you are. The lies are out there, but it is up to you to surpass them.

- Have you had to overcome travel fears?
- What is the difference between fear and caution?
- What travel lies have you heard that you found out did not apply to you?
- Who really knows you?
- How many layers have been piled upon you and by whom?
- How many layers have you peeled off and what do you find?
- How do others react when you peel off the layers of falsehood?
- How do others react when you reveal the real you vs. the you they think they know?

## Savior Lies

Savior Programming says you are supposed to save everyone, but in doing so you forget to save your Self. But no worries, because someone or something will be there to save you. This is anywhere from Jesus Christ to space brothers to the lottery.

Some people want the government to save them. Sick people want the doctors to save them. Parents want the schools to save their children. Even love is supposed to save everyone and everything if you love them enough. Children fantasize about superheroes saving them.

You are imprinted that the military, police, doctors, teachers, and other authority figures are looking out for you, you can trust them and they will save you.

When I was 17 I turned my Self into Child Protective Services because I didn't know what to do. I had a horrible issue with my Mother that was not going away and for which at that time in my mind, there seemed to be no resolution. I didn't realize that turning my Self in was much easier than getting out. I could walk in but I could not just walk out.

The people there yelled at me and told me how horrible I was; how ungrateful I was and did not listen to what I had to say. When I realized what was happening, I wanted to leave. But I wasn't allowed to. My parents were called, but my dad was working and couldn't come to get me; my mom wouldn't, so I was sent home in a police car. Needless to say, my home situation only worsened. I realized then that the authorities would not save me.

When I was 19 I was farming and sued my landlord for not honoring the terms of my lease. After a few months, I realized that the attorneys involved were friends and using me and the landlord as pawns to pad their pockets. I vowed never to get involved in legal battles again because attorneys would not save me.

I found that there are few doctors, both conventional and alternative who don't play on your vulnerability when you are sick and really need them. I learned that the medical system in any form would not save me.

The only person I found that I could rely on to get me through the maze of life is me. I have many other examples, but this gives you the idea. Help was never out there. Help is only in here.

- What authority figures did you think would save you?
- When you were a child, did you ever fantasize about someone coming to save you?
- Does Savior Programming disempower you?

## Lies of Safety

Growing up, I was imprinted with the horrible things that were going to happen in the year 2000. All the proposed scenarios filled me with fear. This was one reason why I didn't want to have children. I worried about how I could protect and keep them safe. I worried extensively about my pets, who were like my children.

Many people during that time period stored food and water in case something happened. Now, people worldwide create doomsday bunkers and have getaway plans.

The lie is that things are going to protect you and keep you safe. Perhaps these things help to alleviate a mind-pattern of fear, but these things can also feed a mind-pattern of fear.

I thought about storing food and water but I also thought that was a fear mind-pattern I didn't want to buy into. I finally settled on buying a nonelectric, portable water filter. But then I considered what would happen if my house collapsed and I could not get to the water filter. I finally gave up trying to have enough things to make me feel safe.

For me, all I know is that I have to put my trust and faith in my Oversoul and God-Mind to bring me the experiences that are most beneficial to the growth of my Soul-Personality as well as the Soul-personalities of those who I love.

I still have extra water, extra food, and so forth, but I am not dependent on them. I know that if it is for my benefit, I won't have these things if and when the time should ever come. I don't trust in these things at all. I do trust that I will have what I need.

I do believe in practicing due diligence when it comes to safety. I'm not out to prove anything to anyone. I'm not going to step in front of a moving bus simply because I can. But I know the ultimate decision of what happens to me and how depends on the strength of my own mind-pattern and the effects of my current work.

During our trip to Suriname, we spoke to a direct descendent of a runaway slave. Long story short, the slaves from Africa knew nothing of surviving in the jungles of Suriname. But they chose the uncertainty of the unknown over the certainty of where they had just escaped. They left with only the clothes on their backs. His grandmother was one of the escaped slaves.

The man told us that someone appeared and gave the escaped slaves some seeds to plant and when they woke up in the morning, there was enough food from the seeds to feed everyone. This happened every night as they fled deeper into the jungle until eventually, they met the local indigenous peoples who took them in and taught the former slaves the ways how to live and survive in the jungle.

- What things do you depend on for safety?
- Is the world anymore uncertain now than in any other time period?

## Lies Entrap You

Mass programming is often about focusing you there instead of here. For example, at some point in linear time, humans will evolve into more. In simultaneous existence, humans are already evolved to the point where they function off of pure energy. Programming can only be hooked into something that already exists. On some level you are this; you know this and when you focus "there" instead of "here" you think that this is you now. The lie is that you are here and not there; what works in that reality does not work in this reality at this time.

Lies of Limitations are Self-perpetuating and brilliantly designed to keep you entrapped. The more aware you are, the more sticky the trap becomes. When you start understanding societal programming and imprinting, the first reaction, after disbelief, is usually anger. You feel tricked, vulnerable, and used which makes you angry. This is the perfect response to feed the lies because what you give out comes back to you.

You may also feel bitterness, resentment, and even hate. All of these negative emotions destroy you and feeds the system to keep it going; the very system that you now despise. Now, you are ready to buy into the lie that it is us against them, or maybe even them against us.

The truth is that the reason the people with all the money don't give it to the impoverished is because the impoverished don't have the mind-pattern to receive. The reason there is brutality is because the brutalized have the mind-pattern to be brutalized.

The reason the government is taking away freedoms is because the masses don't have the mind-patterns to attract freedom. Hospitals exist because people have a mind-pattern of illness. McDonald's exists because the people want this kind of physical and thus, mental food. Truths are hidden because the masses have a mind-pattern of lies. Inequality exists because people have mind-patterns of low Self-Worth. People on this end of the stick want to blame the other end of the stick. Look at the other end of the stick.

• What do you see from this perspective?

Usually, people only look at life from their end of the stick. You have been used to looking at life from the way life affects you. Looking at the totality of the system takes you beyond your own limited perspective. To understand life, you have to view the totality from above, from the Oversoul level because the system is the combined energy of all the mind-patterns of those it affects.

Everyone that exists here on this planet contributes something to everything that exists here. The closer you are geographically to something, the more active that something is in your mind-pattern. For example, if there is war on this planet, there is war inside of you. If you have war in your back yard, the war frequency is stronger and more active within you because the physical representation is geographically close.

I have always been fascinated with pyramids. As long as I can remember I wanted to visit the pyramids of Egypt. To me, they were the most fascinating place on Earth. Because pyramids represent Storehouses of Knowledge in Hyperspace, this means that I was always fascinated with my own Storehouse of Knowledge, knowing that this inner sanctum is the most fascinating place on Earth.

When I went to Egypt I was disappointed. It was surrounded by lies, intimidation, aggression and falsehood. I couldn't get in the pyramids; the tour guides actively discouraged this.

When I heard about the possibility of pyramids in Bosnia, I felt hopeless, like it couldn't be true even though a part of me wanted it to be. When I got there I found the pyramids open, welcoming, easily sharing their secrets. Because I was already opening my own Storehouse of Knowledge the outer world had to outpicture that to me.

Hyperspace/Oversoul tools and techniques take you beyond the lies of limitations because quickly learn that you are not powerless. God-Mind is always in balance, even if that balance is hidden or forbidden to you by your Self in some way.

- What does your geographic location symbolize and outpicure about your mind-pattern?
- What do places where you have traveled symbolize and outpicture in your mind-pattern?
- What do places where you want to travel symbolize and outpicture about your mind-pattern?

## No Victims

One of the biggest lie that you buy into and that shapes your belief systems is that the systems in place such as corporations, banking, medical are designed to enslave you. The reason these systems exist is not because the global handlers decided it is so and then forced them upon you. It is the mind-patterns of the masses which decided that they needed these systems which in turn forced the global handlers to create them.

There are no victims, only willing participants. Whatever you don't like represents something within. It is up to you to determine what that is. Change your focus to change the outer world. For example, a house cannot exist without focus. Without focus, the house has no attention and it disintegrates back to the Earth.

Those who share the same roads every day may be going to different places, but while they are on the road, they all have a joint/connected mind-pattern. If people did not have need for the road, the road would not exist. The road exists because a specific group of people out-picture it.

Those who have the need for a specific incident are drawn to it because of existing mind-patterns. Everything exists energetically first before it can be outpictured. Catastrophes exist because a certain group of people outpicture it. On the deeper levels, the mind-patterns emanate, coalesce and create.

Simply because you don't have awareness of something does not mean that it does not exist. McDonald's fast food restaurants exist because the group mind-pattern creates it. Poverty exists because the group mind-pattern creates it. Then the group throws stones at those who they perceive won't stop the impoverishment.

Organizations already exist via the group mind-pattern. Buildings are the outpicturing of that which already exists on the nonphsyical level, providing the physical structure through which the mind-patterns express in this reality. When you realize that everything exists on the nonphsyical level first before it can be physically outpictured, your understanding of reality begins to shift.

When I was a dairy farmer, there were 2 veterinarians who came to my farm on a monthly basis. Sometimes one came, sometimes the other one came. I used to play a game to read the energy to see which one was coming. Because the energy/nonphsyical arrives before the physical, I was correct about 99% of the time.

When I travel, I always say my energy goes first and then my body travels to catch up with where the nonphsyical part of me already is. All of this has to do with understanding the nonphsyical pathways so you can understand how life is playing out here in physical reality.

- What kind of nonphsyical pathways have you experienced?
- Can you rise above to the nonphsyical Oversoul level and then look down on physical reality?
- Can you see the energy of the house before it is built; the garden before it is planted; the yard before it is landscaped; the game before it is played; the catastrophe before it happens?

Pure frequency is clear; it has no color; tone; or archetype. It simply exists. It is the color, tone and archetype which bring it into physical reality. You have to look behind anything in physical reality to see what supports it. This opens your awareness to a deeper level of what already exists in the Eternal Now.

You are going to be amazed at what you already know. This isn't something only a special few can do. All you have to do is follow the energies to see what they create and then ask your Oversoul for explanation. This is something anyone can do with awareness and a little guidance. Label what you know so you can repeat the experience at will.

All the lies out there only exist because it is in your mind-pattern. No one is doing anything to you. A mirror is being held up. You are looking in the mirror. What you see is you. It can only exist if you feed it. When you correct your own mind-pattern what you don't like goes away; it cannot exist in your world.

It is therefore important to study what you see in the mirror; to be aware of your surroundings as you move through your own reflection. Otherwise, you will become enamored of your own reflection and stay stuck in it; round and round; lifeline after lifeline; the wheel of Karma that is spoken about.

People love drama, regardless of what they say. Which story would most people rather hear: "I got on a plane; flew from here to there and got off"; or, "I got on a plane; it was hijacked; almost crashed; missed the runway; had to sit on it for hours, but after x-y-z, I finally made it off; exhausted; tired; starved; half-dead"? The latter is a much more exciting and memorable tale. An experience of a lifetime that attracts a lot of attention and interest.

- In which part of what drama do you want to participate?
- Are you ready to only observe?
- Do you want to remove/unhook your frequency from a specific play?

When you understand which lies you feed into, you may feel angry. However, anger, shock and disbelief are potent emotions that can shake up your energetic system ultimately to your benefit. The shakeup allows a different path to open along with a new way of thinking.

Next, you may experience a sense of wasted time, wasted effort, wasted life a la "if only I had known I could have done this or that and been here or there instead of where I am now; instead of what I have done." All of these negative emotions surfacing at once may make you feel like you are caught in a hamster wheel. You need a period of commiseration, adjustment, grief and even outrage.

But you don't want to get stuck there such as people do in support groups where you pour your heart out to people who have been there, are there. Too often support groups allow you to dump and get petted, but do not teach you how to move on. You have the tools to move on. You know that when you feed into release and move on. When you feed into "nothing", "nothing" has its hold in you. You begin to understand how powerful you truly are when you stop giving your power away

You have to know you are in the forest first before you can find your way out. You have to know what a tree looks like so you know to avoid the tree. You need your strength and personal power to do this. Whatever you feel is okay. The most important thing is to feel it, acknowledge it, and then release it. Don't stay in the lie, because what you give out comes back to you. Be thankful for your adversaries who provide the foil that makes you strong.

## AFFIRMATIONS—BREAKING FREE

Break free of your lies of limitations by using the strength of your mind. But, be prepared for your world as you know it to shatter. This work is only for those with the willpower to be challenged into the most correct and beneficial path of Soul-Growth.

*I identify the bonds of my own mind-pattern.*
*I redefine my definition of Free.*

*I identify who I allowed to define me.*
*I review my early childhood years.*

*I identify my own true nature.*
*I explore the positive and negative aspects of Self.*

*I identify Self-aspects that are greater than I acknowledge.*
*I break Free of my own false Self-perceptions.*

*I identify Self-aspects that are lessor than I acknowledge.*
*I break Free of my own false Self-perceptions.*

*I identify early life circumstances that shape what I express today.*
*I give thanks to all my life teachers.*

*I identify the Self-aspects I closed down based upon how I was treated.*
*I observe the positives and negatives of Self-aspects not expressed.*

*I observe the Self-aspects I opened up based upon how I was treated.*

*I observe the positives and negatives of Self-aspects expressed.*

*I identify the mind-pattern that I agreed upon before birth.*

*I identify the person "I might have been" without current life experiences.*

*I identify the balance of life experiences that created my present persona.*

*I give thanks for all influencing factors as opportunities for growth.*

*I identify the existence of my Soul-Personality within the Eternal Now.*

*I AM a finger of the God-Mind, existing so It can explore It Self.*

*I identify the needs of the Soul-Personality.*

*My Soul-Personality exists outside of time and space.*

*I identify the necessity of forging the Soul-Personality to extract or imbed specific characteristics for this lifeline.*

*I release the need to fight the forces that forge my Soul-Personality.*

*I realize I AM already Free to choose my path.*

*I Freely chose to come to this planet at this time.*

*I chose my own personal Soul-Personality forging methods.*

*I AM on Planet Earth as a result of my own Free Will.*

*My Soul-Personality exists within Eternal Freedom.*
*I AM always Free within the Eternal Now.*

*Breaking Free is only an illusion.*
*I always have a choice.*

*No one and no thing holds me against my will.*
*I AM not a victim; I AM a willing participant.*

*I Break Free of my own illusions of confinement.*
*I open my own mind-pattern to accept Freedom.*

*I Break Free of my own internal barriers and concepts of limitations.*
*I expand into my own inner space.*

*I experience the vastness of my Soul-Personality.*
*My internal vastness opens doors to external vastness.*

*My choices determine which pathways Freely open to me.*
*I choose to walk the pathways that open up new positive vistas to explore.*

*I see no blocks, only stairs to Freedom.*
*I release the last vestiges of my crumbling past as I choose a stabilizing now.*

*I stand upon a New Foundational Mind-Pattern of
my own conscious choosing.*

*My New Foundational Mind-pattern is in perfect alignment with
my Oversoul and God-Mind.*

*My Freedom is always here.*

*My Oversoul and God-Mind guide me.*

*I wisely use my newly-realized freedom.*

*I maintain my humility and Self-Worth.*

*I AM Free wherever I go.*

*Freedom is a function of mind-pattern.*

*I AM Free to wander inside my Self.*

*I AM Safe as I Self-Explore.*

*I exist beyond the lies of limitations.*

*I exist in any world in any way that I can imagine.*

*I move physical reality with my mind every second that I AM here.*

*I AM constantly creating.*

*I answer only to my Oversoul and God-Mind.*

*I live in Total Freedom at all times.*

# Stress or No Stress?

I t is a mystery why everyone fights change when change is what the God-Mind is all about. Change is more natural than stagnation, yet, most people want to get comfortable and maintain the status quo.

Before I had my dogs, my life was much more calm and relaxed. Yet, as busy as I am, it was too relaxed. I realize that it is too easy to be too complacent and do nothing. The dogs help motivate me to get up and get going. I sit at my computer a good share of the day. With the dogs I get up and down a lot more, I take a few minutes here and there to go outside and play with them, as well as walk them every day. Even though I knew the dogs would bring a lot more stress into my life, I also knew that it would be good for me.

No Stress Programming that is thrust upon the masses is turning people into a society off zombies. If it is too stressful, don't do it; if you are uncomfortable, don't do it; if you have to change too much, don't do it. I have re-examined my own attitude toward stress, what it is, and why we do/do not need it. The deeper I look, the more I realize that divesting your Self of all stress is not healthy. Stress is an extremely important aspect of growth.

The more I observe and question, the more I feel my own attitude changing. Like with the dogs. They definitely are a stressor, yet they provide another dimension of life that I need.

- Do you think of stress as a positive?
- Or only something that is unavoidable so you have to deal with it?
- Do you grow through stress?
- Do you avoid being uncomfortable?
- Is being uncomfortable stressful?
- Are you trying to divest your life of all stress?
- Do you think that social media is pushing/promoting no stress?
- Does "change" equal "stress"?
- Do you fight change?
- Or, do you like change, but only so much and only when you want it, how you want it?
- Is unexpected change stressful?
- When you think that change is okay, are you thinking planned change is okay?
- Is change more natural than stagnation?
- If change is natural, why do people fight it?
- Is stress a part of change?

## Unplanned Stress

When you plan for stress, it is much easier to handle—a new job, a new place to visit, a move to a bigger, nicer home. Even before we added the 2 new dogs and 2 new kittens, we knew that they would bring stress as much as pleasure.

So even if you do not know exactly what that stress is going to be you have a rough idea that you may be challenged once you start your job, move into your home and your pets settle/do not settle in.

Planned stress can be challenging, but unplanned stress is a billion times more challenging. You lose your job, your home; your flight is cancelled and/or your pets run away, or maybe someone in your home has pet allergies so the pets cannot stay. Maybe a pet gets ill or has an accident. Maybe someone you love gets sick or even passes away. Maybe someone smashes into your brand new car; you don't/can't get along with your boss; the plumbing in your new home leaks and the air conditioner needs replacing. You move into a beautiful apartment but then you have heat issues and noisy neighbors.

What once brought you joy now is an ironstone around your neck that you can't take off. You are where you are, you have to deal with your situation and now you are stressfully challenged. This is the place where it is easy to go into meltdown.

- Have you had a meltdown when what you expected to go well, did not?
- Have you had something that you thought would bring you joy and happiness only to find the opposite happening?
- What kind of unplanned change has happened in your life which was totally unexpected?
- How did you react when your status quo was interrupted?
- Have your planned changes gone as expected?
- Do you want what you want when you want it?
- Have you fought the changes until you realized that doing so did not accomplish anything?
- How challenging is it to embrace unplanned change?

I often use this example to illustrate my point:

First, you take a glass and fill it with stones.

- Is the glass full?

Then you add gravel.

- Is the glass full now?

Next, you pour in sand.

- Now is the glass full?

Finally, you add water and the glass is now full.

When I was first starting out in my life, when the glass was filled with stones, I thought my life was full/busy. As I grew, gravel was added into the same glass and I felt overwhelmed. Then came the sand. I really had to push to do what I needed to do. When I thought I absolutely could not do one more thing, in came the water. Yes, I felt overwhelmed like I was going to drown in that water. But I didn't. I figured things out and I got stronger.

I see a lot of people with only stones in their glass who think their glass is full. Compared to my life, what they deal with is nothing. Yet I understand where they are coming from because I have been there. I have compassion for their struggles. They think they are at the end, but I know they are only beginning.

- Have you seen this happen in your own life?
- Every time you think you cannot deal with one more thing, another thing comes along?
- And you survive?
- And then something else comes along and you still survive?
- Do you know people who think their lives are full, yet you know that they are just beginning the journey?

- As you push through one level and survive, do you learn another layer/level of stressors?

- And the purpose is not to break you, but to strengthen you?

- Does stress make you more efficient?

- The more you have to do, the more you do it better?

- The less you have to do, the longer it takes you to do it?

A few nights ago, I could not sleep. I had too much on my mind. I tossed and turned until about 5:30 am. Then I slept for 1 hour and then woke up again. At 7 am I had to get up to start my day. At one point in my life, I was a serious insomniac, meaning I did not sleep for several years. During this time period, I would get so frustrated and stressed that I could not sleep that I would even start to cry. I knew I needed my sleep and could not function unless I had some kind of rest. Ideally, I like to get about 9 to 10 hours of sleep. Some people can get by on less, but I know how I function best.

I rarely have insomnia now, but every once in awhile I have one of those nights when tossing and turning doesn't stop until I get up. I used to use that as an excuse to not function well, but now, I tell my Oversoul that if it isn't going to help me get to sleep, then it has to provide the energy for me to get through my day. And it does. My other choice is to sink into the stress-mode of no sleep so I'm no good for the day, but I refuse.

- Do you ever have insomnia?

- Do you stress if you cannot sleep and you know you need your sleep?

- Do you tell your Oversoul to provide the energy that you need if it doesn't provide sleep?

- Why do you think people need sleep?

- Even if the body needs rest, why do you actually need to sleep?

- Your brain functions while you sleep, so is it to provide dreams?
- Or other nighttime experiences?
- Does purposeful sleep deprivation, such as elite military forces go through in their training, prove beneficial?
- Have you had long periods of your life where you were sleep deprived?
- If so, how did you survive?
- Do you believe the many articles that say not enough sleep is bad for your health?
- Do you believe the constant bombardment of information about how sleep deprived people are at risk and cannot make up lost sleep?
- Does the thought of being sleep-deprived stress you?
- Can you turn sleep deprivation in your favor?
- Do you like to sleep?

You do not realize how much you are indoctrinated in what you should/should not be doing. Just like sleep. You are told that you need sleep, how much, and if you do not have it then "xxx" is going to happen.

When I had my second son, both my babies were on different schedules, so I went for about 1 week with extremely little sleep. I began to truly feel mentally/emotionally out of balance. I then realized that I never slept enough at one time to dream. If you do not dream, your mind/emotions/body never reset. There are case studies of people who do not dream who eventually have a lot of mental/emotional and physical issues. The following is a short article I pulled up on dream deprivation.

### Dream Deprivation Is Just as Unhealthy as Sleep Deprivation—Here's Why

You might already know how important sleep is and how **sleep deprivation can cause a slew of health problems**. But have you thought about your dreams? Do you dream? And can you remember your dreams from last night? If you're not dreaming—and more and more people aren't, according to new research—you're putting your Self at higher risk for obesity, memory loss, and inflammation throughout your body, which can lead to autoimmune troubles.

A review of research on **dream deprivation**, published in the Annals of the New York Academy of Sciences in 2017, delves into the dangers of missing out on the rapid-eye-movement (REM) phase of sleep and the potential reasons why we're not dreaming as much. The article's author, **Rubin Naiman**, Ph.D., a sleep and dream specialist at the Andrew Weil Center for Integrative Medicine at the University of Arizona, calls dream deprivation "a striking epidemic" and "a public health hazard," and one that is seriously impacting our quality of life.

### Quality dreaming is restorative

While you may think that you get your most restful sleep when you don't remember a thing and you're "out cold," Naiman says that if you dream well, you will actually feel better in the morning. Dreaming also seems to be crucial for the body's repair systems and for the brain's learning and memory processes. "Poor dreaming, or damaged dreaming, is strongly linked to emotional disturbance and to anxiety, depression, and other forms of mental illness," he says. "Dreaming also processes and consolidates memory, and both mild cognitive disturbances and serious neurological disorders like Alzheimer's disease are associated with damaged dreaming. If we don't dream well, we won't remember well."

As the paper notes, scientific concern regarding the link between dream deprivation and poor health has been a slow progression. Back in the 1960s, researchers discovered that subjects selectively deprived of REM sleep experienced weight gain, concentration difficulties, irritability, anxiety, tension, delusions, and hallucinations. But the findings took a back seat to the discovery that dreaming also took place in non-REM sleep.

They also took a back seat to other medical discoveries, like sleep aids, psychiatric drugs, and allergy medications. "We've known for years that the most commonly used medications significantly suppress REM sleep," says Naiman. "But even knowing what we know about the importance of REM sleep, with memory and mental health, there's a general tendency to dismiss its value. It's striking that medical science pays virtually no attention to it."

Naiman cites the late-evening use of tablets, smartphones, computers, and artificial light in general, along with early alarms and early risings, which cut into REM sleep, most of which happens in the second half of your sleep time. (Don't miss these 50 easy ways to sleep better.) Alcohol and cannabis are also big culprits, even though they're ironically often used to alleviate stress and promote sleep. Alcohol, for instance, permits the release of hormones that are known to interrupt REM and, therefore, dreaming.

While Naiman says that a glass of wine is fine, too many people drink an inordinate amount. "I think there's an innocent goal: People want to relax and expand their consciousness," he explains. "That actually happens naturally in dreaming, and if we don't dream well, it increases the pressure to find other ways of doing that."

https://www.rd.com/health/wellness/dream-sleep-deprivation/

Dreams help funnel in the messages from the subconscious/super-conscious minds that you need to help you on your journey in life. When this connection to Source is continually interrupted, then you have issues. However, when you take the time to consciously connect in your waking state you are, in effect, having waking dreams.

This means that the messages that most people have to go to sleep to get, you are pulling to you while you are awake doing your Hyperspace/Oversoul work. This is why you can tell your Oversoul to either help you sleep so you can get that sub/superconscious mind connection, or you consciously create this while you are awake. Doing your Hyperspace/Oversoul work also means that you have an increasingly more conscious connection to your sub/superconscious message highway which allows you to do more resetting while conscious.

I love to sleep because I love to dream. I have had various phases of my life which have included fantastic nighttime experiences, such scary nighttime experiences that I was afraid to go to sleep; dreams so wonderful I could not wait to sleep/dream, and such scary nightmares that I was afraid to go to sleep. Interestingly, now I am never afraid in the dreams like I was in the past. Nighttime brings a lot of stress, both real and imagined, for many people for many reasons.

- Have you had nighttime stress at any time in your life?
- Dreams, nightmares, experiences?
- Have you had recurring dreams or dream themes?
- Are you able to interpret your dreams?
- Do you keep a dream journal?
- Can you tell the difference between an Oversoul dream and a programming dream?
- Do you do regular Hyperspace/Oversoul mental work?
- If so, have your sleep patterns changed in any way?

- Do you get answers to your personal issues while you sleep or upon waking in the morning?
- Do you get more answers to your life's conundrums while you are awake since doing Hyperspace/ Oversoul work?
- Is your message highway from Source expanding, either during sleep or waking, or both?
- Do you have a middle name?
- Do you know the importance of having a middle name so that your message highway actually works?

## Coping Skills

Stress teaches coping skills. If you try to remove all the stress, you have less life coping skills. My oldest son was very much loved and taken care of at home. When he went to school he was not prepared for all the negative events that occurred there. The negatives tended to escalate as he grew older to the point where eventually I took him out of public school and put him in private school. His private school years were much less stressing than his public school years.

However, he really learned coping skills at a very young age. The negative events he encountered helped him to be more prepared for the world at large and what to expect. Consider the preceding example of filling the glass. Using this as an analogy to your life, the more that goes into your glass, the more you learn, grow, organize, and are able to cope. You are forced to learn, i.e., what doesn't kill you, makes you stronger. No matter what anyone tries to tell you, this planet is designed to get as much growth out of you as possible.

While I teach proactively getting control of your life, there is usually more reactive learning than proactive learning going on. The reactive learning is definitely more stressful because you have to learn to act and react on the fly. The more you are stressed, the more you perfect your ability to react under pressure under a myriad of life situations.

- Does "uncomfortable" equal "stress"?
- If so, is stress always uncomfortable?
- Do you consciously thrive off of stress?
- Do you like stress?
- Can you like stress yet still be uncomfortable?
- Do you appreciate stress and what it does?
- Do you dislike stress?
- Can you become addicted to stress?
- Is life a continual stress or is it up and down, with stress always an underlying factor?
- Does "no stress" equal "no growth"?
- Is proactive learning stressful?
- Is it as stressful as reactive learning?
- Does stress teach you coping skills?
- Can you be calm on the outside but feeling stressed on the inside?
- Is feeling stressed on the inside "bad"?

Every year, there is a fundraiser going on for a classical music station in my area. We are always told how much it costs to run the station, how much costs have gone up, and your monthly pledge of any amount helps cover the cost of the almost $60 per hour cost of operation.

I have listened to these fundraisers for years. To me, the hosts sound stressed because it seems that their salaries depend on the donations received. Every $5, $10, and $20 pledge is celebrated. I feel stressed just listening to the hosts trying to convince their audience to give anything to help the cause.

Then I think about the people who give money and how stressed they must feel, knowing that their small monthly donation does not even cover 1 hour of air time for the station, yet they give. I wonder if they stress about their pledge not being enough, if they can really afford to give anything at all, and so on. Based on their hourly operating rate, I calculated that the station needs about $500,000.00 per year to operate.

So what if every year, someone just wrote one huge check and there were no more fundraisers and no need for the hosts to raise money for their salaries and no community participation in donations.

- Would the radio station lose its connectedness to the community?
- Does the stress of giving to the station make people feel a part of something important?
- Would no need for donations disconnect the community and make them take the station for granted?
- Would the hosts not be so personally invested in the station and take their jobs for granted?
- Does the stress created by trying to support this station teach a lot of people a lot of lessons?
- Does the stress force them to determine what is important or not important?
- Is fundraising, in general, a stressful activity?
- Have you participated in fundraising activities?
- If you organized them, what kind of stress were you under?
- If you gave, were you stressed to consider the cause, the amount of your donation, and if you could really afford what you were giving?
- Does giving make you feel a part of something?

- If there was no giving would you feel less a part of life in general?
- Does making a payment on a home, car, or any purchase make you feel more emotionally invested in it?
- Does your stress level/blood, sweat, tears mean you are more appreciative of what you have?
- Or resentful of what you had to do to get it?

Yes, when you donate to a cause you unknowingly tie in your psychic energy via your money/energy. If you know what psychic energy is, then you know how to clean up what you are giving so you are not tied in. Most people do not know this, so giving to anything psychically ties you in. Receiving from anyone/anything psychically ties you in.

Always ask if it is even most correct and beneficial to give or receive. And if so, then you have the tools to clean up your involvement so you are not attached to anyone, any place, or anything energetically. There are also lots of hidden hooks which is why you feel stressed when you give, take or think about giving/taking.

I do not give to blood banks because I do not want to be in the position to receive from them. The same with various charities. I do give within my own family because I AM tied into them, but in the way that is most correct and beneficial. This can make me feel stressed. But the stress forces me to re-focus, re-fine and re-define what I want to do vs. what is most correct and beneficial. I can spend many sleepless nights fighting with my Self over what I want to do and what I am being told to do.

If the money isn't there, well, that is an easy answer. This means I'm not supposed to help. There is no guesswork when this is the case. The more I observe and study money as an energetic tool that helps guide and direct my decisions, the more I appreciate the stress that is tied into the money conundrum.

- Do you think that money is one of your biggest stressors?
- Does money help you re-focus, re-fine, and re-define what you want to do to help guide you into what is most correct and beneficial?
- If you have too much money with too many choices, would it be easy to make choices that are not the most correct and beneficial?
- Can too many choices make life stressful?
- When you have little money does having fewer choices make your decisions easier?
- Do easier choices mean you like the choices available?
- Do the choices available help you focus on what you need vs. what you want?
- Does wanting more stress you?
- To get more, do you need to be stressed?
- Are you challenged to really know your purpose and mission in life?
- Does stress keep you on your path whether you want to be on it or not?
- Is having enough energy one of your biggest stressors?
- Do you have to sleep to re-energize?
- Do you allow your Oversoul to re-energize you?
- Does your Oversoul show you the amount of energy available to you via your income stream?
- Does "income stream" equal "stress"?
- Does "energy stream" equal "stress"?
- Do you have enough energy to do what you want to do?

One of my cousins that was my age passed away over the weekend. She was a very important part of my childhood. She lost her mother when she was 7 years old and in my opinion, never recovered. She had a very rare disease that basically shuts down all of the organs, called Erdheim Chester Disease. There are less than 500 diagnosed cases in the world. All the money in the world could not save her. She was given an experimental medication that cost $15,000.00 per month that was finally approved by her insurance company. A lot of stress does revolve around money because a lot of stress revolves around energy. My cousin had no energy; she lost her will to live and her organs simply gave up along with her spirit.

But, the experiences you have are more important than the money. As stressed as you may be, your experiences are priceless. Money cannot buy your health, as much as you may think it does. If my cousin had several million dollars to give to the healthcare system, her health care would not have been better or different. Sometimes the more money you have, the more tests you are given and the more they experiment on you because your insurance allows it. But this does not make you well.

Your mind has to be in order first to pull your health. Money is secondary. You must work on the mind-pattern that brings what you mentally need first, and then the money/energy follows. Sometimes you have to stress your Self first to get your mind where it needs to be. You cannot keep doing the same things and expecting different results.

Stretching your mind is stressing your mind; stretching your energy is stressing the physical body. Every experience you have is going to stress you. Even "no stress" can be stressing. Sometimes you have to stretch your financial capabilities to get more. You have to demonstrate to your Source that you are ready and strong enough to wield more resources. Every part of you must stretch/be stressed for any kind of growth.

- Do you understand why stress is portrayed as bad?
- If you quit stretching, do you quit growing?

- Have you stretched your financial capabilities and then received more?
- Have you done this and received less?
- If so, what did you do differently to get different results?
- Are you stressed to think of money as secondary?
- Is energy secondary?
- Is health secondary?
- Is mind always the most important focus, above health, energy, money?
- Is it easy to use money as an excuse for not getting what you want?
- Does more money mean better health care?
- Or simply more health care?
- Does "more" equal "better"?
- Do you value experience over things?
- In this reality is there a balance between experience and things?

**Prices**

I use sales to buy what I need when I need it. Sales give me a guideline whether it is food, clothing, supplements, and so forth. I actually feel stressed when I buy something that is not on sale. I feel like I am doing something wrong and I am working diligently to overcome these feelings. I do my mental work, visualizing what I need and then paying full price. To me, paying full price feels wasteful.

I visualize having millions of dollars sitting in my bank account and then paying full price. The multiple vitamins I buy at vitacost.com, for example, come on sale from time to time at 20% off. I always make sure I have an extra bottle, so I wait for the sale to replenish my stock. The 20% off is about $10.00 that I save.

It is truly challenging for me to pay full price knowing that these are going to come on sale soon. So far, I managed to never pay full price. I cannot say that in the long term of my mind-pattern that this is a good thing; nor can I say that it is a bad thing. I do not want to be wasteful with the energy/money that I have, regardless of the bottom line sitting in my bank account.

I recently made a purchase at a clothing store and used my 30% off coupon. Then I made another purchase of some T-shirts for my son in Texas to be shipped directly to him. I found out the 30% coupon was only good for one use. So, I made the purchase and paid full price, only to find out I had another coupon that I could have used. I chose to not call and ask for the difference to be applied to my account, but I had to sit on my hands, release resentment up, and tell my Self that I was doing the correct thing. It was truly tough.

I know a lot of people with a lot of money who are truly cheap. I do not want to be cheap regardless of the amount of money that I have or do not have. Yet, I do not want to be wasteful simply because I can. Sales do keep me focused on what to buy and when, especially on items I purchase regularly such as vitamins and supplements.

If I go out to eat, I look at the cost of the item vs. what I could buy it for at the supermarket; then I have to stop and think about the cost of the restaurant and staff and what I don't have to do to justify what I pay for eating out. These little financial stressors play through my head almost every day.

- What little financial stressors play through your head?
- Do you stress about being wasteful?
- If God-Mind is limitless, is it possible to even be wasteful?
- Do you stress about being cheap?
- Do sales help you focus on what to buy/not buy?
- Are you challenged to pay full price for everyday items?

- Are you challenged to pay full price for big ticket items, such as appliances, electronics, furniture, homes?
- Do you/can you visualize millions of dollars sitting in your bank account?
- Do you visualize paying full price for everything?
- Or do you consider that wasteful?
- Do you feel like you are doing something wrong when you pay full price when you know that a sale will be/could be imminent?
- If so, is this stress all based on low Self-Worth?
- Not trusting Source?
- Feeling limited?
- Not recognizing the limitlessness of Source?
- Something else?

In the mountains of Italy where we go on our *Clear Health & Healing* tour, there is plenty of wood, water and stone. In a way, the water tap is open all the time, as the rivers are always flowing with water from the melting snow. Where water is so plentiful, it cannot be wasted because there is always more. When I first started visiting my cousin and saw her throwing out bottles of water so she could get fresh water, my breathing stopped for a few seconds. I am so accustomed to being mindful of water I was challenged to think there is a place in the world where there is plenty of water, all of the time. I soon learned to do exactly as she does; throw out the old water and fill up with new. It really is a freeing feeling to do this.

People are totally stressing over limited resources. I have been indoctrinated with this concept all of my life. For example, if you don't get enough sleep, then you should stress about that. If you don't have enough money, then stress over that.

Money equals energy and everyone is supposed to be stressed about both.

You are always supposed to be stressed over anything perceived as finite. This imprints you with "there isn't enough". You buy into the loop and you fulfill the prophecy. All of my imprinting is definitely challenging to discard and surpass. Paying full price vs. sale items could stress me for days. I still have to talk my Self through the process, focusing on the limitlessness of the God-Mind.

If you have a 9-5 job and you make minimum wage, your linearly-trained mind is most likely challenged to think about millions of dollars in the bank. However, if you are at a minimum wage job it is because you need to learn how to handle money/energy on this level. You can stretch the boundaries here and there to establish growth.

But ultimately, if you are messing up with a little money/energy, then you are going to mess up even bigger with more money/energy. You are going to be squeezed by your Oversoul until you do what you are supposed to do in the way that you are supposed to do it. The stress that you feel is to point you in the correct direction.

### *Necessity is the mother of invention.*

- Does stress force you to become more creative?
- Does stress focus you on what you need to prioritize?
- Can you mess up with a lot of money just as easily as with a little money?
- Do you talk your Self through the process of being stressed so that you can remain as calm inwardly as possible?
- Does knowing the law mean that you can practice the law?
- How challenged are you to overcome your initial imprinting?
- If God-Mind is limitless, why is it so easy to buy into the idea of finite resources?

- Can you accept that you are where you are because your Soul has growth to accomplish that can only be accomplished in your exact circumstance?

- Is it reasonable to conjecture that when you have accomplished what your Soul needs to accomplish in your current circumstances then your life will change?

- Are you stressed to find the patience that you need to stay your course?

- Are you often stressed by the feeling that there isn't enough?

- Are you stressed because you are told that people are killing the planet?

- Do you stress about what the planet will be like for generations to come?

Not too long ago, my dad was scheduled for an outpatient procedure at the hospital. But, they decided to keep him overnight. I left the house at 10 am and did not get home until 9 pm. When I checked the website, it was down so I could not post. I went to bed instead.

The next day, I went to the hospital to get him in the morning. When I arrived, they decided to keep him through the weekend. So, I went home, did a few necessities, got some reading material for him, then Stewart and I went back to see him for a couple of hours. When we got home, I told Stewart that I had had enough and was going to bed. So I did.

I slept about 10 hours, was getting things settled in the morning when my dad phoned to tell me he was being released. Okay, so I got my Self together, went to get him and he was still in the hospital bed when I arrived a couple of hours later. I finally had him home by 4 pm and of course, had to drive during the worst part of a snowstorm.

**Stress or No Stress?**

Surprisingly, I have felt very little stress. I usually do not care to participate in the conventional medical community. However, I have to say that I have been extremely impressed with the medical care that my dad has received.

This all started the day after Stewart left to go to the Bahamas when I took my dad to the emergency room. But not once have I felt that he was not receiving proper care. Every single person we have dealt with has been extremely kind, caring, and competent. The surgeon recently moved his 94-year-old father here from another state, so my dad was not simply an old man but a person/father.

My father had a health issue before his move here, which in our opinion, was not properly treated, so thank goodness he changed his moving date to Michigan 2 weeks earlier than planned. So, he was here, and not there, when his health crisis recurred. Yes, I am tired and yes, emotionally it has not been easy, but I have not stressed about his medical care in any way. I know he is getting the proper treatment and I know he will be better than ever when all of this is behind him.

I know that many people do not care for conventional medical care. However, all things come from one Source and when it is necessary, there is a reason. I am grateful for all those people who took the time to go through conventional medical school so they could be there for my dad, and for other family members and friends who have found medical personnel who care. Ultimately, it is always your mind that heals, but like all things, your body sometimes needs a boost so that the mind can heal. To me, this is another example of trusting Source to provide.

- Have you stressed over having to use conventional medical care?
- Have you used it when you need/needed it?
- Do you still look for the mind for ultimate healing?

- Do you take the time to be grateful for what is available for those who need it?
- Are you afraid of the conventional medical community?
- Do you remember that all things come from Source?
- Do you think there is a level of programming that makes you fear the medical community?
- If you fear the medical community does that hinder your healing?
- Does trust and confidence promote healing on all levels?
- Can you be emotionally pushed without feeling stressed?
- Does emotional pushing tire you out?
- Is this the same as feeling stressed?
- Do you take the time to rest/sleep when you have had enough?
- Can you feel stressed even when you know what you are going through is for the best and you know the outcome will put everyone in a better place?

Today was one of those days. I had to phone the pharmacy to get meds for my dad. Because he was discharged on a Sunday and all the pharmacies are closed, I managed to convince the hospital to give him 4 pills until I could get to an open pharmacy. That added an extra 2 hours to his discharge from the hospital, but he needed the medication.

Somehow, those 4 pills showed up on the pharmacy's forms so this confused the pharmacist over how many pills my dad needed. The pharmacist thought the script was for 4 pills even though I had phoned the prescription in at 8:00 am. He needed 78 pills, not 4 pills. Finally, the pharmacist asked me to tell him how many pills my dad needed. This did not leave me feeling confident in him at all.

Stewart had an interview this morning for Russian television, so I watched the dogs to keep them quiet. When he was done, I put them outside. Then, a few minutes later I looked out when I heard Jade barking to see Jasmine standing outside our neighbors' fence.

Of course, we had snow on the ground and I didn't have any boots on, but I grabbed the leash, dashed outside to find out that she was not outside our neighbor's fence, but inside their totally enclosed backyard! How did she get out of our yard and into theirs?

I pushed on the bottom of their chain-link fence, and Jasmine poked her head out and then wiggled her way out through an opening about 2 inches high by 6 inches wide. Thank goodness I managed to get a leash on her and bring her home, all covered in mud. Stewart carried her upstairs where we put her in the bathtub and I rinsed her off with a shower hose.

The morning wasn't over yet. I went online to check my business bank account to find that several fraudulent charges had been placed over the weekend, putting my account in the negative. Great. I spent the next hour or so calling the bank, speaking to someone, getting disconnected, and then calling another department that put me over to another department. Of course, that card is no longer valid as it had to be cancelled and so all of my online bill paying that uses that card has to be changed.

One reason I have stayed with my bank is because I have not wanted to change all the accounts; now it is mandatory and the card will be here in 7-14 business days. I decided to move forward with changing banks because I'm going to have to change all the account numbers anyway. I take this as my Oversoul telling me to "do it", so I am working on that.

And my morning was not over yet. I had to go to the bank to transfer funds from my personal account to my business so I can pay my business bills. I had to do it as cash to get my bank account out of the hole until the dispute department is able to get the funds back in my account, again, in another 7-10 business days.

They wouldn't let me do this through the drive-through, so I had to go into the bank that I detest, but the manager was on duty. Not too long ago, a person who called me into the bank to try to sell me some kind of bank bonds when I was making a deposit through the drive-through. I took the opportunity to tell the manager about the incident. Apparently, he had been in the bank that day, asked her why I was so upset and she said because their bank would not remortgage my home. So, I filled him on her calling me in from the drive-through while I was just trying to make a deposit and get my dad to his doctor's appointment.

## Aggravation

I feel more aggravated than stressed. Aggravation is not good. I did not feel peaceful and calm inside through any of it. Yes, I can do it and yes, everything managed to fall into place. I'm aggravated that I had to phone the pharmacy 3 times and tell the pharmacist how to do his job; aggravated that Jasmine escaped through a fence that I thought was repaired; aggravated that someone fraudulently used my card; overdrew my account; that the bank rep hung up on me; that I had to phone the bank more than once; that I had to make a special trip to town to put money in my account; had to go into the bank instead of using the drive-through; and that the bank rep lied to the manager about why I was upset that day in the bank.

Aggravate reminds me of aggregate, as defined by Wikipedia;

> In mineralogy and petrology, an *aggregate* is a mass of mineral crystals, mineraloid particles or rock particles. ...In the construction industry, an *aggregate* (often referred to as a construction *aggregate*) is sand, gravel or crushed rock that has been mined or quarried for use as a building material.

Aggregate (geology) - Wikipedia

https://en.wikipedia.org/wiki/Aggregate_(geology)

Grains of sand for me to pass up.

- Can you tell the difference between aggravate and stress?
- Does aggravation cause stress?
- Does aggravation cause movement, like my example of another push to open bank accounts at a different bank?
- Do these kinds of days push you into deeper realizations of what needs to be done?
- Have you been in the position of having to tell professionals, or anyone, how to do their job?
- If so, is this stressful or aggravating?
- Do you avoid making significant changes?
- Or changes that are going to take some time?
- Are these kinds of changes stressful, aggravating or simply inconvenient?

**Planned Stress**

Today was a planned day of stress. Both dogs went into the vet to be altered, so even though we have confidence in the vet, the Animal Mind can't help but be worried while the Spiritual Mind knows that all is okay.

Jasmine is totally passed out, which is a good thing, as she does seem to have some discomfort. Jade is half awake and even though I put him on his bed he's not too happy about it. Stewart petted Jasmine to sleep and now he is working on Jade. The blinds are pulled, the lights are out and our plan is that they sleep through the night.

- Are there times when your Spiritual Mind knows that "all is okay" yet your Animal Mind wants to fret and worry?

- Why does one part of you know that all is okay and the other part has to wonder how it is all going to happen?
- Are planned days of stress any less stressful than unexpected days of stress?
- Is the anticipation of what is to come stressful?
- Why does stress push you into your Animal Mind?
- Is stressing the Animal Mind an opportunity to control it?
- How is it possible to be peaceful in the Spiritual Mind yet so uncomfortable in the Animal Mind, all at the same time?

The dogs are doing well. They are quite active today, almost like nothing had ever happened, so that is a relief. If it were up to me, I would not alter either one of them, but all the research shows that if they are not altered they are at a higher risk for testicular cancer as well as mammary and uterine cancers. Apparently, if females do not have puppies and are not altered they are also at higher risks for these ailments. I read in Norway that it is illegal to alter dogs and cats. Even if there are medical reasons involved it is challenging to find a vet who would do this.

I was worried about Jasmine last night because she was so groggy when I went to bed. She woke up at 4 am whining, so I got up to check on her. She was wide awake and hungry. I fed her and then took her outside on a leash in the moonlight for a few minutes so she could relieve her Self, then back to bed for both of us. So, that is one stress that is completed. Jasmine still has to go back for removal of her stitches, but that is minor compared to what she has been through.

As previously mentioned 3 days ago, I wanted to open new bank accounts with a different bank, but as of today it still was not completed. The person helping me kept asking me the same questions that I had already answered, so I decided that this is the same aggravations I have had with the current bank. I was aggravated enough to call a larger national bank and was told that they could open my account within 1 hour and put a rush on my new debit card.

Again, I would prefer a smaller more local bank, but if it takes more than 3 days just to open an account, in a to-me-emergency-type-situation, then what else can I expect. So, even though I have known the VP of this smaller bank for almost 20 years I wrote her to say that her bank is unfortunately not a good fit for me at this time. My appointment with the new-bank-to-be isn't until the end of the week because of my schedule, but if they can do what I need done in 1 hour, then that is where I need to be.

Even though I was on the correct track to get out of my current bank situation, the track needed more refining to get me desperate enough to call a national bank. I am doing my best to trust the process. I am doing my best to use the stressors as signposts that something needs to change, and then to stop procrastinating and do something.

- How easy is it to keep doing the same thing, simply because it is what you know?
- How many times have you said that you are going to change something, and then didn't?
- How inconvenient is change?
- Does change ever come at a convenient time?
- Have you started to change something because of stress, then become even more stressed because you question your decision to change because the change is more challenging than you thought it would be?
- Are you sometimes stressed to accept your second choice rather than your first choice because first choice wasn't working out?
- Have you been forced to choose the lesser of the evils because none of the above is what you really want?

- Are you doing your best to trust the process?
- Does trusting the process feel rather bumpy more often than not?
- Does trusting the process cause you stress?
- Is there anything in life that is not stressful?

This morning I woke up to emails saying my FedEx account has been suspended and my website hosting payment could not be processed. I was able to switch the website hosting payment to a credit card as an intermediary. FedEx accepted the credit card but for some reason, I could not get the balance processed, so I will have to phone to get this corrected. I imagine these kinds of emails will continue to roll in until my new bank is in place.

I had 3 doctor appointments with my dad today; the good news is he will not need a third surgery, so that felt like a major victory. He still has some follow-up appointments but we know that the worst is behind him. Tomorrow I will be at the new bank at 9 am to get my accounts going; then take my dad to have his new hearing aids adjusted. Progress!

**Sleep**

I am truly tired; I did not sleep well thinking about all that needed to be accomplished today. Yet, everything got accomplished and ended on a positive note. The relief of letting go of this stress definitely has left me ready for bed. Holding stress in your mind and body is extremely tiring. It takes a lot of energy to keep your body tense and rigid, even when you do your best to relax.

Last night as I was lying awake, I continued to contemplate the reason why we need to sleep and reset. Everything in the world sleeps. Sleep gives you the time to subconsciously connect to your Source. As I was lying in bed, my body was still and quiet, I thought perhaps I need to sleep to connect to the Original Energy Generator/Source to fully recharge the body for the next day.

- Why cannot humans keep going 24/7?
- Why do all animals take time to sleep?
- Can sleep be an escape from stress of daily challenges?
- Can sleep elude you because your brain continues to process your life while your body rests?
- Can your body reset/recharge/reset if your brain is busy?
- Does your body tense when your mind is stressed?
- Do you monitor your body for the tension of stress, such as closed fists, hunched shoulders and shallow breathing?
- Do you consciously take the time to relax areas of physical stress as well as take a few deep breaths to calm down?
- Do you remember that your brain is your most oxygen intensive organ of the body and that without oxygen/deep breathing your brain cannot function at full capacity?
- When you feel stress, are you challenged to think?
- Is learning to think with a balanced brain under stress, challenging?
- Does utilizing stress properly enhance your ability to think with a balanced brain under stress?
- Do you think nighttime stress is different than daytime stress?
- Do you grow from nighttime stress as much as daytime stress?
- Do you do your protection/merger work before sleeping?
- Is your nightly mental work routine different than what you do in the day?

Not getting what you want is extremely stressful. Most people have a picture of who they are, how they want their life to turn out, and the way they envision it happening. When life does not match what you have in your head, it takes a lot of mental and emotional adjustment to accept what is happening in the way that it is happening.

As a child, I felt like I was in a survival mode. As an adult, my life did not flow the way I thought it would. In fact, it has never flowed like I thought it would. At this stage in my life, I have given up and allowed it to be what it is instead of continually trying to force the outcome that I originally intended. I think this attitude of giving up allows each day to bring what it does; I experience each day more fully because I am more present than worrying about the future or what was or wasn't.

Sooner or later everything does work out; the more I stress about how the more pressure I am under. The pressure actually makes the adjustment to life more challenging, not less challenging. As an example, when a person faints, the body goes limp. When the body falls, it is much less likely to be injured when it is limp/gives up than if it is stiff. Going limp/giving up is a protective mechanism for the body in this case.

If you are ever in an accident, if you can think fast enough to go limp you are much less likely to be injured than if you stiffen up from pressure/stress/fear. In the same way, becoming more flaccid means that as you are bounced around in the river of life you are less likely to break mentally and emotionally. This also makes you more buoyant and less likely to be damaged by the turbulence you encounter.

However, this also means doing the opposite of what you feel like doing. The Animal Mind wants to get tense; ready for fight or flight. The Spiritual Mind must stay connected and ready to do as Source directs. This is extremely challenging when you are in a human body that wants to react as a human.

- Does focusing on the present challenge you?
- Are you most likely to think about the past, what was/wasn't?
- Or on the future and stress about what is to come/how it is to come?
- Why does the Animal Mind fight with the Spiritual Mind?

- Why does the Animal Mind want to fight or flight?

- Why does the Spiritual Mind always tell you that everything is already okay?

- Why is it challenging to listen to the Spiritual Mind and override the Animal Mind?

- Have you ever been in a situation where you fainted but your body was physically okay?

- Or some kind of accident where you somehow knew to go limp so your body would be less likely to be injured?

- Is it challenging to know that all is well when the linear world is telling you that it is not?

- Are you able to do the opposite of what you feel; i.e., stay where you are and deal with life vs. fight or flight?

- If other people are more in their Animal Minds, are they reflections of your own Animal Mind?

- Do you have compassion for people who are in their Animal Mind?

- Do people who are in their Animal Mind get you wound up and ready to fight/flight vs. reach higher for unconditional love and compassion for them?

- When life does not match what you have in your head, are you emotionally and mentally challenged, i.e., stressed?

- Is not getting what you want stressful?

Watching others get what you want can be extremely stressful. It took me many years to realize that everyone and everything has a time and place. I had a time table in my mind of how things should happen and when. When things did not come together the way I thought they should, I was extremely disappointed and my Self-Worth plummeted.

I also had to learn that not every experience that I wanted was destined for my path in life. Eventually, many hopes and dreams had to be released with new ones taking their place. But again, this doesn't mean that the new hopes and dreams materialized either.

Such is life, at least in this reality. However, watching what others go through who do have what you want forces you to focus on not only the up side of what you think you want but also the down side. Sometimes it is easy to see why you didn't get what you want; other times it is not so easy. Or, if you logically understand why, emotionally can still be challenging to accept.

- Are there things in life that you would have liked, that you saw other people get?
- If so, did this/does this make you feel stressed?
- Is it challenging to accept that others can have what you want, but for whatever reason, their path is not your path in life?
- When you have not gotten what you wanted, is it easy to fall into disappointment and low Self-Worth?
- Is it challenging to think that there is a better plan?
- Is there always that part of you that wants to know what that better plan is?
- Do you observe others who have what you think you want so you can see the down side as well as the up side?
- Have you let go of some of your hopes and dreams, replaced them with new hopes and dreams, and then those hopes and dreams also did not materialize?
- Can you sometimes logically understand why certain things did not work out in your life as you wanted, but emotionally you are challenged to let go of not getting what you wanted when you wanted?
- Can you use other people as in inspiration to help focus you on what you do want without feeling stressed by their success?

- Because of what you know, do you think your Soul holds you to higher standards than the average person?
- Can you compare one person to another?
- Can you compare a tulip to a daffodil?

On the weekends, I like to have a couple of slower days than during the week. I like to sleep in until about 8 am if I can and then slowly make my way out of my bed to get ready for my day.

I try to only do the necessities and save the more involved tasks for my Monday-Friday heavier work days. During the week my days are long. My work days are anywhere from 12-16 hours. Once I am up and going I rarely slow down. As I have mentioned, being Self-employed has its upsides as well as downsides. But for now, this is my life and here I am.

I do find that the busier I am the more organized I am; the more I get accomplished, and actually, the more energized I feel. On my lazy weekend days, I move a lot slower and enjoy the slower pace. I have established a rhythm that works for me. If I work at the same pace through the weekend as I do during the week, I find that I am not as productive as I want to be. I have that burned out feeling. If I need to, I can keep going.

- Do you think that rest has to do with the inbreath and the outbreath of the God-Mind as It creates?
- You rest because the God-Mind breathes in?
- You are active when the God-Mind breathes out?
- Is the breathing of your body a re-creation of the creative force of the God-Mind?
- Without breath, your body cannot continue on?
- With breath, your body is active?

- Is it possible that when you sleep you ride the inbreath of the God-Mind and this is why it feels easier to subconsciously connect to Source?

- Because in True Reality you are actually more in the present moment/closer to God?

- Is it possible that the God-Mind created life in all realities in waves?

- Could you be on one wave while others in humanity are on a wave of creation that came after you?

- And perhaps there was one wave (or more) that came before you?

- Do you try to create your life so that it has a rhythm to it?

- Do you have regular rest or irregular rest, in general?

- If so, with what do you try to align your rest?

- Is the night dark because this is when you are deeper within the God-Mind?

- Do you rest as well in the day as you do at night?

- Is sleeping at night more in alignment with the body's natural rhythm?

- Why does one not sleep as well in the day?

- How important is it to align with the natural rhythm of the God-Mind?

- Is there always order within the God-Mind?

- Are you always looking for your place within this rhythm on some level?

Sometimes you do not understand why you did not get what you want when you wanted until many years later. Your path is not that of the ordinary person. You are striving to be more than the Animal Mind; you are striving to go beyond personal and societal programming; you are striving for conscious answers from the God-Mind in the way that is most correct and beneficial for you.

To accomplish all of this, to know that you have surpassed your tests, you are shown every reason in your life why you should follow your Animal Mind, fall into programming as well as get what you can any way you can. Most people buy into this way of thinking; then they judge you because you do not think like them. And because there are more of them than you, it is easy to look at others and then stress about your perceived failures rather than celebrate your accomplishments.

Often, these types of people seem to know your weak spots and which buttons to push to get you even further upset. These too, are tests so you can decide if you want to follow the low road or the high road. Many people fall off their paths because they cannot take the stress of what other people give them. I have noticed through the years that I care less and less about what other people think of me and more and more about what I think of me.

As unpleasant as my trial by fire has been/can be, I keep marching on. The more I accept that my life is what it is, the less stress I feel to make it something different. I feel like the path of life is already set and I am now walking on it vs. always trying to change it here or there. One day at a time is a much easier concept for me to grasp now than when I was in my earlier decades. Each day becomes more meaningful for what it is rather than for what I want it to be. Every day teaches me and gives me the opportunity to be better at whatever it is I am currently working on. Even my nightmares are no longer nightmares. I am rarely even afraid in my dreams.

- Do you live a less-stressed life than you used to?
- Does knowing what you know help you focus on one day at a time?
- Do you have nightmares?

- Are you afraid in your dreams?
- Do you have recurring dreams or recurring dream themes?
- Do you do your best to learn from each day rather than being stressed about what the future might hold?
- Do you think your path of life is already set?
- Do you try to change it?
- Do other people try to force you off your path?
- Have you seen others fall off of their paths?
- Do you consider your trial by fire unpleasant?
- Do you think others are in your life to tempt you to turn your back on your correct path?
- Are you challenged to think like the ordinary person?
- Does the ordinary person understand you?
- Do you stress because you are so different than most people?
- Do you stress because ordinary people think you are a failure?

Astronauts in space are challenged to stay physically healthy because there is no gravity for their muscles to push against. Without gravity, their bodies are not stressed. In essence, it is more important for an astronaut to be an athlete than a scientist.

When I was in my 20s I cut a tendon on one of my fingers. It was in a cast for 6 weeks; the finger had no stress and while it healed, it atrophied. It was a few years before I felt that finger was as strong as the other ones.

When I was pregnant with my first child, I was on bed rest for 3 months. It is amazing how quickly the body deteriorates without stress. It took me a long time to regain the strength in my legs.

The body can be stressed in a variety of ways. You often see the Russians in the winter out in the cold water and snow with very little clothing to stress the body and build up the immune system. The body needs stress to be healthy. In the same way, the mind needs stress to be healthy; keeping your mind active keeps you mentally alert and your brain in good shape.

And, your emotions need stress to be healthy. You need to feel what you feel, but then learn how to appropriately express or not express your feelings. You are challenged to create balanced stress in your life to keep body, mind, and Soul healthy. Without stress, all the aspects that create you can wither away.

- Do you manage your stress or does your stress manage you?
- Can you have so much stress in life that you become numb to what is happening?
- Have you had experiences where you go through the motions of life, but you are so stressed that your emotions were not functioning, meaning you were numb?
- If so, is it challenging to find your way back to being a feeling, caring, loving person?
- If your emotions are on overwhelm, does your mental capacity increase to get you through the tough times?
- Or, do you suddenly find the physical strength to push through when all else fails?
- Is your goal to have balanced stress evenly spread throughout your life?
- If so, what happens when one stressor takes over all other stressors?
- Does stressing the body create health?
- Have you experienced body atrophy due to lack of use/stress?
- If so, how long did it take you to build it back up?
- Is the body meant to be used?
- If the body is not used, does it waste away?

- Is the mind meant to be used?
- If not, does the mind waste away?
- Are emotions meant to be used?
- If not, do you grow numb and become robotic-like?
- When body, mind and emotions are stressed, are you forced into deeper and greater Spiritual Growth of the Soul?
- Is this the purpose of stress?

## Programming

Stress can easily push you into your programming as well as back into old patterns and behaviors that you thought were behind you. With awareness, you now have direction and focus on what still needs to go. When you start to feel stressed/overwhelmed, you are challenged to use your energy to keep moving forward vs. go backwards. There are many temptations to go back and not too many carrots to keep you moving forward.

You have to dig deeper into that well of inner strength and connectedness to Source to stay on the path, even if you sometimes wonder exactly where that path is leading you. There will be some days when you surpass and some days when you totally lose it. This is the process as you build up strength to keep on keeping on. Stress challenges you to do something different, if for no other reason than as a survival tool. Stress also challenges you with options of going back rather than going forward.

Sometimes you go forward kicking and screaming even when it is for your own highest good. You can easily get triggered into anger and fits of rage. Some people get triggered into emotional eating or other forms of Self-abuse.

Stress continually tests you to see if you are getting stronger, moving forward, making more correct and beneficial choices. This is why I give you the basics; so that when the going gets tough (and it will) you have some basic tools that you can use to keep moving in the direction that is most correct and beneficial for you.

Health crises are opportunities to fix your mind-pattern or bow out of the game of physical reality. You see some people who change completely; others who choose to leave. As long as you are here, it is important that you make the most of every opportunity. The more stress you have and surpass, the stronger you become.

- Do times of stress sometimes make you want to give up?
- Do times of stress sometimes make you want to dig your heels in deeper and charge forward to prove to Self (and maybe to others) that you are bigger and more powerful than anyone could ever have imagined?
- Do you have broad shoulders, meaning that you can carry a lot of mental/emotional/spiritual and physical burdens?
- Just because you can carry so much, is it always most correct and beneficial that you do so?
- When you realize your own capacities are you sometimes challenged to have compassion for those with their own burdens which compared to yours, seem lightweight?
- When you feel stressed and overwhelmed, do you remember to use your Hyperspace/Oversoul tools? sometimes? almost? all the time? every now and then?
- Do you get stressed if you use these tools and they do not work the way you think they should?
- Are these moments opportunities to beat your Self up or to dig into Source even deeper?
- If you beat your Self up, do you stress over how you feel?
- Does stress make you question what you are doing and how?
- Is it important to always question?

- When you are stressed how easy is it to fall back into old habits that you thought you were past?
- If you do this, then are you stressed that you went backwards?
- Do you feel stress forces you to make the most of every opportunity, even on days when there is a part of you that wants to run away?
- Are your wanting to run away days lessening in power over you?
- Are you increasingly more willing to stay and do what needs to be done, regardless of how uncomfortable the situation?

A huge stressor for most people is not wanting to be here. I went through this phase for many, many years. It took a lot of Self-talk and pep talks to keep my Self going and growing. That is why I eventually started *Expansions*. I figured that if I was lonely with my belief system there had to be other people in the same situation. It took a lot of courage to step out of my metaphysical closet in the 1980s in a rural community. But I did and I found others who were interested in the same subjects that I was.

This doesn't mean that we were all 100% alike. And that I didn't have issues with people. The daughter of one of my students first thought I was of the devil; then she joined our group so she could spy on me; then she decided that I was okay; then she got frightened of having to face her Self; then she dropped out of the group and kept me at a distance. Another one of my student's husband despised me so much that if he met me on the street he walked right past me. And so on and so forth.

You take the good with the bad; the bad with the good. And no matter where you are in any universe, you are going to be dealing with others because you are not meant to be A-Lone, and you are not, nor will you ever be.

When you have micro-people experiences that you cannot get through; or should I say, you don't want to get through, you set up the scenario so you fail. Then you can get back into your victim-mentality looping of not wanting to be here. If you are lonely, reach out and touch someone. Most likely you will not be 100% alike and you will not agree on everything. In fact, you may not agree more than you do agree. But that is okay. No one is going to like all of you until you like all of you.

It is challenging to work on the parts of you that you do not like so much. You can do little things. For example, when you look in the mirror you may see body parts that you do not like. Instead of thinking about how much you do not like them, focus on how much you do like them. If you didn't like them this way, they would not be this way. It is your mind-pattern that built them. Give them some positive attention instead of negative attention.

There are always going to be positives and negatives to every person, place and/or thing. You can use the negatives as an excuse to avoid your life or you can march into the negative and face it, using it as a teacher and looking at what you can learn. When things aren't going your way, keep looking at you until you realize why the situation is most correct and beneficial. Then, use the situation to your advantage.

I told how I used the fraudulent use of my credit card to get my Self to another bank. Then, after the inconvenience/redirection of a second bank which pushed me to a third bank. Yes, there were bits and pieces of anger, annoyance, irritation, bitterness and victim-mentality floating around in me, but I have done my best to release these thoughts and feelings and know that I am now in a better place.

And, it is going to take some time to get all my automatic payments changed, and stored credit card payments changed, but I am working at it every day and eventually, it will get done. It would have been much easier to stay with the original bank and continue to bemoan my situation, but I used it to my advantage.

- What kind of negative experiences have you had that you used to your advantage?
- Do you use your negative experiences to motivate you to get to a better place?
- Is transition ever easy?
- Can you expect to be stressed?
- Is it okay to be stressed?
- If you feel you have to avoid a situation, is it because you do not feel strong enough to handle it?
- Are you too nervous/stressed about the outcome rather than the process?
- And if the outcome isn't what you want, is it okay to be flexible, knowing that whatever the outcome, it is what is most correct and beneficial for you?
- Are you challenged to work on the parts of you that you do not like so much?
- Is it easier to avoid what you do not like?
- Is this your pattern in life?
- Have you ever met anyone who liked you 100%?
- Or who you liked 100%?
- How much do you allow other people to stress you?
- How much do you not want to be here because of other people?
- Does that even make any sense?
- Why would Beings of any kind be any different if your mind-pattern is the same?
- And if they are higher level then don't you think that you are going to irritate them?
- And if you are here to help those who are here, then how can you help them if you avoid them?

- Can being an example help others?
- Are you an example for others?
- Do you take the good with the bad and the bad with the good?
- Do you reject people and situations that you do not consider all good?
- Can you get through any situation when you decide to do so?
- Does getting through the situation make it easy?
- Do you expect life to be easy?
- Can you easily get through stress/use stress when you have the correct attitude?

Suicide programming is very strong in heavily programmed people. I spent the first 30 years of my life praying to die. When I was around 30, I realized that I was here for a reason and made up my mind to stay.

I have known many people through the years who wanted to die. They stated this until they created the situation where they willed themselves into deep illnesses. When it came down to really dying the person then often wanted to live. But for many of these types of people, it was too little, too late because of what they set in motion and then fed for many years. Each eventually passed away.

Through my years of study, I have concluded that it is the little child within who wants to die. The child feels hopeless, without solutions, without resources and alone. When you grow up the child within and realize that your childhood is not your identity, that you already are everything that you ever were and will be, then you stop going into this childhood alter that feels trapped without anywhere to turn.

The *Child Within* visualization in **Hyperspace Helper** is one of the most basic and powerful things that you can do. I do not know one person who has not experienced some kind of childhood trauma, then replays that drama/s throughout his/her entire life. You have to get over it if you want to get on with life. There are so many people who avoid this or that type of person, or cut people out of their lives because these people represent parental/authority figures from childhood with whom they have unresolved issues.

Simply because that person is not in your life does not mean that his/her influence is not in your life. This is why you continually bring people into your life who stress you. On some level, they remind you of someone at some time in your life who did horrible things to you. You are not reacting to that person. You are reacting to what that person reminds you of—some parental/authority figure of your childhood that traumatized you in some way and you never got over it.

- Why does childhood trauma still influence people, regardless of age?
- Why does everyone have some kind of trauma that influences all of their days?
- Why is life set up to imprint you with something so mind-blowing at an early age that without constant work, you continue to repeat that cycle?
- Do you have childhood trauma because this tells you what your lessons are that you are to pay attention to while you are here?
- Is it okay to remove these types of people from your life until you are able to face them?
- Can you ever remove them or do you just continue to draw in the same type of person over and over again?
- Do you do the *Child Within* visualization on a consistent basis?
- Do you think you react to your life as a child?
- Is it easy to fall into despair and hopelessness when you feel stressed?

- Did you feel despair and hopelessness, or similar emotions when you were a child?

- Have you known people who willed themselves to die?

- Or people who willed themselves to be ill?

- Or people who said they wanted to die until it was time to pass away?

- When you are stressed are you/were you challenged to stay here and complete your mission here on this Earth?

- When people are stressed, why do they consciously choose death over life?

- Do animals choose death over life or do they do what they can to live?

- Does the Animal Mind fight to stay here?

- Can the Animal Mind help move through suicide programming?

As a child, "fight" was never in my vocabulary. I just wanted to give up. I was never allowed to fight or have any feelings of controversy. So, fighting never entered my mind. I do not think I even realized that fighting was an option. I did not know about programming and mind-control until I met Stewart at age 40.

The fact that you are aware of what you are up against is a tremendous advantage that I did not have until Stewart came into my life. Programming is designed to either control your mind or break you. You are finding your inner strength, power and yes, fight through your anguish. And, you are learning where all of this comes from.

You may not be comfortable, but you are growing and gaining much more ground than you give your Self credit. Your mind-pattern has pulled to you the gift of understanding so you can make more conscious choices. You have more knowledge of your options. As you are discovering, more knowledge does not mean easy. More knowledge gives you more responsibility than other people. This means more stress because you can handle more. The more stress you have, the more you grow.

There is something different in you that other people recognize and feel threatened by. As a child, you do not understand this; as an adult, you realize that people are afraid of themselves. You are facing your Self in ways that most people are not. They do not want to see their positive potentials in you; they want to wallow in their own unique experiences for now.

There are many paths to God; ultimately each person is already at his/her destination because in True Reality there is no time or space. This is why there is no judgment of the path of another. Your responsibility is to stay on your path so your Soul uses every opportunity it has in the linear time it is allotted here on this Earth.

One day, when others are ready to walk the same linear path, they will be able to follow the frequency that you walked and strengthened for them. Just like Stewart and I have helped each other by blending our 2 paths; my dad opened the frequency for the path that Stewart and I walk together. If you are on this path, your life has been stressful and blessedly so, or you would not be where you are today regarding your Soul growth.

- Do you feel blessed by stress?
- Has stress forced you to look for answers in places you would not have thought to look?
- Have others walked similar paths to yours, thus strengthening the frequency to help you better stay on your unique Soul journey?
- Does the stress in your life make you less judgmental of the paths of others?

- Does stress keep you focused on getting the most out of each Soul growth opportunity?
- Does more knowledge of Spiritual Law make you more responsible?
- Do you keep in mind that the higher you are, the harder
- you fall?
- Is it just as important to do what is most correct and beneficial whether anyone sees you or knows what you do?
- Does more knowledge make life easier?
- Is understanding a gift?
- Does understanding open your range of options, whether you like the options or not?
- Can you use your programming to develop your inner fight?
- Can you use your programming as a springboard into who and what you are?
- Can you use your programming as a blessing in disguise?

Because programming is hooked into who you are, programming can help you discover deeper layers of Self. For example, you cannot have Isolation Programming unless you have some lifeline where you are isolated. You cannot have Warrior Programming unless you have some lifeline where you are a warrior. You cannot have Prince/Princess Programming unless you are this in some lifeline.

Many people become quite stressed when they realize that they are programmed. However, once you realize that these alters are built on top of what you already are, you can use this to your advantage to go into deeper layers of Self. You cannot have Suicide Programming, for example, unless you did this in some lifeline. Maybe you gave your life to save others, so this is the hook for Suicide Programming. And, this could also be tied into Savior Programming. Rather than stress about the programming, you have a lot of information about who and what you are.

- Have you determined your various Programs that most affect you?
- Is Programming designed to negatively stress you?
- Are people more controllable when they are negatively stressed?
- If people are told that stress is bad, are you programmed to think that something is wrong when you feel stressed?
- Does knowing that stress plays a positive role make you less likely to be controllable by outside forces as well as inside artificially installed mind-patterns/Programming?
- Does stress force you to think more carefully about your choices when you realize that stress is not bad?
- Does "stress" equal "Soul growth/potential Soul growth"?
- Does societal programming always say that stress is bad?
- Are there ways that societal programming says stress is good?

Societal programming is an ongoing issue for you to buy into or not buy into. You are supposed to be stressed about saving the planet. Everything is about the death of the human population. Not only are you supposed to be stressed about the future of all humanity, but you are also supposedly killing the planet. Talk about attempting to negatively stress you.

You are told that plastic is killing everything from whales, deep sea life, and oceans, for example. People believe these stories. The global elite need you focused and stressed about something; they must be shaking their heads over how gullible people are. People are killing the planet one way or the other, according to them. As if everyday stressors are not enough, now this one on top of your daily stressors. So every time you use anything with plastic, buy anything with plastic or throw anything away with plastic, you are stressing with a lot of guilt thrown in.

My favorite thing you are not supposed to do is use straws and/or those little plastic cocktail stirrers. You are supposed to buy stainless steel straws to take everywhere with you instead. Like, who really needs straws, anyway. And how much money are the stainless steel straw manufacturers think they will clear before people wise up?

You aren't supposed to use plastic bags or paper bags; you are supposed to buy cloth bags. The retailers not only do not have to buy plastic/paper bags, but they can sell you cloth bags. Brilliant idea for the big guys to save money and get you to part with more of your hard-earned cash.

Everywhere you look there is a reason for you to feel bad simply because you exist. Now, you should feel especially bad if you are White. Or, if you have a family vs. those who are from broken families. And all of these stories somehow tie into climate change including alien abductions and human-alien hybridization theories from prestigious universities.

You can either buy into these stories or break through the societal programming to know truth vs. lies. You can use these stories to feel bad because you exist or know that part of your existence is to see through these societal programming stories. These are tests to determine if the Animal Mind is in charge; if you will fight; flight; or go up into the Spiritual Mind and look to Source for guidance vs. fall into the trap of humankind.

- How easy is it to become stressed simply because you exist?
- Are there guilt traps everywhere?
- Do you think your parents felt guilty about their existence?
- If guilt is installed in your parents, then is this automatically passed on to you?

- How many ways can society be bombarded with guilt?
- If you feel guilty, do you automatically feel bad?
- If you feel bad and have low Self-Worth, are you easier to control?
- Does this cause more societal infighting?
- Do people look for others to blame vs. take Self-responsibility?
- Can taking Self-responsibility lead to guilt?
- How easy is it to get society looping on guilt? fear? fighting? flighting? Animal Mind?
- If you do not buy into societal programming, are you more apt to be odd man out?
- Does this force you deeper into programming or deeper into Source?
- Is it better to be alone than wish you were alone?
- How challenging is it to obey human law while still upholding Spiritual Law?

Young people are not being taught to respect elders, their history and/or their knowledge. Even when my boys were young what I said was disputed whenever the teacher at school said something different. After all, the schools have your children for many more hours every day than you.

Young children are so impressionable that they are the easiest ones to program. Just like the "Drag Queen" storytime, for example at libraries around the US. While the adults are arguing over how horrible it is, the children have already been exposed and now their normal is much different than your normal.

Every generation is given something different to stress about than their parents so they are continually separated from their elders. Or, they are given a different verse to the same song so parental programming is intensified. The sooner the programmers get into the minds of the children, the easier the children are controlled and manipulated. Children have a new normal that they have always known they accept with little if any, questioning. Parents help perpetuate this new normal by following what the schools want them to do with their children.

I can remember thinking how old-fashioned my mother was for cleaning with white vinegar and water. I was thrilled when I discovered 409 and Windex for cleaning; it did such a better job in an easier way than my mother's vinegar method. Of course, vinegar is cheap compared to other cleaning products.

The more decades you live, the more you see the same stories repeated in different ways for each upcoming generation. There will always be something for you to stress about, feel guilty and bad about, and question your own Self-Worth and value. Instead of doing your own mental, emotional, physical and spiritual work, you spend your time stressing in negative ways that bring you down and accomplish nothing but destruction, usually your own.

The more you understand societal as well as personal programming, the sooner you get off that loop to realize that you have been stressing for the wrong reasons. Now you can focus on stress/stretching for the correct reasons so you can accomplish some real personal growth and Self-awareness.

- How different would the world be if people ignored the societal stressors that are foisted upon them?

- How many times have you seen societal stressors placed on the public but they have refused to bite?

- How many new programs are put out at one time so if you don't choose one in which to participate it is highly likely that you will choose another without even realizing that you are doing this?

- Why is it to the advantage of the global controllers to get into the minds of the young at an early stage?
- Can you pinpoint societal programming that was instilled in you at a young age?
- Did you think your parents and grandparents were old-fashioned in their thinking?
- Were you around elders when you were growing up?
- If so, did you listen to them and turn to them for guidance?
- Did you respect their knowledge and history?
- Have you observed that each generation has new stressors foisted upon it?
- Do you think those who organize these stressors are part of the global agenda?
- How about the children who speak at events or appear to organize activities or create new inventions, are these real or staged?
- Is your normal different than the normal of your parents and/or grandparents?
- Are you learning to focus on stress/stretching for the correct reasons?
- Is stress a naturally inherent part of growth?
- Do you react to stress from Oversoul/God-Mind level or wounded child or Animal Mind level?
- Does "calm" equal "numb"?

## AFFIRMATIONS—DIGESTING LIFE

A well-functioning digestion system is more unusual than a functioning one, despite greater access to more information. Digestion of food relates to what /how you digest your life. Any physical digestion issues you have is a reflection of mental/emotional issues you have with digesting whatever is going on in your life.

*I easily digest my life.*
*My body easily digests the food that I feed it.*


*I remember to keep Pale Yellow in my Solar Plexus Chakra Band.*
*I easily absorb the information my life provides.*


*I accept the discomforts of life.*
*Being uncomfortable in life is normal.*


*I release the need to numb my feelings.*
*I allow my Self to feel what life is.*


*It is okay to feel negative emotions.*
*Negative emotions are a part of the God-Mind.*


*All experience comes from Source, whether I like the experience or not.*
*I appreciate the totality of the God-Mind.*


*I release the need to fight what I do not like.*
*I realize that what I do not like might be exactly what my*
*Soul needs to grow.*

*I release the need to judge and criticize those people who I do not like.*
*I realize that those people might hold the key to my Soul growth.*

*I embrace what I do not like as directed by my Oversoul and God-Mind.*
*I reject what I do not like as directed by my Oversoul and God-Mind.*

*I do not have to like everything that exists within the God-Mind.*
*My Oversoul and God-Mind directs me in what to*
*participate/not participate.*

*I always ask my Oversoul to guide me in what is most correct and*
*beneficial in every moment.*
*I release the need to judge what others do/not do.*

*I allow others to have their experiences without judging their*
*actions/reactions.*
*I release the need to judge my own actions/reactions.*

*I accept that this world is God's world*
*I release the need to judge/criticize God-s world.*

*Everything comes from One Source.*
*Everything exists for a reason/purpose.*

*I realize I may or may not understand all the purposes in God's world.*
*I ask my Oversoul/god-Mind to explain the world to me.*

*I accept the answers from my Oversoul and God-Mind.*
*I accept that sometimes the answers to my questions are no answers.*

*I accept the timing of my Oversoul and God-Mind.*
*I release the need to force my timing and my way into my understanding.*

*I do my best to trust the process of my life.*
*On some level "I already know."*

*I allow my patience to grow.*
*I allow my True Parent to teach me in its way.*

*I give my attention to my Source.*
*I do my best to absorb the life lessons from my Source*
*in the way It gives them.*

*I AM guided into Divine Order at all times.*
*I know that chaos is simply Divine Order not yet understood.*

*I patiently find clarity in the way my Source directs me.*
*I release the need to follow the timetable of humankind.*

*I follow the timetable of Source at all times.*
*I release the need to fall into the trap of human-sanctioned time.*

*I do my best to exist in the Eternal Now.*
*I do my best to understand and follow Universal Law.*

*I do my best to apply Universal Law.*
*I allow my Source to correct and guide my Soul growth as needed.*

*It is okay when Soul growth is not easy.*
*I look for growth before I look for easy.*

*My trials strengthen me.*
*I AM here for Soul growth.*

*I have compassion for my Self.*
*I have compassion for others.*

*I know my Self for what I AM.*
*I grow my Self into my own I AM.*

*My life is customized for my personal Soul growth.*
*I utilize my life that I AM given to the best of my ability at all times.*

# Be The Change

I have seen the phrase "Be the Change" so many times, I could almost say that it has become repetitive and boring. Originally, I thought I made up the phrase, but then I had to chuckle when I started seeing it everywhere. And like the majority of repetitive phrases, most people kind of stop seeing it. Just like when there are items in your home that need to be cleaned up, but you stop seeing them, even though they are right in front of you. I still like the "Be the Change" phrase because you are already the change, even if you do not feel like it.

Societal media is filled with so many platitudes that most people do not have a clue how to accomplish. There is this odd layer beneath the platitudes that seems to say if you wish upon a star long enough, what you want comes to you.

This seems to be the general attitude. People want something better, but they do not have a clue how to bring it to themselves. And something better seems to be either all tied to money, wanting to win the lottery, or throwing all your money away since you can't get it anyway to live out in nature without anything. One extreme to the other. No balance and no knowledge.

On social media, I post a lot of photos from the Waldensian Valleys. These are real people with real lives interacting with each other and nature; working diligently and hard, with inner satisfaction as well as a sense of belonging.

There are pictures of families hiking, herding their animals, family-owned restaurants, cheese-makers, chestnuts gathered from local trees being roasted, mushrooms that are seasonally gathered, maintaining hiking trails, as a few examples. Real people, real lives, connected to the Earth and to each other; definitely connected to their own inner moral/ethical/spiritual compass that directs their daily lives. They know their neighbors, the townspeople and vendors, and they help each other.

They still have their struggles with each other and within families. People are people. And here we are in our corner of the world, doing our best to be real, to support each other and our Selves so we can do whatever is most correct and beneficial for each Soul.

You have an inner moral/ethical/spiritual compass; you are doing your best to be who you are; to work diligently and hard; to find a sense of belonging; to know/help Self and each other; to find a place of balance; to improve and elevate not by wishing on a star and hoping, but by aligning with your Source and thereby charting your Personal Course. In this moment, you are the balance between all the extremes of the world.

*You are eliminating right and wrong and judgment.*

*You are releasing your need to swing from one extreme to another.*

*You are forgiving.*

*You are letting go of extraneous thoughts and feelings that could weigh you down.*

*You are releasing the mind-control and programming.*

*You are willing to put in the time, effort and work so that you can harvest your rewards when it is appropriate for you to do so.*

*You are learning patience, even when you feel impatient.*

- Do you think about your Self as "the Change"?
- Do you realize the impact that you have on this Earth and others simply by Being and doing?
- Do you think about your own inner moral/ethical/spiritual compass?
- Where did that come from?
- Why is it within you?
- What propels you to keep going, even when it feels like the odds are against you?
- Do you feel the hold of mind-control and programming lessening?
- Are you learning patience, even when you feel impatient?
- Are you learning to follow the timing of your Soul vs. the body/Animal Mind?
- Are you learning to mitigate the extremes in your life?
- Is forgiving easier than it was?
- Are you consistently agreeing to not carry the weight of your past with you?
- Are you learning to be steadfast even when you want to run?
- Do you think that you are holding a space for those who are brave enough to take up a similar path of Being?
- Does it matter who is or who is not watching you, as long as you know that you are connected and anchored deep within your Source?

The stronger you become, the bigger the battles. You are developing your mind in a way that few people on this planet are willing to do. You are engaging in a unique path that puts what is most correct and beneficial as your goal. Most people only want what they want when they want it. You are learning to determine what is most correct and beneficial for you as well as to wait for the most correct and beneficial timing. Your mind is getting stronger because of what you are going through. You are not only a mental warrior, but you are an unsung mental hero.

Yes, programming is intense; both personal and societal. You can choose to feed into it or you can get out of it. Just like an alcoholic or a drug addict. You can become addicted to your programming and go deeper into it. Programming addicts are everywhere. They like to call themselves Targeted Individuals amongst other things. Well, hello! If this is what you are going to label your Self, then you cannot expect something different to happen.

You will always find people to feed the lower aspects of Self in this Earthly and astral soup of existence.

- Why do you think you came here?
- To live a life of love, light and peace?
- Or to determine your own strengths amongst the cesspool?
- How tempting is it to give in to the masses?
- To argue, fight, gossip and slander?
- How long do people last before it pulls them under?
- Do you want to get in the dirt with them?
- Or, do you want to allow them their process while you get on with yours?
- Would you really want to sit back and do nothing?
- Would you get bored after a few days of resting without any battles to challenge you?

- When you watch movies and read books, aren't the heroes invigorated when their next battle is on the horizon?
- Do the real heroes run from the battles or do they embrace the fight because they know they are the only ones who can do what needs to be done?
- Are you a mental hero?
- As a hero, do you need to be recognized by others?
- Or only by Self and Source?
- Do you really care if other people do not understand your process, as long as you know what you are doing and why?

Decades ago, my brother told me that I could never change anything from the outside; all change had to come from within. I was a bit more militant in my attitude and what I was going to do for the world. I have certainly watched this happen all over the world, in every aspect and corner.

Infiltrators either gather people to form a group that they can direct, or join an already-formed group and then jockey to direct the opinion of the group. Look at the transgender issue—who ever thought Bruce Jenner would agree to become a woman! What a great spokesperson to hold up to already confused people to get them to make their own choice to follow this trend.

After he had surgery on his Adam's Apple, he looked in the mirror and exclaimed, "What have I done!" Now he is dating a 23 year old young woman. So, if he's interested in females, why did he want to become a female? None of it makes sense, but this is the idea—to confuse you with the agenda of controlling you.

The global handlers know exactly what they are doing. They lay out the path for people to willingly follow, and people go. No one forces anyone to do anything. People willingly become the change that the global handlers want. Your goal, is to "Be the Change" that your Oversoul/Source wants you to be. Refusing to participate in the global

100 • Heights of Wealth

handler agenda is building your character and making you strong. This does not mean easy. It means strong.

- How easy is it to become the change that you consciously never intended to become?
- How easy is it to fall into the agenda of someone else without realizing that you are giving away your Self?
- Is a confused society easier to control?
- Is an angry society easier to control?
- Is there an agenda to make victims feel empowered, only to control those who feel victimized?
- Is a person like Bruce Jenner a victim?
- If people make the conscious choice to do something, does this still mean they are victims?
- When you are looking for Self-empowerment, how easy is it to find someone who tells you what you want to hear vs. what you need to hear?
- Were parents and family the voice of what you needed to hear?
- Does society need a restructuring?
- What can you, one person, do to aid in the restructuring of society?
- If so, is violence, anger and marching in the street the way to go?
- How challenged are you to pick your way through all the choices that are presented to you?
- How challenged are you to stop looking outside for answers and go deeper within, getting your answers from your Source?
- Does observing the outer world, even with all its craziness, give you Self-direction on how to proceed?

When you realize that you already are the change, and you hunker down to "Be the Change" that you came here to be, you are going to be attacked. That is a fact of life. Attacked really means that you are being tested so you can determine who you are and how strong you are. You have two options---to run away in fear or to greet your attackers fearlessly with the courage to stand up for your Self.

In my earlier years I always ran away; I ran away from my mother and from my university professors; from bosses and co-workers. There is a huge school of thought that says to leave these toxic people behind. But, wherever you go there you are. So, I kept getting the same experiences except with different people. Same song, different verse.

My first husband was never happy wherever we were. He bought and sold property with the pledge that the next one would be better; that he would happier; that life would change. I believed this until after a while, nothing got better; in fact, in my opinion, it only got worse. Finally I stopped and I left. I had enough. And then he got sick and he died.

When you stagnate, you leave this reality because if you do not change with your opportunities, your Soul recognizes that you are not learning so why waste the opportunity. You are extracted so you can go somewhere else and learn in a different environment. But learn you will, in or out of body. Here or there.

Your Soul has a plan; you have things to do and you are supposed to be doing them. So, here you are. When I met Stewart, I stopped running. I stopped making excuses. And, the attacks increased.

- Do you think you should leave toxic people behind?
- Have you shut out toxic people only to find more when you turned around?
- Have you realized that you cannot run away from your Self?

- Have you thought you found supportive people, only to be attacked?
- Have you thought you were attacked when others were only trying to help you see who and what you are?
- What is the best method to deal with an attacker?
- Can anyone attack you if you are not attacking your Self, somehow, some way?
- How many times have you run away from uncomfortable situations?
- How many times have you run toward uncomfortable situations?
- Have you observed people who are stagnating, leave this reality?
- How easy is it to get strong—mentally, emotionally, physically, spiritually?
- Is getting strong supposed to mean easy?
- Have you taken the time to be grateful for the attackers, through which your Soul spiritually grew and prospered?

In this reality, there are always so many options and opportunities that life can be exceedingly overwhelming. This does not mean that your options and opportunities are what you think they should be, yet, they still exist. Most people reading this book have shelter, food and clothing. It may not be your ideal, but you have it. Think about how many people in the world do not even have this much. This means that every morning, it is important to give thanks for shelter food and clothing rather than take it for granted.

I have lost so many pets this past year that I have tended to focus on the loss instead of the fact that I had them for so many years. There are still too many areas in my life where I focus on what I do not have instead of what I have.

I lost one of my favorite aunts 2 weeks ago and my other favorite aunt is now at a major cancer center discussing treatment options. I can feel this aunt's loneliness as her sister who passed was her rock. Additionally, she lost her husband, my uncle, less than 1 year ago. Another fresh loss, as well, for me. While I am trying to "Be the Change", the past is pulling me back into it; all the memories of what was and the physical anchors that held the memories are passing.

- How can you "Be the Change" when it feels like your past won't let you go?
- Or is it that you won't let go of your past?
- Are you pulled back into your past so you can conclude what needs to be concluded?
- Can you "Be the Change" while you are grieving?
- Is grieving part of the change?
- Can you "Be the Change" when you fight some changes?
- Do you only accept the change that you want to accept?
- Are you grateful for what you have, right now?
- Is it too easy to focus on what you do not have?

## Toxic People

There is always a lot of focus on toxic people in your life. Many people say to leave them and move on. This is easier said than done, because usually you just exchange one toxic person for another. And yes, it can be worse.

In a way, the word toxic is a misnomer, because having toxic people in your life can only happen when you are toxic. There is a reason why toxic people show up. Ignoring them only puts off what you eventually must face within your Self. Sometimes you need a breather to build your strength so you can face the toxic people, but sooner or later, similar people are going to reveal themselves. Usually, people are toxic because of some kind of trauma, either in this life or another. They are so traumatized that they cannot get over their experiences. When they do not know what to do about it, they take it out on you.

- Is it best to avoid traumatized people if you want to be the change?
- If you are an example of how to be, is avoidance the best course of action?
- Do toxic people teach you to set boundaries?
- Do you teach toxic people about boundaries?
- Can you have compassion for people, yet still remove your Self from their lives?
- If the toxic person is someone with whom you must interact on a daily basis, can you do Oversoul communication with them?
- Can you have compassion for someone but not buy into their toxicity?
- If a toxic person throws toxins on you, can you refuse to accept them?
- When you deal with your own underlying issues of toxicity, do these people go away or change their behavior toward you?
- Do you know people who smile to others, yet are venomous toward you?
- Do toxic people have health issues?
- If you do not clear out your own toxicity, are you setting your Self up for health issues?

There was a time in my life when I did not listen to anyone. Then, I realized that others actually had something to say. So, I listened to everyone. And realized that was also not the way to be.

Finding your own internal balance always challenges you on so many different levels. One of my goals is not only to appear calm, but to be calm. Regardless of what comes at me, I want to be calm and consciously connected to my Source at all times. When life is flowing smoothly along, this is not so difficult. When life is throwing you around, or you are tired or not feeling well, or the unexpected happens, I am more challenged to be calm.

This is why you always have to ask what is most correct and beneficial for your own unique situation. Sometimes, you do have to yell back; sometimes, you do have to walk out and never look back; sometimes you have to be silent; sometimes you have to stay. You have to determine what is going on in the outer world, what you need to learn, what you have learned, what you are done learning, what is going on in your inner world.

When I was working on my fear of heights, I did a lot of things that I did not like. The last thing I did was go down a water slide that was 5 stories tall. At the top, I was given a little wooden sled to sit on so my bathing suit would not ride up. Sitting in this little sled, I could not see the bottom of the slide, only my legs and feet sticking straight out in front of me. I went down the slide, congratulated my Self and decided to never do it again. I could do it, but did I have to keep doing it.

- If you are the change, how do you know how much to do before you are done?
- How do you determine when it is time to walk out the door and never look back?
- If you keep getting the same situation over and over again, do you need to keep looking within and stop running?
- If you close the door and you do not get the same situation, are you done?
- Or maybe, you do not need the same severe lesson again?

- But you need a few gentle reminders?
- Can you be calm inside and still yell at someone because this is what the other person needs?
- Do you sometimes have to match your tone with what the other person can actually hear?
- If you are calm, and the other person is turbulent, can that other person actually hear a calm person?
- If you are the change, do you need practice dealing with a variety of people in a variety of ways?
- How do you determine what is most correct and beneficial in the moment?
- How challenged are you to do the correct action for the correct reason in the correct timing?

One of the biggest challenges when you are the change, is to know when to keep moving forward and when to change directions. So many times I have tried to push my way into a situation that needed changing, only to realize it was not going to change the way I envisioned. When you know more than the other person, it is so easy to want to share what you know. I am always too eager to help, so I definitely have had to learn to know my audience and back off.

Just like my aunt who is now in Houston getting evaluated for proton therapy. When I heard she was going to Houston, I told her I would meet her there if she needed someone to help her. No answer. Then, I found out my cousin was taking her. Instead of being disturbed, I looked at it as being relieved of that duty. But I did offer and I would have gone had she needed me.

She will have an extended stay during treatments, maybe as long as 2 months. I know people in the area and offered to help find a short term place. No one took me up on that offer or even said thank you. Again, I am relieved of any responsibility, but I stepped forward.

I have 3 cousins who are brothers who said they will take turns being with her during the long-term treatment. I told them that if they need to be relieved, I would be willing to help. They all live in Texas, so they are closer than I am. But the offer is on the table and I will not push nor will I get my feelings hurt if I am not asked to help. I have to allow them their matching color, tone and archetypes.

I really did not want anymore pets after this past year of losing so many, plus the 2 cats that remain are 13 and 14 years old. Stewart found 2 dogs. But before he found them I told him I kept seeing 2 white puppies. I wasn't looking for them, they just kept coming in my head. Then, guess what, surprise! He was looking at these dogs that I kept seeing in my head. I could have shut the door and said no way, but the energy of the dogs are already here and every signpost says to let them in.

Knowing when to push on doors and when to close them is another layer of balance. You have to learn the subtle signs of when to move forward and when to back off, even when you do not want to. This has definitely taken me time to learn and I am still refining this, just like you. You have to know:

### *When doors are opening.*

### *When doors are already open.*

### *When doors are closing.*

### *When doors are already closed.*

Each frequency is different, with many variations of each one. Sometimes, you can push your way in, only to find out why you should not have. Or, not go through an open door only to find out why you should have. All lessons. All challenging you to find your balance with Source.

- Have you pushed your way in, only to find out why you should not have?

- Or, not gone through an open door only to find out why you should have?

- Does being the change mean you have to stretch your Self-expectations?

- If you stretch your own Self-expectations is it challenging to realize that others may not want to stretch theirs?

- If you are changing frequency streams from within, is it natural to challenge all frequencies that come your way?

- Do you naturally want to help others upgrade and be their own change, too?

- Do you think that you can overwhelm people simply by Being?

- If you are the change, from another's perspective, could you be seen as a negative rather than a positive?

- What if others think being the change means marching in the streets?

- How do you know what "Be the Change" means for you as opposed to how others may define it?

- How challenged are you to figure out how much to give to your audience as well as how to give it?

You most likely have seen social media videos circulating of pets that are surprised by something. One popular video is of a cat that turns around to find a cucumber lying on the floor behind it. The cat jumps straight up in the air because it has seen a cucumber. Animals notice whenever something or someone is different. Animals have to be physically aware to stay physically safe.

So, if you are different, you awaken the Animal Mind of others. You stand out and this means others have a need to explore you. Think of how a pet acts. They poke, sniff, smell, prod, dance around, hiss/bark, trying to get whatever it is to act/react so they can determine if it is friend or foe; if they should fight or flight.

In the same way, people do this to others who they perceive as different. They have to get you to do something that will tell them if you are a danger. If you challenge their mind, or challenge their status quo, or what they know to be true, then you are a danger.

At the post office, here in the US, whenever you mail a package, the postal clerk asks if you are shipping anything dangerous. At one point I would say with a big smile on my face, well, I am shipping books, I guess some people consider knowledge dangerous.

You are a kind of living book that is a danger to many people. If you are the change, the Animal Mind of other people are going to know this on some level. You are a danger, especially if you challenge them to evaluate their own lives.

If the idea to challenge their life comes from within them, they can deal with it. But if it comes from someone who they consider a peer, then you are a danger/threat. If they cannot flight, (such as family member, co-worker, neighbor, then they do the other thing that animals do—they fight. They do not see you the person. Their Animal Minds perk up and see you, the danger/threat to their status quo way of Being.

- Have you had people fight with you for no reason?
- Or be afraid of you?
- Or ostracize, humiliate and do other horrible things which from your perspective seemed totally unreasonable?
- Have you thought of your Self as a Living Book?
- Does Knowledge scare people?
- Do you think people feel threatened by you?
- Do you think people like you until they get to know you?
- Are people curious about you?
- Do people poke at you?

- Do you attract passive-aggressive behavior?
- Do you think people poke at whatever they do not understand?
- Is Animal Mind behavior an attempt by people to understand that which they do not understand?
- If people do not have the correct questions to ask, do they resort to what they do know, such as poking, prodding, pushing, fighting?
- If you are the change are you up to the challenge of being explored by the Animal Mind of others in an animal mind way?
- Can you stay centered and know that it is them and not you?
- Can you give them the space to be who they are in the same way you want your space to be who you are?

Being the change means being different. Being different makes you a target. Your goal is to stay steadfast in place, doing what you came here to do and accomplishing your goals regardless of what comes at you. All the naysayers and challengers are reflections of your own doubts and Self-questioning. They provide the opportunity for you to go inside and define who you are and who you are not.

- Are you who they say you are?
- Should you listen to them or listen to Self?
- Are they giving you words of wisdom?
- Or words that help you define your choices?
- Have you had someone scream and yell at you, telling you what they think you are?
- Has this made you stand up and declare your own inner knowing of Self?
- Does it sometimes take pushing and cajoling before you finally have the gumption to stand up for your Self?

- Do you remember that it is your mind-pattern that pulls this behavior out of people?
- And whatever they are saying, you need to hear?
- Even if it is to make that choice of who you are vs. who they are saying you are?
- Do you need to step up and stay stop?
- Do you stand up for your Self?
- Do you ask your Oversoul how best to respond?
- If you get out of your center, is that part of your process?
- Are you still too strict on your Self?
- Do you need to be strict but when you fall down, know that is okay?
- Do you know that you will get up again and keep going simply because you are the change?
- And you are never stagnant, even when some days, you may want to be?

When I first started to teach publicly, one of my older students told me that no one likes a prophet in their own backyard. I was very disheartened that my attempts to reach out to various establishments were rejected with patronizing comments such as, "Oh, you wrote a book. How nice."

It took me a long time to realize that the world was not waiting for me, at least not in the way I thought it would be. Now, I realize how much I still had to learn and that the world was waiting for me to learn from it. I also realized that what my student said is true. Most people want to learn from someone who does not too closely represent them. Because when you too closely represent them, they stop thinking you are so wonderful. They see your negatives as well as your positives and then quickly become disillusioned that you are not perfect.

- Where did the illusion of a perfect teacher come from, anyway?

Even when I tell people that the reason Stewart and I do what we do is because we have so many issues, people are still disappointed when they realize that yes, we do have issues. Most people do not want to look at themselves. They want to look at you and admire you from afar.

I love scrolling through social media and looking at all of the people who are out there teaching.

A man with long-hair walks up to a gong, hits it with a rubber mallet and then turns, faces his audience, closes his eyes and melts into the sound of the gong. Another man wearing African apparel sits with his eyes closed before an incense burner on another live feed.

I'm sure you have seen such things and more. They are all actors and they will all draw an audience, because people want to be entertained as well as think that these people can do it but they cannot. Because that would be too close to home if they could do it, too. The people want something that they cannot be; if they cannot attain it, then they do not have to try. They can sit back and only wish for something. If you never start, you cannot fail, you cannot lose, you don't have to work hard and no one can say you failed because you never even tried. People always want something "out there" instead of "in here".

- Have you ever fallen into the trap of people who tell you that they have something special, but you do not?
- Or seen this happen to other people?
- Have you wondered why it is so easy to fall for the actors who portray what you can never be?
- Is it easier to watch other people fulfill their dreams then think about fulfilling your own?

- Do you think this is another trap that the global handlers know about?
- If the star seems too far away, you will never even begin, because a part of you says you will never reach it, why try?
- Is it easier to live vicariously through others?
- How many thousands of people line up to watch athletes play?
- If you want to "Be the Change", how much impact are you going to have as one of the global handlers' programming icons?
- How much impact can you have as an average person hanging out with other average people?
- What if every average person tried just a little bit to be more than he/she already is?
- Do you think the age game plays a part in the average person wanting to "Be the Change"?
- Do people give up hope?
- Can you be a prophet in your own back yard?

There are wild fires that are raging in California. I seriously doubt that all those people who are losing their homes, who at some point wanted change in their lives anticipated that this was the change that was coming to them. Yes, they are cleaning out and clearing out, but what a huge way to be forced into change. Even those people whose homes are still standing also have forever changes. Their neighbors are gone along with businesses, jobs, schools and recreational areas. Change, change, change.

Their change is coming by way of fire; fire purifies and cleanses; it is about suppressed anger; rage; resentment and hate. I bet those people who lost their way of living would not agree with this assessment. If these emotions were not within them, their mind-patterns could not have attracted such atrocities.

But, those who survived the tragedies are being given another opportunity to move on and rebuild. They are now in a reactive situation because they did not choose to be proactive. It is the emanations of their mind-patterns which brought these situations to them. Think of how many people moved out of California just before all of this happened.

- What is the difference between those who proactively left and those who are now reactively being forced to evacuate?
- Do you have compassion for those who are forced to change?
- Do you have compassion for Self when you procrastinate so long that you are forced?
- Does your Oversoul has compassion for you when it has to force you to change?
- Does your Oversoul have tough love for you?
- Does your Oversoul give you every opportunity to change?
- Do those people who survived the fire have new opportunities?
- Have those who did not survive the fires reached the end of their roads, so their new opportunities are in different realities?
- Even when you consciously decide to "Be the Change", can you expect to be uncomfortable?
- Do you think being uncomfortable is part of change?
- And if change means no stagnation does this mean that you most likely, will always be uncomfortable?
- Do you know how to be comfortable in the midst of your discomfort?

You most likely have been the change since you were born and you are just now identifying it. When you move with the change, there is less discomfort and more excitement. Like riding a raft down a winding river. You don't exactly know what is around the bend, but you know how to shift your balance, you have your skills, you are wearing your life jacket, have your oars, and whatever it is, you will go with it, bumps and dumps, twists and turns, smooth water, rough water, whatever else is in your path, you are prepared.

All of your experiences up to this point are making you the strong person that you are. The more you are stressed, without breaking, the stronger you become. And if you do break, and are able to Self-repair, then another feather in your cap. Good can always get better; strong can get stronger; skills can be honed and improved. You started out with Class 1 Rapids and you are moving up the ladder so you are ready for the more challenging rides along the way. You are learning that while your Oversoul directs the river, how you ride that raft is all up to you.

- Do you think of your Self as a strong person?
- Do you feel like you are equipping your Self for life?
- Are you ever done equipping your Self?
- Should people who feel old give up or keep going?
- Do people use age as an excuse not to do?
- Do people get tired of riding life's rapids?
- If so, does this cause them to give up?
- Do you think people realize they need more tools to be adequately equipped for life?
- Have ever felt like you were broken, with no return?
- What made you take another breath and try again?
- Did you come out on top stronger than ever?
- How many times have you felt like giving up?
- How many times have you started again?
- Can change be scary and exciting at the same time?
- Do you think you have been the change since you were born?

If you have ever walked into a roomful of people feeling happy, only to find your Self sad, angry and/or depressed, you understand that what emanates from the mind-patterns of others does change and influence you without a word being said. In the same way, if you are sad, angry and/or depressed, being with people who are having a good time can definitely pick up your spirits.

This is why it is important that you always ask your Oversoul to hold you in protection so that you stay clean and clear regardless of who you are around. And when you are clean and clear, simply by being, you do affect those around you in some way. Yes, you can be on a bus, train or airplane and never speak a word to anyone, but on some level still affect the people around you. You affect everyone with whom you interact from a store clerk to wait staff in a restaurant; from your neighbor to your colleagues at work.

Whether anyone consciously knows it or not, what emanates from you does impact their lives on some level. You do not need to speak to anyone; others may not even be aware of your presence. But who you are, simply by being always has an impact.

There are many articles of how trees in a forest communicate with each other, passing messages along.

> There is now a substantial body of scientific evidence that refutes that idea. It shows instead that trees of the same species are communal, and will often form alliances with trees of other species. Forest trees have evolved to live in cooperative, interdependent relationships, maintained by communication and a collective intelligence similar to an insect colony. These soaring columns of living wood draw the eye upward to their outspreading crowns, but the real action is taking place underground, just a few inches below our feet. https://www.smithsonianmag.com/science-nature/the-whispering-trees-180968084/

In much the same way, your Soul is always in communication with other Souls, with or without awareness. In fact, if you were aware of every communication it would probably drive you crazy. Again, another reason why your Oversoul is so useful protecting you in more ways than you know.

- Do you think about all the ways you impact others simply by being?
- Does "impact" mean "positive"?
- Does "impact" mean "most correct and beneficial"?
- Would you want conscious awareness of all your inner level communications?
- Does your Oversoul protect you from overload?
- Do the Oversouls of the populace protect them from overload?
- If others knew what was going on within you would they be on overload?
- Or, if they consciously tried to do what you do, would this put them on overload?
- On some level, do you think others are afraid of you because they know their own limits?
- Has anyone ever made you feel like you were on overload?
- Have you been around people who are too intense, whether they open their mouths or sit quietly?
- Do you maintain your protection 24/7 via the Oversoul level?
- Do you think your energy field is cleaner and clearer than the average person?
- Or, does your energy field have an ebb and flow?
- What does your energy field look like when you dig into the dark recesses of your mind and how could this impact others?

- Have you been in situations where your mood changed simply by being around others?

The human collective consciousness is like a huge, energetic soup. You may feel when you absorb the energy of others. If you think you do not, this is because you may be so accustomed to what you feel, you do not even realize what you feel. It is like standing in tub of ice cold water. Eventually, you do not even realize that you are cold.

In the same way, this explains why you do not realize that you are even part of the energetic soup. If you think you are not feeling and absorbing, pay attention. However, the cleaner and clearer you become with more defined boundaries, the less you absorb.

Visualize a group of people in the midst of this energetic soup. Into the mix comes a person who is energetically clearer and cleaner plus has a boundary around him/her Self. This confuses the other people. They are going to question what is in their soup; the soup that they know so well, since they were born and maybe even for eons of time. You are going to stick out like a sore thumb.

When people do not understand something, they turn their back and ignore it. If it doesn't go away and they have no choice, they will either challenge it or poke and push at it. They will do what they can to keep this oddity from infringing upon their status quo. You know from your personal work how much effort you have to put into correcting and balancing your own mind-pattern.

- How can you even begin to explain your inner work to someone who does not want to know?
- What you are doing is not a quick fix. What you are doing changes you and changes your world; it changes your interactions with everything in your existence. Because this change occurs over linear time, you may not even appreciate the magnitude of your own work and your personal accomplishments.

- Do you take the time to be grateful for where you were and how far you have come?
- Do you look at others and recognize how much inner change you have manifested?
- Is all outer experience only about inner change?
- Can the outer world change without inner change first?
- Is the outer world the tool your Oversoul uses to get your inner attention?
- Do you sometimes need to be hit over the head to get whatever it is that your Oversoul wants you to get?
- Is it easy to ignore your own energetic soup, hoping that it will go away?
- Have you ever tried to explain to someone your inner work, only to realize you should never have started the conversation?
- Are people curious about you, only because they cannot figure you out, not because they actually want to know you as a person?
- Does your inner level work make others feel threatened because on some level they know they need to move out of the status quo?
- Do you know that the trials and tribulations of others are there so they can grow?
- If you absorb their trials and tribulations, are they less likely to grow?
- Does absorbing their stuff help them and hurt you?
- Can you release the need to feel sorry for people, but still have compassion for their struggles?
- Do you go to the Oversoul level and silently ask for help for these kinds of people?

What your mind-pattern emanates does change people; energetically digging into the recesses of their minds. Even if you are not within their visual range, your clarity and cleanness is going to impact the energetic soup, reverberating out to impact others in some way.

Before Stewart and I met, we spoke on the phone. I was in Oregon and he was in New York. On our first phone call, he told me that he saw me with a baby and that baby was his! Okay, here is this guy I have never met before, 3000 miles away, I am 39 years old, never been pregnant nor wanted to be, married to another man, and this guy on the end of the phone still married to another woman is telling me that I am going to have his baby.

I felt like I had a huge bell put over my energy field and he had hit it with a huge sledge hammer. I became physically violently ill for almost a month. And this is after all the work that I had done for 39 years.

When Stewart first started doing seminars, he had people running from the room crying, vomiting and hysterical, often never to return. One week-long class, a young man came for 2 hours, left and we never, ever heard from him again. I could tell you tons of other stories, but you get the picture. This work shakes people up.

To Stewart, what he knows is ordinary so he did not realize the impact of words on the recipients, those who willingly came, paid money and consciously wanted to know. He definitely has toned down his presentations and learned better ways to approach his audience. Even when people want to know, they are challenged because energetically, they get shaken up.

Just by Being, without saying one word, your presence is going to shake up those around you. You are emanating something different and on some level, others know and they fear. People fear change, even when they see your courage and want to know what you know.

- Do you feel courageous?
- Can you be courageous and fearful at the same time?

- Does it take courage to push through fear?
- Can positive experiences pull out your fear?
- When life is going well, are you sometimes afraid that you will not be able to maintain it?
- Do you need courage to keep going in your direction vs. the direction others want for you?
- Can you courageously move forward while feeling fear trying to pull you into the crowd?
- Sometimes when you think about the direction you are going, do you feel others try to stop you before you even begin?
- Do you feel that others think you are too intense?
- How many people change with you?
-  How many people have walked away from you?
- When people change with you, do you acknowledge their courage and strength?

Being the change is not an easy task. Being the change automatically makes you an unspoken leader. When I was appointed by the Governor of Washington State to a Small Business Development Council, I was intrigued but extremely intimidated. I was dealing with the Governor, his personal assistants and bodyguards, his relatives and many other high level government officials.

After I had been on the Council for a few short months, his personal assistant came to me and told me how impressed everyone was with my leadership abilities. Internally, my jaw dropped open, because from my viewpoint, I had barely spoken. I chose to sit back and observe as I tried to figure out exactly what was going on and what I could possibly contribute.

I was then voted into the leadership of the council which positioned me for much insider information. I was nervous but excited; I loved my time on the Council and I really learned a lot during those years.

The woman who headed the Council was about 10 years older than me. I admired her greatly, but she felt threatened by me. I was told that I was another one of her in the making and I was asked if nominated, would I be willing to lead the Council at the end of this woman's term.

I was again nervous but excited, but the bottom line was this woman who I admired blocked me. The only reason she could give, I was told, was that I did not speak loud enough. There you have it. It wasn't to be and I eventually quit the Council, which then eventually was dissolved by the Governor. I was an unspoken leader. I did not recognize my own inherent leadership qualities. Others had to tell me. Others were jealous of something that I wasn't even really sure about. Being the change is not an easy task.

- Do you see your Self as a leader?
- Do you have leadership qualities?
- Is being a leader a lonely place?
- Does a leader see things that others do not?
- Does a leader have to stand up against a lot of scrutiny, both true and false?
- Does a leader have to be strong?
- Do others like a leader who rises from their own ranks?
- Have you ever been somehow thrust into a leadership role that you did not expect or feel prepared for?
- Do others see more positive in you than you see in you?
- Have you found your path blocked by the limited view of others?
- If so, is it possible that your Oversoul was protecting you in some way?
- Does "Being the Change" mean that you came here already a leader?

- Does being a leader mean you want people to follow you?
- If you are a leader, do you have to tell people that you are a leader?
- Or are you automatically viewed as a leader?
- Is a leader automatically a threat, whether you are an officially recognized leader, or a leader simply because you exist?
- Do you think people say they want a leader until they have one?

Often those who are in command need people under them who will do as they are told and not think for themselves. So the best way to let you know that you are not appreciated is tell you that you are not exactly what you already are. If you are a natural leader, those in command may feel threatened that you will be a better leader than they are. There are always layers for those people who do not fit the conventional mold.

It took me a lot of years to get over not being able to be the leader of the Small Business Development Council. I really loved being on the Council Board, so to me, being the leader of it was an incredible opportunity. I even thought that perhaps they wanted me because they thought they could control me. Even when I do not always understand why emotionally, logically I go to the *rejection is God's protection* to get me through when I do not get what I want.

Many people are silent leaders. Your leadership is unspoken and most likely not consciously acknowledged, you are here paving the way for others to someday, someway follow. Opening and setting frequencies that need to be here. Acknowledgment from the outer world is never as important as acknowledgment by Source. It is always the inner level acknowledgments that build and support the Soul, which is exactly what you are doing.

- Do you like being acknowledged by others?
- Are you disappointed when you are not?

- While the ego in-balance is necessary, can too much outer acknowledgement give people a false sense of importance?

- Is inner level acknowledgment more subtle?

- Is building and supporting the Soul less easy to identify?

- Does outer acknowledgement give you more things to define you, such as awards and certificates?

- Does anyone else really see your inner level acknowledgments in the same way that you do?

- Have you been around people who have to tell you who they are?

- Does a lion have to tell you that it is a lion?

- Do those who are in tune with you see you vs. those who are not will more likely dismiss you?

- Do you still carry disappointments inside from positions that you wanted but did not get?

- Do you think you have been passed over for leadership positions because others felt threatened by you?

- Or felt that they could not control you?

- Is rejection God's protection?

**Nice**

Life isn't nice. Life is not designed to be nice. Life is designed to rough you up so you can change and grow. Your mind-pattern becomes like hard, compacted dirt that needs to be roughened up so the old weeds can come out, roots and all, and new seeds can be planted. Those new seeds need fertilizer and manure is the best kind.

All these people who are in your way are providing the roughing up of the hardened soil of your mind-pattern so the ground is ready for new seeds. As an ex-farmer, I can tell you that it is amazing to till the soil. First, you mow the old plants down. Then, you disc the soil to cut everything up. Then comes the plow to turn the topsoil upside down, bringing the deeper roots to the surface. Next, you disc the ground again to break up the clumps of dirt roots and hardened soil.

Then, you disk it again and again until the field smooths out. Finally, you harrow the field. A harrow is a farm implement with long metal finger-like claws to start smoothing out the surface. Sometimes, you may even need to lightly irrigate before the seeds are planted. Depending on the crop, you may also have to apply fertilizer, pesticide, or herbicides or a combination of all at various points in the process.

You cannot use fresh manure as fertilizer. The manure has to age. The methane gas has to come out of it, the solids have to be stirred into the liquids, and everything needs time to break down because when it is too fresh it is too strong and will kill any plants.

If you are not familiar with farming life, you most likely to do not stop to think about all the steps that have to happen before a new crop is planted. But trust me, it is much more complicated than a non-farmer could ever realize. In the same way, what you go through to get your old mind-pattern roughed up and ready for change, isn't going to happen overnight. You need a variety of experiences provided by a variety of people to rough you up enough so all the old stuff inside can be torn up and ripped out. The more you resist, the longer it takes.

Imagine a farmer trying to prepare a field where the hardened soil refuses to roughen up; where the roots won't give and clumps of dirt won't break down; where fertilizer/manure and even water is rejected. It is not going to be easy for that farmer, the perceived adversary of the field, to do what he needs to do.

- Who or what is in your life to rough up your mind-pattern?
- Do you give thanks at the end of every day that this person/ farmer, is persistent in his/her efforts to get your mind-pattern roughened up and ready for planting?

- Are you like the hardened soil, hanging on to your stuff because you do not want anything disturbed except how and when you say?
- What if the season for planting is now but you aren't going to be ready until 4 months from now?
- Are you going to let the planting season pass you by…again?
- Or, are you going to tell that person/farmer, to give it all he/she has because you want to get your lessons/roughening up done and over with so you are ready for those new seeds that are coming your way?
- How challenged are you to get that attitude of gratitude going for the person/farmer who is trying to help you turn the soil of your field/mind?
- Are you graciously accepting the fertilizer/manure?
- Or are you refusing to accept it?
- Do you want to keep that hardened soil of your mind?
- Do you then wonder why new seeds you try to plant are not growing and flourishing; and instead are dying?
- Are you trying to use manure that is too fresh and needs to age?
- Are you trying to rush a process that cannot be rushed?
- Do you expect life to be nice?
- If so, why?
- Has it ever been nice 100% of the time?
- Does the hard soil that is being roughed up think the farmer is nice?
- Do you need people to rough up your mind-pattern?

I love the definition of nice as someone who does not want to rock the boat. How true. In my earlier years I always thought if I did my work, my life would become easier, life would be smooth and simplicity would set in. Instead, I found my life increasingly challenging, bumpy and complex. Yet, I must say that I enjoy challenges. Of course, like everyone else, I prefer challenges of my own conscious choosing, and I want them to be resolved in the way I want them resolved.

Resolving them via the Oversoul level means I have to be more creative; i.e., I have to change my mind; become more creative and therefore more open to the flow of Source.

The reason I gave you the farming example of working the soil is so you can truly start to understand that there are a lot of steps between the thought that I should change to actually making the change. People do not realize that change is a complex task; anyone who thinks that change should be easy is falling into the programming of the masses.

This idea that life is nice and easy is a huge trap that the majority of people fall into. I also thought the same thing decades ago. When you have this idea in your head, and your life is not nice or easy, then you immediately think that something is wrong with you.

- How many times has the outer world had you questioning "what is wrong with me"?
- Is any change you have ever made been harder/more challenging than you originally thought?
- Have you thought, "I'm going to change this!" only to fall back into old habits and patterns?
- If so, why couldn't you keep the change going?
- Was the change too challenging?
- Was the process monotonous and boring?
- Did you lose interest?
- When change doesn't go your way, are you forced to get more creative, dig deeper and utilize more inner/personal resources?

- If you can easily weight lift 20 pounds, would you want to challenge your Self to lift more?
- Would you be satisfied to have someone show up with a few more pounds with which you could challenge your Self?
- Do you look for challenges in your life?
- Do you like to walk longer or lift heavier weights?
- Do you like to try new foods?
- Do you like to explore different parts of your country or the world?
- If this life was only smooth sailing, would you consider it a wasted life?
- Do those people who rough up your life serve a purpose in a way that no one else can?
- Is it too easy to have hissy fits when you are challenged?
- Is growth painful?
- Can it make you cry and weep?
- Is crying and weeping cleansing?
- Does change involve mourning for the passing of the old to truly be prepared to receive the new?
- Is mourning different for everyone?
- Is mourning always a part of the process?

Change is an interesting process. As much as people resist it, they also crave change. It is exciting to travel, try new food, meet new people, read a new book, get a new house, start a new career, begin a new relationship and so forth. All of this means change. All these changes sound exciting and wonderful. Yet, there is always the reality that goes along with the daydreams.

Most people daydream about the positives, forgetting to fill in the rest of the story. All life experiences contain both positive and negative. For example, our 2 new puppies. Puppies are adorable, sweet and loving. But the rest of the reality is that they are also a mess. Today, they got out of the area where we have them contained and almost gave our 13 year old cat a heart attack. They chased her all over the house, finally cornering her in the basement where our furnace is. We got the dogs but couldn't find the cat all day. Finally, we were able to locate her after dinner tonight, still hiding in the basement and afraid to come out.

That is the reality of getting a puppy. What you do not plan for happens. This is the same thing in life. No matter what you plan for, something is going to happen for which you did not plan; something that is going to test your resiliency; flexibility; patience and most likely your temper.

- How are you going to act and react?
- Are you going to go with the flow, or get angry about it?
- Are you going to hang onto your daydream and be upset because reality doesn't fit the picture you have in your mind?
- Are you going to be flexible and turn left when you were focused on turning right?
- How many times have you implemented a change, any change, where it has gone 100% exactly as you had imagined?
- How many people have gotten in the way of your daydream?
- How many people have turned your beautifully imagined scenario into a living nightmare?
- When you think change why do most people not include the full picture?
- Or how about people who only focus on the negative side of change, forgetting about the positives?
- Have you wanted to implement a change, but stayed focused on why I can't?

- Does change seem to be emotional, either plus or minus, without considering that several scenarios could happen?

- Do you think it is important to know that whenever you plan change, there will be positives and negatives?

- Can you stop there, or do you have to outline in your mind what those might be?

- And if you have done this, how many times are you caught off guard when something unexpected and unplanned for happens?

- How easy is it for you to turn left when all your focus was on turning right?

Life truly is one continuous change. Even when people think they have a status quo, something is always moving and changing. For most people, this is their physical structure/body. Your body is never going to look exactly like what it did last year or the year before or the year before. Every thought that you think creates a reaction in your body because body follows mind.

It is always interesting to me that when I haven't seen someone in a while, I will often think this person looks the best that I have ever seen him/her. When I make this comment, the person then proceeds to tell me what a stressful time he/she has been through. Then, I usually say, "Well, stress becomes you."

And this does seem to be true. Stress is a result of change that you are resisting, but is happening anyway. That fight is what gives you the spunk to get up and get going. When life is too calm and placid, you lounge around without pushing your body or your mind. Both need to be well exercised for you to get stronger on all levels. This means your body gets stronger as your mind becomes more alive, even if it is more alive simply because you must survive. People without much to do often lose their spark. I have seen this happen. They become depressed and despondent and give up.

All the challenges that you have are designed to get you to move; the more you move the more alive the Soul becomes. The more alive the Soul becomes, the more your energy field shines. And, your body changes to match the glow. This is why you must take good care of the body so it can upgrade as your mind-pattern upgrades.

Change, change and more change, at least linearly, because in True Reality, you already are and have everything that you can possibly imagine. It is the strength of your mind-pattern that manifests here what you already have there.

- Have you thought about what you already have there?
- And why you are so challenged to bring it here?
- Is there some kind of a lag between there and here?
- Do you think it has to do with the different realities of existence with different rules and different players?
- Do your challenges push you to delve deeper into the necessary changes to bring what you see into this reality?
- When you change, do you envision what already exists, and then pull it to you?
- Just like the layers of your mind, are there layers to moving energy from one reality into another?
- Does everything you do force you to become more creative?
- Or, more appropriately, reach into the creative recesses of your mind?
- Do you feel the more you push your Self the more you become alive?
- Do your changes cause your Soul to glow and light up?
- Does your body react to increased Soul energy pouring in and through it?
- Are you careful to take good care of your body so it can hold more Soul energy?

- Have you witnessed others lose their spark?
- Have you your own spark waning but then something happens that ignites it?
- Does stress happen when you resist change?
- Does too much change feel overwhelming?
- Do you resist change rather than go with it?
- Have you had periods in your life without too much activity where you are surprised to find that you feel bored and listless?
- Whether positive or negative, does change invigorate you and breathe new life into your mind and body?

When you are so locked into the narrow focus of your linear life, you are challenged to look at the multidimensional Being that you are. This is the beauty of Hyperspace/Oversoul work that teaches you how to be present and focused here, yet stretch your mind so that it can go there.

For example, you want to increase your income stream. If you can imagine something, it already exists, somewhere. This means that you really are not imagining anything; technically you are viewing whatever already exists; somewhere; someplace; some time; some reality.

- Because it exists there does that make it most correct and beneficial for here?

This is what you have to determine with the aid of your Oversoul. Your Hyperspace/Oversoul work gives you the tools and techniques to clear the path for what is in alignment with the wishes of Source for you, to come to you. Like any energetic stream, whatever you see isn't just going to zip straight to you. There are energetic blockages that have to be cleared before what you see can manifest in this reality.

If you bring something in too soon and you are not ready for it, then it can destroy instead of help. This is why you are learning what your specific balance is for your specific and unique Soul-Personality.

And, this is why you continue to want. Wanting something forces you to continue to use your creativity, reaching deeper into the recesses of your mind to pull out what is already within you.

- Is wanting a part of change?
- Is there a part of you that feels guilty or undeserving when you want something?
- Does wanting make you search deeper?
- Does wanting improved finances make you feel guilty?
- Does money feel like a forbidden fruit?
- Is money often the prize at the end of whatever you want?
- Does the amount of money you have determine the energy that you have in this reality to move about freely?
- If what you want isn't here do you think it is on its way?
- Do your changes facilitate whatever you need to find its way to you?
- Are the people who you perceive block your path, preparing you to be strong enough for the rest of your life?
- Does holding onto your past hold your attention, focus, strength and energy here?
- Do you forget to view there with its multitude of possibilities?
- Do you have the potential to manifest there, here?

## Money

Money is the physical form of nonphysical energy. When you are priming your pump and setting the pathway, it is challenging to know how much to put on your credit card to say "I trust the process" and when it is best to not do anything. I tend to be on the conservative side; I do not like to use credit cards, but there are times when that is the only option. Then, I am grateful that I even have a credit card.

Credit cards are designed to be used against you, but with correct mind-set, you can use them to open the frequency flow of funding. The issue for most people is the mind-pattern of doubt and guilt get in the way. I used to think about everything that I could do for everyone else if I had the funds, but as time grows on, I can see why I haven't had the funds. I need to be clear on how to hand it out. The people I would have given it to would not have used it to Self-elevate.

Being the change is challenging on all levels in the same way. Everyone wants an improved income stream, but not everyone knows how to make that work for them instead of against them. Money/income stream really translates into energy. Too much energy can be dangerous; too much money can be dangerous; too much knowledge without the wisdom to use it correctly can be dangerous.

Being the change means being strong enough to not fall into danger zones. Being the change means that if you do fall into danger zones, you are strong enough to get your Self out. This is a challenging concept for most people to grasp. People visualize what they want, they envision the positive and they forget to include the negative.

- Have you fallen into danger zones and then worried about how to get out?
- Yet, somehow, someway, you do get out and you are wiser and smarter?
- Does getting out help everyone on some level?
- Is it challenging to change life by Being, rather than by talk or action?
- How many things have you tried to change by talk or action without success?
- Are you strong enough to open your income stream and not help those you love in financial need?
- Or, only give what they need, not what they want?

- Can you teach others to fish, so they can get their own food with your mental work?
- If people you know suddenly had all their basic needs met, would they stop stretching their own creativity?
- Does Being the Change mean watching those behind you struggle?

Change means you have to be flexible at a moment's notice. During my farming days in rural America, life was at a slower pace than those who live in the city. Whenever I wanted something, I waited for it to come on sale and then I made my purchase.

When I moved to New York, my first experience about moving too slowly was when Stewart and I were looking for a washer/dryer for our rental apartment. We found a great pair at a great deal. He wanted to buy immediately, but immediately was not really in my frequency, so I told him I wanted to think about it overnight. That was my process.

Of course, the next day when we went back to get them, they were already sold and out the door. I had to learn to step up my pace. To me, thinking about something is a part of the process. In fact, I like to think more than I like to act. It is like savoring the experience. My issue is also that once the act is completed, I have a tendency then to hold onto the past as part of my savoring of the experience.

- Do you think that holding onto the past is about savoring experience even when it is to your detriment?
- When you are in change mode, and you know that you need to let go so you can move on, why is letting go so challenging?
- Do you like to think before acting?
- Do you procrastinate and never act?
- Or think too long before acting?
- Do people who rough you up mentally and emotionally push you to act before you are ready?

- Is it challenging for you to ever be ready?
- Do you act too quickly without enough forethought?
- Do you know your process for change?
- If you act/change too quickly, does that upset the people around you?
- If you act/change too slowly, does that upset the people around you?
- Can you be flexible at a moment's notice?
- Does your flexibility depend on whether you want to be flexible or not?
- How challenging is it to change on a moment's notice when it is something you do not want to do?
- Do you have to be flexible in your life to survive?

How others react to your change continues to be a huge issue. This is part of hanging onto your past. My mother did not allow change. It was her way or the highway. My way was never good enough for her. Therefore, I had to think before I did anything new and ask my Self if it was going to get me in trouble someway, somehow. I had to remember the past, which as a child could have been anywhere from a few minutes to a few days ago. I had to think about what I did as well as the consequences of my actions. I always had to think carefully because I was trying to avoid any negative reaction/consequences.

This pattern with her followed me my entire life with her. I was always afraid of what she would think and her consequences. Even when she could no longer physically abuse me as an adult, I was still terrified of mental/emotional abuse. Internally, I still reacted like the scared child. When something burns you, your natural inclination is to avoid it. And that is what I did the majority of my adult life. I avoided her because I never knew when she was going to verbally attack me.

In the first few years after I left home, whenever I spent any time with my mother I would become physically ill. Vomiting, nausea, migraine headaches. This lasted about 10 years or so. I was always an extremely sensitive child and of course this carried over into my adulthood. This is why I say, when you look at your process of change, you must look at how your childhood affected that process.

- Were you allowed to change?
- Was it your parents' way or the highway?
- If you made a change without permission, were there consequences to pay?
- Did you make quick changes before your parents could tell you no?
- Did you do what you wanted to do regardless of parental consequences?
- Were you rebellious?
- Were you externally rebellious?
- Were you internally rebellious, desperately wanting to make changes but afraid of the consequences?
- Were you the change in your family?
- Were you/are you the silent change in your family?
- Do you carry these same change characteristics into your adult life?
- Are you afraid to "Be the Change" because of negative childhood imprinting?
- If you came here to "Be the Change", can anyone stop you now, but you and your own fears?
- Do you insulate and isolate because you are repeating childhood imprinting?
- If so, is it time to let that go?

- Do you still react like other people are your parents, ready to scold or cajole you?
- Can you release the little child within who is afraid of adults?
- Can you stand up for Self as an adult?
- How deep are your roots that anchor you into Source at all times?
- Does holding onto your childhood prevent your adulthood from happening?

## Parents as People

Sometimes, parents are afraid for you as you are growing up. When you are growing up with a limited view of the world, often you wonder what the big deal is, thinking that your parents are over-reacting. As a child, you only think about your parents as parents. But they are people first who had a life, long before you came along.

As children, you are usually so focused on your Self that you do not have a clue as to how your parents cope with the issues that they are going through; what is inside them; what is making them tick. It is easy to hold onto what they did to you. In the same way, you have to take into consideration what you did to them. Even though my mother passed on, she is still teaching me. I am still studying her as a person instead of only as a parent. I am still finding new areas of what she did right vs. only focusing on what she did wrong.

All of this continues to tie into objective observing your life so you can understand what really happened vs. what you thought happened. You were affected as a child, your memories and feelings are those of a child. This affects your entire life with repeated patterns that loop and hold you in place. You had to come in with something different to be doing what you are doing today. In spite of what you suffered, both perceived and real, you kept going and you continue to "Be the Change".

- With all you know, how can you expect others who know less, to be more than they are?
- Are you still challenged to forgive and move on?
- Are you still studying your childhood so you can objectively understand it?
- Do you know who your parents were as people?
- What were their personal issues when you were a child?
- From their perspective, what did you do to them?
- Did they know you, the person, or only you, the child?
- Were your parents afraid for you?
- Did they install fear?
- Did you pick up that fear by osmosis?
- Do you think your parents felt threatened because you are different?
- Did you have a mentor growing up?
- Did you mentor your Self?
- What is it within that drives you to maintain your own uniqueness amongst the crowd?

When you realize who your parents were as people when you were growing up as well as who you were to them, you start to get a better objective perspective of what actually happened in your childhood vs. what you think happened. Whatever you experienced, you experienced through the mind of a little unexperienced-in-the-world child. This means that what could have seemed like nothing to your parents could have been a major trauma for you. And, what might have been something to even your parents might be so horrific that you never get over it.

Your whole body can be fine, but if your little toe hurts, that is where you focus. Well, as a child, let's say you have an arm and a leg that hurts. Still, the majority of your body is well, but you still focus on what hurts. Before my mother passed away, she apologized to me; she said that if she hadn't been so hard on me that maybe my life would have been easier. It was heartfelt and I know she meant that. I was on top of the world, thinking that my work with her was done.

Then, when she passed away, I found out that she basically had written me out of her will. She left me a vase and one/half of her car, the other one/half went to my brother. Everything else went to her 2 sisters. I was devastated and crushed. I went from being on top of the world to down at the bottom again.

I will also repeat that I am still hurt and angry over this last thing she did to me in this world, but bit by bit I continue to examine what I know and put more pieces together, like you are doing. And just the other day I was thinking that maybe cutting me out of her will was her way of forcing me to continue evaluating my relationship with her. Otherwise, I would definitely have thought that I was done when I was not.

One adult memory that pops up every now and then, is my mother emphatically telling me that she was a good mother, and me thinking, uh, no you were not.

But, after her apology, I thought about all the good things she did do, and I wrote her a letter listing them and thanking her. Then, after the smack in the face with her will, I have had to dig even deeper into my relationship with her. And guess what, through the years, I have found even more good things that she did. And in many ways she was a good mother. Even many more ways than I originally listed.

In other words, part of "Being the Change" is me changing my opinion through my objective observations about my mother in a major way. I am still not at peace with her, but I continue to dig; I AM willing to change. And I AM.

- Are you willing to change your opinions about others?
- Are you working on your objective observations?
- Is what you thought traumatic as a child not so traumatic through the eyes of an adult?
- Are you allowing others to play the part of traumatizer-parent to you?
- Do you now have the tools to deal with those who play the role of traumatizer-parent?
- Who do you react to like they are your parent? Boss? Colleague? Neighbor? Relative?
- Do you have compassion for the lifestream that shaped the persona of your parents?
- Or anyone who plays the role of traumatizer-parent?
- Are you changing your mind-pattern so you no longer react as a child?

Ostracizing or punishing you as a child did not change you; instead you became more determined to be who you came here to be. As an adult and you do things differently than your parents, or others, you are a threat. If you do it the same way as they do, people can say that they are okay. When you do things differently, then they think your actions are statements that tell them they are not okay.

Good can always get better. Look at your parents' parents. Regardless of how bad you thought you had it, it is possible that your parents' had it even worse. For those of you with children, hopefully, they will improve on however you raised them. And for those of you without children, you are influencing other young people in your lives, often nieces and nephews, in ways that their parents cannot do.

You are impacting people, but this does not mean that they like your impact. This is why it is important to be respect and compassionate. They do not know what you know; you cannot expect them to behave differently than their influences. You are proactively making your good, better. But most people do not know how; and they are afraid of change.

- Do you have respect and compassion for others who live their lives in fear?
- Do you let others who live their lives in fear, get the better of you?
- When others push your buttons, do you release what you feel up to your Oversoul rather than out your mouth?
- Do you stop to think, *"There but for the Grace of God, go I"*?
- Who are you influencing with your changes?
- Who are you proactively helping in ways that their parents cannot?
- Does your way of doing things make other people feel threatened and feel like they and their ways were not good enough?
- Did ostracizing or punishing you as a child make you more determined to "Be the Change" that your parents could not be?
- Without the punishments and ostracizing, do you think you would have been so determined to do something different?
- Were the punishments and ostracizing the roughing up you needed to strengthen your resolve to not do this to others?
- Are people who are different always a threat to the status quo?

New beginnings always means change, which as you are discovering, is exactly what you were born to be. People in general do not like change, preferring the status quo. Or, if they do embrace change, this usually means they like change in their way, their reasons and their timing. You are learning to go one step higher and receive your guidance from Source 24/7, as best as you can.

You will always be tempted to go back to the old way or join the way of others. You have to prove to your Self that nothing can tempt you; nothing tempting you means no matching color, tone, and archetype and you can finally move into something else. If you want to show people the way out of their current path, you have to jump in there with them. This encourages them to know that if you can do it, so can they. You have been born into challenging circumstances with often challenging people. You must understand the journey and the people if you are to clear a path out for those who wish to follow. To do this, the first person out must be you.

The person clearing the path has the most struggles and the most challenging burdens to bear. You are the one doing the dirtiest, grubbiest work with the most primitive tools that you must build as you go. "Be the Change" is a catchy slogan, but there is a lot more to this than simply sitting back and talking about it. You need action on all levels, mental, emotional, spiritual and physical. You are an amazing person. You are the most important person who must recognize how amazing you are.

- Do you pat your Self on the back for everything that you have managed to accomplish, even when it is against the odds?

- Do you give gratitude for your knowledge and the wisdom you are developing to use it in the way that is most correct and beneficial?

- Do you feel like you have jumped into the middle of an unknown forest and now you must forage for everything you need to get out?

- Do you think your current work is helping to clear the path for others when they wish to leave the forest?

- How many times are you/were you tempted to go back to the way you used to be, or to join the crowd simply to fit in?

- How much strength does it take to keep doing what you know is most correct and beneficial when others pull you every which way except the way that Source is directing you to go?
- Is "Being the Change" part of your mission and purpose in this life line?

# Affirmations—I AM Grateful

New Beginnings, Change and Gratitude. You cannot have new until you are grateful for what you already have. It is challenging some days to be grateful, but your life is as it is for a reason. Build your attitude of gratitude to receive new blessings of positive abundance.

*I AM grateful to be here on this planet at this time.*

*I have incredible opportunities.*

*I AM grateful to my biological parents for giving life to my body.*

*I have unique genetics and mind-patterns.*

*I AM grateful to understand the agelessness of my Soul.*

*I have everything I need already within.*

*I AM grateful to know what I know.*

*I have knowledge beyond that of the average person in this reality.*

*I AM grateful to understand the stream of consciousness from the nonphysical to the physical.*

*I have the ability to use this reality to expand Soul-knowledge.*

*I AM grateful to understand Self-Responsibility.*

*I can change what is to what needs to be.*

*I AM grateful to know that this reality is a school for my Soul.*

*I exist here for many reasons with many layers.*

*I AM grateful to know that I do not have to like all that is most correct and beneficial for my Soul.*

*I agree to grow through what is most correct and beneficial for my Soul.*

*I AM grateful to be able to objectively view what was.*

*I AM different than I was.*

*I AM grateful for everything I have, regardless of how much or how little.*

*I know my Source always gives me what I need.*

*I AM grateful for the challenges that focus my attention on where I need to grow.*

*I know I never have more than I can bear.*

*I AM grateful for my Soul-strength.*

*I upgrade and elevate my mind-patterns through my trials.*

*I AM grateful that every day is an opportunity.*

*I treat every day as a blessing.*

*I AM grateful to know that I AM okay, as is.*

*I do my best, each and every day.*

*I AM grateful that I AM never A-lone.*

*I know that my Source guides, directs and supports me every step of my journey.*

*I AM grateful to have my Source as my best teacher.*

*I AM always consciously acquiring new knowledge and the wisdom to use it correctly.*

*I AM grateful when what/who I no longer need, moves out of my life.*

*I know that it is okay to grieve during the releasing process.*

*I AM grateful that I can find a place of peace within my Self.*

*I allow others the space to be who they are, without judgment from me.*

*I AM grateful that I find compassion for my Self and my journey.*

*I have compassion for others and their journeys.*

*I AM grateful that I understand and accept the necessary struggles of life.*

*I do what I need to do to develop Soul-strength.*

*I AM grateful for repetitive lessons that push me into my potential.*

*I stop repetitive cycles as soon as I AM able.*

*I AM grateful to observe when I loop in repetitive cycles.*

*I step off my loops and into something better.*

*I AM grateful to be an agent for balanced, positive elevating change.*
*I realize that not everyone appreciates balanced, positive elevating change.*

*I AM grateful that I embrace balanced, positive elevating change.*
*I easily identify programming that sabotages my efforts.*

*I AM grateful that I know how to persevere against the odds.*
*I use the odds in my favor.*

*I AM grateful that I know how to keep trying.*
*I find the doors that lead to my most correct and beneficial opportunities.*

*I AM grateful to "Be the Change" that is most correct and beneficial.*
*I get up and keep going, each and every day.*

*I AM grateful to know when to "hold 'em and when to fold 'em".*
*I know when to start and when to stop.*

*I AM grateful to always be in the correct place at the correct time.*
*I align the correct place at the correct time with the correct action.*

*I AM grateful to be who I AM in the Eternal Now.*
*I already have within me everything that I will ever be.*

# Problem/Challenge/Growth

I am the first person to tell you not to use the word problem, but instead use the frequency of challenge. However, for most people whenever an issue arises, the first word that enters their head is problem. Then, they start worrying and wondering what to do about it. As you are advancing and moving forward there are going to be a lot of problems along the way.

You have to hone your problem-solving skills so that problems turn into challenges that you can use to propel your Self forward. And, you cannot stay in problem-mode because of what you know. Some people without your problem-solving skills do stay in problem-mode because they do not know how to extricate themselves. Even with your problem-solving skills, when you are especially stressed or upset you may not be able to extricate your Self easily.

As you are learning, your entire life is a process. If you strive to maintain societal goals you will literally drive your Self crazy. You have to forget about the societal markers and focus on the aspect of your Soul-Personality that is in this moment of the Eternal Now. As you know, easier said than done. The more you focus on your Soul first, the more the rest of your life comes into place.

- Does come into place mean what you want or what you need?
- Do you easily let go of what you want?
- Do you easily accept what you need?
- Is it easy to put more focus on the Soul than the physical world?
- How do you focus on the Soul while using the physical world for Soul-growth?
- Do you feel like it has to be either "Soul" or "physical world"?
- How do you blend the two worlds together?
- Are you supposed to blend them or learn from each separately?
- Does the physical world sometimes feel diametrically opposed to the nonphysical world?
- When you feel stressed or upset, do you forget to do your Hyperspace/Oversoul work ?
- Do you know people who stay in problem-mode and never get out of it?
- Have you ever found your Self in problem-mode and been unable to get out of it?
- Does problem-mode feel like it will last forever?
- Does problem-mode exist to give you a taste of timelessness?
- Is the concept of time a huge issue for most people?

People are consistently trying to gather more energy/money as a way to resolve their problems. They are trying to take a physical representation of something nonphysical to solve nonphysical problems. But, they do not realize that their problems are nonphysical which is why physical wealth does not make them happy. Happy is nonphysical; emotions are nonphysical. You cannot solve something nonphysical with something physical.

Physical only exists to boost the nonphysical. But in this reality, people try to use the physical in place of the nonphysical. This school of thought is what traps people in the physical. For example, right next to my town is another town called Benton Harbor. On New Year's Eve, a local woman conspired with her boyfriend to kill her husband while all 3 were home on leave from the military to visit family. She said she did not want to divorce her husband because she wanted his death benefits. The husband, aged 23, is dead; the wife and boyfriend will now both be in prison for life, both in their early 20s.

I wish I could say that this a rare incident, but I see this type of story repeatedly in the news. People do terrible things for physical wealth without thinking of the physical consequences of their actions, much less the nonphysical consequences of their actions. Too many people do too many bad things to advance their physical wealth while not considering that without the nonphysical in place they are not going to get what they think they are going to get.

They have a problem and they think they are going to solve it with physical wealth; instead, their problems are complicated rather than resolved. Instead of waiting for whatever is most correct and beneficial, they reach out and grab what they want. They are not accepting they have what they need vs. what they want. They are not following human law. They are not even thinking about what is right or wrong. They definitely are not following Spiritual Law.

While these actions may seem extreme to the average person, many people are resorting to these kinds of tactics to solve their problems. I have a cousin who helped one of my great-aunts change her will entirely in my cousin's favor when my great-aunt was on her deathbed. In my opinion, my cousin complicated her problems on the Soul level once she did this. This cousin eventually died after a short illness at the relatively young age of 70.

These are all inner tests of doing the correct action for the correct reason in the correct timing. Problem solving is challenging. Temptation is real.

- Have you been in situations where you could have solved your physical problems but definitely complicated your nonphysical ones?
- Do you do what is right because you don't want to be caught or face physical punishment in this reality?
- Or do you do what is right because that is the correct thing to do?
- Do you know people who tried to solve their problems in bad ways and complicated their lives?
- Do you know people who only do the right thing because they are afraid of going to hell?
- Do you see people in general look for the shortcut to solve their problems rather than take a longer but more permanent road to problem-solving/resolution?
- Do you find problem-solving challenging?
- Is temptation real?
- Why do some people go to the extreme rather than try to resolve problems amicably so that all involved can come out in the best way possible?
- Is a grab for physical wealth an unconscious grab for nonphysical energy?
- Are people really after energy?
- Are people intent on gathering as much energy as possible for use now or later?
- Is a grab for physical wealth a statement of not believing in the continual energy supply of Source?
- Does the physical only exist to boost the nonphysical?

- Do people try to substitute physical for nonphysical?
- Is money almost always seen as the ultimate problem-solver?

**Journey vs. Goal**

When you discuss problems, you usually think: problem, resolution/goal, finished, move on. You need the resolution/goal to finish and move on. This society is goal-oriented. If you see money as the answer to your problems, then your goal/resolution is to get money and move on with your life. But, having money is not the problem-solver that most people think it is.

- Yet, you need money so if it isn't the problem-solver, what is?
- Your focus on getting more money is almost like a game.
- How do you get more?
- What do you do with it once you have it?
- How do you maintain/sustain your money/energy to continuously flow?
- How can you put as much focus on enjoying your journey as attaining your goal/resolution?
- There are many journeys that I have been on that I have definitely not enjoyed, yet in retrospect what I learned was priceless.
- Is the concept of "enjoying your journey" a falsehood to make you feel somehow less than when you do not enjoy your journey?
- Is your journey always educational, even if it is in unexpected ways?
- Would it be more appropriate to say your journey to your goal definitely will be educational; appreciate the educational process?
- Is education always enjoyable?

- Do most people think "enjoyable" when they think "educational"?
- Does a goal give you a talking point with others?
- If they cannot understand your journey, is it easier to tell them your goal?
- Is money one topic to which almost everyone can relate?
- Is the goal a temptation that can distract you from the journey?

While scrolling the Internet I often see homes that entertainment people are selling for a few million dollars. To the normal person, this sounds like a huge house. But when you read the following statistics below, what is a multimillion dollar home for people like this:

> The Hollywood Reporter estimates that A-list movie stars routinely make $15 million to $20 million for top roles in big-budget films. Secondary lead actors in a movie such as The Force Awakens earned an estimated $1.5 million to $4.5 million. Oct 3, 2017

Yet, when you see a multimillion dollar home you may oooh and aaaaah, but the pictures reinforces that this happens to someone else, not you. Now, look at what the stars of the film take in, per film:

| Actor | Film | Total Income |
|---|---|---|
| Tom Cruise | Mission: Impossible | $70,000,000 |
| Harrison Ford | Indiana Jones and the Kingdom of the Crystal Skull | $65,000,000 |
| Jack Nicholson | Batman | $60,000,000 |
| Leonardo DiCaprio | Inception | $59,000,000 |

https://en.m.wikipedia.org/wiki/List_of_highest_paid_film_actors

This is another place where you stop thinking about your own income because you think you can never measure up to this kind of income stream. That is one of the points of all this publicity about how much these people are making because you rarely go any further. Because if this is what the entertainment people are making, you cannot even begin to imagine the income of the people who pay the entertainers to distract you.

With this in mind, you automatically lower your goal of making money because the only way to make this kind of money is to be an entertainer or win the lottery. Most people bet on the lottery even though they have a greater chance of being struck by lightning.

Yes, if you hang out under tall trees or on top of cleared hills during thunderstorms, it might not be too surprising if you're struck by lightning. But overall, each of us has a very, very low chance of being hit by lightning: In fact, it's about 1 in 1 million. In a group of 292 million people, only one is likely to win a Powerball jackpot, but 292 are likely to be zapped by lightning. https://www.fool.com/slideshow/25-things-more-likely-happen-you-winning-lottery/?slide=8

Everything is put out there to tempt you, but you can't have it. This emotional taunt is what pushes people to prove that "I can have it". They want others to see that they are as good as everyone else, if not better. This goal of having money is a huge emotional game that the global handlers play with your emotions. Many people succumb to the temptation of the goal instead of following Spiritual Law. In the short term, they may win, but under Spiritual Law, there will be a huge price to pay.

Layers upon layers within layers. All of these layers of societal imprinting are designed to make you think that you are a nothing, have always been a nothing and most likely will always be a nothing. Problem solved!

You buy right into it with negative Self-talk such as: I don't have a multimillion dollar home, I have never had a multimillion dollar home, and most likely I will never have a multimillion dollar home.

Problem solved because what is the point of even trying to solve something that you already know is done, over, finis.

- Have you ever been jealous of people who have more physical wealth than you do?
- Do people who have more physical wealth like to flaunt what they have?
- How about the super-wealthy who you rarely see?
- If they have so much money why aren't they flaunting it like everyone else?
- Do you now feel, or have you felt, that your income level is a done thing with little chance of improvement?
- Would you be happy with a home, any home, as long as you have some kind of a home?
- Or, once you have a home do you keep wanting to improve on whatever you have?
- Do you think the global handlers emotionally taunt society with what exists but the average person cannot have?
- Who do you think the entertainers buy their multimillion dollar homes from?
- Do you think the global handers think "what is mine is mine and what is yours is mine"?
- Does this attitude help you to focus on what is important to you?

The opposite end of the spectrum is what is now called a minimalist, which means owning very little, if anything. I read an article about a minimalist who lives with her sister who is an extreme minimalist. The extreme minimalist said that her cat has more things than she does. Okay…

Not having much is supposed to solve all your problems. I'm not exactly sure how, but in my opinion being a minimalist is a method of denying your Self the pleasures of the world, as well as what some people would consider necessities. If you have low Self-Worth being a minimalist is an excuse to justify to the world why you don't have what society expects you to have. Plus, you can get attention because you don't want what others have and you have a unique lifestyle that others can envy. Plus others may even view you as more spiritual because you are not attached to things. Kind of like a vegan is more disciplined than a vegetarian and therefore most envied. All are mind-patterns of low Self-Worth, Self-punishment and Self-deprivation.

- Are necessities objective or subjective?
- Since you are here, should you be experiencing the pleasures of the world?
- What are the pleasures of the world?
- Is it important to know which pleasures of the world are most correct and beneficial for you?
- Is this a case of the correct thing in the correct timing in the correct way?
- Is being a minimalist another version of experiencing the pleasure of pain?
- Do you like sleeping on a bed and sitting on a chair vs. sleeping/sitting on the floor?
- Why would the minimalist have a cat with more things than she has?
- Does she think more of the cat than she does of her Self?
- What kinds of mind-patterns would be inherent in a minimalist?
- What about influences of Simultaneous Existences?
- How about programming?

- Do people envy those who they perceive are most disciplined?
- Is it enviable to not want?
- If so, where does the idea of "not wanting" come from in a world of abundance?
- Does not wanting solve your problems?
- Could being a minimalist, extreme minimalist, vegetarian or vegan be most correct and beneficial for some people?
- What is the difference between a poor person and a minimalist?
- How about a poor person and a vegan/vegetarian?

Too many things aren't going to solve your problems nor are too few things. Because as you know, your problems are nonphysical and cannot be solved by physical things. People who have too much can have too much because those who have too little believe that they deserve little. They work hard but do not reap the fruits of their energy.

The physical representation of their energy has to go somewhere, so those who believe that they deserve too much, scoop up that unclaimed energy for themselves. In fact, in 2013 CNN Money reported:

> Currently, states, federal agencies and other organizations collectively hold more than $58 billion in unclaimed cash and benefits. That's roughly $186 for every U.S. resident. The unclaimed property comes from a variety of sources, including abandoned bank accounts and stock holdings, unclaimed life insurance payouts and forgotten pension benefits.
>
> Some people are owed serious cash. Last year, a Connecticut resident claimed $32.8 million, proceeds from the sale of nearly 1.3 million shares of stock. The recipient of the funds requested to remain anonymous and no further details were provided.
>
> More than $300 million in pension benefits is currently owed to some 38,000 people, according to the Pension Benefit Guaranty Corp. The unclaimed benefits currently range from

12 cents to a whopping $704,621, with an average benefit of $9,100. Benefits may go unclaimed because an employee is unaware they had accrued retirement benefits at a previous employer, the agency.

https://money.cnn.com/2013/01/24/pf/unclaimed-money/index.html

Be sure to check the following website link because every once in a while one of our members reports that he/she has found some unclaimed money. Search any state where you have ever lived and put in every surname you have ever used. If you have any deceased relative you can try searching that person's name/states where he/she lived in case something shows up:

https://www.unclaimed.org/

Those people who have too much have earned what they have in some way, shape or form. Those who have too little are reaping what they have sown. Here we have the extremes. I think people with too much teach the people with "too little" in such a way that the too much people gradually scale down their wealth while gradually increasing the wealth of those with too little.

- Just because they can have too much, does this make it correct?
- Do you think they can hold onto their too much for too long in the same way that you may hold onto your no-longer-necessary emotions for too long?
- Can the people with too little hold onto their low Self-Worth for too long?
- Does each extreme group of people blame the other group for their problems?
- If you have too much it is because the other group doesn't deserve it?

- If you have too little it is because the other group doesn't deserve it?

- Is this an example of people helping or blaming each other?

- If everyone on the Earth helped to elevate each other, would there be a new balance with better health and wealth for all?

- Why does the group with too little admire those with too much?

- Why does the group with too little patronize the businesses of those with too much?

- Is it possible to balance outer wealth by balancing inner energy?

## The System

The system invites you to participate; this is your temptation. However, because everything has a positive and a negative, as well as neutral, if you find the positive and make it work for you, you are not participating in their system the way it was intended. For example, the societal programming tells you that technology isolates people. This is the programming that tells older people to dwell on the way things were vs. what is.

I like technology and I use technology in a way that works for me and not against me. Social media helps me spread the word about my business. When I first started publishing the only way you could get the word out about your products was through expensive advertisement in papers and magazines. Social media connects me to the world and I like that. Technology lets me print 100 books at a time instead of 5000. Regardless of how many memes I see, I am grateful for technology and how it connects me to the world. I feel much less isolated because of technology.

Before technology people carried books, newspapers, game books, handcrafts, even transistor radios. If people are going to isolate they are going to isolate. Isolation is a function of mind-pattern. Interesting that now, you are being told and shown how dependent you are on technology and how you are isolating your Self. Social media is portrayed as bad rather than helpful. You can participate in the negativity and negative imprinting or you can disconnect from this and choose to use the tool for positive enhancement. As Stewart often says you can use a pen to write a beautiful story or you can choose to stab someone with it. The choice is yours.

The same with gun control that is being pushed on us here in the US. The issue will never be about any weapon. The issue is with the people. As you already know, take away all the guns and those who want a weapon will find something else to weaponize. The problem is not about guns. When I was studying statistics at my university, I did a statistical analysis that actually proved that the more police officers that were present the more crime in the area. The data could be interpreted to say that by putting police in certain areas that crime increased.

Disconnecting and not participating are ways to solve some of societal issues as well as your own. In addition, sometimes the best way to change something is from the inside out, such as how you personally Self-correct. I am doing my best to change me for the better while at the same time disconnecting/not participating unless my Oversoul says that it is what is most correct and beneficial.

- Have you ever resolved any of your own issues by disconnecting and not participating?
- Do people want to blame guns for people getting hurt?
- How do you feel about gun control?
- Do we need guns as a society?
- Can you resolve your personal safety with mind-pattern?
- Are guns necessary in the meantime until your mind-pattern stays 100% safe 100% of the time?

- Do you like or dislike social media?
- Does social media control you or are you in control of it?
- Do you like or dislike technology?
- Does social media and/or technology lead to social isolation?
- Does pushing how isolating technology is actually isolating older people from younger people, thus another division of generations?
- Is system temptation a negative?
- Is the system what you make it?
- Can the system turn you into something/someone that you are not?

Guns are a phallic symbol that represent power. Guns physically manifest the thoughts that are in your mind. Take away the guns and take away people's perception of power.

As you know, the Waldensians in the mountains of Italy were poor in physical assets and few in physical numbers. Yet, they fought valiantly for centuries with very few to none guns, destroying thousands and thousands of troops. In fact, one Roman Catholic author, Rainier Sacho wrote: "There is no sect so dangerous as the Leonists (another name for Waldensians because they were from the Lyons section of France) for three reasons, first, it is the most ancient; some say it is as old as Sylvester, others say it is as old as the Apostles themselves, second it is very generally disseminated; there is no country where it has not gained some footing. Third, while other sects are profane and blasphemous, this retains the utmost show of piety; they live justly before men and believe nothing concerning God which is not good."

I highly recommend that you read our **True World History** book as well as **Rorà** which is considered Christian historical fiction. by James Byron Huggins. I am proud to say that Rorà is the town where my family comes from.

My point is that the Waldensians did not see their power lying in guns, but instead in God. They were masters at Self-defense, using their natural surroundings to outwit those with guns, cannons and horses. Of course many Waldensians did perish and in despicable ways, but they still believed that it was better to sacrifice the flesh than the Soul.

People are not imprinted to perceive power outside of Self, i.e., they have faith in guns over God. In the same way, during war if the leader is captured, the entire psyche of the followers can be destroyed. Or even capturing the flag of the opposing team can sap the energy right out of the people whose flag has been captured.

People need a rallying point. Here in the US, they are trying to take away our flag as a sign of national respect. They are trying to turn it into a symbol of shame instead of pride. I am against gun control simply because guns do not kill, people kill. It does not matter what you regulate or how, those people who want to kill will find a way. I saw a meme with one person holding a sign wanting to ban guns; another person had a sign wanting to ban spoons because spoons made him fat.

Right now the frequency of the people needs the outer display of guns to focus on their own internal power. Right now, owning a gun is a physical representation of what people feel they lack in the nonphysical.

- Why are flags important?
- Why does a nation or a group need a flag?
- What is it about a flag that makes a nation or a group feel powerful?
- How can a piece of cloth with symbols on it that is paraded around all over the place give people a sense of power/pride?

- Why is kneeling in front of US flag seen as a sign of disrespect when kneeling before anything is generally seen as a sign of fidelity and allegiance?
- Is this part of linguistic/social engineering?
- Why do people need a rallying point to feel powerful?
- Do people have more faith in guns than in God?
- Is it better to sacrifice the flesh than the Soul?
- Or, is it important to save the flesh so the Soul has a place to learn its lessons?
- Is saving the flesh an Animal Mind function?
- Or is Animal Mind most correct and beneficial to save the species?
- Without guns do people feel powerless?
- Why is gun control so emotional?

Owning a gun may set you up to have to use it someday; a Self-fulfilling prophecy. Guns and weapons are the epitome of using an outside force to solve inner problems. Every day in the news there is story after story of people who try to solve their issues with guns and/or other weapons. Nothing is ever solved this way only complicated. This is a variation of winning the battle but losing the war.

## Conflict Resolution

Everyone has inner conflict. All conflict is enhanced by outer temptations. You are always tempted to leave the straight and narrow path that your Soul needs because there are so many outer distractions designed to do exactly this. You are conflicted about what to do, where to go, who to be with so you are given many temptations to choose from with only one being the most correct and beneficial. When you wander off the path then new temptations are set up to see how far you will wander before you realize that what you are doing is not working and you need to do something else.

One of my downfalls is that I have always had so many ideas I am challenged to narrow my focus and then maintain that narrow focus. My ideas were my temptations. Then, I listened to people who said they could help me fulfill my ideas instead of listening to my Self. Every single time I listened to others I had a major problem in my business.

- What kinds of temptations have you faced that have caused you to wander off your narrow path?
- Were you conflicted before you wandered off?
- Were you gullible because of what you wanted to do or have?
- Are temptations designed to test your gullibility?
- When you wander off your narrow path does it take a long time to find your way back?
- Does inner conflict cause sleepless nights and restless days?
- Is it easier to solve the conflicts of others than your own?
- Is it easier to play the blame game than recognize your inner weaknesses that allowed you to wander off?
- In your ideal world, what is the best way to discover/uncover your inner weaknesses?
- In your ideal world, what is the best way to strengthen your weaknesses?
- Have you been in situations where you won the battle but lost the war?

There are so many easy ways to get lost in the forest; all of the various trails are definitely temptations, but you must not stay too long—you must get back on your path. When you think about the entire forest, you definitely can feel overwhelmed. When I used to think about my entire life and what I wanted to accomplish I felt that I must hurry up and get it all done. Time felt very limited. What I felt I needed to accomplish seemed massive.

Rushing through your life makes it much easier to get side-tracked and off your path. You miss the obvious signs of where you are supposed to be as you try to process all the distractions. It is easy to think that the distraction is on your path when in retrospect it most definitely is not. I have learned that the more I slow my Self down, the more I see, the more accurate my processing and the easier it is to stay on my path.

I do my best to take one day at a time; one step at a time. And when one step at a time seems too much, then take ½ step or ¼ step. As my cousin in the Cottian Alps says, what is important is that you keep moving and do not stop. Because once you stop, it takes more energy to start again and more energy to get your momentum going.

Many years ago I had a client whose husband was an avid boater, yet she was terrified of water. To conquer her fear of water I taught her to first stand beside the water. Then, put in her toes, then her entire feet and over time she was able to dispel many of her fears. It was not an overnight process, but she started in a place where she could focus without distraction and be successful.

There are too many issues in life that cannot be solved overnight no matter how much you want them to be. When you focus on your problems and feel the pressure of time, you can easily feel overwhelmed, give up and not accomplish anything that you came here to do. The feeling of being overwhelmed can paralyze you to inaction. I have had this experience many times; when you do not begin you do not fail.

- When a task seems too big, is it easy to just not begin so you do not fail?
- Have you had a sense of failure before you ever even began a project or tackled an issue?
- Does the sense of failure cause you to procrastinate or never begin?

- When you have a problem, do you feel the pressure of time to solve/resolve it?

- By doing Hyperspace/Oversoul work, have you learned to slow down?

- Does slowing down feel dull and boring compared to a fast-paced life?

- Does slowing down slow down the illusion of time?

- Does slowing down actually give you more time because you are more focused on the tasks at hand?

- Does rushing through your life make it much easier to get side-tracked and off your path?

- Is it easy to think that the distraction/temptation is on your path when it is not?

- Is it more challenging to start and stop than to keep going?

- Do you feel limited by time?

- Is it easier to think of only one tree in a forest than the entire forest?

- Why do problems feel so overwhelming if they are Self-tests designed to help you grow?

## Perfectionism

I googled the definition of perfection and this is what I got:

> The condition, state, or quality of being free or as free as possible from all flaws or defects.

The word perfectionist when googled has almost 25,000,000 results. Then I googled "what to do if you are a perfectionist" and I got over 14,000,000 results. Oh my gosh!

I used to be a perfectionist until I finally stopped to ask my Self what exactly was a perfectionist and who was I trying to please? I realized that I was always trying to live up to the standards of my mother; I was conditioned to fear my mother's watchful eye because nothing I ever did was good enough for her. So my perfection that I was always trying to attain was what I perceived to be my mother's expectations.

When I realized what I was doing and why, I stopped trying to please everyone else. I started working on pleasing my Self. Apparently, according to my google searches, I wasn't the only one kowtowing to someone else's expectations and trying to live my life according to someone else's standards. Plus, I found out repeatedly that I cannot compare my Self to others except in general.

When I think, *"There but for the Grace of God, go I"*, I am thinking about what I might have been like had I not done my personal work. Every person is a unique flower in the garden of the God-Mind. No two people are alike. I cannot compare the beauty of a tulip to a daisy to a rose to a lily. Each flower adds something unique to the garden of life.

- Do you compare your Self and your Self-expectations to others ?
- Can you observe others in general to give your Self an idea of what to do/not do?
- Do you compare your Self to others in minute detail?
- Is trying to compare your Self in minute detail a fruitless task?
- Can you compare a tulip to a daisy to a rose to a lily?
- How can you say one is more lovely or important than the other?
- Is comparing your Self to others a temptation that leads you into trying to be a perfectionist?
- Are you trying to be better or just as good as others?
- If so, then what is the point?
- Is one flower better than another?

- Should a tulip try to be like a daisy or a rose like a lily?
- How does a perfectionist define perfect?
- Does everyone have a definition of perfect?
- Do you strive to please others over your Self?
- Do you think you are striving to please your Self when in reality you are trying to please someone else?
- Do you do what you do so that others will like you?
- Do you appreciate your own uniqueness in the flower garden of the God-Mind?

Trying to be a perfectionist has caused a vast majority of people to develop depression and anxiety. When you can't be or do whatever your version of perfect is, you feel like a failure causing you to question even the point of living.

You will never solve any problem perfectly according to someone else's standards. If you are stressed over what perfect is, you have to look within to find out where that mind-pattern began. Only then can you pull the energy out of your energy field, giving it back up to your Oversoul and into God-Mind. Keep reviewing **Decoding Your Life**. Universal Law as outlined in this book helped me then, helps me now and can help you, too, if you follow the law and principles.

Whenever you are not satisfied with whatever issue you are trying to resolve, you begin judging and criticizing Self. This is why I am very explicit in this book about using the affirmation:

### *I release the need to judge and criticize my Self.*

This was my go-to affirmation for many, many years. Every time I was judging/criticizing my Self for not reaching some level of perfection, I started with this affirmation repeatedly until I was energetically able to pull my Self up and out of depression and Self-criticism.

Then, my next go-to affirmation was:

*I AM okay, as is.*

***I AM doing my best because if I could do better I would.***

Even when you are Self-sabotaging and know that you are Self-sabotaging you are still doing your best or you would not be Self-sabotaging. I have learned through the years that I AM doing my best in every moment. Whatever you do in any moment is your best at that moment or you would be doing something else.

Knowing better does not mean that you can practice better. Knowing something does not really become a part of you until you use it. Even if you think "I shouldn't be doing this" but you do it anyway, that is still your best or you would not be doing something that you know you should not be doing.

It is challenging to pull out the old imprints, but it can be done. But it takes a lot of diligence to get to this point. Reading is a great first step. Then you have to practice to see what you know and do not know; what kind of results you get; and if you consistently get similar results.

There is a lot to do when you Self-study. Intellectually you can know a lot of things. It is the practice that challenges you to change your Self. If one step is too much then take ½ step, or even ¼ step. As long as you keep going you are going to get somewhere.

You have your unique process and it cannot be compared to the process of others. However, you can use the behavior of others as a kind of guideline and inspiration on what to do/not do. You can share your process and others may be able to take bits and pieces to create their own process.

- Can you think too much?
- Is thinking without action pointless?

- Do you need action to truly understand any issue as well as to adequately problem-solve?

- Do you use the behavior of others as a kind of guideline and/ or inspiration on what to do/not do?

- Do you want to see immediate results when you start something new?

- Does doing Hyperspace/Oversoul work require patience?

- Do you think about how long your Soul has existed in comparison to the physical body?

- Does it make sense that this life is simply a little blip in the process of your Soul?

- Does everything in this reality have a place?

- Do you have a place?

- Can you be so worried about what you are/are not going to do that you never start?

- Do you know people who are always talking about something but never doing it?

- Do you know when you are not doing your best?

- Or is "not doing your best" a fallacy in the same way as perfectionism ?

- Can you only do your best in any given moment?

- Can you ever solve any problem if you are constantly judging and criticizing your Self?

- Does constant judgment and criticism of Self mean that there can be no solution because the solution will never be right/ perfect/doable?

- Is judging and criticizing your Self another way to say "I AM a victim"?

- Can you accept Self as is?

- If you are not okay as is, can any solution you come up with be okay?

Many people criticize themselves because they think they should have done better. Sometimes intellectually you know what you should be doing but emotionally you want what you want and so you do it anyway. Then, people intellectually judge and criticize themselves because they gave way to their emotions. This is why you need to balance your brain.

Many people function with either intellect or emotions. Balancing your T-Bar Archetype or using the Pineal Gland Archetype at the Pineal Gland helps to balance the brain. So does keeping your brain in Royal Blue. So does breathing into your center as discussed in **Decoding Your Life** and also walking; anything that moves your physical body left/right; left/right.

Intellectually people know a lot of things are wrong but they do them anyway. Think how many people drink and drive; or text and drive; shoplift; overeat; don't exercise; open their mouths when they should be shut. If you could do better, you would.

You do the best that you can in the moment with what you have. You release what you did; think about what you can do better next time, and then do your best to do better next time. Then repeat the process. It takes a long time to stop any habit response, from overeating to not exercising to talking when you need to be silent, or being silent when you need to be talking. If you could do better, you would. Yes, I know that I am repeating this sentence because it is so important that you "get this". When you "get this" then you can finally stop judging and criticizing your Self for not doing better.

- If I told you to go put on a pair of ballet shoes and dance Swan Lake, could you do it?
- Would you expect your Self to?
- Would you feel horrible if you did not succeed the first time?

- Do you need practice to perform ballet?
- Is trying the same as doing?
- Is trying an important step in the process?
- At some point do you have to stop "trying" and start "doing"?
- Can you try to dance?
- Or is dancing "doing" regardless of how you judge your performance?
- Can you observe your performance without judging it?
- Can you want to dance Swan Lake but acknowledge that you need more practice without judging your Self?
- Or, maybe you never really wanted to dance Swan Lake and it is time to admit that this is not your area of interest or expertise?
- And if it is not, do you have to criticize your Self for feeling this way?
- Why does the intellect want to judge and criticize the emotions?
- Do you feel what you feel regardless of what the intellect tells you?
- How do you align intellect with emotions so all parts of your brain are going in the same direction?

You have to tell your Self that if you could have done better, you would have. You did a good job with what you know and the practice you have. Keep practicing and you will continue to get better and improve.

In the *Star Wars* movies, Yoda says, "there is no try, only do". If I throw a pencil on the floor then tell you to try to pick it up, you are going to either try and not pick it up, or you are going to "do" and actually pick it up. No one is asking you to judge if you did it well or not well. The same with the dance of Swan Lake. This is an analogy that pushes you outside your comfort zone. The minute you start to dance you are "doing" not "trying". Either you dance or you don't.

Sometimes life does not seem to be in your favor. Even if you cannot see it, life is always in your favor. For example, a few years ago we had a great client who wanted to come to several seminars and she wanted to pay all of it up front. It was great to have a nice chunk of money. However at the seminar she decided that Stewart was eyeing her girlfriend, then starting phoning and harassing us. Finally she demanded back that large chunk of money which I had gratefully received and used to pay a lot of bills.

So while it looked like receiving that initial money was in my favor, it was not in my favor in the long run. If I had not received the money initially I might have been upset. But, I would not have to borrow the money to pay her back. I obviously could not keep money for services that were not going to be rendered. I trusted this person because she had been a client for many, many years. In the end my life was much more complicated because I had to give back money that was already spent.

This is why I always, always tell you that *rejection is God's protection*. Life is always in your favor; you always have what you need. You most likely do not always have what you want. Most likely you do not even get what you need in the way that you want. Intellectually these are extremely simple concepts. Emotionally, it is challenging to accept. When you put together a jigsaw puzzle, it is always amazing that the smallest bit of color on one piece can absolutely define the entire puzzle when it is put in its correct place.

There are a lot of things in my life that I know are the way they are supposed to be, but a part of me wants "what was" instead of "what is". Intellectually I can talk about it all day long, but emotionally I still feel what I feel. I work on being grateful for what is and some days are better than others. You cannot reason with your emotions but you can build another pathway. In addition, you can use your affirmations as energetic tools to create new avenues of action. Balancing your brain and getting intellect and emotions to form some kind of partnership will get you further along in the most correct and beneficial way.

- Does "most correct and beneficial" mean the way I want, what I want, when I want?

- When you don't get what you want in the way you want, when you want, is it easy to start criticizing and denigrating Self?

- Is it okay to feel what you feel under these circumstances?

- Can the intellect help bring you out of a depressed state?

- Do emotions sometimes want you to stay in a depressed state?

- Are there parts of Self that want you to feel sorry for Self?

- Can the intellect devise distractions to pull you out of depression, such as gardening, walking, painting, socializing, and using Hyperspace/Oversoul tools and techniques?

- Can distractions be a positive as well as a negative?

- Is life one complication after another?

- Or is life an interesting story that throws unexpected curves to keep you interested and entertained?

- Do you like reading books or watching movies with unexpected plot twists?

- Do these unexpected moments keep you more fully engaged and entertained?

- Is this okay when it happens to someone else, but not you?

- Is it challenging to realize that life is always in your favor?

- Is it always challenging to constantly remind Self that *rejection is God's protection*?

- In your life, do you try or do you do?

Any word that takes whatever you want into the future creates a linear future frequency. This means that even if something is trying to get to you, it cannot because your mind-pattern is projecting future, not now. Hope is great example of this. Hoping that you can do something denotes the future, not now. Planning is about the future rather than now. Both of these words have a frequency. Each letter has a frequency.

This is why affirmations are so powerful. They can build or they can destroy. The more times you say something the more power you give it. You can empower the positive in your life or the negative. With conscious awareness you can make conscious choices to empower the positive. Empowering the positive may feel like a negative in the moment; or conversely, what feels like a positive in the moment may actually be a negative.

For example, now that summer vacations are at their peak, I continue to read about how many horrible things happen to people. For example not too long ago a grandfather accidently dropped his granddaughter out of a cruise ship window, killing her. Yesterday I read about another man who was killed when he went overboard on a cruise ship. A few days ago a 15 year old girl from the UK on a tour with her family in Malaysia disappeared in the night and was found dead.

In the beginning, I'm sure all of the families involved were excited and elated. They did not know what was waiting for them. If they hadn't gone, they never would have known the negatives that transpired. They would have been disappointed and let down. They would have labeled the positive of not going as a negative.

These things that are happening to tourists are in the news everywhere: slipping on rocks while climbing up to see a waterfall: being swept away by rogue waves and rising tides at beaches; being beaten and/or raped at hotels. The list does not stop.

This is why I tell you that whatever happens to you is in your favor. These people all had some kind of lesson to learn that actually was in their favor when you get above the judgment of the event. We do not know why these people had to go through what they had to go through, but you can have compassion for their journey.

In the same way, when you are disappointed or let down, have compassion for Self that you are not getting what you want, in the way you want, in the timing you want. But do your best to defer to the decisions of your Source. Grieve for the loss of your ideas but be grateful that you are protected on a higher, deeper level. Continue to use your affirmations to create your life, but work on being a co-creator rather than the sole creator. When you try to create on your own you are going to find your life much more complicated whether you accurately identify it as this or not.

When you bring in Source as your co-creator you have a greater understanding of the big picture. The more you practice this concept the more you can *"let go and let God"* and trust the process. Not easy, but doable.

- How challenged are you to *"let go and let God"*?
- How often do you think you know best, only to find out that maybe you didn't?
- How easy is it to judge the negative experiences of others rather than have compassion and understanding for their journey?
- Are you challenged to see Self as a co-creator of your life rather than the sole creator of it?
- Do you take time to grieve for the loss of your ideas?
- Is this important even when you know that it is for the best when you do not get what you want?
- Do you have compassion for Self when you do not get what you want?
- Or how about when you get what you want but not in the way you had expected?

- Do you use words like "plan" or "hope" or similar words that place your life in the future instead of the present?

Any words that put the solution/resolution to your problems into the future are words to be avoided. Low Self-confidence makes some part of you think that you do not have the solution now and you must struggle to get the solution which may or may not come.

Poison ivy, for example, grows in the forest alongside jewelweed. Poison ivy can give you a horrible rash and jewelweed is the antidote, which always grows within close proximity to the poison ivy. Problem/solution exists simultaneously whether you are conscious of this or not.

"The whole" always exists within the God-Mind. Problem/Solution is the whole experience. Poison Ivy/Jewelweed is the whole experience. Rash/cure allows you to know everything about this experience. Knowing the rash is only part of the experience. Healing is the other aspect of the experience. You need both sides of the coin to understand the entire experience. Regardless of your problem, the solution is always close at hand. The issue is that you may not like the solution, the way the solution comes and/or the timing of the solution. But always, always the solution is there waiting for you to open your mind and receive it according Source's wishes, not yours.

Just like you can choose to avoid the very words that sink your life. Hope is the word that destroys your chance of getting what you hope for. "I can't stand" so you have leg, back and feet issues. Your words are saying the exact opposite of the health you seek. "Someday, my ship will come in". Someday is the future, so you stop your ship from arriving now.

You know the problem. Your words are giving you the solution. The solution is right in front of your face, actually already in your mind and flowing out your mouth but you do not know how to interpret the solution. Yet, there it is. Observation is a huge part of problem-solving. Asking questions is a huge part of problem-solving. Slowing down is a huge part of problem-solving. All of these qualities help you define the solution that you have perhaps missed your entire life.

- How eager are you to slow down when society tells you to speed up?
- Is every fiber in your Being telling you to go faster?
- Why do people who run fast, ski fast, play tennis fast catch your attention more than those who run slow, ski slow and play tennis slow?
- Do you like to watch golf?
- Is golf a slow sport?
- Why does golf capture the attention of people?
- Do you ask a lot of questions?
- Are questions appreciated or do others get annoyed when you ask too many questions?
- How do you define "too many" questions and according to whom?
- Does asking questions slow you down?
- Do you ask your Oversoul question after question after question?
- Do you observe or only think you observe?
- Do you observe Self as discussed in ***Decoding Your Life***?
- Is challenging to objectively observe others without judgment or criticism?
- How challenging is it to observe Self without judgment or criticism?
- Have you been stumped in any issue, only to find the solution lying right in front of you?

- Have you spent time looking for an object only to discover it was right in front of you all the time, even in your hand or on your body?

- If Source creates a problem does this mean that there must be a solution?

- If there is a solution does this mean there must be a problem?

- Does a part of you feel that you must struggle to be worthy of the solution?

- Does Low Self-confidence mean you are not worthy of having your problem resolved?

When you have a problem you usually have to do the opposite of what you want to do. When you have a problem the first thing most people want to do is run in the opposite direction. Instead, you must stand firm and face it.

When you feel sad, unhappy or depressed then use affirmations such as:

### *I release the need to feel sad, unhappy or depressed.*

There is a part of you that wants to feel these negative emotions or you would not have them. The trick is to feel them and move on. If you have a need to feel bad about your Self then you hang onto the negative emotions. Feeling negative emotions is also a way to hold onto experiences from which you are not ready to release.

For example if someone passes away or maybe even moves, you may feel very sad, unhappy and depressed because that person is no longer in your life. Or, this can even be the passing of a pet. Feeling sad, unhappy or depressed reminds you of that person or pet. You may miss them and do not like the void that person or pet leaves. While you can fill the void with something else you do not want to because the void is for that person/pet. The void is still a connection that you may feel you lose once that void is filled. This is also an example of wanting "what was" vs. "what is". The problem is living in the past and not getting what you want in the Eternal Now. The solution is to move on and fill the void.

When 4 of my pets passed away within 1 year I was not ready to get new ones, but Stewart was insistent. I finally told him I just didn't care; do whatever you want. Long story short, we got 4 new pets and I am grateful that he pushed because the house feels so much better with the 2 dogs and 2 new kittens. In my mind I never wanted anymore pets because the pain of losing them is too horrible. I could have stayed in my suffering but I gave up and gave in. I *"let go and let God"* in the form of my loving husband taking control. I am grateful that I allowed the voids to be filled.

I still have 2 older cats, one 15 and one almost 15. Having the 2 younger kittens will help fill the void when the older ones go. Now I feel like I never want to have that kind of void again.

It is challenging to allow your Self to be happy or excited for living when those who you love are no longer with you, whatever the reason. You miss them. That is the bottom line. Sometimes I grieve for my grandparents who have passed on, or other relatives or friends that I miss. Sometimes I miss friends and family who are still here, so I am grateful for technology that lets us be in touch even if not physically present.

Doors close for a reason. There is always another door, even if you do not like it or think you preferred the old door/old way of living life. Be grateful for what/who you had and the time you had in that experience. God-Mind is always moving and so are you, even when you don't feel like it or want to be.

- Do you wish that you could consciously pick and choose when and how your life experiences could begin, end or change?

- Is it challenging when life takes turns that you consciously do not want to travel?
- Is it challenging to be grateful for what you have when you think about what you had?
- When doors are continually closing, are you left with fewer and fewer choices?
- Do fewer choices narrow your focus?
- Do you sometimes have to step back to spring forward?
- Do you still grieve for people or pets who have moved on?
- Have you filled those voids even if it is with memories that make you smile?
- If you feel sad, unhappy or depressed how challenging is it to force your Self not to be?
- Is it better to force your Self into positive emotions than to stay in the negative ones?
- Do negative emotions tie you to experiences that you are not ready to release?
- Is it challenging when you do not get what you want in the way you want in the timing you want?

Many years ago when I first started my publishing business, I was jealous of other authors who knew somebody who could help place them and their books. I felt totally alone. It was not until I finished my first book that I realized that writing my book was the easy part; selling it was the difficult part. As I was lamenting my lack of contacts, my Oversoul said, "You have me!"

This is a physical world. However, whatever is in your world is still a result of your own mind-pattern. Your Oversoul is protecting you in spite of your Self. Doors closing are protection and redirection. Too many doors open may sound like a positive, but it also means too many choices.

Just like going online to buy something simple like a pair of shoes. There are at least 60 billion different ones to choose from; there are too many choices. So yes, you can have too many doors to choose from. It is a blessing when doors close and you are forced to look at doors that you would not otherwise consider. This does not mean that you like the door at first glance. Nonetheless there is always a door.

And you always have support. You may want someone or something in the physical but you are learning to go within. You are supported in more ways than you could even imagine on the nonphysical level. You are given every opportunity to step up to the most correct and beneficial solution. What is most correct and beneficial does not always mean that you will like what is presented to you.

You are never alone; if you feel alone and affirm that you are alone then there is no way that the nonphysical support can get to you. You have a problem and the solution is trying to get to you but your mind-pattern will not allow the solution in. You know how to use your affirmations as energetic tools that dig around in your energetic field to rearrange what is not working for you and to allow what you need to come into you. Reading about it and doing it are 2 entirely different things. If you read that a coat will keep you warm in the winter but never actually put the coat on and go outside you will never quite understand the experience. Reading and doing are 2 different things.

I have often had people reject my ***Decoding Your Life*** book because it looked too simple. I could tell by looking at them that they needed the information. But, I could not tell them that because there is no way that they would hear what I had to say. They had issues, the book was in their hand, and then rejected as too simple. Solutions do not have to be complicated; you can be holding them in your hand; you can have them circling you in this moment, but you have to be willing to allow the solution in.

- Are you ready to allow a simple solution to solve your conundrum?

- Do you deserve to release the struggle?
- Has your struggle brought you to this point?
- Is it time to reap the rewards of your struggles?
- Do you hold on so tight to your issues that the solutions cannot reach you?
- Do you use your affirmations as energetic tools to rearrange your mind-pattern?
- Do you feel alone?
- Do you go to your Oversoul and God-Mind first for support?
- Has support come to you in ways that you never expected?
- Does your Oversoul works behind the scenes to set up the solutions to your problems?
- Does your Oversoul work behind the scenes to protect you from your Self?
- Do you feel abandoned sometimes by your Oversoul and God-Mind?
- If so, who/what has abandoned you in physical reality?
- Is it a blessing when doors close to force you to look at doors that you would not otherwise consider?
- Can you have too many choices?
- Is it challenging to think of doors closing as protection and redirection?

Every solution to every problem already exists in the present/Eternal Now. You can use your affirmations so that everything is now resolved to your level of understanding. For some reason, the majority of the people always interpret statements like this to mean that they will like the resolution. In this reality, few people really like the resolution because you generally do not get what you want, when you want, how you want. If life only went how you wanted and when you wanted, you probably would ultimately be miserable and unhappy without understanding why.

Sometimes just knowing what is going on is a relief. I have heard many people say that they had a physical issue but went from doctor to doctor without anyone believing them. When they finally found someone who would listen and received a diagnosis they felt a sense of relief. Once the issue is pinpointed and labeled, then you can start the resolution. Same thing if you are depressed and do not know why. This takes a lot of deep internal energetic digging to uncover what might have been suppressed/buried for years and perhaps decades. Once you know what condition underlies the depression then you can make conscious decisions about correcting this.

One of the biggest challenge is always that when your issues are resolved you always think that you are going to like the resolution and you will be happy, satisfied, at peace, feel more balanced, and so forth but this is rarely ever the case. If you are in a rough relationship that requires a divorce or simply a split from one another, the resolution may be what is needed but it might not be what you want or the way that you want. You may not like this resolution. Maybe you have a bug infestation in your home so you resort to an exterminator. Here is the solution but you may not like having to deal with pesticides. You may need a job but when you find the best one for you, transportation may be an issue to actually get there. Or you like your work but have issues with your coworkers.

- How many times in your life have you thought, I will be happy when…?
- And then "when" comes and it wasn't what you thought it was going to be?
- If your solution requires digging around in your own negative emotions, how likely are you to do this?
- Is it easier to not rummage around in past unpleasant emotions?

- Do you think "resolution" equals "happy"?
- Do you feel better when you know the cause of your issue?
- Can knowing the cause make you feel unhappy?

Sometimes when you reach your goal, it feels anticlimactic. this demonstrates the importance of the journey even more than the goal. The more challenging the journey the more interesting the story. In **Decoding Your Life** I used the example of reading a murder mystery. Page 1 someone dies. Page 2 the culprit revealed. Page 3 The End. You enjoy the story more than knowing who did it immediately.

I have a strange way of reading books. I get obsessed with knowing how the story ends so I read and read and read; it is with great difficulty that I can put the book down. So, for most of my life I read the ending first. Then it is easier to relax and read about the journey. Too much focus on the ending never allows me to enjoy the process. This is how I resolve the process.

In this reality, you rarely know the outcome of the journey. You only know that you are on a journey to somewhere. You may have a general trajectory but that can change at any moment over the course of time. When you can view a problem as an interesting journey with some kind of growth along the way, you are finally making headway about your reason for existing at all.

My 2 puppies from Russia have been a problem since Day 1. However, it has been an interesting journey and now that they have been here for about 9 months they seem to finally be really settling in and finding their place. Jasmine isn't digging to China every day; they are eating better; they seem happier with their beds; toys and treats, and they get more loving and cuddly every day toward us.

Our last big hurdle is integrating them with the cats. I trust Jade about 95% and Jasmine only 50%. In the beginning I trusted Jade about 50% and Jasmine 0%. It has taken a huge amount of work and frustration to get them this far. I never dreamed we would have the issues we have had which means that I have had to reach deep for new solutions to new problems. They have forced/challenged me to grow in too many ways that I never expected. But I definitely get a lot of satisfaction for our group accomplishments. I definitely have not reached my goal with them, and the journey has been much longer than I anticipated. I am learning and growing, trusting the process of reaching milestones in the most correct and beneficial timing.

- What journey are you on right now that is taking longer than you expected?
- Have you had accomplishments along the way that encourage you to keep going?
- Or, do you need to keep going whether you feel encouraged or not?
- Do you like the idea of "milestones" instead of "goals"?
- Can you view a problem as an interesting journey?
- Can you appreciate whatever comes your way without being upset about it?
- Do you get upset first, then calm down enough to appreciate it?
- If you only focus on the ending does this stop you from appreciating the process?
- Does the process of any journey give you a template for future journeys?
- Will life always be one journey after another or maybe several journeys simultaneously?
- Does attitude make a difference?
- Or, does "problem" always equal "bad"?
- Does a more difficult problem mean a more interesting story?
- Does "interesting" mean "good or bad"?

When you are in kindergarten, you still have problems. Your years may be few, but you can have big problems. Some things that keep you awake at night might be who is going to ask me to be on their team tomorrow; will I be able to recognize my home address when the teacher reads them off in class; will I get the paintbrush I want when it is time to go to the easel; what will I have in my lunch...For a young child, the list of problems never stops.

At every juncture of your life, you are going to have problems that keep you awake at night. Children often dream of being an adult so they can finally have total control of their lives; adults dream of being children when their problems seemed small. Children do not realize that adults do not have total control of their lives in the way that children think adults do. And adults forget that when you are a child those simple problems were not simple at all. The more problems you solve, the more problems you get. The goal is learn while you are here, so passing your problems mean you earn more.

Simple people have what you might view as simple problems, but to them they are very challenged. Their problems need to be respected and understood as important to them on the same level that your problems are important to you. You cannot compare apples and oranges; you cannot compare your problems to anyone else's. You cannot say that your toe hurts more than my hand. The problems each person faces is unique to that person, but the underlying template is the same for everyone. When you are respectful of others' problems, others are more apt to be respectful of yours.

- Do you respect the problems of others?
- Do you feel that others respect your problems?
- Do you think others can understand your problems?
- Do you sometimes feel like you are the only person on this Earth with your problems?
- Do you realize that others have similar problems?

- Does it help when you realize that you are not the only person facing your specific problems?

- Do you envy people who you think have simple problems?

- Is it important to realize that their problems are not simple for them?

- Does it give you any comfort to know that the more problems you pass the more problems you earn?

- Do you remember some of your seemingly simple childhood problems?

- As a child did you want to be an adult so you would have more control over your life?

- Is being an adult as wonderful as you thought it would be when you were a child?

It is so easy to see how to solve the problems of others, but few rarely want to listen. You see them headed for the cliff and you cannot stop them no matter how hard you try. This means you have to stand back and watch them dive right over knowing you may be the one who has to pick them up when it is all over. If they could have done better, they would have. This is why they won't listen to you. There is something in that experience that they need. They are not yet strong enough to walk the path that you see; instead they need the longer more circuitous route.

I used to judge people quite stringently for their choices that took them straight into the ditch. It took a long time for me to learn to develop compassion for their problem-solving journey because I needed to develop compassion for my own. I had to learn that I could not control their journey and make their life easier. That had to come from within them. In the same way, I needed to focus on my own journey, find my own easier path and be supported solely from within.

I had to step back and allow them to fail because it is in the getting back up that they succeeded. If I took away their fails/falls I took away their opportunity to build their own internal strength. You have to love and care enough about people to stand aside and let them go right into the ditch when that is the best place for them. No one likes to be in the ditch but getting out definitely builds strength and character.

This is what your Oversoul does for you; it allows you to fall in the ditch as much as you need until you have the strength and character to not fall in that ditch again. And each time you get out of that ditch your Oversoul is right there beside you, cheering you on. It cannot do the work for you; it can set you up for success, but you have to be the one who does the work.

In the same way, when you see people around you repeatedly falling in the ditch, you can only lend a helping hand with permission. If you are told on the Oversoul level to stand back, then that is what you must do. You must respect the learning process of everyone in your life, no matter how much you love, care and want to help that person. Ultimately, the only true help comes from within. The more that person is driven to tap into Source, the sooner that person will have his/her problem solved.

- Is it challenging to respect the learning process of others, especially when you see them heading for a ditch?
- Have you tried to warn others only to be ignored?
- Do you feel disgusted when you see them repeatedly falling into the ditch instead of succeeding?
- Is getting out of the ditch part of your success?
- If you fall back in again, does this tell you that you have more work to do?
- Is "falling" the same as "failing"?
- Is falling a status report?
- Does climbing out of the ditch build strength and character?

- Is it especially challenging to watch those you love fall?
- Is trying to steer others away from the ditch trying to control their lives?
- How many times have you tried to do this, only to be rejected?
- How many times have you tried to do this and your help was accepted?
- If your help was accepted are you still on friendly terms with this person?
- On some level, do people resent help?
- Do they want to learn on their own?
- Do you judge people when they fall into a ditch when in your opinion, they could have chosen a different route?
- How do you feel about picking up people who fall when if they would have listened, it would not have happened?
- How many times has your Oversoul picked you up?
- Is there ever a limit to how many times you pick someone up after a fall?
- Does your Oversoul limit how many times it picks you up?
- Does your Oversoul sometimes allow you to stay in the ditch to force you to rely on your inner strength to get out?
- Is this Unconditional Love?

When you do not have compassion for your own Self, it is extremely challenging to have compassion for others. It took me many years before I realized that I had no compassion for my own journey. I did what I did because I needed to do. If I failed I just kept at it until I got it and kept my Self in a continual state of forward movement. As an abused person, I was used to abuse so I was very good at Self-abusing. I had no mercy when I had a goal to reach. I would rather be dead than not reach that goal, surpass it, and then go for the next one. I always thought "If I can do it, you can do it". That part is true, but you don't have to beat your Self up to get to wherever you are going.

The more I learned to slow down, the more I learned to have compassion for my Self as well as realize that most people were not going to drive themselves as hard as I did. Their journey was different and I had to learn that was okay. In the same way, I had to learn to not be so hard on my Self, thus my famous affirmation in **Decoding Your Life** that I refer to all the time:

### *I release the need to judge and/or criticize my Self.*

That was my go-to affirmation for many, many years. I also used:

### *I release the need to judge and/or criticize others.*

because it was so easy to see the faults of others and then wonder why these people did not correct them, like I had done. As you can see, my left brain definitely knew how to solve the problem but my right brain still had more balancing and growing to get my emotions in alignment with my intellect.

You need both halves of your brain in balance to solve all aspects of your problems. Intellect can take you a long ways, as I found out. But it must eventually be balanced with emotion. First I had to stop judging and criticizing my Self which lessened my need to do this to others. Then, I filled the space that this mind-pattern had with Pale Pink for Unconditional Love and Acceptance of Self and Compassion. Only then did I truly understand what others were going through and that it is okay for each person to have his/her process.

I cannot judge God's world. I need to step back and allow God to take care of Its own rather than think that I need to carry the world on my shoulders. I have compassion for my struggles which allows me to have compassion for your struggles. And I have enough Unconditional Love for others to stand back and let them struggle even when I could shoulder their burdens. Tough love. Just like what my Oversoul and God-Mind have for me.

- Do you have compassion for your struggles?
- What does Compassion mean to you?
- What is the difference between Unconditional Love and Love?
- Why are all these emotions important if intellect can solve your problem?
- Can intellect solve problems without emotion?
- Are you challenged to know when to step forward and when to step back when it comes to helping others?
- Do you tend to judge God's world?
- Do you have go to affirmations that you can easily draw upon when your problems get you down?
- If everything comes from one Source and God-Mind allows all/solves all, why do you think bad problems exist?
- Do you have compassion for your journey and all that you have been through?
- When you observe others who are having a bad day, do you think about what that person may or may not be going through?
- When you see people who are mean or bullies do you think about what that person may or may not be going through?
- Do many people develop hard shells so that they can keep moving forward and get through whatever problems are in their lives?
- Do you think some people simply give up?
- If so, do you have Compassion for them?

Every time in my life when I felt like I could not handle one more thing, one more thing appeared. Then I wondered how I was going to do it all, but somehow I managed. I often use the example of the cup full of rocks that looks full; then you add the pea gravel and the cup looks full; then comes the sand—surely the cup is full. But oh, no, you can still add water! This is so descriptive of my life.

I have always been a busy, active person. When my cup was only full of rocks, I only thought I was busy. At each step of the way, when something more was added, I would think about how previously I thought my hands were full but I had no idea then how much busier I could be. In the same way, I have observed others whose cup only has rocks but they think their cup is full, just as I did at one time. There is nothing that I can say until they experience the pea gravel, sand and water. Now we can have a conversation.

When you lift weights, you do not start with the heaviest ones. You start light and as you get stronger you keep adding more and more weights a little at a time. This is the same with life. You start with one problem and when you manage to get that one somewhat resolved, the next problem hits. Now you have two problems, which strengthens your problem-solving skills, so you get another one or two. The more problems you solve, the more you earn.

This is why I started calling my problems challenges because problem indicates that something is wrong. Whatever happens to you is in your favor whether you realize it or not. This means there is no problem because nothing is wrong. Something may need correction but that doesn't make it wrong. Everyone is doing the best that they can do at whatever they do or else they would do something else. And simply because intellectually you know that what you are doing is incorrect that does not mean that emotionally you know it is incorrect.

Look at the life of the pedophile Jeffery Epstein. Intellectually there can be no doubt that he knew what he was doing needed Self-correction. Emotionally he wanted what he wanted and he had the money to make it happen. He had enough money to literally hang him Self. And obviously there are a ton of other people connected to him that intellectually knew what they were doing needed correction, but apparently emotionally they did what they wanted to do as well. Then somehow the emotions convinced the intellect that everything was "okay" and the loop spiraled downhill.

As I always tell you, you can break the Spiritual Law all you want but eventually your actions catch up with you and the Spiritual Law will break you. Whether he is alive or dead is inconsequential. His operation is over and he is done. His Soul-Personality did a huge service to humanity to pull out those kinds of people who prey upon the helpless and victimize those who need protection. You never know why on the Soul level people do what they do. What will happen to him next is between him and his Source.

Those females who were his victims may be well compensated for what they gave to help pull out the perversions and demonic forces of society. Each person knows coming into this reality why they are coming in and what lessons they are here to learn. All those who were complicit in Epstein's activities, including his brother, have all succumbed to temptation/Animal Mind/demonic forces rather than correct themselves and walk away. Each of these people will be faced with more choices and more temptations. That is the way it works. They will have the choice to dig deeper into what they are already doing or correct their mind-pattern with conscious effort and growth.

- How challenged do you think the various layers of Epstein players are?
- Consciously do they view being caught as bad?
- Do you think some have relief because they can correct their mind-pattern?
- Do you think those who were complicit have different lessons than those who actively participated?

- Do you think Epstein should be applauded for helping bring this evil network out of hiding?
- If it wasn't Epstein, would it have been someone else?
- Do you think the exploited females came in knowing what was going to happen to them?
- Do you think they could all be part of a greater plan to rid this Earth of perversion and demonic forces?
- Does the end ever justify the means?
- Would there have been any other way to end this network, other than from the inside?
- Does getting on the inside of your problems mean sometimes you have to get dirty in the process?
- Have you, or someone you know, ever been caught doing something bad?
- Yet, this turned out to be the very situation that saved you/ person you know?
- Do you call your problems "problems" or "challenges"?
- Does the cumulative learning from your problems make you a better problem solver?
- Have you found the more problems you solve, the more you get?
- If so, does this make you feel stronger or weaker?
- Have you felt that your life was full and you could not handle one more thing, and then one more thing showed up?
- Do you see people who only think they are busy, according to your life?
- Do you have Compassion for them, knowing what might be coming for them?
- Are there different layers of Compassion for Self and for others?

Speaking up for me was always an issue. When I was in college I had a professor who was a Marxist and I was a capitalist. He did not like me one bit and made sure I knew it. I went through the entire semester with continual vomiting and diarrhea. Every day was torture but I was determined not to quit. At the end of the semester he gave me a horrible review which absolutely floored me. I realized that I had no choice but to take action; I went to the head of the department where I burst into tears as I explained how horrible the semester was. She was very kind and asked why I had not come to speak to her earlier. Honestly, this had never even crossed my mind. I was so imprinted with not being able to voice my opinion as a child that stating my opinion or asking for help was not even on my radar. However, I did know how to suffer in silence, so suffer in silence I did.

I never really learned how to effectively speak up for my Self until I went to New York to live. As the song goes, "If you can make it in New York, you can make it anywhere." I had a lot of tough lessons there that forced me to finally speak up for my Self. Learning to speak up for my Self sooner rather than later has been a lengthy process for me. I was imprinted in early childhood to not rock the boat, because if you do most likely you are going to get hurt/punished.

This was a mind-pattern that I carried forward for decades. I could have great conversations in my head, but put me face-to-face with someone and not only did my tongue stop working but so did my brain. This is why doing the *Child Within* visualization is so important. This is not a one-time/all done type of visualization. There are so many imprintings from childhood that need to come out that the more you do it, the more you find and the more you are amazed at the buried mind-patterns that continue to affect you to this day.

- When you have a problem, do you address it immediately?
- Do you ever have problems where you absolutely are at a loss on what to do?

- If/when this happens, do you feel out of control and under the control of someone/something else?
- As a child, did you feel like other people controlled you?
- Were you allowed to have problems as well as help to resolve them?
- Were you always told what to do leaving you with minimal problem-solving skills?
- As a child was your opinion valued?
- Did you feel respected?
- Is speaking up to your Source and asking for help part of what you do?

Imagine that you are on a football field carrying the ball, with hundreds and maybe thousands of people cheering you on. Those people cheering you on want you to get that ball across the finish line, but they cannot do it for you. You consciously chose the game but you do not always consciously choose how the ball comes to you or your opponents. This is the same way in life. You consciously chose to be here but once you are in the game of life, you do not always consciously choose your adversaries or how you get what you get. You get so focused on the game that you forget and/or do not hear those who are cheering you on; you always, always have help from the other side/nonphysical.

When you are in a crowded room, you can focus on one conversation because you know how to consciously ignore the other conversations. Eventually you may even not see, hear or notice other people in the room. Your attention and hearing is 100% on the one conversation. This is just like your life. You get so focused on your problems and issues that you are not able to see, hear or notice how much help you have from the other side/nonphysical.

This can come in many forms, from loved ones who have passed on to Angelic Frequencies to Oversoul, God-Mind, Absolute, All That Is.

Regardless of how much nonphysical encouragement, you are still the only one who can do what you need to do. Yes, there will always be entrapments, adversaries, opponents not of your conscious choosing. But all of these seemingly negatives are there for you to surpass and grow stronger. A warrior grows stronger by sparring with a worthy opponent.

- Did you come to this reality for your Soul to grow stronger?

- Have you grown stronger in times of great opposition?

- Have you wished that someone would just step in, take the problem away or solve it for you?

- If problems are meant to make you stronger, why do you wish them away?

- Do you think about how much help you have in the nonphysical protecting and cheering you on?

- Do you breathe your Self into your Center, and anchor deep within Source when you feel out of sorts, as described in *Decoding Your Life*?

- When times are good do you breathe your Self into your Center, and anchor deep within Source as described in *Decoding Your Life*?

- During the day do you touch into your center to know the deep connection of Soul to Source?

- Can you visualize a parent watchfully gazing over a child, allowing the child to learn on his/her own rather than stepping in to solve the issue?

- If a child is reaching for a wooden block would a parent push the block a little closer so the child could reach it?

- Or, even wrap the child's hand around the block so he/she feels what it is like to grab it?

- Would the child know that the parent helped?

- Would the child think, "Look what I did!" because he/she is so focused that he/she does not see/feel the parent's aid?

- Could this be an analogy of what happens to you when you only think you solved the problem on your own?

- Could the nonphysical realms be pushing your solution closer and closer, or even putting your hand on the solution?

The deeper you identify as a Soul in a human body, the deeper your knowing that all is well even when it may not feel like it. The Animal Mind which runs the animal body must always survive to perpetuate the species. This is why there is such fear when life does not go according to your plan. Panic sets in from the Animal Mind. The physical world is all illusion but when your Soul is in an animal human body, it feels very, very real, which is the point.

Every obstacle is set up to tempt you to give in to such emotions as Self-pity, depression, hopelessness and despair along with physical temptations such as food, sex, money, alcohol and drugs. The more obstacles you overcome the more Soul strength you gain, so the more problems you get.

I recently watched Marvel's movie *Thor* and it reminded me of how a true warrior is always looking for a worthy opponent, not running from one. There is that sense of justice and knowing that you are good at what you do.

- Do you know that you are good at what you do?

- Do you have the proper training to deal with your worthy opponents?

- Do you want to know all the facts going in?

- If so, does this give you a sense of control?

- In any real-life situation do you ever know all the facts?

- In real-life situations are you ever always 100% in control?

- Do issues/problems arise when you thought you knew what you were getting into but then realize that you didn't have a clue?
- Do you need the confidence to know that whatever it is, "nothing can disturb the calm peace of my Soul"?
- Do you have to know how to be flexible, twisting and bending so you deflect every obstacle that comes your way?
- Is your physical body flexible?
- What does physical flexibility say about mental flexibility?
- Does problem-solving have to be a lonely ordeal?
- Can problem-solving create a deeper Source connection?
- Do you get angry at Source for your problems?
- Can you ever convince Self that all is well if you do not have Self-Worth and Self-Value?
- Are you worth Source helping you?
- Is it easy to be angry and feel abandoned by Source?

When any problem presents it Self, it is very easy to become distraught and project all kinds of negativity into the situation. I used to stay up all night worrying about the what ifs of any given situation. I worried my Self into the ground. I have learned that worrying about the what ifs is a huge waste of energy. I have so much to do I definitely do not want to be wasting energy, time or my potential sleep.

When I have an issue that I know is full of unforeseen potentials, I do my best to pass the situation up and wait for facts before I start addressing "what to do if". This way I can focus on what is at hand instead of something that may never materialize. I know that my Oversoul will tell me what to do and when to do it as the situation unfolds.

***I wait for the first thing to do to be revealed to me.***

***Then, I wait for the next thing to be revealed to me.***
***I resolve my problems step-by-step as best as I can.***

With that said, like everyone else, every now and then something comes up that especially upsets or disturbs me. Then I have trouble focusing, concentrating, and sleeping. Instead of keeping the disturbing energy up into my Oversoul, I allow it to fall down into my energy field and then of course into my body. This agitates every part of me until I can settle down long enough to know what to do. I do not worry that I won't know what to do or how to do; I just have to get centered enough to push the agitating energy back up to my Oversoul.

Some problems are long-term no matter what you do to try to resolve them sooner. This means that you have a long time to extract the learning from that specific situation. Take court cases, for example. These can be ongoing for months and sometimes years. Anytime anything goes to court, most likely you are not going to get 100% of what you want. These kinds of situations give you ample time to discover what was in your mind-pattern to put you in this situation in the first place. You also discover that you will get what is most correct and beneficial vs. what you want. You truly have to *"let go and let God"* because you have no choice.

- Have you ever been in a long-term court case?
- Did you get what you wanted?
- Did you discover what was in your mind-pattern that put you there in the first place?
- Does such a situation keep you on edge as background noise ?
- What is the mind-pattern for people who relish long-term problems?
- Can you get addicted to this kind of drama/trauma in your life?

- Do you know people who go from one long-term problem to the next?
- Are health problems long-term issues that keep people on edge?
- Or financial problems?
- With the correct knowledge, could a person with a long-term problem create a solution that is more in alignment with what the person wants vs. needs?
- Have you been in situations where you were forced to "*let go and let God*"?
- With all you know, do you still have problems that agitate, keeping you awake at night and disturbed in the day?
- Do you play the what if game?
- Do you work on resolving your problems one step at a time?
- Do you listen to your emotions, intellect or try your best to balance both?

How true it is that you never know the path that life will take you. What you do today affects what happens tomorrow. How you solve your problems today determines what is next in line for you. You will always get a worthy opponent at each step of your journey. You will also get temptations to leave your path at each step of your journey. The more years you live, the more you see how your life comes together in strange and mysterious ways.

When you have a problem the size of a pebble it is easier to reach down and remove it. But when you have a problem the size of a boulder you must be more creative and resourceful. That is why I tell you to amass your tools so that whatever is in your way you have something in your tool bag from which to begin.

Sometimes, all you need to do is breathe, sleep and eat with the problem at your pineal until you are provided with one step. You may not know exactly how that boulder is going to be moved, but you know that it will happen. Sometimes I think a problem is going to be resolved in a short period of time, only to find that it drags on. There may not be any obvious solution but you know you have to start.

If you worry about how and when the problem will resolve, you will waste a lot of energy. As with all things, the best way to solve the problem is to begin. You may wind up with an answer that you had not expected. You may be determined to stay the course of some specific path that you are on but at some juncture you are shown another unexpected path that you need to take.

I was determined to stay in my first marriage because I could not imagine doing anything else. I worked on my Self continually but never expected the pathway out would be to marry a man in New York. I never expected 3 step-children much less 2 children of my own. I never even entertained the thought that there might be someone who would be as metaphysically oriented as I was. It was all a surprise to my conscious mind when everything came together. But, I had to work on my Self to make it happen.

It was a huge challenge to leave the first marriage; I was under threat of death. I could have stayed and I always think that I probably would have died. Or, because he died within a few years maybe I would have had a lot of money, but I would have been all alone. I made a choice and as you know, our lives together have not been easy; we have been attacked with every breath we take. Yet, we have both become stronger and we continue to gain Soul Strength. My life did not turn out the way I expected, yet I did my best at every juncture to learn and grow, regardless of the obstacles.

- Has your life been easy?
- Did you make a decision to learn and grow at every juncture ?
- Does growing always mean better in the eyes of the world?

- Is your Soul growth about pleasing the world or pleasing Source?
- Have you had choices that would have left you alone with a lot of money?
- Have you made choices that gave you people/family/friends instead of money?
- When you have more left brain/right brain balance do you think you can have loving support from people and money?
- Do you sometimes stay where you are because you cannot imagine anything else?
- How often do unexpected solutions show up to your problems?
- Do you often first reject the solutions before you accept them?
- Have you thought your problem was pebble-sized only to find out it was the size of a boulder?
- Do you hold your problems at your pineal gland?
- Do you allow your Self to eat and sleep during the disturbances of your problems?
- Do you think that what you do today affects what happens tomorrow?
- Do you think you waste a lot of energy by worrying?

Life is one problem after another; often it is multiple problems happening simultaneously that you must juggle while doing your best to survive. But once you see your problems as challenges that engage every capacity of your Being, you begin the growth process instead of the shutdown process.

Elite military forces are those people who survive the greatest challenges. If I was ever in need of help, I would certainly trust them to help me. Elite military forces are comprised of only those people who pass the most rigorous physical, mental and emotional challenges.

I would like to add spiritual challenges as well because my guess is that they not only question Self during their training but most likely their Source, too. These people are pushed to their limits and beyond. That is the only way that boundaries and borders get stretched. Determine what you can do, and then push and stretch just a little more beyond your most uncomfortable place. Bit by bit all your strengths are consciously and purposefully enhanced.

This is exactly your mental/emotional and spiritual training that you are going through. Perhaps you are pushing your physical limits as well. All I know is that in any time of crisis, I want the boldest, bravest, smartest people on my side. The way you become bold, brave and smart isn't by sitting on the sidelines; it is about getting dirty in the trenches of life. This is how you grow and expand.

- Are you willing to get dirty in the trenches of life?
- Or have you been put there where you have no choice but to grovel around in the dirt for a while?
- If time of crisis has made you stronger, in retrospect are you glad that you were not just sitting on the sidelines watching?
- Have your mental/emotional/spiritual limits ever been maxed out?
- What about your physical limits?
- Are you the kind of person that you would want on your side in times of crisis?
- Would you survive or would you cave under pressure?
- Does pressure forge strength or make you collapse under its weight?
- How often have you been pushed to your limit?
- And then pushed beyond your limit?
- Is there a difference between stretching your boundaries and being stupid about what you think you can do?

- Would you want a daredevil on your side during times of crisis?

- As problems in your life mount, is there a natural tendency to shut down rather than use them to grow?

- As you grow through your challenges are you more interested in living because you survived and are stronger?

Each problem is unique to each person and is uniquely solved according to the mind-pattern to whom the problem belongs. The answer coming easily does not equal an easy answer. The more you work on your Self, the stronger you become and the more you open to the depth of Self to allow the answers to come in. This does not happen without copious inner level work.

Just like any expert, he/she may make something look easy, but the practice and skill development to get to the point where it looks easy is nothing that you could ever really share with another person. Your problem-solving, skill development methods are always going to be unique to you. Each person is a unique cell within the Mind of God; without exact duplication, no one will ever have the exact same problem that is solved in the exact same way.

Today as I was walking the dogs, I was mentally reviewing all the struggles that I have gone through these past 9 months to get the dogs to walk in tandem with me with minimal pulling; all the various dog collars and leashes; all my sore muscles and frustrations. At one point I even took them to a dog expert to ask for help with training, but just as I always tell you that you can't find anyone to solve your problems, this person did not solve mine. I spent a ton of money for a private lesson plus various dog collars that were supposed to help me. I never implemented his advice; the collars are in a drawer.

What really helped turn the beginning of the resolution in my favor is when I thought to ask the breeder what kind of collar the dogs were used to. The minute I put this specific collar on the dogs, they each knew what to do and training has gone so much easier ever since. So the answer came easily to me once I asked the correct person the correct question. I still had to work with the dogs to get them to walk with me and in tandem, but at least I was over the hump.

- Who amongst you has ever imported 9 month old Yakutian Laika dogs from this specific breeder in Russia?
- Who has gone through exactly what I have gone through?
- Who can identify how challenging working with these dogs the past 9 months has been, much less managed to resolve as many problems as I have with these dogs?

So you see, you can empathize with me all you want, but until you have done exactly what I have done in the exact same way, you do not have a clue as to how to solve my problems. And, each dog has his/her own unique personality, so even if you managed to do all the rest, the personalities of your dogs would be different than my dogs, and on and on.

However, if you have gotten a new dog or puppy and had to adjust to the dog and the dog to you, we can talk in generalities. We can each have a general idea of what the other has gone through. If you have never done even this much then our ability to co-problem solve is going to be even less.

The bottom line for each person is that in general, we can help and support each other, but we cannot solve the problem of another no matter how much we want to do this. This is the way it is supposed to be because the goal of having a problem is to be challenged into growth. The best we can do is support each other; we can troubleshoot and listen; we can learn from the trials of each other; we can acknowledge the struggle; the challenge and the growth. It is wonderful to know that we have support of each other in this reality plus we have the support of Source.

### *I AM better now than I was.*

- What more could we ask for?
- How challenging is it to know that you are the only one who can solve your own problems?
- How often do you wish that someone else would step in and do this for you?
- Have you tried to get others to solve your problems?
- If so, how often are you satisfied with the results?
- How important is it to ask the correct person the correct question to help get your problems resolved?
- How often have you asked person after person without satisfactory results?
- Can Source direct you to the right answer?

## AFFIRMATIONS—FOCUS ON COURAGE

Sometimes, it is easy to focus on your fears. You may find your Self not moving backward because you know you are not going there, yet moving forward contains both positive and negative potentials that frighten you. Time to stop focusing on fear and focus on courage. What you focus on grows!

*I acknowledge all my emotions within.*

*I choose to focus on courage.*


*I release what holds me back.*

*I strengthen what moves me forward.*


*I identify negative comfort.*

*I choose my comfort courageously.*


*I release my disappointments when doors close.*

*I courageously ask for the next door to reveal it Self.*


*I AM willing to release harsh Self-expectations.*

*I courageously accept my Self "as is".*


*I objectively observe my Self with courage.*

*I know my own internal Self-recipe.*

*I courageously remove my blinders.*
*I know my negatives that need correction.*

*I courageously remove my blinders.*
*I know my positives that need correction.*

*My Oversoul guides me in my Self-correction.*
*I courageously face the balancing of my Soul-Personality.*

*I make wise decisions.*
*I courageously face what is vs. what I want to be.*

*I stand upon the strong foundation of my past.*
*I courageously face my linear future.*

*I allow the breath of God-Mind to flow in and through me.*
*I courageously allow the best within to blossom and grow.*

*The Eternal Now is All That Is.*
*I courageously live my life one moment at a time.*

*I emulate the constant movement of the God-Mind.*
*I courageously align my Self with Source.*

*I release the illusion of stagnation.*

*I live in the flow of the God-Mind frequency.*


*I release the need to feel isolated and alone.*

*I courageously allow my Oversoul and God-Mind to support me in all that I do, think, say and feel.*


*I allow my Soul to grow.*

*I courageously take control of my Animal Mind.*


*I gather my strength from within.*

*I courageously accept total responsibility for my life.*


*I release the need to play the blame game.*

*I courageously accept the inner reflections of my outer life.*


*I move forward one step at a time.*

*I courageously slow down to ½ step at a time when necessary.*


*God-Mind sets my pace.*

*I courageously follow the most correct and beneficial pace set by my Oversoul and God-Mind.*

*I observe human law.*
*I courageously follow Spiritual Law.*

*I make my own choices.*
*I courageously accept the consequences of my choices.*

*I recognize opportunity.*
*I courageously accept opportunity.*

*I face my Self to dispel my fears.*
*I courageously accept that all fear comes from within.*

*I release my fear to be afraid of my Self.*
*I courageously face my inner darkness.*

*I release my fear to be afraid of my Self.*
*I courageously face inner magnificence.*

*I find my own power within.*
*I courageously allow my Self to feel my own Power as fueled by Source.*

*I AM always guided and directed by Source.*
*I courageously wield my Power.*

*My mind is the strongest tool I have.*

*I use my mind correctly with Courage.*


*I focus on Courage at all times.*

*I AM Courageous.*

# Money Is Only The Beginning

No matter who you are or what your income is, you most likely always think that you need more. The pursuit of money never goes out of fashion. Some people want to say that money isn't spiritual but as you know everything comes from the same Source, including money. Anytime you deny the existence of anything, whether you like it or not, you deny this part of the Existence of the Creator.

You are learning to not judge the creations, but rather to observe and understand. Most people are highly challenged by this concept because you have an innate sense of right and wrong regardless of what you do or do not do. When you do what you judge as wrong then you open up to a host of feelings within to explore or not explore. Life generally feels quite complicated when you do not understand the basic Universal Laws that govern this reality.

The goal of the global handlers is to keep you from understanding this reality. Instead of going to Source to define Self, you are entrained from before birth to trust the outer world to define you.

This means you give your power away to the global handlers, who gladly take it from you. Your parents did this, their parents did this, and the parents of their parents did this. Thus, this is genetically imprinted to look outside instead of inside as well as feel weak and small in comparison to the rest of the world.

There is already a system in place ready and waiting when you first start to awaken to the magic of money and what it can do for you. You may not quite understand what it is when you first are entrusted with your own, but you soon realize that is what you need to navigate your way through your world to get what you want.

- How can you get more money?
- How young were you when you first asked your Self this question?
- No matter how much oney you have ever had, have you always found your Self wanting more?
- Have you heard people say that money isn't spiritual?
- Have you ever thought this way about money?
- Have you come to terms that everything is spiritual and comes from one Source or, do you still struggle with this concept?
- Do most people have an innate sense of right or wrong?
- Do the global handlers have the same sense of right or wrong as the general populace?
- Do the global handlers use Universal Law?
- Does learning Universal Law help to give your life order?
- Or, does learning Universal Law complicate it more?
- Are you genetically imprinted to look outside of Self for answers?
- Do you think money could be called magic?
- What is your earliest memory of money?

A local chain retailer where I often shop is permanently closing, so since I was out on other errands, I decided to stop to see if there were any sales. Interestingly, there were no sales. I commented on this to one of the clerks and she told me that whatever was not sold was going to other stores in the chain. She said, "It's just business, you know. Nothing for their loyal customers of all these years."

Her words stuck with me, because all through my years in business, this is a common phrase that is repeated over and over again. There is always a complete separation of people and emotions. The people are the left-brain/physical reality representations and the emotions are the right-brain.

The perpetuation of this idea of people as things/chattel belonging to physical reality means that they can be controlled, bought and sold. When you think of the concept of slavery, families were separated all the time. And remember, slavery has been in existence for centuries and within all races, countries and communities. In the US, it is still talked about as a black vs. white issue, but that is another ploy to divide and conquer. Many people talk about all people being slaves to the economic system, which in many ways is true. Most people have car payments, home payments, insurance payments, credit card payments, and a host of other payments all going to the few families who run the world.

Most people dislike those who they feel have the economic hold over them. In their minds, if they had more money, no one could have that economic hold over them and they would be free. They recognize the system, they understand that it is just business because this is the imprinting. Even though they don't like it they feel powerless to change it, so they complain and continue to feed the system. The loop continues on.

- How many times have you heard, it's just business?
- Do you have to accept that, regardless of how you feel?
- How many people do you know that feel like they are a slave to the system, yet don't know how to get off the loop?
- Does the economic system view people as chattel?

- Is the system interested in the health, wealth and wellbeing of the populace?
- Is the populace used and abused, only to be thrown away as soon as their bodies are worn out?
- Do the global handlers care about the emotions of the people?
- Or, do they make a show of caring to keep the slaves in line?
- Do the global handlers imprint the populace with the idea that families must be separated?
- Do the global handlers separate their families?
- Are you aware that all civilizations have used slaves to grow and expand?
- Do you think most people view more money as freedom?
- Does the economic system create a suppression of the emotions of the populace?
- Does the economic system teach/imprint you to divide your left and right brain, rather than teach them to work together?

When I was at my university, one of my professors was a Marxist. He did not like me at all. One of our discussions was about how what he judged as inequities should be corrected. For example, he said if one person had 12 hungry children and I had no children but lots of money, I should give my money to help take care of those children.

- If I choose to not have children, should I be forced or feel obligated to feed hungry children?
- What if I was saving my money for a car or a house?
- Isn't this a conundrum that most people face?

There are lots of hungry, homeless, sick people who need the basics of life while other people are busy saving for a bigger home, fancier car, a vacation or for taking care of themselves later in life. If you lived in an indigenous village, all of your needs would be met by your community. My Grandfather told me how in his small town, everyone knew who was poor and needed help. They would take food and clothing to the families long before the government stepped in and created programs to help those who are struggling. Then, of course, the townspeople quit helping in the same way. My Grandfather did not believe in government handouts. He believed in people helping each other.

- Does moving out of the group-mind into individualized consciousness mean that you should care less about your fellow human?
- Why do we live in a world with so much inequity instead of a world where all our needs are met?
- Is money the answer?
- How does your Soul benefit by being aware of what some people have/some people do not have?
- Why do children choose to come into poor families?
- Why do monied families often have difficulty conceiving?

Both Stewart and I give you techniques to balance your brain. He uses the T-Bar and Pineal Gland Archetypes. I give you the breathing work in **Decoding Your Life** as well as encourage you to walk, which also balances the brain. You also know that you can use the color Royal Blue in the brain to balance and strengthen it. You know about mind-pattern and nutrition to help keep the brain balanced and healthy. There are basic eye exercises to help both eyes to work together instead of separately. Regardless of what you choose, you need to get the left and right brain hemispheres working together.

Remember that programming is used to split the mind, which functions through the brain; and that the physical follows the nonphysical. So, if your mind is traumatized, your brain follows. If your mind is split then your brain is split i.e., it cannot function as a whole.

Right brain holds your emotions, male/father issues, spiritual ideas and helps you tap into the Spiritual Mind. Money represents nonphysical energy—Right brain.

Left brain holds your logic, female/mother issues, physical reality and helps you tap into the Animal Mind. Its physical representation is paper/coin/credits—left brain.

This means that the global handlers splat your brain when you focus on money. In this way, they reinforce specific and societal programming. You are continually focused on the emotions of money and why you need it. First, you are imprinted with taking care of the physical body, such as food, shelter, reproduction/family so human species does not die out. Then, you are imprinted with how challenging it is to get, you don't deserve it and you should give it to others. You are traumatized as are forced to watch others starve, go homeless and see families split apart.

- Why is the topic of money so sensitive?
- Can people be traumatized by money?
- Why do people get so emotional about money?
- Does the economic system use "Kiss Me, Smack Me" Programming?
- Does the economic system teach/imprint you to divide your left and right brain, rather than teach them to work together?

Money can traumatize you and affect your eyesight as well as how your brain functions. I can remember as a child being so upset about all the hungry children in the world. It was traumatic to see people in downtown Seattle who were homeless on the street as my mother would march along holding my hand, constantly reminding me, "Don't look."

I worried about all the people in the world who were hungry, cold and without shelter. I was traumatized by the fact that I had food and shelter and others did not. When you see things that you cannot do anything about, the way you deal with this is to energetically shut down and pull your energy inside, away from your organs; the shrinking violet syndrome. Your body is present, but you are not.

During my vision therapy, I was diagnosed with blindness in my left eye. They proved it to me by having me close my right eye and with my left eye open, everything was black. In addition, when you cannot see far away, it is because you pull your energy in close, away from your eyes so the only energy available is to keep your eye alive, nothing more.

When you cannot see close up, you focus on something "out there" to avoid what is "right in front of you". Maybe your next door neighbor has something that you want, but can't have so you deal with it by emotionally shutting down. You pull your vision in, feeling trauma on some level that this is their life, not mine.

I was traumatized by children in my elementary school who did not wear hand-me-down clothes and got to buy ice cream sandwiches every day for lunch. Why them and not me? I was traumatized by the rich kids who had more and I was traumatized by the poor kids who had less.

People have a lot of trauma over what they are forced to witness whether they want to witness it or not. Even when I have to do some of the research; I have to be sure to breathe my Self into my center before I read or view what I need to know. There are things I prefer not to deal with but know that I must. I really don't want to read about the couple who kept their 13 children chained to beds for years; Islamic women who are killed because they are women; Chinese women giving up their only baby to the state for an apartment; and see a video of a man beating 2 babies. These are traumatic that force you to either shut down or open up to programming.

And if someone walked into my life and plunked down a few million dollars in front of me, after I paid off my debts, I would once

222 • Heights of Wealth

again be traumatized about what to do next. I emotionally shut down when I get a notice from my bank thanking me for my past year of doing business by giving me a two cents reward. Two cents! I don't think there is anything that I can buy for two cents except Low Self-Worth. There is a lot of trauma/drama around money.

Yes, it does affect your eyesight because you don't want to see what is here or there. When your eyes are affected your brain is affected. What you see causes you to shut down your emotions or be run over by them. When you can't think about something anymore, you close your eyes, take a nap, go to bed. You escape with eyes closed from the trauma/drama of the outer world.

- Do you want to see all the trauma/drama on the news?
- Are you forced to see trauma/drama all around you every day?
- As a child, were you traumatized by what others had and you didn't?
- Or by what you had and others didn't?
- Do you have issues with seeing either far away and/or close up?
- How do you think your money or lack of contributes/ed to how you saw/see the world?
- Sometimes, do you want your brain to simply shut down for a while?
- Do you sometimes escape through a nap or an early bedtime?
- Do you think your psychic energy pulls away from your eyes instead of pouring into them?
- Do you want better vision?
- Does better vision allow you to see more trauma?
- So is it easier to have bad eyesight and see less of the outer world?
- Do you have buried trauma in your eyes?

- What happens if you pull out buried traumatic memories out of your eyes?
- Will your eyes improve?
- Can they handle the memories?
- Does trauma/drama keep you more manipulatable and programmable?
- Do the global handlers know that at your income level, you are traumatized by seeing people that you cannot help?

How you see the world makes a big impression on the left and right hemispheres of your brain. The global handlers know this and do not want you to find your place of personal power. They want your bodies strong enough to work, but without the mental creative capacity for upward mobility. All the carefully controlled boxes that you are in give you just enough freedom to think that you are upwardly mobile. You always have people above you so you can strive to get some place; people below you so you can see how far you have come. You have the Death Program going on; this box tells you to hurry up because you are going to die soon without achieving your goals, whatever they may be.

All of these are examples of how seeing this world can traumatize you, affect your eyesight which in turn traumatizes your brain and leaves you open and receptive to more programming.

- How many people do you know who have corrective lenses or corrective vision surgery?
- Why do companies spend millions and billions of dollars on advertising each year?
- If 13 families rule the world and they own all of big business, what does it matter if you buy Coke, Pepsi, Mountain Dew or Sprite?
- Why are you always given so many choices?

- Why are you inundated with advertisements?
- Why are you shown pictures of celebrities' multimillion dollar homes all the time?
- Why do they want strong bodies but not strong minds?
- How do they make you think you have a strong mind?
- Does your opinion count in the overall scheme of things?
- Do you really have healthcare or only think you do?
- How many ways are you purposefully traumatized which splits the brain and leaves you open for more programming?
- How can you spend $100 or $200 on dinner while for many people, this is their food budget for a week?
- If everyone had the same would your life be less traumatic?
- Can you observe trauma without participating?
- Does this take away your humanness or drive you into the Spiritual Mind?
- If you do not allow what you see to traumatize you, can you more effectively utilize this world instead of feel it is against you?

## Advertising is a Show

Kiss Me, Smack Me Programming is rampant. On the same page of news, there will be an article about how good something is for you and the next article tells you how bad it is for you. The entire world is a stage.

- What if they gave a war and nobody came?
- What if they spent millions of dollars on soda advertising and no one bought it?
- If they have to spend millions of dollars to keep people buying soda, then what does this tell you about their products?

- Do they need you to drink it so you get sick and eventually wind up in the hospital where you pay them to experiment on you?
- Without the advertising would people stop purchasing soda?
- Without advertisements would you stop buying nonsensically?
- Would your appetite for things that satisfy the animal mind stop?

When you go to a supermarket, you really have very few choices. If you want soda, you go to the soda aisle, no matter what state in the US, you are going to get the same selections.

I love being in the mountains in Italy because there is no ELF, no Internet, no television, not much access to news. In the mountains, people are connected to one another, to the land, to their food, to being together, to community, to watching out for each other, to culture. Here, the billions of dollars spent on advertisements are pointless. They live, they love, they play, they work, they die.

If you are a small company trying to make your living you cannot compete with a company that spends millions on advertising. Big business wants to make you feel small, pointless, break your spirit, make sure your business is not passed down in your family for generations, make you more susceptible to selling out to a bigger business. As a small publisher, I cannot compete with big ones with advertising dollars. When I started out 40 years ago, my dream was first to be picked up by a big publisher, which I soon realized was never going to happen, which is why I decided to do it my Self.

Next, I envisioned a huge company with everyone on the Earth wanting what I had to offer. But I have never had the marketing dollars. In the beginning, before the Internet, I took out ads in metaphysical magazines and flyers; got articles out; sent out newsletters by post; solicited distributors all over the world. I used to say that I thought I had arrived when I wrote my first book and published it. I realized that was the easy part. Selling it was more challenging than the writing.

I've been through many decades of watching entrepreneurs sell out, give up and go broke. Now, entrepreneurs are people like Elon Musk. Well, I can tell you right now, unless big business is backing him in some way, he cannot be where he is, nor can anyone else. Millions and billions spent on advertising is about destroying the spirit of the people as well as splitting their brain so they can be more easily mind-controlled and manipulated. Advertising has nothing to do with money. It has everything to do with flash and bling. Point you here, point you there, keep you focused outside of Self and confused.

Confused people are easier to control. People whose spirits are broken are easier to control. People whose brains are split are easier to control. The global economic system has nothing to do with money. It focuses you on money so you don't look behind the scenes. Once you understand the show, the mystery is removed and it loses its appeal.

- Do you get caught up in the hype of the Earth is dying and has finite resources?
- Or that people are waking up and now life can get better?
- Do you read one day that some food is good for you and the next day you read that it is bad for you?
- Do you really want to wear ripped jeans if you can buy a pair of unripped jeans?
- What kind of mind-pattern says, I need to wear ripped clothing?
- Without all the hype people would people stop buying soda?
- Do you know people who are addicted to it?
- Does advertising focus you on specific food or drink purposefully knowing it will make you sick?

- Is the purpose of advertising to make you sick on all levels of your Being?
- Is one purpose of advertising to get you sick enough that you voluntarily present your Self as a gift to the medical system to be experimented upon?
- Does advertising break the spirits of small business owners?
- Is entrepreneurship dying out in the US and other developed countries?
- Must you be more creative to survive?
- Do you think about why books are on the *New York Times Bestseller List*?
- Does this list influence which books you buy?
- Why do you think companies that are already globally known continue to advertise?
- Would people stop frequenting their establishments?
- Would fast food chains die?
- What if Monsanto quit advertising?
- Would people stop thinking about all the chemicals in their food?

Advertisements really are about showing you how powerless you are; what is out there; what you can or cannot have. If you can't afford a luxury vacation, simply drink a soda and it like being on a vacation with all kinds of wonderful things happening to you. If you want the real luxury vacation, you can put it on a credit card because you cannot afford it without help from the outside world. And, you get to feel superior over those who stay home.

When you feel powerless, you can gain feelings of superiority over those people who aren't doing the correct thing for the Earth and the environment. You need to be recycling, eating earthworms, eating vegan which is much more superior to eating vegetarianism, driving a small car, and doing whatever you envision to not leaving a footprint on Mother Earth.

- Aren't you supposed to walk on Mother Earth?
- So if you don't leave a "footprint" does that mean that you don't exist?
- Do you see where this narrative is going?

Money spent on advertising isn't about selling you a product, it is about influencing your behavior. The mind of each individual is extremely strong for the global handlers to have to spend so much money to keep the population under control. Maybe there are subliminals in the commercials that say, every time you see soda or whatever, you must buy it, you must drink it, you must share it, give it, and buy more, you must never be without it, it is better for you than water.

The money you use to buy their products feeds their lifestyles. They patronize their own establishments and family-owned companies. The money always stays with them as well as your mind.

- Do people want money or are they looking for control over their own minds?
- Instead of going for Self-control, do people succumb to mind-control and the glorified objects and lifestyles that are thrown around for them to want but never have?
- Does having money give you Self-freedom or does money suck you into the economic system?
- Can you have big money without being part of the economic game?
- Does Self-freedom come from money?
- Are advertisements, money and objects technologically enhanced to make you want them more?

- Why do global handlers spend so much money/energy to keep your mind under control?
- Do you know how extremely powerful your mind is when it is under your control?

As long as your mind is under their control, your physical body cannot revolt against them. There are more of us than there are of them. This is why all the insane money is spent on advertising. The goal is not to get you to buy objects; the goal is to for them to buy your mind.

When most people think about money, they think about paper and coin currency. Now you are often forced to use credit and debit cards. Many places will not take paper and coin currency. The cashless society is upon us. My paternal grandfather was a coin collector. He had a lot of interesting money, including $500 and $1000 bills, now unheard of in the US economy.

Gradually the US economy eliminated these denominations. You used to feel really rich if you had a $100 bill. But, you don't want to carry $100 bills because they might be counterfeit. Most store clerks have to hold them up to the light to ensure that they are real; many stores don't have change when you try to use them. Some businesses even say that they won't take any bills larger than a $20.

Younger people are well entrained in using a card vs. cash. They will never miss cash and their children's children will never know what cash was unless they read about it in a history book. Now, you feel rich by holding a piece of plastic in your hand.

- What kind of frequency is plastic?
- What kind of frequencies are gold, silver, nickel and copper?

I recently saw the movie *Jumanji* and in the film, someone had a small piece of real wood that was valuable because it was real wood.

- What kind of frequency does "real wood" hold as opposed to "imitation wood"?

Some time ago, I told you about this story:

Don Miller, a 90 year old man in Indiana who had his home raided by the FBI and thousands of artifacts confiscated.

Miller, 91, died Sunday, nearly a year after federal agents surrounded his rural Rush County home and began removing thousands of exotic artifacts as television helicopters hovered overhead. Officials at the time cited a desire to catalog the pieces and return them to their countries of origin.

And even after his death, the progress of the federal investigation remains shrouded in mystery. FBI Special Agent Drew Northern declined to comment about the case Tuesday night. Officials from the Indiana University-Purdue University Indianapolis anthropology department, which is assisting the FBI in identifying and preserving the artifacts, also would not comment.

https://www.usatoday.com/story/news/nation/2015/03/26/antiques-collector-dies-fbi-seized-artifacts/70475324/

- Why do you think this happened?
- What was the government looking for?
- Do you think it was a question of money or frequency?
- If this can happen to this man, could it happen to anyone?
- Do you have collectibles in your home that might carry valuable frequency?
- Can you buy frequency?
- Why does art sell for millions of dollars, but is one of the first things to go in public school when there are budget cuts?

- Does the government have the right to raid your home and take your artifacts after you spent decades collecting them?
- Why do the global handlers want you carrying plastic instead of gold, silver, nickel and copper?
- What could you own at one time that you cannot own now?

There is an old saying, "Keep your eye on the prize." Most people think that money is the prize, so this is where you focus. Or, they think what money can buy is the prize, so that is where they focus. You would be surprised at how many people say they wish they had the money for our services, products, classes, events and/or trips. Or, after an event, they say, "I wish I would have been there." These people focus on the money to get to the event, or the event it Self. Lacking money to attend an event means you lack Self-Worth/Self-Value/Self-confidence. These are the areas within Self to focus on.

Expansions.com membership is less than $1 per day. If you don't think Stewart and I are worth that, then you don't think you are worth that. If you cannot manifest even $1 per day, then you are not ready to be a member. You still want to learn our information, you can buy a book. If you can't afford a book, go to your local library and they will order one in. I have people writing to us often about books so I tell them to contact our website customer support to ask about slightly damaged books which we sell for much less. Believe it or not, almost zero people follow through.

Some people are upset that we charge so much for our services. Their excuse is that they cannot afford them. If you can't afford them, then you aren't going to get enough out of them to justify your money and your time/our time. In these circumstances, the prize is what I just told you: Self-Worth/Self-Value/Self-Confidence.

- Do you care more about what the outside world says about you than how you feel about Self inside?

- Do others dictate what you do and do not do?
- If you already have money but don't spend it on what you really, really want, what does this say about your mind-pattern?
- Is money finite?
- Is your ability for Self-Value/Self-Worth/Self-Confidence finite?
- What is your prize that you are currently focused on?
- Is it money you need or mind-pattern to bring it to fruition?
- If you want a new home do you want money or a new home?
- Is the new home a statement of "I AM elevating my Soul"?
- What is the prize, money, a new home, or elevation of the Soul?
- If you focus only on money, will that get you what you need?
- If you focus on getting a new home, will that get you what you need?
- If you focus on elevation of the Soul how can a new home not come to you?

Mind-pattern, mind-pattern, mind-pattern. As you elevate your mind-pattern, the outer world must reflect this back to you. In addition, the elevation of your mind-pattern means others in your household have the opportunity to do the same. The mind-patterns of other family members now reflect what is going on within you.

I have seen people buy really beautiful homes but in a short period of time, practically destroy them. What you need to realize is they found the money to get what they want, but the mind-pattern was not elevated enough to maintain the home. So, they brought the house down to their level instead of going up to the level of the home. Which means you must learn and understand frequency. Money is energy/currency/frequency.

Life is a process. I continually tell you that you think you are going steps 1, 2, 3, 4…, but instead you are going steps 5, 16, 23, 38….you must slow down, go back and fill in the blanks. Be careful what you ask for, you might get it. You might finally get your new home, but then the pipes burst, roof leaks, furnace quits, windows leak, chimney backs up. Doing your inner level work means your mind-pattern does not attract such issues. You have to do your inner level work to reap the rewards. It is tough; you are challenged, you must determine the frequency.

The issue with most people is they focus on money without recognizing the ramifications of getting what they want with the money. They see a shiny object in a window, it catches their attention and so they want it. That is as far as the focus goes for most people.

- Have you ever gotten what you asked for, and then wished you never got it?
- Does life sometimes seem slow for you compared to what you see others doing/having/getting?
- Does your mind-pattern work influence what comes to you?
- Are you learning patience, even if it is after-the-fact?
- Have you gotten what you asked for, but couldn't maintain it?
- Or, it broke, needed repairs, didn't work correctly from the start, and so forth?
- When your mind-pattern is in a specific place, how can its reflections not come to you?
- How can your mind-pattern not attract failure, disappointment, abandonment, lack without mind-pattern correction?
- If your negative mind-patterns already negative, how can you create a strong positive mind-pattern?

- What do you want in your life right now that you are not getting?
- Do you know why it isn't coming to you?
- If it involves money, is it money or what the money represents?
- If it does not involve money, then what is the frequency behind not getting what you want?
- Can time have a different connotation for you than for others?
- Is time limited/finite?

## Mind-Patterns Buy Time

There are always going to be many forks in the road where you have to make choices. When you make the choice to slow down and fill in the missing pieces, time slows down for you. People often say money doesn't buy time or you can buy anything but time. The wealthy buy time by employing others, but they also buy a different set of challenges. Your mind-pattern buys you time. When you pay a little more money than you can afford, you stretch Soul-elevation, Self-Worth, Self-Value, Self-confidence.

My father will be 92 in March, and he is happy, healthy, and drives all over the countryside. The work that he does on his mind-pattern gives him more time. Because I work with my mind-pattern and I still need my dad to help me, this extends my time with him.

I used to ask my mother to move to St. Joseph. There is a wonderful retirement home on the lake, lots of activities right downtown. Then, she would have been close to me, Stewart, and her grandchildren. She made the choice not to move here. I often think that if she had made the choice, she would have suffered fewer body ailments and illness, extending her lifespan as well as increasing her quality of life.

I know one man who could not leave his mother. He wanted to, but she made him feel guilty if he ever tried to establish his own life. He resented this, but he did not want to hurt her, so he left the only way he knew how by unexpectedly passing away after an extremely short illness. I know so many people who made choices that created more or less time for themselves. Time cannot be bought with money, but can it be bought with mind-pattern.

- Do your choices determine the time you have?
- Do you know people whose mind-patterns have lengthened or shortened their life span?
- What about time to develop awareness?
- Does mind-pattern give you what money cannot?
- Does your mind-pattern give you online shopping so you do not have to take time to physically go to stores?
- Does your mind-pattern give you extra time when you cross the ocean by plane rather than ocean liner?
- Can mind-pattern instantly teleport you?
- Does limited mind-pattern say you need funds to travel by car, bus, subway, train, plane?
- Is time flexible based upon your mind-pattern?
- Can money buy you flexible time?
- Can money buy you choice?
- Or is it your mind-pattern that brings the choices to you?

Your choices that you make can give you more or less time. You have much more control over your life than you realize. This is why it takes billions in advertising dollars to control your mind. If you were so easy to control, there would be no need for the elaborate show that the global handlers regularly use for control.

## Protecting Your Money

Fear is huge. So, people are always looking for ways to protect their money and investments. People think investing in precious metals will protect them. What most people don't realize that when times are tough, I'm not going to want your gold coins, I am going to want food and water. If you have gold, then you have to prove it is gold before you can sell it. This is the same for all precious metals and gemstones.

Did you know:

...from 1933 to 1974 it was illegal for U.S. citizens to own gold in the form of gold bullion, without a special license. On January 1, 1975, these restrictions were lifted and gold can now be freely held in the U.S. without any licensing or restrictions of any kind.

https://en.wikipedia.org/wiki/Executive_Order_6102

Beginning in 2016, in Greece citizens have to report their gold holdings to the government.

https://www.marketsandmoney.com.au/greece-gives-wealth-confiscation-a-whole-new-meaning-cw/2015/12/02/

The government can take your possessions, home, bank accounts any time for just about any reason. This is why it is important for you to trust Source to take care of you instead of worrying about your Earth-based valuables. With the correct mind-pattern, valuables cannot not come to you.

- Would a stockpile of gold make you feel wealthy?
- Would you want to spend it or hoard it?
- Is hoarding an Animal Mind or Spiritual Mind action?
- Do animals hoard?
- Do animals depend on the Earth for survival?
- Does the Spirit need sustenance from the Earth to survive?
- In a crisis, do you think people would accept your gold?

- In a crisis, would the laws and rules of society stay intact or fall apart?
- Are most people willing to give up what they have if they think it is for the betterment of the whole?
- If the government can create this scenario, would people willingly give up their money and investments including homes and property?
- Did you know the government can even take your pets?

After Pearl Harbor, the US military asked pet owners to donate their pet dogs to the war effort. The name of this program was Dogs for Defense. The dogs were trained and used for guard and patrol duties. To encourage the donation, they also advertised a program where the dogs would be deprogrammed after the war.

https://en.wikipedia.org/wiki/Dogs_For_Defense

The Government Asked for Pets for Defense in the 1940s. What if the U.S. government wanted your dog to enlist in the military?

That's exactly the request that went out in 1942 shortly after Pearl Harbor. The direct attack on a United States naval base brought to light the reality of what the country faced. The military realized they had missed out by not establishing a canine unit to assist the armed forces, which were going to be stretched very thin.

The worth of dogs in the military had been proven in World War I when European forces used dogs for sentry, for message-carrying, and for clearing the foxholes of rats before the men took up residence in the trenches.

When help was needed, the country turned to its citizens and requested they donate their pets to help the cause. People responded by sending their dogs, some 40,000 of them over a two-year period. Ten thousand of these animals were selected for full training.

https://www.huffpost.com/entry/dogs-world-war-2_b_916760?guccounter=1

Five thousand years later, the value of the Elkhound is not lost on the Norwegian Government: It gave the Norwegian Defense Minister the power to commandeer all privately owned Elkhounds in times of war.

https://nationalpurebreddogday.com/war-dog-of-the-vikings/

When you really think about your freedom to do what you want, you find that there are laws behind laws that can be called on by the governments at any time to take your physical assets.

- Would you give your pet to the government in time of war?
- Would you feel better knowing that if your pet survived, it would be "deprogrammed" before being returned to you?
- Would you get a specific breed of pet knowing that it would have to be turned over to the government in time of war?
- Do you ever stop to think that whatever you have, it could be taken away at any time?
- Do you have insurance?
- Does insurance always pay?
- Does insurance feed the mind-pattern that something will happen?
- Is insurance a tangible/real asset or another pretend way to generate money for the global handlers?

Before health insurance was required, I had a friend who decided to purchase health insurance after many years of doing without it. Within a couple of months, he was hospitalized. He said he asked him Self this question, "Did I get health insurance because I knew something was coming or did something come up because I got the health insurance?"

This is one of those questions that always stays with me. I have home insurance, but when I had an issue with my steps, there was a clause against rain damage. When my backyard was practically destroyed a couple of years ago, the estimate was under my deductible. Many years ago when California went through a lot of mudslides, so many homes were destroyed that the insurance companies went broke and the homeowners lost it all. Insurance really is about giving you assurance that you are going to be okay.

The value of a stock or the currency of your country is all artificially determined. This means that your net worth can change at any given moment or even be completely taken away from you. If the government doesn't get it, thieves could be out after your assets. Read this story about a now very wealthy man with a new set of challenges.

### Man Goes Into Hiding Out Of Fear For His Life After Finding A Massive Emerald

Unfortunately for one Brazilian man, his good fortune resulted in a lot of bad luck. He hired a team to help him mine for precious stones, hoping that he would find something of enough value that would take care of his expenses for the next couple of months. What he unearthed instead, however, had him in fear for his very life.

A giant, emerald-studded rock—worth a stunning $304 million—was recently discovered in Brazil by a 50-year-old man who was looking for nothing more than to cover his expenses for a few months. Unfortunately, his incredible find didn't lead to a life of luxury at all. In fact, the man was forced to go into hiding after news of his discovery broke—and he feared he could be the target of kidnapping, extortion, and even armed robbery.

Of course, robbery might be difficult for any thief; the massive emerald weighed 794 pounds and stood at four feet tall! The man claimed it would take a forklift to even transport the rock. Still, in a country where criminals are known to use explosives and automatic weapons, the threat against this stone's owner was very much real. The stones, which were mined about a month ago, were found 656 feet deep inside the bowels of the Carnaiba Mine, a gem-rich area in Bahia in the northeastern corner of Brazil. The owner wouldn't say exactly where in the mine they were discovered; he feared that doing so would help criminals more easily track him down.

https://www.twoeggz.com/int/5355750.html

I've even heard people who donate to the blood banks say they do this in case they ever need it.

- Does donating mean you are setting the scene to make a withdrawal?
- Does giving to the needy because you think about how you would feel if you were in that position set up the mind-pattern for you to be needy in some area of your life?
- Does stockpiling food in case of an emergency create the mind-pattern for the emergency to happen?
- Is hoarding a left-brain activity?
- Is spending a right-brain activity?
- Do you fear for your assets?
- Are you attached to your assets?
- Do you love your assets?

Many people feel comfortable because of a job with a well-established company, only to find the company merges with another one and their job goes out the window. I've seen people close to retirement who are laid off as well as large companies who take away benefits and stock options.

People are imprinted to put their faith in material objects. Accumulate something you can see. At one time, that was a property of some kind that you could hold in your hands.

I know people who have lived like paupers but had huge net worth on paper. They love to hold the paper that says they have wealth. Holding that paper is their enjoyment. In a time of crisis, that paper is going to be meaningless. Food, water, and toilet paper will mean much more to you than a piece of paper that says you have $1 million dollars in the bank that you can't even get to because the computers are shut down.

In Suriname, the grandson of a former slave told us the story told to him by his grandmother. One day, the Dutch slave owners hid their slaves in the jungle because the Dutch tax collectors had arrived from Holland. They were there to count the slaves so they could tax the plantation owners on their property. Well, once hidden safely in the jungle and without their Dutch overseers, the slaves took off into the jungles of South America, knowing absolutely nothing about how they were going to find food and shelter or survive.

The grandmother says that during their flight they were given seeds by an angel and told to plant the seeds at night and in the morning they would have food. And this is how they made their way into the jungle until eventually, they found the Amerindians who took in the slaves. In times of crisis, people often turn to prayer and look to a higher power. When the physical world folds, then people turn to the nonphysical.

- Why not choose prayer first?
- Why do people wait until times of crisis to turn to a higher power?
- If you do not fight, does your fear go away?
- Does fear go away when it has nothing to hold onto?

- If you never fear going without food, will you always find food?
- If you never fear going without water, will water always be available?
- If you don't fear the death of the physical body does that change your attitude toward life?
- Do your choices determine how you are taken care of?
- If you are greedy and hoard, are you directing Source to stay away because you have everything covered?
- Are you so busy directing how your bills get paid that you forget to thank Source for all?
- Do you let Source direct the show?

The idea of ownership is not something that indigenous peoples ascribed to. There were territories that people stayed within, but these territories had to do with Earth frequencies that matched the frequencies of the varying tribes. Anything that was made of precious metals and stones belonged to all the people, with inherent frequencies that the people respected.

In addition, the indigenous people used the astral to help protect what belonged to the people. The astral forces were the curses and are the reasons why ancestral objects and grounds should not be disturbed. Ownership is now just the opposite. Instead of making sure that everyone has what he/she needs, it is only about the needs of the individual.

- Do you think indigenous peoples took into account what each unique individual needed?
- Would life be boring if everyone had the same?
- What do you think of Universal Income where people get a basic income to spend how he/she wants?

- Who would determine what basic food, shelter, clothing means?
- Is there room for individuality in societies and cultures that are more community-based, such as Amish, Hutterites, Hassidic Jews, Muslims?
- Once basic body/Animal Mind needs are satisfied, does one seek to satisfy the Soul?

I decided to see what $65,000,000 and $200,000,000 homes look like, so I found a youtube channel with these types of properties and took a video tour. When you look at these mansions you can tell how everything is staged. Everything has a place and a reason. Natural materials are used for construction as well as displayed throughout the homes. The grounds are impeccably manicured. You can feel the frequency and the flow of energy.

I thought about how people who have this much money would laugh at my paltry financial debt. This made my debt feel small from their perspective. These kinds of people would probably find my entire financial picture laughable.

Then I imagined them out in the real world. They probably view the majority of humans like animals. Except their animals probably live better than most humans. Not too long ago I clicked on a link that took me to a description of the Queen's Balmoral Palace. I was surprised that this one palace is on 50,000 acres and has several guest cottages that you can rent. To maintain these estates would be a huge financial undertaking.

- What kinds of mind-patterns would a person like this have?
- Do you think he/she would find your own debt paltry and your living circumstances laughable?
- Would they worry and fear about losing what they have?
- Or would they never even think such thoughts?

- If something happened and their estates were given to people of lesser means, what would happen to the estates?
- Would they maintain their grandeur or would they fall into ruins?
- Do you think with the correct mind-pattern that everyone could live like this?
- Or, are resources on this planet limited and this type of lifestyle is only for a few?
- Do these estates beautify and uplift the planet or are they wasteful?
- How does how the poor live affect the planet?
- Does it take money to beautify and uplift?
- What if these people with these estates are charged on the Soul level of maintaining beauty for those who cannot...yet?
- Is it possible the super wealthy are Guardians of Beauty?
- Did these people come in with a mind-pattern that exudes beauty, elevation, and upliftment?
- Is beauty frequency?
- Are the various stages of frequency coming into alignment beautiful?
- Is beauty subjective?
- To create a mind-pattern that attracts money, is beauty a mind-pattern that you should/could cultivate?

I had a friend who loves to organize who said would organize my pantry and drawers for me. If it was me, I would have had my pantry done in an hour or two but she took 2 days! But, when she was done, my pantry was a work of art. It felt like a musical instrument was playing when I opened the pantry door. I never thought that an organized pantry could be so beautiful. I don't think she consciously realized it, but she knows how to organize by frequency. Everything has a frequency/sound and when she aligned all the frequencies/sounds, I was transported by what I saw and heard. This took absolutely no money, but definitely uplifted and elevated my entire home.

When you walk into a clothing store, some stores are beautiful and some are not. If you walk into a store designed for lower income/lower Self-Worth people, the presentation is not the same as when you walk into a store in Beverly Hills, that is if they will even buzz you in.

- Is your home beautiful?
- Is the frequency of your home in alignment?
- Do you influence your environment or does your environment influence you?
- Is your environment frequency?
- Do you need money to align the frequency of your environment?
- If you cannot align the frequency of your current environment, why would you want more than you cannot align?
- Have you seen a portrait photograph that captures the beauty of the old, young, rich, poor, healthy, sick?
- Do these people see their own inner beauty?
- Do the subjects of these photos always have money to make themselves beautiful?
- Do you want to see a face full of make-up to make it beautiful?
- Or, do you want to see the face under the mask?
- Will the increasing use of cosmetics by men make them more beautiful?
- Do you see the beauty within your Self?
- Is your inner beauty reflected back in your environment?

- If you were destitute poor would you beautify your environment?
- Do you ever think, I would be more beautiful/handsome if I had more money?
- Can you choose whether to allow your environment to take you down or to boost your mind-pattern?
- If you find a $600 piece of clothing on sale for $150, do you need $600 or just the piece of clothing?
- If $150 stretches your finances, does spending that much on an item of clothing declare your Self-Worth?

All frequency when it comes out of God-Mind is neutral. This is why it is imperative that you learn how to objectively observe so you know what is vs. how you perceive/judge something. Whether you want a new home or new clothing, you have to ask your Self why you want it. Most people decide what they want and then try to figure out how to get the money.

If you want a new car, this is because you want a new path in life. If you want to travel, this is because you need to go to places within your own mind. If you want gold, this is because you are looking for God-Mind wisdom. So, instead of starting with money start with the mind-pattern that creates what you are looking for.

This is where most people lose patience. Most people want instant gratification because the Animal Mind needs instant gratification to survive. The Animal Mind needs food, shelter, sex to continue the species. If it doesn't happen, the species dies. When your Animal Mind is in control and you don't get what you want, then you feel like a failure.

Spiritual Mind knows that it is ageless. When the Spiritual Mind is in alignment with what is most correct and beneficial, whatever is most correct and beneficial comes to you. Sometimes, what is most correct and beneficial isn't fun and puts you through a school that no money can buy. If money was the most correct and beneficial thing for you to have, nothing could keep it away from you. If you want money so you can run away from your issues, what is most correct and beneficial is for you to not have it.

- Can material wealth keep you in an Earth-bound loop?
- Can you have material wealth without it controlling you?
- Does objective observation mean that you stop judging what you see/experience?
- How challenging is it to objectively observe without judgment?
- Do the global handlers set you up to judge the outer world?
- What happens to your skills of discernment when you judge?
- When you think of what you would do with money, do you know the mind-pattern behind what you want?
- Do you know what mind-pattern to cultivate to attract what you want?

Many years ago, I got a call from our local supermarket. When I saw their name come up on my caller ID, my first thought was wondering what I did wrong. But, it turns out, they were giving away a cruise a day in January, and I had won a cruise!

I wasn't looking to win anything; I didn't even know there was a contest, but obviously, my mind-pattern prepared me to travel. A ship represents your Oversoul; the ocean; the ocean of life/your emotions of life. It was a really fabulous trip and was the first of many cruises that Stewart and I eventually took. In fact, I sometimes even have dreams of being on a huge white ship. My mind-pattern outpictured this for me. I still had to get the money to get to the ship and pay for incidentals, but I did not need actual cash-in-hand to go on the cruise. My point is you do not always need cash to get what you want.

This same supermarket has begun sending personalized coupons and each coupon is good only on certain days. This means you have to hold onto their folder of coupons and remember to look at them all the time to see which ones you can use. While cleaning off the top of my desk, I came across some expired coupons of theirs. Each one was good for $5.00 each week. I guess I forgot about them, but I still held onto them. There were also some that were not expired good for 25 cents to one dollar off specific items. My dilemma is if I toss the coupons I feel like I am throwing away money. If I hold the coupons this indicates that I don't have 25 cents or one dollar so I better keep these. I have always been respectful of money and its representation.

Tossing coupons I actually can use is like tossing money carelessly out the door. Holding onto the coupons means I can't spend money now, I have to wait until I need that specific item which has to be during this specific week, which to me is Self-limiting. Using the coupons makes me feel worthless because this means that I need to save 25 cents which in turn does not add to a mind-pattern of abundance. Whoever invented the idea of coupons knew what he/she was doing. I've come a long way from being a dedicated coupon clipper yet there are increasingly more ways to entrap my mind.

- Have you ever won anything of significance?
- Do you know what it represents and why your mind-pattern drew your winnings to you?
- What have you received that did not require you to pay with cash-in-hand?
- Are you able to accept what is given to you, regardless of how it comes to you?
- Do you always need cash to get what you need?
- Do you have coupon dilemmas?
- Are you respectful of money?

## Hoarding

It is very easy to focus on what you need/don't have/still want, but when you focus on what has come to you and is coming to you, this opens the frequency for more to pour in. For example, I purchased gift cards over the holidays which in turn gave me a gift card for my own use. A small bonus but I'll take it with gratitude.

Once I ordered some meat online and the incorrect order was sent to me. I received a larger order of other types of meat. When I phoned the company to let them know, they told me to keep the shipment plus they sent my original order. When we go to New York for Stewart's nephew's wedding in a couple of months, his sister offered to let us stay in her home and use her car as well as provide meals for us, so we won't need a hotel, rental car and restaurants. Both my sons received scholarships to their university which greatly reduced our cash outlay while giving my sons an education.

I have a friend who told me she cleaned out her closet and had some nice clothes she thought would fit me. I thought how nice until she showed up with price tags on them. I wanted to judge how they came to me, but instead, I bought a few things. She was happy and I did get a good bargain on some clothes that looked brand new. Even a credit card says that you can have something now and you know that the funds are manifested to pay it off.

- Can you name times when something unexpected has come to you?
- Or you manifested something without a direct cash outlay?
- Or received credit to allow you to move forward?
- And was challenging for you to accept in any way?
- Or did you feel resentful or guilty about accepting it?
- Does focusing on what you don't have keep you closed to receiving/accepting what might be waiting for you right now, at this moment?

- If you get what you want, do you stop working on strengthening your mind-pattern?

This evening when I was cleaning up after dinner, I was thinking about how I was raised to save/hoard everything. We wiped off the aluminum foil for everything, all plastic bags were saved, even wrapping paper and bows were carefully cleaned up for re-use. Growing up, I never thought anything about it as this was a part of life.

When I was on my own, I decided that I would no longer clean off the aluminum foil for re-use, only because I didn't like doing it. I still did everything else, though. It was easy to accumulate boxes, bows, jars, paper bags, plastic bags, old clothes in case I wanted to use the cloth for something else, and so forth.

At some point, I decided I was limiting my mind-pattern and gradually the hoarding is stopping. Notice I did not say stop, because lately I have been eying my cabinets again thinking that it is time for another major clear out.

What I find most interesting is that when I go to the mountains to see my family in Italy, they also hoard out of necessity. They pick herbs and flowers for their medicinal liquors when they are in season. On our hikes, my cousin points out the leaves that they use to store their homemade cheeses and another variety of leaves used to store butter. She talks about the cave where items are stored to keep them cool. And the tree from which you can use the pitch as a band-aid.

In the fall, they gather chestnuts and pick mushrooms, as well as harvest grapes to make wine. They also prepare their winter wood for heating their homes. They even bring water from their mountain home to their home on the lower part of the mountain. The list goes on and on. Hoarding and storing is a way of life. This is working with nature and protecting the Animal Mind. I want my cousin to write a book about all she knows—but she cannot imagine that people would be interested in what to her are mundane and ordinary everyday/seasonal occurrences. I do not see her operating from fear or angst. She is doing what must be done in the way she knows how to do it.

I consider my own hoarding and see that this is a result of my natural and inherent genetics gone awry. Since I don't have herbs and chestnuts and mushrooms to gather, I gather substitutes, boxes, glass jars, wrapping paper, plastic bags and other items that eventually prove useless and must be tossed. I save them because I might need them someday, but often someday doesn't come. Unlike my cousin, who uses what she gathers and trusts that each year, Nature replenishes.

I also gather rocks and stones. I have done this my entire life. I love them. My Waldensian grandfather built everything on his property, most of it from stone.

And so, I don't know how to build with stone like my family, so I do the next best thing. I collect stones. I love going to the Waldensian country and looking at their magnificent stonework, homes, barns, animal hutches, patios, picnic tables/benches, sinks, floor tiles and even roof tiles, all hand-hewn from stone. When I am in the mountains, I learn so much about why I do what I do and why I love what I love. My hoarding comes from fear that I won't have enough or what I want when I need it. I recognize another layer that is genetically inherent in me.

- Does hoarding come from genetics gone awry because you are not doing what your ancestors did?
- Do you feel wasteful when you clear and clean out whatever you choose to hoard?
- Does recycling help your feelings of guilt?
- Does recycling perpetuate the myth that resources are limited?
- Do you feel better when your cabinets are empty, full, or stuffed full?
- Did your ancestors depend on Nature to provide?

- Do you think ancestors had more trust in the process?
- Or, do you think they worried about years of scarcity?
- Is scarcity a human/Animal Mind concept?
- Or, only human?
- Do animals living in the wild trust in Nature to provide?
- Is trust instinctual?
- Do we have genetic/inherent trust gone awry?
- How strong is your mind-pattern of trust?
- Do you trust your Source to provide, regardless of how bleak the moment appears?

When I farmed, there was nothing I loved better than preparing food for the winter. I canned and froze all kinds of fruits and vegetables. I read books and taught my Self. No one told me to do it or showed me how. It was already within me, and I did it. The entire process fed my Soul. In addition, my Animal Mind was happy because it knew it had physical food until the next harvest season.

## Manifesting

You manifest with each thought you think, each word you speak, every action you make, even if you manifest a mess. You are still manifesting. The issue for everyone is you don't know how you manifested what you have. With Hyperspace/Oversoul tools you are determining what you have already manifested and then what you want to do about it.

- Do you want to keep it?
- Discard it?
- Modify?
- Start over?
- Go back?

- Are you becoming more conscious of your manifestations?
- Do you need more money so you can manifest more messes?
- Do you need to clean up what you have, so you do not bring your messes forward?
- Does having less money focus you on the specific messes that need to be cleaned up?
- Does a bigger house mean more closets and cabinets to stuff full?
- Does a smaller home focus you on not stuffing?
- Is a bigger home more opportunity to make bigger messes?
- Does a smaller home force you to be more orderly?
- Does having more money make you more responsible?
- Or, do you need to be more responsible first so you can handle more money?

Flexibility is a fabulous mind-pattern to attract what you need. Sometimes, you decide what you need and focus on that specific need until you make it happen. You must always be mindful that what you think you need is not the most correct and beneficial. In fact, there might be something even better waiting, but if you focus "here" you do not see what is "over there".

The more you dig, the more you realize how many mind-patterns need to come into balance before you bring on the money. Money is only the outer representation that gives you focus so you know where you need to grow. When the necessary mind-patterns are in place, the money comes to you or the object of your desires comes to you.

You focus on money because you focus on lack. You are taught that lack means you need more money. Then you are told money can't buy everything like health, time, happiness, peace so you always look for money to resolve your issues instead of the mind-pattern that brings to you what you need.

When we were on Nevis, I fell down the steps and badly sprained my ankle. I know exactly my mind-pattern that caused it. But guess what, I was at a health and healing clinic. I was taken care of and got exactly what I needed. No one asked for any money. They were generous with their time, supplements, heating pads, oils, kindness, compassion, care, you name it, I had it. And, I did my own mental work and used what they had to offer as a boost to my own mind-pattern. Three days later, I was well enough to walk through the airport on my way home instead of deal with the complications of a wheelchair.

It is too easy to focus on the mind-pattern of lack instead of what you do have. Or fear that says you won't have it when you need it. It is challenging for most people to focus on trusting that you have what you need, when you need it. And the Animal Mind is active thinking that if you spend it, you will have to look for more, just like you must hoard to get ready for the coming year.

- What kind of mind-patterns do you need to have money?
- Do you need money or do you need what you need?
- Do you think money is the only way you get what you need?
- Can money buy you time to build supportive money mind-patterns?
- Is it easy to get in a money coming in, money going out loop?
- Is it important to have a storehouse of money "just in case"?
- Or does the storehouse of money mean you will someday need to use that storehouse?
- Can a storehouse of money feed a mind-pattern of lack because then you don't want to spend the storehouse?
- Do you need the mind-pattern of flexibility before you need more money?

I am doing my best to dig deeper into what mind-pattern I need to cultivate so my mind can automatically bring to me what is most correct and beneficial. I do not want to be dependent on money to fulfill my needs. I want to be dependent upon mind-pattern and Source. If something is trying to get to me another way, but I only focus on money as the only way I could block other ways of what I need getting to me. I've read about people digging in their fields to unearth coins, jewels and other antiquities. Sometimes people walking on the beach find ambergris, otherwise known as whale vomit, that is worth hundreds of thousands of dollars in the perfume industry.

I had a friend in my farming days who did not get along with his father. So, he worked for another farmer who had no children. This farmer eventually willed his farm to my friend. No money exchanged hands, but my friend's mind-pattern attracted a farm complete with home, equipment and everything else he needed.

When I was pregnant with my first child, Stewart's sister gave me everything I needed for the baby, from crib to clothes. No money changed hands, but my needs were met.

- Have you been focused and dependent on money to fulfill your needs?
- Can you focus on the mind-patterns behind the money so that when you do receive money you are better equipped to handle it?
- Can you broaden your perspective, be flexible and allow Source to fulfill your needs in Its way instead of Your way?
- Are you able to accept from unconventional sources, even if you don't know what those are?
- Do you think you have blocked something that might be trying to get to you, but you haven't been ready to accept?
- What came to you that you needed without money changing hands?
- Can you be grateful instead of always wishing for more?

- Does guilt make you give to others rather than keep what you need for Self?

- Can things boost your mind pattern?

## AFFIRMATIONS—SPIRITUAL MIND

Programming activations and triggers are all around. Every conceivable way to throw you into Animal Mind/fight or flight scenarios is possible. It is especially important that you stay vigilant with deep protection and use your Self-Integration Archetypes in your energy field at all times. Use these affirmations to anchor into your Spiritual Mind.

*I AM that I AM.*
*I AM deeply anchored into my Source at all times.*

*Nothing disturbs the calm peace of my Soul.*
*I AM centered and flexible.*

*I objectively observe.*
*I make conscious choices about my actions and reactions.*

*I ask my Oversoul before I open my mouth or move my body.*
*I AM guided and directed by my Source.*

*I greet all growth opportunities with courage.*
*I AM fortified and empowered by my Source.*

*I AM patient with my Self.*
*I give my Self time to grow.*

*I AM patient with others.*

*I allow others their time to grow.*

*I allow my Self to feel what I feel.*

*In conscious awareness I choose how I react to what I feel.*

*I recognize when I feel pushed into fight or flight mode.*

*I release the need to allow the outer world to push me into fight or flight mode.*

*I maintain my Self-Integration Brown Merger Archetype at my pineal gland and Reptilian brainstem 24/7.*

*My Self-Integration/Brown Merger Archetype helps keep me whole and complete.*

*I recognize when I lose control of my actions and reactions.*

*I focus on going up to my Spiritual Mind.*

*I remove my Self from programming triggers as much as possible.*

*I release the need to be pulled into the Animal Mind.*

*I recognize the attempts of my Animal Mind to take control.*

*My Spiritual Mind controls my Animal Mind at all times.*

*I release the need to live in fear.*
*I AM anchored into the Courage of my Oversoul and God-Mind.*

*Nothing and no one controls me and/or my emotions.*
*I AM anchored into my own internal knowing.*

*Nothing and no one can attack me unless I allow it in.*
*I release the need to allow external attacks to affect me in any way.*

*I release the need for internal programming attacks and activations.*
*I AM stronger than my programming.*

*I release the need for external programming attacks and activations.*
*I AM in control of me at all times.*

*I release my need to give my power away to programming attacks*
*and activations.*
*I AM always centered and grounded in Source.*

*Nothing and no one is stronger than Source.*
*I live in the protection of my Source.*

*I release my need to fear technology.*
*My mind is the strongest tool I have.*

*I release my need to fear the power of the global handlers.*

*My mind is powered by Source.*

*Nothing and no one can chase me if I do not run.*

*I choose to face all challenges with Courage.*

*I release the need to hide from all reflections of my Self.*

*I face all levels of my Self with wisdom and understanding.*

*I chose my life.*

*I choose my methods of Self-Understanding.*

*I appreciate all opportunities for growth in this Reality, whether I like them or not.*

*I grow, in spite of my Self.*

*I release the need to hinder my own growth.*

*I pass and surpass my Earth School lessons.*

*I release the need to use programming triggers and activations as excuses.*

*I AM in my power at all times, anchored deep within my Oversoul and God-Mind.*

# Where Energy Flows Money Goes

The majority of the people, if not all if they would admit it, always want more money. Most people always think that that they do not have enough. Past issues, meaning emotions unresolved and buried, wreak havoc in your life. This includes getting your most basic needs met, such as money for shelter, clothing and food.

Interestingly enough, eating has to do with energy to run your body. Energy is represented by money in physical reality. In the nonphysical all energy comes from your Source. More energy flowing through your physical body translates into more energy coming in from Source. This sets the frequency for an increased flow of money into physical reality to represent what is coming into you on the nonphysical levels from your Source..

Fasting is one way of cleansing your physical body so it can hold more energy. However, if you need to build your body with food and supplements, then continue to practice mindful eating so you prepare and strengthen your body to hold more energy. Increasing physical energy in the body can translate into more of its physical manifestations such as more money flowing in.

You also need to chip away at the blocks you have of feeling limited. With the correct flow and alignment of nonphysical energy and the correct mind-pattern, you can manifest more of what you need in this reality. There is more than enough for everyone. Pulling out your past issues and emotional blocks is like opening the floodgates to the dam. But, as with all your inner work, you must open the floodgates in the way that is most correct and beneficial for you.

- Is it possible that the feelings of not having enough are buried alongside repressed emotions and past issues?
- How is it that you can have enough food and drink, but never enough money?
- Why do even those with the most physical wealth on the planet still search for more?
- Why is the Soul never satisfied with the amount of money that it has?
- If God-Mind is limitless, how can this be?
- How many ways does society tell you that you do not have enough money?
- How many ways are you imprinted with struggling to get your basic needs met?
- How many people are struggling to put food on the table, pay for their housing, auto and clothing?
- How many people buy into the mind-patterns of low Self-Worth and Self-Value?
- Do you do the Green Psychic Flush visualization?
- Why is Medium Green the color for healing?

**Mindful Eating**

More mindful eating means more mindful thinking. Interesting that there is a special banana cake that I rarely ever think of except when it's my birthday. My mother told me that her mother used to make a yellow cake, slice bananas lengthwise on the cake, and cover it all in meringue and then bake it in the oven. This is the origin of the modified version that I make. My mother's mother had a wood stove in which she baked for her family of 8. So, when I eat this cake, I think about all of the times I have eaten it, the places where I have made it, childhood memories, my mother's childhood and her mother cooking in the kitchen of their farmhouse which was built by my grandfather. Weirdly enough, I am not even especially fond of bananas.

Eating this cake is always a walk down memory lane for me. Perhaps this is why I only think of it one time per year. The physical cake ties me into the nonphysical energy of my birth. Maybe this is what makes it special. If I had it every day, it would lose its nonphysical impact on me.

- Do you have a favorite cake made in a favorite way that you eat on your birthday?
- If so, do you eat it any other time of year?
- What is the cake's nonphysical impact on you?
- Are there any specific foods that you eat that bring up nonphysical memories, pleasant or not-so-pleasant?
- Why is physical food associated with nonphysical memories?
- Do you think it is tied into "as above, so below"?
- Are you okay with eating cake?
- Do you feel guilty when you eat cake?
- Does cake represent sweetness in your life?
- Do you feel guilty accepting sweetness in your life?
- Does society imprint you to feel guilty when you eat something sweet?
- Do you crave sweet experiences in life?
- Does feeling guilty while eating sweet food program you to feel guilty when a sweet experience comes into your life?
- Do you feel guilty when you have something sweet and others do not?

- Do you accept sweetness in your life?
- Or, does sweetness always come with strings, that most likely pull you down instead of elevate you?

One day not too long ago, as I was walking through the supermarket, I was thinking about how you can get just about any food you desire. You do not have to go to a specific place, and often you do not have to wait for a specific season. You can get pretty much what you want when you want it for the right price. I found some frozen crab legs from Russia. The price was $30.00 for one pound, and about half of that pound is shell.

When I picked up the package and looked at the price, my first thought was it was way too expensive. But of course, it would have cost me a lot more to go all the way to Russia to get them. Then I started thinking about how worthless a person feels when you are shopping for something as basic as food and you cannot afford the price. So I definitely decided to buy them, plus they were for my birthday dinner, which meant I could definitely justify the price.

After my birthday I was shopping at another store. I found frozen crab legs that were about the same price as the other store and decided to get more. It was on a rather cold snow day, so there were very few people in the store. But no matter where I put my shopping cart there was a mother with her daughter who was about 8 years old and my shopping cart was in their way. I actually was beginning to get annoyed because I was trying to have a bit of quiet time as I shopped, but no matter how many aisles I skipped, there they were, conversing quite loudly.

Just before I was about to get further annoyed, the mother muttered that she wished she was coming home to my house for dinner. When I realized that she was actually speaking to me I looked up. She mentioned that she loved crab legs and I simply said that I had them before and they were very good. From then on, I did not see her again until time to check out, but instead of feeling annoyed, I felt compassion for her. She probably felt she could not afford them and therefore not having them re-enforced low Self-Worth, her income strata, and the fact that having a family is expensive, plus more. I did not justify why I was buying them. At one time I would have had to say that I had them for my birthday, so I was trying them again.

- Have you ever bought something relatively expensive at any store where you felt you had to justify your purchase to someone?
- Do you judge that it is okay to pay more for a special occasion but not when it is "just because"?
- Do you think high-priced food is purposefully designed to make you feel worthless because you cannot afford it?
- Is it important to pay more than what you think you can pay to stretch the frequency of positive abundance?
- Does the price justify why not to buy something?
- If you really want something, can you find a way to pay for it?
- If it is most correct and beneficial for you to have something, does it find its way to you one way or the other?

I like to think about food when I am fasting because I feel that I actually make better choices when my Animal Mind is not in charge. I made some delicious pizzas from scratch this past Friday and Saturday nights. As I made my pizzas, I realized that the pizzas have to do with many layers that I am digging through within my Self. When I fast, the foods that I want to eat change. Well, after I made my banana layer cake, I had a piece for a couple of evenings, skipped an evening and now that I am fasting, there is still more in the refrigerator. At one time, that cake would have been gone in about 2 days. Now, it is practically a week later and there is still one-fourth of the cake left. This is what I mean by how fasts change what you want.

Last night I made 2 roast chickens as well as mashed potatoes filled with onions, garlic, cream and tons of butter. Onions and garlic are comprised of many layers. Then, I peeled my remaining shallots, so more layers.

I have been wanting to make a cream of onion soup, so I am thinking about that. I will probably boil up the chicken bones for broth tomorrow and then look for a recipe. I made my version of French Onion soup a few days before the 3 day fast began. So many foods that my body is wanting has to do with layers.

When I fast, rarely do my thoughts turn to sweet foods, because my body craves other things. When I first started fasting many decades ago, I craved sweet foods because they give you a quick boost of energy that makes you feel good. After the fast, I ate the things I craved only to find out that they no longer satisfied me in the same way. Then, I was disappointed that I had indulged my cravings. Even the banana layer cake that I made after the last 3 day fast does not contain much sugar: 1/3 cup for the pudding; 2 tablespoons in the whipped cream; 1 cup for the cake itself. However, the flour, milk, and bananas are all sugar/carbs that need to be considered.

- When you think about sugar do you also think about the carbs that you eat as sugar?
- Do you think that your body needs sugar so carbohydrates are okay to eat?
- Do you beat your Self up for eating carbs or only for eating sugar?
- If you have a piece of fruit for dessert instead of a piece of cake, do you think you are doing well?
- If so, do you think about how they are both sugar, so if you want the cake, why not just eat the cake?
- Do you practice Self-denial when you eat, meaning you deny your Self what you really want?

- Does Self-denial carry through into the rest of your life, meaning you deny your Self what you really want often settling for less or something you really do not want?
- Does fasting help you change what your body craves as well as what you want to stuff into your body?
- Even without fasting, does mindful eating make you stop and think before you eat or even after you eat?
- Does mindful eating extrapolate into the rest of your life so that your decisions and choices become more mindful and less haphazard and emotional?
- When you fast, what kinds of food do you dream of eating?
- After the fast, do you eat them?
- If so, do they taste as good as what you thought they would?
- Does your portion size change after your fast or during more mindful eating?
- Does the food you crave come in layers?

I had a cup of strong coffee with unsweetened chocolate almond milk to break my fast at about 2 pm this afternoon. Even though it is not as cold in Michigan as it was last week, it is damp and feels colder than when it was a dry cold. Today I made sesame seed bagels and tried my hand at cinnamon raisin bagels. I finished taking the meat off of my roast chickens for Chicken Alfredo for dinner tonight and put the bones in with some steam-distilled water to start a nice chicken broth for whatever soup I choose to make next. It was another cooking day.

Even though I cook a lot, I rarely stuff my body anymore when I eat. Stuffing comes from a mind-pattern of lack that you better eat it/get it now because you do not know when you will get it/afford it again. I used to love to eat at buffets because for a low price you could eat all you wanted. I got to pick and choose exactly what I wanted and how much I wanted; I had control of my eating and portion supply. When I did not eat as a child, my mother had control over my food/

energy. I am fortunate to say that we always had food in the house, but if I did not eat what she prepared in the way she prepared it, I was often sent to bed hungry. For this reason, I am very cognizant about giving people food that they like.

I still like buffets, but I prefer to pay more and get a higher quality of food. And I do not stuff my Self as I did at one time. What I really like is a nice sit-down dinner. I enjoy being served and taken care of; that feels very nurturing to me.

- Does he who controls the food supply, control the people?
- Did anyone have control of your food supply in your life?
- If yes, did that person have control of you?
- Do you like to eat at buffets?
- Do you like to stuff your body full of food so you get your money's worth?
- Or because you don't know when you will get that specific food again?
- How do you feel about eating at an expensive restaurant where your portion is quite small compared to an all-you-can-eat buffet?
- What is the difference in mind-pattern between eating at an expensive restaurant with a small portion and an all-you-can-eat buffet?
- If you eat less, is this telling your Self that you have plenty, you will get that food again, you will have more positive experiences?
- A that you do not have to stuff because have exactly what you need, when you need, and as much as you need?
- Is your home or living environment stuffed with stuff?

## Coupons

Recently I made a $100.00 purchase at a clothing store. Immediately after I placed my order, I received a coupon for 30% off. I wondered if they sent me the coupon because I just placed an order, or was this a coincidence. I have fought with my Self over coupons and discounts my entire life. I often buy based upon what is on sale. My conscious reasoning is to get more for my money. But I have realized that buying on sale helps me narrow the choices that I must choose from.

For example, if I go to a clothing store, I check out the sale rack first. I buy from a website for organic food and products as well as supplements. When food is on sale, I buy food. When vitamins and supplements are on sale, I buy those items. I organize what I purchase around sales. So, when the 30% off coupon came in, I fought with my Self about phoning the store to ask them to take the 30% off, which would have been $30.00. In previous times, I would have called, because I have felt resentful that I had to pay extra. The stores are generally accommodating when this happens, so I know doing this is productive.

However, since I am working on increasing my financial flow, I asked my Self if using that coupon would imprint me with I need that $30.00 for something else. Or, would not using the coupon imprint me with "I have so much money that I do not need that $30. I can buy whatever I want, when I want." This time I practically sat on my hands so I didn't dial the store while passing resentment up. If I had received the coupon before I made the purchase, I would have interpreted that as the Universe handing me $30.00. But because the coupon came in after-the-fact I had to really think about what I was doing and why.

Some people choose to sell their old clothing through thrift shops rather than give them away. I wonder if the few dollars these people receive is more beneficial than giving the clothes to those who are needy. I had a garage sale once. Once. Because for me, sitting around all day to make $25 was not a good use of my time. It was my old stuff that I wanted out of my house. That was the goal.

- Does getting money for what you do not want justify getting rid of it?
- Do you feel like you deserve to remove old stuff from your home?
- Does releasing your stuff make you feel wasteful?
- If you give it away, do you care who gets it and what they do with it?
- How does throwing your stuff away vs. giving it away or selling it?
- If God-Mind is limitless why do you hold onto your old stuff?
- How do you feel about using coupons and discounts?
- Or buying things on sale?
- Do you arrange your shopping around sales?
- Are coupons and sales designed to manipulate the buying of consumers?
- Have you ever bought something on sale and then wished you hadn't?
- Do you use sales and coupons to justify your purchases?
- Do you think there are too many choices when it comes to items that are offered for purchase?

There are so many subtle ways that imprint you with lack I sometimes wonder how long it will take to dig them all out. I have always used coupons and looked for discounts. In fact, a long time ago I used to bargain with people to get them to reduce their pricing on products/services. I enjoyed talking them down and paying less than they asked. It had nothing to do with whether I had the money or not. It was about getting more for less. At some point along the way, I realized that these people were asking what they thought they deserved. I was not honoring their process, and by not honoring their process, I was not honoring my Self. When I came to this conclusion, I stopped trying to bargain. Either I paid the asking price or I did not buy at all.

In the same way, I am learning that when you need coupons and discounts, use them. But the idea is not to be dependent on them. Being dependent on them says that you can only have certain items if you pay less than. You pay less than because you feel less than; you do not deserve to pay full price because you are not worth full price. Using coupons to determine when you buy restricts the flow of positive abundance because you cannot have what you want now, you have to wait until the product/service is less than. You also enhance the imprinting that your income stream is limited so you have to spread out the little income that you have to get the most for your money.

- Why do you sell old clothing and possessions rather than give them away?
- Is there a fine line between using coupons and discounts and not using them?
- Should coupons and discounts only be used when necessary so you begin to set the mind-pattern that you can have what you want when you want it?
- If you find a $20 bill laying on the floor do you take it?
- Or leave it because someone else might need it more?
- What if paying more now means that you are priming the pump for more money to come in?
- Can using coupons and discounts continually keep you in a poverty mind-pattern loop?
- What if you had so much money that when you are done with your car, you could give it to the most correct and beneficial person who needs it?

- What if you had so much money that when you were done with your home, you could give it to the most correct and beneficial person who needed that home?

I have a friend who a few years ago cleaned out her closet and brought some of her nicer things over to see if I liked them. I really thought that was nice of her until I noticed that each item had a price tag on it. Oh, well. Then, at some point, she told me that she had a friend who paid hundreds of dollars for her name brand clothes that she barely wore. Every year, this woman had a party, invited her friends over to go through her closet, and then only charged about $100 per item. My friend was bragging to me about how she could get such great clothes from her friend for only a few hundred dollars every year.

I would never think to ask my friends to purchase my old things. I have always given away what I cannot use, except for the one garage sale. However, if my friends would have wanted any of the items I would have gladly given these items away. Generally, it is very easy for me to give my things away, once I make the decision that I no longer want/need them. No matter what I paid for something, I am happy that I got use out of whatever it is, and I am happy to think someone else might continue to enjoy the item for as long as the item holds together.

When I really want something, the cost of the item does not matter to me. I will find a way and yes, Source does provide. I love going to see my family in Italy and Source provides by bringing the correct group of people together to tour with me. It is a lot of work to put the tours together. I work while I am there. Working keeps my journey in Italy interesting with people who I might not otherwise interact with on such a personal level. Source provides.

Some people think travel is a luxury, so when they hear that I go to work, in their minds, my travel is justified. I never appreciated travel until I began traveling. To me, travel is an important part of a well-rounded person. I appreciate my experiences and what they add to my Soul-nurturing and growth.

When we got the new animal additions to our family, we put money aside every month to make it happen. Yet, it is impossible to put a price on the love and joy that these amazing creatures add to our household. Even the issues that come as a responsible pet owner are acknowledged as part of the process. The animals are in my opinion, priceless. If you walked into my home today and offered me millions of dollars for them, I would not part with them. It is most correct and beneficial that my pets stay with me.

- Do you have items in your home that are not for sale no matter how much money someone offers you?
- Is your home for sale if someone gave you a great price?
- If you give freely, does this set the imprinting for your Source to give freely to you?
- If you accept freely, does this set the imprinting to receive freely from Source?
- When you give or accept freely, do you stop to ask if what you are doing is most correct and beneficial?
- What if you give freely to someone who is not the most correct and beneficial recipient of whatever you are giving?
- What if you accept freely something that is not most correct and beneficial for you to receive?
- Do you practice discernment in your giving and receiving?
- If there is something that you really want, do you find a way to make it happen?
- If so, do you first ask your Source if it is most correct and beneficial?

**Source Provides**

I have told you the story of the descendant of slaves of Suriname, whose grandmother escaped through the jungles and survived because each night before going to sleep, they planted a seed that grew food for the slaves to have in the morning. Source provides. Often when you least expect it, when you have given up, is when your ship finally comes in.

There is a parable of a wicked man who found $20 and a good man who twisted and sprained his ankle. An angel appeared and told the wicked man that he had been destined to find a treasure chest full of gold, but because he was so wicked all he got was $20. And the good man had been destined for a major accident, but because he was good, he only sprained his ankle.

When you look at what other people have vs. what you have, remember that each person is on a unique path. As much as you want to compare Self to others, it is virtually impossible. If you feel like you have less, you might actually have more because of your exemplary life. Each person is learning his/her own unique lessons. This does not translate to easy. The stress that you may feel is what helps you get up and keep going, even when you feel like you want to stop. Stress is not bad; stress is an important attribute that helps build your physical body and also helps build your mind and character. Fasting is a conscious stress of the body to force it to let go of whatever it is holding onto. The body thus releases the physical representation of the nonphysical mind-patterns that you have been holding onto.

- Do you think of stress as bad?
- Do you want life to be easy?
- Would you be bored with easy?
- Have your toughest times been the ones that forced you to really declare who you are and what you know?
- Is it challenging to not compare Self to others?

- Are you making a conscious effort to accept your life "as is"?
- Does accepting anything open your frequency to accept more positive abundance?
- Do you easily accept help and advice from others?
- Are you receptive to accepting lessons even when they challenge you, or do you complain and feel sorry for your Self?
- If you accept the lessons Source gives you, do you think this can translate into accepting financial abundance?
- Have you had the experience of giving up, only to have your challenges come to a conclusion, even if it was not how you expected?
- Do you do your best to focus on Source provides even when you doubt that this can ever happen?

One of the biggest lessons in life is to realize and accept that life rarely goes as you expect it to go. By observing my repetitive cycles, I have found that what I thought I was going to learn/do, rarely happens. I always learn something, but usually not what I thought in the way I thought I was going to learn it. When this happens, it is so easy to label Self "failure". I have been there, done that, too. But with distance, I realize how much each of these failure situations taught me; I may not have appreciated the lessons at the time, but in retrospect, I always learned a lot.

This is why now instead of labeling my Self "failure" when life does not go my way, I label the process re-direction. Yes, sometimes I am disappointed that circumstances did not go as I planned. Yet, even with my disappointment, I do know that there is a reason that will reveal it Self. Because of this, my lows are not so low which means my highs are not so high. My emotions are leveling out which makes life easier; not easy, but easier. There is a difference.

When your emotions dip low, so do your finances because where your energy goes, its physical counterpart, money, flows. When your energy is low/depressed, money cannot find you. When your energy is high, money can come into you. However, you must have the energy to keep/maintain your income stream. When your emotions are low is when you need money/energy the most. When money does come in then you have to spend it to compensate for the emotional/financial deficit. Up and down, up and down. This is what happens to the financial flow of most people. Whatever you get is spent about as quickly as it comes in. A never-ending cycle for most people. Where your energy goes, money flows. Managing your energy is a huge task.

- Is it easy to accumulate bills and debt that must be paid as soon as money comes in?
- Is your financial stream tied to your emotions?
- Or, are your emotions tied to your financial stream?
- Do you feel energized when you have funds?
- And de-energized when you have no/low funds?
- Has your life gone the way you planned?
- Have you spent a lot of time being disappointed?
- Do negative energy frequencies set the state for negative/restricted financial flow?
- Do you still label your Self as a failure?
- Do you know that what did not work out the way you hoped/planned/intended was most correct and beneficial for your Soul growth?
- Is physical food the only source of energy for your body?

## Limited Resources Imprinting/Programming

Your emotions fuel your energy level. When you have money, you feel good so you feel energized and you have the potential to attract more. This is where most people falter. If you never have money, your dreams are limitless. Once you have money, you go into fear mode thinking that once you spend the money, it is gone. So this is what you create. It is truly challenging for most people to have a constant flow of money because having money actually promotes fear of not having money. This is why when you get it, you spend it, and then it is gone. Or, when you have it, you worry about losing it.

When I first started farming many years ago, there was a government program to help young farmers get started. I borrowed $48,000.00 to start farming. Because I had never dealt with that kind of money it really didn't mean much other than it was a lot. I had nothing to lose, so it did not seem risky in the moment. However, as my assets accumulated and grew, the full force of losing something hit me. When I had nothing to lose, I was not afraid of losing anything. When I had something to lose, I was afraid of not being able to keep what I had. When you feel that fear of losing what you do have, the money flow is automatically restricted.

All of this is definitely a mental game; a game for your mind. Because where your attention flows, the money goes. Your attention goes to fear of losing, so you create loss. This can mean something breaks down, so you have to pay that bill; someone gets ill, so the money goes for medical bills; maybe taxes that you owe are more than you expected, and so forth. You cannot keep the money flowing because your energy is focused on the fear of not having, so you do not have.

- How easy is it to become afraid of losing what you have?
- How challenging is it to know without a shadow of a doubt that Source provides?
- Have thought that you were all set with your budget only to have unexpected expenses that put you back into fear mode?
- If you cannot handle what you have, why do you think you should have more?

- How much do you need so you do not have to fear spending it all, losing it, or needing more?
- Have you been in the situation of not having anything but endless dreams?
- Have you had finances but were afraid to spend?
- Have you been afraid of losing your financial streams?
- Do you worry about replacing your money before you even spend it?
- When you have had money, have you not been able to hold onto it or generate more?
- Does fear of dealing with the money you have take the joy out of having it?

I ended my fast late morning with a nice hot cup of strong black coffee with unsweetened chocolate almond milk. We are in the middle of an ice storm/snow storm, so that was really wonderful. I simmered some turkey thighs on the stove which we had for dinner along with some mashed potatoes, broccoli and biscuits that I had previously made and frozen. I made cranberry sauce from cranberries in the freezer this morning. I plan on making a nice onion, garlic, sausage and greens soup with the turkey broth in the next day or two. You can also make turkey thighs in your crockpot, too, if you are working away from home. I like to smell food on the stove simmering while I am working in the day.

You are highly imprinted with the fallacy of limited resources vs. the limitlessness that exists. I have done my best to imprint my sons with "they can have anything they want" as well as with discernment of what that might be. I also told them many times that they both have great money-attracting mind-patterns and I explained why my money-attracting mind-pattern is not as wonderful as theirs. They know that I have struggled on and off through the years. This is not a secret in our household.

Interestingly, they are both extremely mindful of their spending. Even when we have traveled and they have had the money to buy souvenirs, they are mindful of what they purchase. They both have savings accounts; they both have always had jobs, sometimes more than 1 at a time; they both think and research before they make their choices. They both use a lot of discretion about their eating, usually choosing proteins and vegetables with a few carbs/sweets thrown in the mix.

I do see them influenced by peers who always talk about how they don't have money. My youngest son prefers to go to a nice restaurant and pay between $5 and $10 for a burger. His peers want to go to McDonald's so they only have to pay $2 for a burger. If he accompanies them to McDonald's, he chooses not to eat there. He will come home and eat after. My son understands the value of nutrition and quality food. Quality food means a quality mind-pattern. Sometimes he feels guilty because he does not have money issues and his friends do. Or, at least they think they do. If my son was raised differently, he would be saying and doing the same things. He is discerning in what he wants and chooses. His friends were not taught discernment so they do not understand that they are making choices on the negative side of money rather than the positive side.

Many of his friends want to be doctors because doctors make a lot of money. My son chose his career field because he enjoys it. He may make money doing it, but it is not the reason he chose the field. Interestingly, now that my son is paying for his own clothes, he no longer likes to shop at family-oriented chain clothing stores. He prefers to pay more and have fewer clothes of higher quality. He does watch for sales, which is okay at his stage in life. Sometimes I even tell him that I will help him pay for some of his necessities but he insists on paying for them him Self. My sons have always had what they wanted. When what they want changes, they figure out a way to make what they want happen.

- Do you know what it is you really want?
- Or do you simply think that you know what you want?
- Do you shop for quantity or quality?
- Are you in your chosen career field because you want to make money or because you enjoy it?
- Did you choose your field of work or did your field of work choose you?
- What is the difference?
- Do you enjoy your work?
- Do you learn at work?
- Are you being paid to learn?
- Do you take full advantage of the learning opportunities at your work place?
- Or do you complain because you do not like it there?
- Do you view your work place as a school from which one day you will graduate?
- Do you love your work so much that you never want to graduate into something different?
- Are you looking forward to the time when you can retire from work?
- Are you as mindful of what you eat as you are with your spending?
- How many ways are you imprinted with limited resources?
- Do you think about the limitless of the resources around you?
- What about people who live in the middle of big cities and towns, yet cannot partake in its food and shelter?
- What kind of mind-pattern do homeless people have?
- What are the mind-patterns of the people who live in these big cities and towns who allow this to happen?

- Are there homeless people who truly want to be homeless?
- What types of occupations/non-occupations might these homeless have had in other lifelines that lead them to take up this type of lifestyle?
- Are the homeless allowed to be here to hold you in fear that you could be homeless, too?
- Is fear a Self-perpetuating trap that is ever-so-challenging to get out of?

I really enjoyed my time as an art director in an art gallery. I was always experimenting with different arts and crafts media, so this was like a dream job that I loved. As I watched the artists bringing their work in for sale, I often thought about all the things that I could make and sell. The issue was, I did not have a passion for what I could make and sell and still get something for my time.

During these years, I taught my Self how to do Hardanger embroidery which is openwork having elaborate symmetrical designs created by blocks of satin stitches within which threads of the embroidery fabric are removed. I absolutely loved doing it, people admired it, so I decided to sell some of my pieces. But there was no way that I could recoup anything for my time. I wound up resenting selling the pieces because I received so little compared to the time involved making them. So, I stopped selling them. Then, I decided to make and sell crafts because I calculated the cost of the materials, how quickly I could make them and realized that I could make a reasonable profit. I even bought all the materials to put the crafts together, but I did not have any passion. I just could not bring my Self to actually make the crafts. I eventually gave all the craft materials away.

During these years I was also a farmer. I was good at farming, and I was proud of the challenges I faced and overcame. Farming was not my passion, but I could do it and make money. I could make more

282 • HEIGHTS OF WEALTH

money farming than working for someone else. The art gallery job was my passion and entertainment, but farming was my main source of income.

The reason I am laying this out for you is because there are many ways that you can make money or not make money. And you can do many things at one time if you want to, if you do not want to, no matter what you do, you most likely will not succeed. You have to put effort into whatever you decide to do. When I dairied, I worked 24/7 round the clock. When I was a hay farmer I worked 24/7 round the clock except in the off-season. Then I had more time, except I also had a trucking company. The art gallery job was year-round. Plus, I taught my metaphysical classes, gave lectures, wrote and mailed newsletters, and wrote my books. And did my arts and crafts, had my pets, cooking, gardening, and so forth. Where there is a will, there is a way.

In my opinion, the structure of a 9-5 job can be very beneficial. Or even one or two part time jobs. But you have to decide that you are going to learn what you need to learn. If you are fortunate, you also have benefits and a steady paycheck that you can count on. This does not mean easy. My farming days were not easy. But I could do it, it supported me, and I was working on farming my Self.

Use that money to fund your passion, whatever that is. And work on your Self-Worth so that money finds you. There are many people who work really, really hard for very little money. And some people, who do very little, if anything, with mind-patterns that pull in wonderful income streams. All of this together creates a balanced individual. All of it is important.

- Does your work provide structure?
- Does it provide a steady paycheck with benefits?
- Does your work allow you to enjoy your passion?
- Do you know what your passion is?
- If not, why do you not have a passion?

- In your dream world, what would you do for work?
- Is work important?
- If you had all the money you wanted, what would be your motivation for learning?
- Does work provide a motivation that you would not otherwise have?
- Does work provide lessons/learning that you would not consciously choose?
- Are you willing to work 24/7 to accomplish your income stream goals?
- Have you ever had work that you absolutely loved?
- Do you have to absolutely love your work?
- Is there a reason that work is called work and not play?
- Do you feel stuck in your work?
- Why is work a dirty word?
- Is it to keep you programmed to hate/dislike/tolerate what you do the majority of your time?

Having money/not having money keeps your focus on what you need to do for you. With what you have, you get to decide how to best benefit Self. Then, you have to learn to be grateful for what you have vs. resenting what you do not have. When your income stream gradually opens up, your choices gradually open up. When your income explodes then your choices explode. Sometimes it is better to have fewer choices.

I do as much of my shopping online as possible. I continually give a heavy sigh when I am looking for shoes, for example, and I click on a website that says 800 shoes. I really do not want to sort through 800 pairs of shoes. So I look for another website and it only has 650 pairs of shoes. I do not want to sort through this many either. This is why I like to shop sales. Sales narrow my focus as well as conserve time and energy. If I go to a website, put in sale shoes I may only have 50 or 60 pairs to look at. Even if I had all the money in the world, I really, really do not like sorting through almost 1500 pairs of shoes if I were to look at all the shoes on only 2 websites.

Most people do not appreciate exactly where they are and what they have. There is always a honeymoon period when everything is new. So if you all of a sudden have the money you think you want, you elevate into a new and exciting lifestyle. But like all things, eventually the new and exciting wears off. This is really no different than people who take recreational drugs. They start small, but then they need more and more to get that high feeling. When you have money, you feel good. But having money is relevant. When your income increases, you eventually reach a plateau and then you want more. When you get more, you enjoy it for a while, but then you want more. You need more and more to get that positive feeling that money gives you.

This is why you need to get that positive feeling now, rather than waiting to get it from money. Otherwise, you still allow the outer world/money to control you. As the saying goes, "Give a poor man a million dollars and he will soon be poor again; take a million dollars away from a rich man and he will soon be rich again."

This means that wealth comes from inside, not from the outside. You have to develop your inner wealth first to then attract outer wealth. Otherwise, Soul growth is nil.

- What does "inner wealth" mean to you?
- Are you developing inner wealth?
- Have you had money, only to lose/spend it quickly and then be without it once more?
- Have you had money, lost/spent it only to rebuild once more?
- Either way, what was your mind-pattern that caused your circumstances?

- Have you received increased income, been happy for a while, only to then be unhappy because you still want more?
- Is it challenging to not allow money to control you?
- Is it challenging to feel positive without money?
- Do you fully appreciate where you are now?
- Does having too many choices make you feel overwhelmed?
- Is having too many choices a distraction?
- Does having too many choices focus you on buying what you want vs. buying what you need?
- Is it sometimes better to have fewer choices?
- Do you continue to build your attitude of gratitude?
- Do you release resentment for what you see but cannot have?
- If you cannot appreciate "now" what makes you think you will appreciate "later"?

As much as people say they want choices, sometimes it is really nice to have others make the choice for you. When we are in the mountains in Italy, every night the hotel owner prepares dinner for us and never gives us a choice. He prepares one menu each night and no one has ever told me that they have left hungry. It is really nice to go into the dining room, sit down, be served, and not have to make choices. When we need a picnic lunch I tell him how many and he has them ready for us. When we are out on the trails we are happy with whatever we are given. The weather determines where we go hiking and for how long. My cousin Elisa is in charge of making these decisions. We go with the van. When we eat lunch in the valleys, the restaurants also have one set menu. We show up, we are served, we eat, we relax and we are grateful.

If your career chose you, in many ways, it is a blessing that you did not have to worry about what you were going to do and how. So often people do not know what they want to do for their work and they spend their days wandering from job to job, unsatisfied and financially unsupported. When other people are making decisions for you, sometimes you do not realize how much responsibility is taken off your shoulders.

Growing up I never thought about not having a roof over my head. Now, I know many people who worried about that as a child or even now as an adult. In the same way, when you work with your Oversoul, your Oversoul makes choices for you. You may not like the choices, but if you made your own choices you might like the results a lot less. I always think that life can be better; life can be worse. This helps put life in perspective to help keep you motivated and continuing on your unique journey.

The more you realize why life is as it is, the more inner wealth you accumulate; the more you can be satisfied with "now" instead of always focusing on something else. However, purposefully and proactively shaking up your own life is better than waiting for someone or something else to do it for you. Best to stay on the proactive side of life, but this can be a fine dance.

- How challenging is it to always be finding the balance in your life?
- How challenging is it to keep your finances growing without sabotaging what you have or get?
- Can you have so much that you become complacent or lazy?
- Or so little that you lose your motivation, thus become complacent or lazy?
- Do you like having your Oversoul choose for you?
- Do you resent when life plans go your Oversoul's way, but not your way?
- Do you like having choices?
- Do you prefer to be taken care of without any choices?
- Or somewhere in between?

- Do you want to make choices but then resent the responsibility of your choices?
- Do you want to make choices that are consequence-free?
- Can any choice ever be consequence-free?
- Do all choices have positive and negative aspects to them?
- How often do you wish you had more choices?
- Does more money mean more choices and therefore more opportunities to fall flat on your face?

## Is Sharing Caring

I often see headlines where public figures owe millions in back taxes. You have to make a lot of money to owe that much in back taxes. This is because more money means more chances to fail—or be re-directed. In other words, you may get more money just so you know why you should not have more money.

One of the biggest issues of getting more money is other people. First, of course, you want to take care of your own bills and debts. But after the essentials are paid then you may have family and friends that you want to help. But sometimes, helping them is actually hurting them. Sometimes, they need the struggle to grow. Yet, if you do not help them then your relationship with them may be broken forever. You do not want to take away the lessons of others, yet perhaps with extra money you can help them mitigate their lessons. Just like your Oversoul has to decide how to help you in the most correct and beneficial way, you now take on this role for your loved ones.

- If you have a cousin who is losing his house because of a drinking issue, do you help save the house knowing that your cousin is going to do this again?
- Do you give with strings attached, such as he has to attend AA, get a doctor's appointment, eat correctly, and so forth?

- If you give with strings attached, who is going to monitor the cousin?
- What if you have a retirement fund but one of your children has legal issues and needs your financial help?
- If you give that financial help will he/she learn his/her lesson?
- Or even if they do, what if this compromises your ability to live comfortably?

If you do not have the money, you do not have to choose. You are, in a way, protected from having to say no. You cannot give what you do not have, which then forces the other person to make decisions that you do not have to make. You don't look bad in their eyes and your relationship is preserved. Not having money can save you from making truly challenging choices. Maybe you have a ton of money and someone you know needs a car. Yet, if you buy them a beautiful new car and they have low Self-Worth, they might crash the car, potentially injuring Self and others, not to mention destroying the gift. This may mean that you buy them a low budget car just so they can get around because this is all their Self-Worth can handle, even though you could buy them a gorgeous brand-new car. There is tremendous responsibility when helping others.

- If you came into a lot of money, do you know people who you could help financially?
- Would you ask your Oversoul if it would be most correct and beneficial to help them?
- Would you worry about taking away their lessons?
- Would you worry about your relationship with them?
- Can giving money to people you love ruin relationships?
- Does not having money to help others take away your choice to do so?
- Does not having the choice help you breathe a sigh of relief?

- Have you ever done something financial for another person only to have it backfire on you?
- How much money do you have to give to another person to really help them?
- To help someone, must you give them money for food, shelter, education, job training, life coaching?
- How long do you have to give money to someone to really help him/her?
- If you give a person $5,000, or $10,000, what happens to that person when the money is gone?
- What if you give someone a car, but they cannot afford the license, tax and insurance?
- Or a home but they cannot afford to maintain it, much less taxes and insurance?
- How can you help others open their mind-patterns and upgrade Self-Worth so they could use the money you give them as a way to prime their own pump?

If you give others too much, you are going to see them heading for disaster. If you give them a little and you see them doing well, you can give a little more. This can put you in a position of control, power and manipulation. This is why you work with all the Oversouls involved to see what is "most correct and beneficial" vs. just passing out money because you have it. When you have money and do not give it to someone who is losing their car and/or home, having health challenges, legal issues or simply struggling to pay daily bills and eat, you have to always stop and ask what is most correct and beneficial for that person.

People do not understand that money is not about money. Money is about energy and the mind-pattern that is needed to support that flow of energy that in turn allows the money to flow in. This is why people stockpile money. It is their "energy reserve". People who spend freely keep that frequency open so that more can come to them.

Think of the celebrities with their dozens of homes, cars and luxury items. They do support the economy, but it is at their discretion. They are in charge, they have the buying/spending power, and they get what they want when they want it. Behind them are all the global handlers who own all the businesses that the celebrities support. So, the global handlers pay the celebrities who then spend the money at the establishments owned by the global handlers. In effect, the global handlers get their money back so they can hand it out again.

But if you spend too freely without the mind-pattern to support it, then you are going to wind up with zero. If you give too freely to someone without the mind-pattern to support it, they will wind up with zero. But you must have the inner strength and resolve to not give too much to someone who is drowning. That drowning person is going to curse you to the end if you do not throw them a life rope.

- Can you give without wanting to control and manipulate the person so he/she does not fall flat on their face again, perhaps taking you down with the ship?
- If you want to control and manipulate the outcome of your monetary gifts, is there a fine line between doing it your way vs. the way their Oversoul wants for them?
- Do you see how easy it is for the global handlers to keep all the money reserves within their circles?
- Do people who work hard without much financial compensation have the mind-patterns to be well paid?
- If the struggling working class poor get too much too fast could this be the end of them?
- If the struggling working class poor have their basic needs of food and shelter met, then what will happen?

- Will they elevate into something better or degenerate into something worse?

- Does the struggle keep them focused so they cannot get into trouble by having too much money?

- Is allowing others to struggle sometimes the kindest thing you can do for them?

- Would it feel kind to the person?

- Does your Oversoul have to make these same choices about you such as when to give you a life rope and when to withhold it?

- Do you think your Oversoul does a dance as it decides how, when and why to help you?

I have thought a lot about the homeless and the working poor and how best to help them elevate. At first, I thought about a small community with tiny houses; teach them how to take care of the home; have a community center where they can eat properly and learn about nutrition and exercise; perhaps have a garden and/or a greenhouse; teach then skills/trades, maybe arts and crafts so they can earn a living and help fund the community.

Then I look at the people who are on the streets helping the homeless. They pass out meals, give warm clothes, give them haircuts, bring them to shelters. This is a stop-gap, but does not correct the problem. Next, I thought about an apartment complex that could house many such homeless people. Yet the same questions remain except on a larger scale and perhaps less manageable simply because too many people are together with too many issues.

When I was growing up in Seattle, and it was a much smaller city at the time than it is now, whenever we took the bus to go downtown, there would always be homeless people lining the streets. My mother would always tell me not to look at them, but I couldn't help but notice them as we marched along. Sometimes she would say that they wanted to be that way or that they just want you to look at them, so don't look. It was challenging for me to envision people who wanted to be like that, or who looked like that for attention. However, when you look at the homeless just here in the US, there are so many everywhere, I wonder how one tiny community could make a difference.

- What about people who do not want this in their backyard?
- Who would accept as neighbors people who get out of prison with nowhere to go, few funds, skilled or unskilled and have a record?
- Where would such a community of former homeless people be welcomed?
- What kind of issues would these people have?
- How would you help them develop a better mind-pattern?
- Would starting one small community pave the way for more?
- Is it better to begin helping a few than helping no one?
- Do you think the homeless would be more receptive to mind-pattern analysis than people with money because they are desperate?
- Or are they desperate?
- Are animals treated better than the homeless?
- Can you compare the mind-patterns of well-treated animals to the mind-patterns of the homeless?
- Does allowing homelessness in society make you think, I don't want to be like that?
- Do the homeless serve as a reminder that *"There but for the Grace of God, go I"*?
- What would be your solution to homelessness?
- Is money the answer?

Many people have at some point in their lives have either experienced homelessness or been close to people who have/are. Money and shelter are not enough to end homelessness. They just mask the underlying issues which are then going to surface in another way.

- Stop-gap measures may encourage the homeless to try to do something different, but without guidance of some kind, is this even possible?
- If they get a hot meal 1x per week, what about the other 20 meals per week that they don't get?
- What is within those people that do get out of homelessness that is not within/active in those who remain homeless?

There is a spectrum of homelessness, with a variety of people who are homeless for a variety of reasons, which means not every solution is going to fit every situation. Taking care of your own homeless feelings will help everyone. This is why it is so important to know that you are home, wherever you are. If within you there is a sense of not belonging, of not being in your real home then this has to be outpictured in some way. So, you have homeless people to do it for you.

- If you do not feel like this is your real home, are you rejecting Mother Earth and all that She provides?
- Are you also rejecting physical reality?
- If you reject physical reality then how can you accept the energy provided to be here?
- If you don't want to be here, how can you expect to be able to accept the money/energy that allows you to move freely about this reality?
- You don't want to be here but you want money/energy to do whatever it is that you want to do in a place where you don't want to be?

- Do the global handlers have all the money/energy they want and more because they do want to be here, they like physical reality and they want to do everything they can and live in this world forever?

- Does religion teach people that they will get their reward in Heaven to help de-focus them away from wanting to be in this reality?

- Does religion teach rejection of money/energy?

- When people reject the abundant storehouse of material wealth does this allow the global handlers to scoop it up?

- Do the global handlers have so much money/energy because they love being here so much?

- Do you think the global handlers view their resources as limitless?

- How many people do you know who love living here on this planet?

- Should you feel at home wherever you are?

- Do you?

## Home and Belonging

The food that best nurtures your body comes from the area in which you were born. Every region of the world has food unique to it. For example, in the Pacific Northwest, I ate salmon berries and thimbleberries that grow on bushes in the forests. I also picked seedless wild blackberries that grow on vines on the ground. Even the milk from the cows in the Pacific Northwest is different because they eat differently than cows from the Midwest or other parts of the country. What an animal eats affects the final product of their meat and milk products. Your genetics tell you what kinds of food best feed your body.

The food in your place of origin in this lifeline is what your physical body builds it Self from. This means that your body resonates to specific frequencies in specific areas. And, that section of the Earth has a specific frequency which is why that food grows there and your Soul chose that specific locale. This further explains why you feel at home more in some areas than others. For example, I love the feel/frequency of the Pacific Northwest where I was born and I miss it terribly.

I love the feel/frequency of the Ozarks where my parents are from; I love the feel/frequency of the Cottian Alps and also France where my great-grandparents were born. Every part of my genetics resonates to specific places around the planet which gives me a sense of home and belonging. Because of easy mobility, there are a lot of people living in places that do not match their frequency, which is one reason why life is challenging for them. You cannot plant a cactus in a forest and expect it to easily grow or a fern in a desert and expect it to thrive.

If you are a cactus, your Oversoul may tell you to live in a forest for a while to get lessons that you can only get in the forest. This means that you may have to ingest food/ideas/energy that do not have the best overall match, but for your Soul growth it matches perfectly in the moment. When your lessons are learned, your Oversoul may want you somewhere else.

I never liked New York in the seven years I lived there, although I enjoyed parts of my life. But, I learned so much that it was worth my sojourn, as challenging as it was.

- Can you make your home anywhere?
- If you have mixed genetics, does this cause you to wander from place to place?
- Do you need to live in one area that matches your genetics for a while, and then move on to another area that matches another set of genetics?

- Can simply visiting an area that matches your genetics provide Soul growth?

- Do you have to have money to create your home?

- Is your body your home?

- If your Soul feels comfortable in your physical body, then does your physical body feel more comfortable wherever it is?

- Do you need money to create a comfortable physical body?

- Does correct thinking about your body extrapolate into correct thinking about your home?

- How do you think the homeless feel about their bodies?

- How challenged are they to keep their bodies clean, orderly, exercised and fed?

- How much work is it to keep your body in order?

- Does society tell you that you need money to upkeep your body?

- Or can it be done with what you easily have on hand?

- If you feel depressed or upset, are you more challenged to keep your body up?

- When you feel depressed or upset, is this the time to pay extra attention to your body?

- If money and shelter are not the answers for the homeless, can you say the same for your Self?

- Is what you need deep within so that you feel at home wherever your Oversoul plants you?

## Existence is Home

This kind of sounds like wherever you are planted, you open the door to your home, walk in, put your feet up, relax, and then when it is time, you move on.

Perhaps homeless people have nomadic simultaneous existences, but in a way, everyone is a nomad. Perhaps the homeless represent your own nomadic journey through the God-Mind It Self. Until you return to your Creator the homeless have to exist to make this statement so that some part of you is aware that you are just passing through wherever that may be at the moment.

And on this journey, right now, right here, the currency/energy that you need to exist is money. Money is the intermediary between what you need and how you get it. You believe you must have money to get what you want. Yet, there are people who get what they need without any exchange of money. Someone may give you a place to live, free meals and clothing. There are people who bypass the money system to get what they need.

Some people go to college with beautiful scholarships; others take out huge loans with which they are burdened for life. Some people have fabulous health insurance plans; others struggle to pay minimal medical bills. Some employers cover gym memberships and child care; other people pay this out of pocket. Maybe you forage for wild foods that are free for the taking; or have a neighbor who grows too much produce who gives you some for free; or a friend who hunts and/or fishes and shares with you. Perhaps you have a colleague who lends you his/her condo for a few days, or invites you to spend some time with them, thus giving you a free vacation. There are many, many ways that you can pull what you need/want to you without that intermediary of money.

Perhaps with the correct mind-pattern, the positive side of buying on sale is that you get what you need and use less of the intermediary known as money and more of your mind-pattern that brings to you what you need, when you need. Some people even hand out coupons in stores for items you may need or want. Sometimes customers give their unused coupons to other customers waiting in line at the cash register.

- How important is money vs. mind-pattern?
- Does purchasing sale/discounted items show how strong your wealth mind-pattern is?
- Have you had people give to you unexpectedly in ways that show your mind-pattern was pulling in what you needed/wanted?
- Is money necessary because you do not believe that Source provides?
- Is money something tangible that you can actually hold, see, count that gives you confidence that Source provides?
- If you do not have that tangible thing/money in your hands are you less inclined to believe that Source provides?
- Have you observed people you know get something for free when you had to struggle to pay for the same thing?
- Have you wondered why "them" and "not me"?
- In retrospect, can you determine the difference in mind-patterns?
- Do you believe you must have money to get what you want/need?
- Do you ask Source to bring to you what is most correct and beneficial in the most correct and beneficial way, or do you only ask for money?
- Do some people think it is wrong to ask Source for money?
- How do you feel about asking Source for money/energy/currency?
- Is your Soul a nomad?
- Do you think that Existence is Home?

Homelessness can be a step for those who need to be more aware of the body. When you are able to objectively understand why people have the experiences they have, as well as the reflections in your own life, you start to lose the guilt for having more. For example, I fly business class when I travel. If it was up to me, I would go economy, but Stewart has impressed upon me that "we deserve" and we must open these frequencies. Generally, the business/first class customers board the plane first. Then you are given drinks and snacks.

So, I board first, get comfortable, and then must watch all the other people boarding including older people who can barely move, young parents with young children, people from all walks of life parade past as I sit comfortably in my large seat with plenty of leg room holding my drink and eating my snacks. This has been an extremely uncomfortable lesson accepting more. Most airplanes only have a few rows of business/first class seats with the rest economy. I have had to realize that it is the mind-pattern of those people in economy that put them there. With the correct mind-pattern there would be more business/first class seats and only a very few if any, economy seats. I accept that I am an example for them to aspire to; they can either be resentful or wishful when they see me sitting there, or they can be inspired to open their mind-patterns to receive more.

I do like going business/first class; I like being able to use the lounges where there are drinks/food; the nicer bathrooms and it is much quieter. I like being able to board first; I like being treated like a person rather than cattle; I like being served food; I like being closer to the bathrooms when in flight; and getting off the plane first. In addition, if there are any changes, issues or delays, business/first class customers are given priorities and are well-taken care of. But I still push through my guilt that I have and others do not; I work on "I deserve" and "I accept" and all my Self-Worth issues. Every flight is a challenge for me but I keep working on it. I am better than I was. I like flying business/first class with my sons because this imprints them with Self-Worth so they do not struggle with it like I do. Because of what I want them to be imprinted with, I push my Self even harder to be an example for them.

Everywhere on this Earth, there are people with more and much more; less and much less. The more you understand mind-pattern the more you understand "why" which then stops your judgment of their situation as good or bad which in turn allows you to focus on your own mind-pattern. You are then able to accept the positives without guilt that your mind-pattern draws to you.

- How challenged are you to accept without guilt, knowing that others have less?
- Do you realize that others have less for a reason?
- Do you know that it is okay for others to have less?
- Can you accept more than others without guilt?
- Do you know people who have more who look down at people who have less?
- Is wanting others to have more judging their life and then deciding what they should or should not have?
- Do you feel bad that you have what you do when others do not have the basics?
- Do you have ongoing inner struggles about why you have more and others have less?
- Or why others have more and you have less?
- Do your own inner struggles help you find a balance?
- Can having more be an example and inspiration to others?
- Does having more help to hold open the frequency for others to follow?
- Do you observe the mind-patterns of those who have more to learn about your own mind-pattern?
- Is it possible to ever have too much or is too much a judgment?

When you are not used to having so much goodness in your life, you can be overwhelmed. This is often why homeless people do not take advantage of all the kind offers that others gave them. They may actually want something better for themselves, but they just do not feel like they deserve it. As strange as it sounds, you cannot give a person too much goodness at once. Too much positive is just as overwhelming as too much negative.

When I was first married to Stewart, I was not used to getting gifts. He gave me gifts for my birthday, Valentine's day, Mother's day, holidays, or just because. Every time he did this I was so surprised that I would cry. It took me a few years to get used to getting gifts. When you have low Self-Value, it is truly challenging to accept that you deserve much of anything. This is why having things is a challenge. You may want it in the worst way, but without that inner Self-Value, you are not going to keep it if indeed it can even get through to you.

This is why when you clean you interpret what nonphysical value it represents in the physical world. The main value of physical things is to outpicture the nonphysical. You must have the nonphysical attributes in place for them to be outpictured in the physical. When everything is in place, the physical must come to you. In this moment, most people have the negative nonphysical attributes firmly established within. Therefore the negative nonphysical is going to come to them. Remember that negative is not bad; it is what you need at the time to learn and grow. Now, you are changing everything up; pulling back the negative nonphysical attributes to your Oversoul so the positive nonphysical attributes can come forward. Money is not what you need to solve your issues. Mind-pattern is what you need and then your issues solve themselves.

- How challenging is it to put mind-pattern before money?
- How easy is it to say "if I only had the money, life would be different"?

- Do you think some people use not having the money as an easy excuse to not be motivated to change?
- For example, "I only make minimum wage, so I will never get what I want"?
- How challenged are you to build the mind-pattern that draws to you what you need, when you need it?
- How easy is it to be discouraged and depressed rather than motivated and enthused?
- Is it challenging to think that negative is not bad?
- If you do not like something, do you label it bad?
- If you need negative for your Soul Growth, are you willing to go through rough times?
- Are rough times bad?
- Do you think of every single physical item that is in your environment as an outpicturing of your nonphysical mind-patterns?
- Have you ever been positively overwhelmed to the point of tears?
- When you realize that you do deserve, is there a limit on what you deserve?
- Do you feel that you deserve unlimited fantastic experiences?
- Or only a finite number of fantastic experiences that are not too expensive and ostentatious because then you would start to feel guilty?
- What came to you that you did not have to use money to obtain?
- Do you want what you want for the correct reasons?

**Self-Abuse**

Not getting what you want is another form of Self-abuse. Sometimes, you manifest, but then you cannot accept. This is because of the need to Self-abuse and Self-punish. When you feel guilt, you are Self-abusing and Self-punishing. When you do not eat properly, or digest what you are eating, you are rejecting your life experiences. Even joyous occasions. I know people who cannot eat during celebratory events, for a myriad of reasons, from excitement to fear. Often, people feel guilty for feeling happy, because on some level they feel like they do not deserve to feel happy. Or, thinking about those people who are not happy makes them feel bad.

Not having money, watching everyone else enjoying life, feeling like you are sitting on the sidelines, all of these things feed your need to Self-abuse and Self-punish. No one ever does anything to you; this is challenging to remember.

When I did not have money I often worked several jobs at the same time. I have done the most menial jobs from a maid/cleaning person in a nursing home to dairy farming where I wore knee-high rubber boots because of the daily cow manure that I had to wade through. I am not too good to do what needs to be done, but on the other hand, I have elevated my Self out of working with body waste. Just because you can, does not mean that it is correct and beneficial. And, what is correct and beneficial for your Soul Growth may no longer be necessary once your Soul learns.

Knowing when to move on can be challenging because usually, you feel the pull of concluding where you are before the next opportunity is in full view. Or, you may have several opportunities so you may be confused which is the most correct and beneficial. Every choice you make is an opportunity to move forward, stay where you are or even go backwards. You will choose what your Soul needs to fine-tune your process. When you learn to ask first what is most correct and beneficial you may find the speed of your Soul Growth accelerating.

- Do some people stay with a lower income stream because they have an internal need to Self-punish and/or Self-abuse?

- Do people with this mind-pattern come out of childhoods where this was imprinted upon them?

- Is it easier to sit back and blame the system, or even a specific person or group of people, than to take responsibility for where you are in your life?

- If you blame others, what do you think happens to the growth of your Soul?

- Does blaming others give you the motivation to get out of your deficit position or provide another excuse to stay there?

- Are you willing to do the lowliest job if that is most correct and beneficial for your Soul Growth?

- Is there really any lowly job or is that a judgment?

- Why is one job considered low and another high?

- Why is physical work not as revered as mental work?

- Do you feel like sometimes you are sitting on the sidelines and watching the world go by?

- Are you Self-punishing?

- Did you sit on the sidelines as a child?

- Are you repeating childhood mind-patterns that need to be released?

- Have you been at joyous occasions and not been able to eat?

- Do you Self-abuse and/or Self-punish in some way or another?

- Do you have guilt when you have money?

- Is this a form of Self-abuse and Self-punishment for you?

- Is there a part of you that needs to feel bad, so you find a reason for this to happen?

- How skilled are you at manifesting the negative and accepting it?

It is challenging to do the correct thing for the correct reason in the correct timing. When it comes to increasing your personal wealth, if you intend to keep it, then this is an especially important rule to follow. And, this may be why you do not have the wealth that you want. You need to accumulate/acquire it for the correct reasons. Once you have it you must have the correct mind-pattern in place to keep it. Finally, the timing must be correct because you do not consciously know how it will affect your life and or the lives around you.

People who are born into wealth already have that mind-pattern in place. Just like any mind-pattern, the wealth mind-pattern is also generational. You never hear anything about the global elite being spoiled or spoiling their children. Yet, in our income class, we are told constantly that you have to work hard for what you get; if you get what you want you are spoiled; if you give too much time to your children then you are hovering over them and they will never grow up; if you give too much material things then they will take everything for granted, not appreciate it, and expect the world to give them everything.

Even in sports, academics and arts there are always competitions with winners and losers. In my opinion, simply showing up makes you a winner. Rather than participation to compete, it seems people could participate for the enjoyment of participation. Years ago I played a card game called Pinochle on a semi-regular basis with neighbors. I loved to play simply so I could play. Yes, I enjoyed winning but I primarily liked to play for fun. I liked to play tennis, but it wasn't to kill the other player. I liked to see how long we could keep the ball going back and forth. Even in school I was taught about the glass ceiling that exists and is practically impossible to break through. There is a general perception that race, sex and class can prevent your upward advancement.

All of these are easy mindsets to buy into that make you angry and resentful at others because you don't have what they have and you feel that it is impossible to get it. Ultimately, this is not about money. This is about division; another way to divide and thus conquer the masses. All the global handlers do is hold up a big mirror to tell our income class about our fears and insecurities. You look in the mirror and buy the lie which keeps everyone divided because you have less than others. It also keeps you in fear that you may lose what little bit of the pie you manage to scrape together. This is why I constantly tell you that no one ever does anything to you; everything that comes to you is a testament to the power of your own mind-pattern. This means all positive and all negative.

- Does it take a strong mind-pattern to keep wealth away from you when there is so much abundance around you?
- Do you have to be firmly anchored in the belief that you do not deserve, that you have little value and little Self-Worth to keep all the abundance that is around you, away from you?
- Is division of wealth more about divide and conquer than money?
- Do the global handlers keep you giving out anger at your peers so that anger can come back at you from your peers?
- Does this mean that the anger continues to circulate back and forth, thus never even touching the real instigators?
- If you have a mindset of advancement can anything hold you back?
- Can the meaning of advancement change?
- Is competition a positive or a negative?
- Is it more important that you show up than win?
- Do you even expect the world to support you like the global elite?

- How challenging is it to do the correct thing for the correct reason in the correct timing?
- How challenging is it to accumulate wealth for the correct things for the correct reasons in the correct timing?

You do not have to explain your Self to anyone for anything, unless specifically directed to by your Oversoul. This is one mind-pattern I have noticed about wealthy people. They never explain why they do what they do to anyone. In addition, they never justify what they bought and why they bought it. They never try to justify the price nor would they even try to tell you about what a good deal they got because that would mean that they were concerned about the price, which they are not. They do not talk about money because money is not an issue for them. Our class talks about money because it is an issue for us.

With all of this in mind, recognize that in your life, you do not have to explain your Self. People are going to think all kinds of things about you and say all kinds of things based on assumptions they make because of their own lives. You have to learn to not let them get to you in any way, shape or form. When you know who you are and what you are, the attacks slow down and someday, will actually stop. All these people do is give you the opportunity to either acquiesce to their demands or stay anchored in Self, Oversoul and God-Mind without giving your power away.

These people are opportunities that you can utilize to build your character and strength, or you can fall beneath their constant pummeling. This is why I tell you not to complain to others because most people do not really care about you, they only care about themselves. All of these mind-patterns have to do with your maintaining your Personal Power vs. giving it to others. When you have Personal Power, you have energy flow directly from Source. No one can take that from you unless you give it away. These people and situations are tests so you know if you are going to keep your Personal Power or give it away and let someone else have power over you.

- Are you going to only give your Personal Power to your Oversoul and God-Mind so they can return it to you, even stronger than before?
- Do you "ass-u-me" things about others?
- Does Money give you Personal Power/Energy or does Personal Power/Energy bring you money?
- Have you complained and made so much noise that you got what you wanted because the other person needed you to be quiet and go away?
- How easy is it to fall vs. maintain your Personal Power?
- Do people who try to take control of you put you in an emotional fight?
- Do you care what others think of you?
- Can you control what others think of you?
- Do you know people who are always talking about what they got on sale, or what a good deal they got?
- If you really have money, do you have to talk about it all the time?
- In the same way, do you have to tell people how good you are at something?
- If you are good at something do your actions speak for themselves?
- Do you think you can implement in your own life the mind-patterns of wealthy people?
- Do you focus on what you do not have?

- Does hoarding money create stagnation?
- Does spending money enhance cash flow when you have the correct mind-pattern?

While I'm not a fan of debt, it serves a purpose. When you have debt, you are saying that you expect money and you expect to be able to pay the debt. In its own way, debt helps get the money flowing. There is a fine line between using the money to flow and sinking in so deep you cannot get out. I have so many credit cards that if I used all of them I would owe enough to go to the moon and back. Yet, if you close out a credit card, it actually counts against you on your credit score.

I keep them only because I can't close them out. I got them because once you have 1-2 cards, then the card issuer raises the interest rates until they are prohibitive. As the rates on the old cards went up, I was offered new ones with lower rates. I do my best not to use them at all. And since I do have them, I use them to boost my mind-pattern to say that I can get all the money I want if it was most correct and beneficial.

A long time ago my father told me to carry a $100 bill in my wallet to help me feel wealthy. At that time $100 had more value than it does today. I used to do that for many years. He also told me that once he gave a $100 bill to a woman he was trying to help grow her prosperity mind-pattern. He told her to carry it and feel wealthy. A couple of weeks later he asked how she felt carrying the $100 bill and she said, "oh, I spent it on pizza for me and my kids". Money is not about money. It is about mind-pattern.

- What do you think of carrying money around with you to give you that feeling of abundance?
- Do you think carrying it is enough or does it need to be spent and replenished?

- Can you use debt to impact you in a positive way?
- Is it a fine line between debt building you up and tearing you down?
- Why do you think you are not allowed to close out a credit card without it negatively impacting your credit score?

## AFFIRMATIONS—THE FREQUENCY OF ACCEPTANCE

Everyone looks for more energy, deeper Source connections and more money, all different layers of the same thing. Surprisingly, you may be more challenged to accept these 3 things than to create them. This is a greater conundrum than most people realize, heavily influenced by deep Self and societal programming.

*I accept that I chose to be here on this planet in this moment in time and space.*

*I AM grateful for my opportunity for life.*

*I accept that I AM a fantastic and marvelous Soul.*

*I AM able to see my own inner Beauty.*

*I accept that I AM a multidimensional package.*

*I play my role on Earth as is most correct and beneficial.*

*I accept that we are All One.*

*I AM always connected to my Source.*

*I accept that I like sweet food in my life.*

*I allow sugar in the most correct and beneficial form/amount to energize my body.*

*I accept sweet experiences in my life without guilt.*

*I deserve to enjoy sweetness in my life.*

*I release the need to accept whatever the outer world wants to give me.*
*I AM learning discernment on what I accept.*

*I graciously accept whatever my Oversoul and God-Mind give me.*
*I accept the lessons of my life because they build fortitude and strength.*

*I accept what Source gives me without justification to the outer world.*
*All that Source gives me elevates, uplifts and allows my Soul to grow.*

*I accept help and advice from others when it is most correct and beneficial.*
*I stretch the frequency of positive abundance to increase the flow.*

*I accept the limitlessness of the God-Mind.*
*I accept the limitlessness of positive physical abundance on all levels.*

*I accept my responsibility to learn discernment.*
*I accept the consequences of my choices as learning opportunities.*

*I accept that there is no failure.*
*I accept the redirections of life as most correct and beneficial*
*for my Soul growth.*

*I accept the Intelligence that propels All of Creation.*
*I accept the intelligence of All That Exists.*

*I accept that I only save my Self.*
*I accept that the Earth can save her Self.*

*I accept my ability to discern Truth.*
*I easily see through programming traps.*

*I accept that everything comes from the same Source.*
*I AM filled with kindness and compassion for All.*

*I accept that each Soul comes to Earth for its unique Soul growth.*
*I release the need to judge, criticize and/or change the paths of other individuals.*

*I accept that I must tend to my own Soul business.*
*I objectively observe to best enhance my own Soul growth.*

*I accept the energy provided by Source to complete my mission and purpose here on Earth.*
*I accept daily energy and sustenance from Source as is most correct and beneficial.*

*I accept the money provided by Source as a physical representation of nonphysical energy.*
*I accept that I have what I need to help focus me on my mission and purpose.*

*I accept my ability to expand my nonphysical resources.*

*As my nonphysical resources grow, my physical resources grow as is most correct and beneficial.*

*I accept the strength of my mind to create.*

*I create with conscious discretion.*

*I accept my ability to reevaluate my creations.*

*I change my mental/emotional course as is most correct and beneficial.*

*I accept my ability to release nonproductive mind-patterns.*

*I allow Source to direct my expansion of positively productive mind-patterns.*

*I accept the transmutation of positively productive mind-patterns into physical resources.*

*As my mind-pattern corrects, my financial flow follows.*

*I accept my financial flow.*

*I allow my financial flow to expand as my positively productive mind-pattern expands.*

*I accept support from my Source on all levels.*

*I AM grateful for and accept positive support from wherever my Source gives it to me.*

# Increase Your Financial Stream

I have never met anyone yet who says they have too much money and they just don't know what to do with it all. You cannot have financial health unless your mind is in order. Financial issues direct your attention to what needs correction in your mind. Your mind must be in order to allow your financial stream to open up. When your finances are not flowing the way that you would like, you are directed to what needs correction in your mind.

You are learning to balance the left and right hemispheres of the brain so that what you do bring in does not overpower and destroy rather than help you. Too many people think that more money means their life immediately changes for the better. But too much money too fast often proves destructive instead of constructive. People with too much money for them to handle means the money proves to be their downfall instead of their upliftment.

You must build constructive mind-patterns that enhance what you need so when you get it, you are ready, open and receptive. You must also balance your brain so that you use your financial stream and it does not use you. As with all things, what at first glance looks like it should be easy, is a bit more complex. Building your mind-pattern step by step allows what you do need to come in a way that you can handle, accept, keep, and build upon.

- Can you visualize your Self with multiple income streams?
- Do you know where they would all come from?
- Have you ever received unexpected funds?
- Do you feel worthy of multiple income streams?
- Do you want to be here in this lifeline?
- Do you want to correct everything now so you don't have to come back?
- Does an attitude of not wanting to be here open or close your income stream?
- Do you resent the bills you have or are you grateful for them?
- Do you resent the corporations to which you send money every month?
- Or landlords or family members?
- What are you choosing to do that stops financial streams from coming to you?

I do not think that humanity will ever change the world. When you observe all the various levels of existence, you can understand why they are needed for the Soul-Personality to grow. Even though you are indoctrinated into the theory of overpopulation, there are always Souls waiting for the opportunity to come in. They want to experience this planet as it is for the lessons that are unique and can only be found here. Here, there is abject poverty, where people do not have even basic necessities such as food, water and shelter all the way up to people who have material wealth beyond the imagination of most people.

- If this planet changes, then where will they go to get the lessons that their Souls need?

- What is the mind-pattern of someone who would enter this life without even the basics?
- What is the mind-pattern of someone who has an overabundance of material wealth?
- Why would he/she hold onto this abundance without sharing it?
- Why are there so many options in between material poverty and material overabundance?
- Does the person with material poverty work as hard as the person with material wealth?
- Is the work of one person more valuable than the work of another?
- Is the output of each person important?
- Is the responsibility of the hunter providing for his/her family the same as a CEO of a corporation?
- Is the responsibility of the mother looking for clean water for her child the same as an engineer designing a city waterworks for an entire town?
- Is one person more valuable than the next?
- Do you think lifelines build one upon the other?
- What might a hunter choose in his/her next lifeline?
- Or a mother looking for clean water for her child choose in her next lifeline?
- How big of a step can each person handle from one lifeline to another?
- How big of a step can you handle in this lifeline?

I think a lot about finances because the economic climate is not really conducive to small business as it once was. While no one says you can't be a small business owner, there are a lot of obstacles that do their best to stop small business beginnings as well as growth. But, this is like all other challenges. Think about the obstacles that make it difficult for you to be physically healthy. In the same way, there are a billion obstacles that make it difficult for you to be financially healthy. Instead of giving in, you have to use the obstacles to make your mind-pattern strong enough to move over, through and/or past these obstacles.

• Why do you think people keep coming back to this Earth plane?

Many want to say that it is the "Law of Karma." But really, it is more than that. You keep coming back because you have not exhausted all the lessons that this Earth plane has to offer. Generally, you stay in the same family lineage because you helped to mess it up and now you help to correct it. Or, perhaps you helped make it prosperous and now you get to reap the rewards. If your metaphorical clothes fit, then there is no need to change them. And in this reality, obstacles either make you or break you. When they break you, you get simpler and simpler chances which narrow your focus until you get the lesson. Keep in mind that "simple" does not mean "easy".

You already know this reality, so there is no point to move on to another one before you have extracted all the knowledge that you need from here. For example, if you misuse money, maybe you choose a life stream where there is no money at all. Perhaps you then choose a very poor country without food, water and/or adequate shelter. Or maybe you wind up in a country like this because you believe that money is evil, or you are determined to live off the grid without understanding that all things come from One Source. Maybe you dreamed what life would be like in so-called simpler times, so your mind-pattern drew you to such a time period. Why you choose your lifestyle and lessons is truly unique based upon what your Soul-Personality needs. These experiences are food for your Soul in the same way there is food for your body.

- Why do people attach such negativity to money?
- Do you perceive your current financial obstacle course doable or overwhelming?
- If you perceive it as doable do you have days where you feel overwhelmed?
- Is the understanding of money important enough to keep you coming back into this reality?
- Do you think you are ready to move off of this Earth Plane?
- Do you think you have exhausted all that it has to teach you?

## No Expectations

I often read about how to raise your children without expectations. Young people are berated in these articles because they expect to be given everything. These stories make the young people feel bad, the parents feel bad, and parents make the decision to be tougher on their kids. Yet, a lot of the berating because they got this or that handed to them is exactly how I raised my sons without the negative effects. This is why I tell you to do the opposite of whatever mainstream is pushing. Keep in mind the children of the global elite as you read through this next section.

Basically, all the information says that the millennials are spoiled and have been given too much, therefore they don't want to work and they expect everything to be given to them. My two sons were very fortunate in their raising because they always got what they wanted. I wanted them to have this mind-pattern that they could have or do whatever they wanted. However, together we made choices about what they really wanted so they also learned discernment. I never told them no, we can't afford this; you can't have that. Instead, together we evaluated what they would or would not use and why; if something was really worthy of its price; how long they would use something if it was purchased, and so forth.

We also discussed how the most important thing we have as a family is each other. That our home, vehicles, possessions would mean nothing if each person was alone with his/her things. We discussed how each person was wanted, loved, cared for and how much we like our things but if we had to choose between each other and our things, the family won out.

In addition, my sons are not sports-minded so they witnessed a lot of children get awards, but they never received any. They were disappointed because they loved the glitz of the big golden statues. When they went to their Adventist school, those with high academic ratings were given paper awards so my sons were excited to get these. Children like being acknowledged. This enhances their Self-Value. Those who never win and are never acknowledged have issues. Everyone is good at something. Everyone needs to be acknowledged as a child, in my opinion.

Teaching your children that you can't have everything; you can't always win so don't expect it is a huge difference in the way the children of the masses are raised vs. the global elite's children. You most likely were raised with the "you can't have everything" mentality and "you aren't always the best" and "you aren't always going to win, so don't expect to". Sometimes these are told directly to your face; other times you simply get that via osmosis.

Your financial issues today are a result of your upbringing. On a very deep cellular level, you know your place in this society. This is what you have to extricate out of you. And the more years you have living this lie, the more challenging it is to uproot it from your cellular structure.

- Have you observed what you are told vs. how you see the children of the global elite are raised?
- Are you okay with they can have it but I can't type of mentality?

- From an Oversoul level, why would one family have billions of dollars while some families don't even have clean drinking water?

- If the global elite pooled their resources that everyone could have the basics?

- If the global elite pooled their resources to provide the basics for everyone, then what would happen to the Souls who need the experience of abject poverty?

- Do poor people work as hard as the global elite?

- Should the poor be compensated for their labors?

- Is the street sweeper as important as the CEO of the biggest corporation?

- Why do people see such disparity and say that it is okay?

- What happens if you give the basic necessities to the person in need of food, water, clothing and shelter before he/she is ready?

- Why wouldn't they be ready?

Here are the primary reasons why most people do not have money:

### *You don't feel worthy.*

### *You feel guilty.*

Poor people are poor because they need the lesson. The lessons vary from person to person from having money in one life stream and not appreciating it, to taking it away from others, to not having the Self-Value to have even the basics. Others need the opportunity to figure out what you are figuring out. This doesn't make it easy, but it does mean that once you get it you don't forget it. And if you do, then you find your Self repeatedly in the same position until the lesson really sticks.

When I was farming in the high mountain desert of Eastern Washington State, my house water was from a community well that was originally drilled to support 30 homes. By the time I was farming in the area, there were almost 90 homes on the well. This meant that we did run out of water from time to time, especially in the summer when temperatures could reach well over 100°F. I truly learned to appreciate water. Water represents emotions. These were extremely volatile times for me, so no wonder my external "well went dry" when my internal "well went dry".

- When you see photos of people carrying water, looking for water, bathing in dirty water, what do you see?
- Do you put your Self in their situation and think about how you would feel?
- Does this make you want to correct it for them?
- Do you think about the Golden Rule, Do unto others as I would have done unto me?
- Do you think about how you would want people to help you if you were in that situation?
- Do you think about the next step after the Golden Rule, which I tell you is, Do unto others as others would have done unto them?
- Do you go to the Oversoul level to see why they are in this situation?
- Do you think about how you know another way of life, but these people do not?
- Is this like aliens who observe but do not interfere?
- Is helping people get something so basic as water, before they are ready for that help, is interfering?
- Can your heart be in the correct place but your logical thinking is not?

- Can your logical thinking be in the correct place but your heart is not?

The reason you need to consider all of these ideas when observing others is because when you allow your financial assets to grow, you have to deal with everyone around you. Remember, you are moving out of the pack mentality. If you are with a pack of dogs, you fight to see who is the strongest and he/she becomes the leader of the pack. When you realize that people operated first from the Animal Mind, then you begin to see people for who they are vs. who you want them to be. You see each person as a unique individual instead of putting your Self in their place.

Knowing what I know, I really don't want to walk 20 miles to find water. But if I didn't know any better, and that was my life, I would just accept that this is the way life is. You cannot judge the life experience of another once you move above the Animal Mind. You can observe it and understand it with permission via the Oversoul level. Judging can only come from Source.

As your financial stream increases, you need Self-Value to know that you earned it. Therefore you use your finances as determined via the Oversoul level. If you increase your income stream and you think about the person who has to walk 20 miles for water, you have to make choices:

- Do I dig a well for that person?
- If I do, does this mean that I have to do without?
- Do I let that person walk for his/her water and take a luxury vacation?

Recognize how easy it is to get pulled into feeling guilty. The person who has to walk for the 20 miles to get water does not even know you exist; does not understand the possibilities, or maybe has heard that some people don't have to do such things. But that person has come here for a reason. And when that person learns the lessons, the mind-pattern of that person will pull what he/she needs. Maybe, water will be discovered near where the person lives; maybe a huge company with tons of money will show up and pipe the water to his/her home. You cannot take away the lessons of others without consequences for Self. You cannot judge their life experiences as good or bad. Their life experiences are what they need for Soul-growth.

- Is it better to not have more money so you do not have to feel guilty?
- When your income stream increases, do you then attract more expenses so you do not have to feel guilty?
- Do you give away your money so you don't feel guilty?
- Do you buy friendship with money?
- Do you give money to those with less than so you can feel more than?
- Do you give it to big corporate charities that do not need it, thus you feel angry instead of guilty?
- Do you get angry at friends and family who want what you have rather than feel guilty for not giving it to them?
- How many ways can guilt affect your income stream?
- Does guilt ever positively affect your income stream?

People limit their possible income streams, for example, by thinking about winning the lottery. They are so narrow-focused that they think this is the only way that their income is going to exponentially increase. I know one woman who won $1 million when the lottery was first implemented in Washington State almost 40 years ago. Most people do not know even one person who ever won the lottery, yet they continue to put their faith in what they consider something tangible rather than their Oversoul and God-Mind. If you can only think of gambling as a way to open up your income stream, you automatically close off other possibilities.

Money represents energy. You are learning how to open your energy flow on all levels. And, not only open the flow, but accept that which you open up. Most likely, you know how to open the negative flow as well as you accept and receive the negative. While negative is rich with experience, you are now learning to do the opposite.

Just as you are learning to open up your positive energy flow step by step, the global handlers close society down step by step. For example, the upper middle class have one income level. Middle class has another income level. Lower class has another. Below this are the poorest who have comparatively nothing materialistically. Each class lives within its own section of society, from homes to available places to shop. If you live above your means you are looked down upon by your social strata. Or, if you climb to the next social strata, you are not too welcomed by the one you left and maybe not too welcomed by the one you are entering.

As a management tool, these classes help the global handlers know how to target you to keep you producing but not elevating, or moving just enough to make you think you are getting somewhere even when you are not. For example, minimum wage is increased by fifty cents or even one or two dollars every so often. Then, some benefits are taken away or your paycheck deductibles are increased. They may give you something else, like childcare in the workplace or an extra day off.

- Doesn't this confuse, depress and disturb you further so you do not know if you are getting ahead or only think you are getting ahead?

- When you are confused, depressed and disturbed are you easier to control?

- If you can't focus on your own life because it is too confusing, then why not have a pretend life?

- Is pretending to be a healer, channeler, Reiki master, different gender, race or species easier to focus on than your day-to-day reality?
- When you do open up your money flow, does something happen to take it, like an unexpected medical, home repair, or auto bill?
- Do you think there are general frequencies that target anyone who opens up his/her financial flow?
- Do challenges make you more discerning?
- Do challenges keep you more focused?
- Do challenges make you consider giving up but then force you to define what giving up means?
- Is it healthy for those in power if too many people elevate?
- Why is money so darn important anyway?

Some people think they shouldn't have it; others think they should not only have theirs, but yours too. Money is a physical representation of energy that you feel you have nonphysically expended. You can expend a lot of energy but not feel that you are worthy of physical compensation. This is why there even is a bottom of the pyramid. If you are on the level above the bottom, you can look down and appreciate how much better off you are. If you look up, you can see that there is room for growth.

If you are on the bottom and you suddenly jump to the top, you would not know how to handle that kind of material wealth. You would take care of your basic, immediate needs but then your real issues would begin.

- How would you decide what to do with the rest of your money?
- If you hire people to help you, would they help you or steal from you?

- Why is it that people constantly try to take yours instead of being satisfied with what they have?
- Do you have a tendency to give too much and not keep enough for you?
- What can you do to stop that mind-pattern that allows people to steal from you?
- What else can they steal from you besides money?
- Can others take from you without your permission?
- Do you think you have unconsciously taken from others without their permission?
- Are you okay with moving up the pyramid at your current pace?
- If you moved faster, would this mean more challenging lessons?
- Would you want the responsibility of running the world or being a billionaire?

I finally started clearing the top of my desk. I have a habit of accumulating too many papers that need to be tossed. I am clearing and cleaning in the corners of places; drawers; freezers; bits and pieces here and there. My desk represents my finances. And if it is cluttered and tangled, then my finances can't get to me, because somewhere in my mind is clutter and entanglement. I haven't finished my desk, but I am picking away at it like I am other areas of my life. The cleaning and clearing of clutter and entanglements has been easy. I feel better about my Self because I've gotten quite of bit of house cleaning done. The smoother I can make my outer life the smoother the flow of my mind-pattern.

When my house is in order, I feel better. This improves my energy flow which in turn improves my financial flow. I was speaking to a young man a few days ago who just got a new job. At his old job, he was not treated with much respect. There was junk food available, and he was not allowed to take tips from his customers. At his new job, he is treated with respect, he has access to quality food at excellent prices, and he can take tips from customers. This is a giant upgrade in mind-pattern. The better he feels about him Self, the better the outer world treats him and rewards him. This is the way in all of life. The better you feel about your Self, the better you are treated and rewarded.

Like mice in a maze, when you find the correct path, you get a reward. When you are off-course, you are not rewarded. The more frustrated you get, the further the reward because you don't feel good about you so your mind-pattern does not let anything positive come back to you. This is a weird type of loop upon which you can easily find your Self. You have to then go back to doing the opposite of what you feel like doing to change the focus.

- What do you do to feel better about your Self?
- Does feeling better about your Self improves your financial flow?
- What kinds of rewards have you received from the outer world when you were on-course?
- What represents finances in your life, a desk, wallet, purse, drawer?
- Is the physical area where you take care of your finances neat and orderly, or cluttered and disheveled?
- When you feel financially discouraged, is it easy to get on a loop that feeds it Self in a negative way?
- When/if this happens, how do you get off of the negative loop?

Yesterday I bagged up some leftover vegetables from my son's salad that I was saving to eat later. As I was bagging it up, my mind went to what Stewart would say. In his family, they would throw things like this away. In my family, we saved everything. We used to wash the foil for re-use, save wrapping paper and ribbons/bows, turn off the lights if no one was in the room and did whatever we could to lower our expenditures. Stewart says my family was cheap. I felt like we were being economical.

I think about this a lot because there are some things I have quit doing. Like washing out every bottle of liquid soap until there are absolutely no bubbles inside, showing that every speck of liquid soap is absolutely gone. I've quit washing foil for re-use but big pieces that can be used again, are definitely used again. I contemplate whether this is lack mentality or respectful mentality of what I have.

When I was in the Cottian Alps and spending time with my family there, I see that they are exactly like I am. In fact, when my cousin and I went on a picnic where we ate chicken, she collected all the bones to take home to her dogs. They are extremely conservative in how they monitor what they have. I understand why. Up in the mountains, you just don't run into town to get what you want. You either make it, find it, save it, or do without. My mother's family was very poor growing up, but she liked to say that during the depression when other families were hungry and without shelter, that her family always had food and a home.

When I moved to New York, I found that I could get 18 fresh bagels for $5 so I bought them for less money and effort than I could make them for. I used to make all of my clothes growing up, but in my adult years, I found I could purchase clothes cheaper than I could even purchase material for them. I am still pretty conservative. Even washing dishes, I wash the least dirtiest pot, then the next until I reach the final dirtiest pot.

As I observe the global elite, I wonder if they throw everything out. They know they can always get more, any time, any place, from anywhere.

- Are they wasteful or do they have the mind-pattern that says they always will have what they need and what they want?

- Does my family have a poor mentality or a mentality that is respectful of what they do have?
- Do you think the Earth really has limited resources or is this another way of creating a lack mentality?
- If everything we have comes from the Earth, then won't everything eventually go back to the Earth?
- Why do people choose to be born in overcrowded cities with inaccessible goods and services or allow garbage and waste to accumulate in the streets?
- Why do others choose to be born up in the mountains or out in the desert or in the countryside where they have to make everything or do without?
- Does throwing out what you don't use or need mean that you trust Source to provide?
- Does keeping and utilizing all the bits and pieces mean that you respect all that you have?
- Is there a balance?
- Is an opulent mind-pattern a throwaway mentality?

## Earth Has More Than Enough

The Earth has more than enough to sustain its populations or the populations would not be here. By populations, I mean animals, flora, fauna, and everything that exists here. Just today I read about a new product that could replace plastic water bottles made from chloride and brown algae extract. It is made to be eaten. I don't think my mind saw this one coming. There must be tons of other things that have not been brought into existence yet to solve this issue or that issue.

Opulence is all around, but you don't see it, just like I didn't see the edible water bottle concept until someone else brought it into this reality. I read about someone in a poor country taking old tires to make shoes; and one person who made a bicycle, including the tires, completely out of wood. A man in New York City waits in line for people; in fact, he now employs about 20 other people who also wait in line. These people are all bringing opulence into their mind-patterns.

When I was the director of an art gallery, I found a few simple crafts that I could make and I knew I could sell, but the issue was that I was not passionate about making these things. I bought the materials and never made them. What I really loved to do was my hardanger embroidery. Hours and hours to create magnificent pieces. But I knew that no one would ever pay me enough for the hours that I put in, so I priced them low enough to sell but then I felt resentment for not being adequately compensated for my time.

I've come a long way in Self-Value, but I honestly can say that I don't feel I have an opulent mind-pattern. One of my stepsons rents airplanes and helicopters to wealthy clients. One client spends $12,500 every day to rent a helicopter that picks him up at his home and drops him off at his office building. Every day! This is definitely an opulent mind-pattern.

- But is his expenditure wasteful?
- Is this a throwaway mentality?
- Do you think he cares about using up the world's fossil fuel resources?
- Are people who use private planes wasteful with a throwaway mentality or do they have opulent mind-patterns?
- Are you imprinted to feel guilty for any vehicle that uses less than 50 miles per gallon on fossil fuel?
- Is not being wasteful a mind-control trick by the global elite to keep you in a limiting loop?
- Should you develop a throwaway mentality to open your door to opulence?

- Are limited resources another way to tell you that you can't have what you want while the global elite has unlimited resources?

- Do you think the global elite recycles or cares about recycling?

- Is recycling another mind-control program that the global elite set in motion and the populace picked up?

- Do you think the global elite clip coupons?

Sometimes because you are so close to you, you must step back to see what is really happening. You have to go beyond your own income strata so you can understand it. You have to look beneath and above. Sometimes, you need an extreme reference point, or what may feel like an extreme reference point, so you can even begin thinking about questions to ask. Questions/affirmations are energetic tools that help you dig within your own energy field. Questions/affirmations are color, tone and archetypes that combine into something that you can actually use to create change.

You literally use these to dig around inside of Self. This is why new thoughts, ideas, comments, questions and yes, answers, come to the surface the more we come together and explore. The group mind here is focused on the same challenge because everybody here has the same challenge. We have this huge boulder sitting amongst us all that we are trying to remove so we can see what is underneath it. We have to be prepared for whatever we find. You might loosen up a corner; I loosen up a corner, and together we literally get that boulder rocking and rolling back and forth until we can roll it right out of way.

The Queen of England employs a keeper of the swans. She owns all the swans in the United Kingdom and only the Queen can eat swan. She actually has someone who goes through the United Kingdom counting swans. That is an opulent mind-pattern.

I am technically challenged, I have had a lot of trouble with the people who create/run my website since its inception decades ago. The Internet is a blessing because it opens up my market. Yet, it comes with the dark side that can also destroy. This is the same thing with your own income stream. You never really know how it is going to come to you. But, if you aren't ready, it can take you down as fast as it can take you up. The power people know how to handle money because they understand and can handle energy. This does not make them good or bad; positive or negative. They are excellent at what they do, even if you don't agree with how they do it.

- Can you observe people with opulent mind-patterns without judging them?
- Is your understanding of the global elite growing?
- Are you less reactive and more investigative?
- Are you learning how to apply what you need to do or not do in your own life by observing them?
- Are you okay that they exist?
- Are you okay that poor people exist?
- Are you okay that you cannot save the world?
- Do you give money and things away because you don't Self-Value?
- Or because you feel guilty that you have something that someone else doesn't?
- Can you do tough love of withholding what others want because that is what is most correct and beneficial for all involved?
- Can you enjoy an opulent life while you know others are suffering?
- Are you respectful of the paths of others and the way they need to learn their lessons?

334 • Heights of Wealth

Sometimes you must be willing to go backward so you can go forward. There are so many people here who have gone back to their origins, living at home with parents. To some, this may at first feel like a failure because they couldn't make it on their own. However, the global elite never leave home. But they set the masses up to do exactly this. The imprinting of failure when you return home is high, not only externally, but how you view your Self. When I lived on the East Coast, there are more family generations living together. When I told this to people on the West Coast, where families are generally smaller, I could hear the judgment in the voices of those to whom I told this.

Economically, it makes a lot of sense to live together, so another reason why the global elite doesn't want you living with family. Not only do you give up emotional/mental/spiritual support when you don't live with family, but you buy more. When you live together, you can share cars, kitchen appliances, utilities and more. You pool your resources so that ultimately everyone has more with fewer expenditures.

When I lived in Washington State, I visited a Hutterite Colony. The Hutterites are an offshoot of the Amish/Mennonites. Within these colonies, people are definitely interdependent. What I like about the Hutterites is the way they pool economic resources. They do not reject the outside world in the same way the Amish do and are more communal than the Mennonites. The Hutterites do not have kitchens in their homes; instead, each colony has a huge communal kitchen with commercial appliances. Instead of a laundry room in each home, they have a building with beautiful commercial appliances.

The colony I visited had 22 families. So, instead of 22 washers, dryers, refrigerators, stoves/ovens, dishwashers, kitchen cabinets, laundry rooms, the colony invests in commercial appliances. This saves a lot of money for the colony but takes away a lot from the global elite. The women share in the laundry/cooking chores on a rotating basis. Great meals, home grown food, laundry done and you don't have to do it alone and all the time.

In the same way, they combine farming equipment expenditures. Unless you are a farmer, you may not be able to appreciate the value, but much farm equipment sells for over $100,000. To set up a dairy barn you need about one million dollars. Instead of having many farmers heavy in debt to make this happen, they communally own bigger tractors and other pieces of farm equipment as well as larger dairies. This means millions of dollars are not going into the pockets of the global elite. Each colony is much more economically stable because of their communal arrangement.

- How much more would the elite make if these colonies were broken apart?
- How much more stress on each family because now they are all alone?
- How much more physical workload without their interdependence on each other?
- Are the elite better off if they can focus you on independence vs. interdependence?
- Are the elite better off to keep you feuding amongst one another rather than helping each other?
- Why do the elite focus you on helping those beneath you economically instead of those who are on par with you economically?
- Who benefits economically for each failed colony?
- What are the weaknesses of the colonies and how best to strengthen the weaknesses?
- Do you think the global elite work on dividing the strongest or weakest families first?
- Does weakening families increase the financial stream of the global elite?

When your outer environment is cluttered up, usually this is because there is something you don't want to look at. When I start to worry about my finances, the condition of my desk begins to deteriorate. I don't want to look at what is going on, but I need to face my desk and clean it up. As I clean up my desk I pick through the clutter of my mind. Most people don't clean up external clutter because they are so accustomed to it that they don't see it. It is easy to have one piece, 2 pieces, 4 pieces, 8 pieces of clutter sitting around. Many people do this with their cars, which represent your path in life. Both of my sons have told me at various times that people who get in their vehicles say they are surprised at how neat and clean their vehicles are.

- How many people's vehicles have you gotten into and can't even find a place to put your feet?
- Is your vehicle this way?
- A car is your path in life, so why would that be cluttered?
- How does your entire home get cluttered?
- What is the mind-pattern of the global elite who have housekeepers and staff to keep their environments clutter free?
- Do you think the homes of the global elite are ever cluttered?
- How does moving into discomfort help you to improve your financial stream?

Your vehicle represents your path in life. The clutter represents what prevents you from success on your path in life. As you clean it out, think about what each piece of debris represents. As you toss the debris, toss the mind-pattern that supports the debris. There are so many ways that you can clear your path, but few want to take the time to actually do the work. Maybe you don't have the motivation or the energy at the moment, but when the mind-pattern is aligned, the motivation and energy suddenly appear.

When you know your mind-pattern is not in alignment, then you have to force the alignment until everything clicks in. All of this is about releasing the need to Self-sabotage. You know what you need to do; you can see it; you may even feel guilty that you aren't doing it and it doesn't cost anything. I often have thought this about poor areas. Often the yards are messy, the houses are in disrepair, and the area is usually littered with garbage. It costs nothing to very little to clean, weed, paint, pick up garbage.

- Where is the pride of the people?
- Have you looked at seemingly downtrodden people and thought the same thing?
- If they don't have food, why don't they plant vegetable gardens?
- What is in their mind-pattern that they don't think about these foundational activities that might markedly improve their lives?
- Why are they not motivated to clean and clear out the garbage?
- Why are you not cleaning and clearing?
- Why are you not exercising your physical body?
- Why are you not exercising your mind?
- Would all of these things help your financial stream?
- Would these activities pave the way for the poor and downtrodden to open their financial streams?
- Do these activities open the energetic flow?
- How do unmotivated, downtrodden and depressed people change their lives?
- If they live in the "Eternal Now" how do they change that when they simply struggle from day to day without basic food/water/shelter?

- Do you feel like you are destined to remain in your financial stream forever?

I have been slowly but surely picking my way through the accumulated extra paperwork on my desk. Today I threw out a stack of magazines and cleared out a few folders. As much as I have thrown out, I doubt the average person would even notice. However, I am feeling better; cleaner; clearer; lighter. I think some days I get discouraged because there are always more bills waiting to be paid. This is federal tax month here in the US. I was thinking about how all year long I want to make money, but when it's income tax time, I'm holding my breath hoping I don't owe taxes, or at least not too much or maybe I'll even get a refund. Refunds mean you didn't make money last year, so you get some of your pre-paid taxes back.

- Isn't this another way to sabotage?

The year we took a tour group to France, we took in a lot of money for the trip, which pushed our income into a higher tax bracket. We paid that money out to cover the expenses, so it wasn't really income in my opinion, but we had to still say it was for the few minutes that it passed through our accounts. That learning experience meant I had to pay $20,000.00 in taxes that year. 2008. I borrowed against the equity in my home to do it and I still haven't paid it off yet. This is why we only take our fees and have you pay the rest to everybody else on our group tours. I learned the hard way.

The truly working poor get refunds. They have worked, not earned much money, so now let's give them back what they shouldn't have paid in the first place.

I hire a bookkeeper to keep my records in order and let me know every month when my $1500 monthly tax payment is due. I pray every month that the money will be there when the automatic payment is taken. I pay the bookkeeper every month to keep me on task and then

I have a CPA that lets me pay her fees off over a few months the first of the year.

The system is not set up for me, the small business person. I am allowed to be a small business owner, but the system is in place to do everything it can to keep me from succeeding. Which means I have to do my mental work to keep my Self going. I have a lot of opportunities to fail. I have a lot of opportunities to succeed. The global handlers do everything they can to see that I fail. I do everything that I can to ensure my success.

- Do you feel that the taxes in your country are designed to keep you subjugated to the global elite?
- Do you feel the services you receive in return are justification for the taxes that you pay?
- Do you feel like taxes are part of the obstacle course that you must surpass to succeed?
- Do you try to avoid even talking about taxes?
- Are taxes something that you don't want to see?
- Are you grateful for the ability to pay your taxes?
- Do taxes feed the system that supports you?

Many people have the dream of working for themselves. I think this is a great dream, but you have to consider the practical sides. To me, this is another "grass is greener on the other side of the fence" scenario. You may think you have a lot of freedom, but in many ways, you have less. When you are the owner, you never get away. There is always something to be done; always something you want to invest in; a project you want to bring to fruition that needs funding; you have to pay all your own taxes and healthcare; you don't have an automatic retirement plan or stock options; you take all the risk and responsibility. If you have employees, it is up to you to make sure that you are solvent and can meet payroll so they can meet their obligations. There are a lot of reasons why not to be Self-employed.

There are as many reasons why to be Self-employed, but the "why" reasons are shrinking from the viewpoint of the global handlers. They do not tell you that you can't be in business, but they continually take away the rights of small business owners, or make you pay more for rights you used to have for free.

When I was appointed by the Governor's Office of the State of Washington in the late 1980's as a small business representative to testify before the Washington State Legislature, I was thrilled. And testify, I did. I spoke very much from the heart. I was passionate about the plight of small business people, not only my own, but my colleagues and peers who comprised this special council. We all had very real concerns specific to our own unique businesses.

One day, I woke up when I heard someone say that the bill we were testifying against had been with a particular office for the past year. It was being written, reviewed and rewritten by staff, attorneys, legislators and so forth for one year. The bill was thicker than a Bible. And in that one moment, I realized, that if that much time, effort and money had already gone into that bill, that my puny, heart-felt testimony, and that of my colleagues, was really not going to matter one iota. The bill was going to be passed. But, the legislature could go on record saying that they had heard from small business people, had taken all the testimonies into consideration, and still decided it was in the best interest to pass the bill. I really was deflated when I made that realization. I learned a lot about the system and government in general during my time on this Council.

I have watched how the government has shut down small business through the years, again, not by telling you no but by increasing taxation and making compliance astronomically unaffordable to many industries. In the dairy industry, they offered millions of dollars to not produce so much milk. This was appealing to farmers with bad management practices as well as older farmers, those with ill health, or those who wanted to take their several million dollars and run. This was the beginning of the end of the small farmer.

Most small gas station owners were forced out in the 1980s-90s when new environmental regulations were put into place, forcing them to dig up old tanks and replace them with new tanks. This not only meant huge loans to make this happen, but no income stream while this was in process. And so on. I can cite more stories, but this gives you the idea. No one says you can't but they make it pretty darned challenging for you to say why you can. Now, it might be best to combine the best of both worlds. Work for a larger employer so you have all the benefits and develop your own small business on the side.

I actually think small business should be split into another branch called "micro –business". Here is the definition of small business from the US Small Business Association's website:

> Small business size standards define the largest that a business concern, together with its affiliates, may be and yet qualify as a small business concern for SBA and most other federal programs. SBA has established two widely used size standards – 500 employees for most manufacturing and mining industries and $7.5 million in average annual receipts for many nonmanufacturing industries.
>
> https://www.sba.gov/contracting/getting-started-contractor/make-sure-you-meet-sba-size-standards/summary-size-standards-industry-sector

According to the Small Business Administration, a small business person such as me does not fit these parameters, or even come close.

- Have you ever wanted to be Self-employed?
- Have you ever been, but you are not now?
- What do you consider to be the plus side of Self-employment?
- Have you looked at the negatives, or only dreamed about the positives?

- What business would you like to be in?
- If you are employed by others, what are your biggest complaints?
- Have you looked at the issues from the company's viewpoint?
- Have you considered working for someone else plus have your own business on the side?
- Did you realize how big the US government definition of small business is?
- Is your mind-pattern big enough to be a small business owner?

A couple of years ago, someone I know told me the story of going to the family home of her boyfriend. The boyfriend's family is fairly wealthy. The event was a picnic and the meal was served on plastic plates that were then discarded. Now, apparently these plastic plates weren't the kind you get from the supermarket where you spend $5.00 and get 50 plates. These were thick, heavy duty plates. So, as her boyfriend's family finished eating and threw the plates away, this person was digging through the trash, retrieving the plates, and washing them to take home. I can only imagine what the family thought about this action. While this person thought she was being thrifty and was thrilled with her find, you have to think about her mind-pattern that allowed her to do this.

- Is this being thrifty or Self-limiting?

One person told me about her friend that spent thousands of dollars on designer clothes, wore them once, and then invited her over to go through these clothes. Brand new, designer clothes, my friend said, for only about $100 each. So she got thousands of dollars of clothes for only a few hundred dollars. If the friend can afford to do this, I wondered why she would not give her unwanted clothes away.

There is an old saying "Penny-wise, pound-foolish". One summer, while visiting my family in Missouri, one of my uncles refused to get fuel at a close gas station because he had seen one down the road for 1 cent per gallon cheaper. 1 cent! And when my mother was living, he would take her car to the car wash (that was nice) but then he made her pay him the amount: $1.50. My family would have garage sales, invite each other and sell their old possessions to one another. Because of my upbringing, I've really had to examine what I do to stop/limit my income stream.

- How many ways do you stop/limit your financial stream?
- How many times are finances coming your way, but there is a part of you that prevents the money from actually reaching you?
- Have you ever gone through someone's garbage and been thrilled with your find?
- Is this a mind-pattern that opens financial streams?
- Can the saying "penny-wise, pound-foolish" be applied to you?
- How do you balance thrifty with Opulence?
- Is opulence wasteful and indulgent or telling Source you trust It to provide?
- If someone else was cleaning out your house, what percentage of your things would get tossed?
- If you were cleaning out your home to move, what percentage of your things would you toss?

I grew up with the constant reminder that "money doesn't grow on trees, you know." I don't know if I heard this from my parents, peers, teachers, or other adults, I just know that was definitely imprinted deep into my subconscious mind. Maybe it was said on television programs. I can remember being fascinated by money tree plants as a child. I couldn't believe that there was actually a plant called a money tree. I really loved the seed pods that came on every autumn. Maybe people who don't think so much about money really do have a mental money tree mind-pattern. No matter how much they pluck from the tree, it still comes back.

Today, I was thinking about how much discretion I've learned regarding money through the years. I've had a lot of painful money lessons, but I have been thinking about the doors that open and the doors that close when it comes to finances. I had a friend from a family that was relatively well off. Her father refused to eat leftovers. They were either thrown away, given to the dog, or sometimes the mother and my friend had them for lunch. But I was under the impression that most often, leftovers were thrown away. My friend would often tell me after seeing her parents that her father had insisted on giving her $1000.00 for pocket money; he insisted on buying her this beautiful emerald necklace and so on.

Sometimes, I asked her to pick something up for me since I was more tied to my home via family and work. The minute she walked in my door with my items, she had the receipt out and wanted payment immediately. She was very clear about her expectations; almost brutally clear. I had other friends at the time who also picked up things for me from time to time, and I picked up things for them. Sooner or later we would gather up our receipts and decide who owed who what. Usually, we were about even by the time we got around to settling our bills. These friends struggled financially and were more in the same financial boat that I was. Perhaps the friend who always demanded her money now, whose father threw away the leftovers and gave her hundreds of dollars in pocket money, had a better financial mind-pattern than I did. Yet, I would not want to be like her.

- Do you think accountability is better for increasing and holding onto your income stream?

- Do you keep your leftover food, or do you throw it away?
- Were you told money doesn't grow on trees or something similar?
- If so, did this embed in your mind-pattern?
- If you suddenly had enough money to pay off your debts and put money in the bank what would you do with the leftover money?
- Do you have discernment when it comes to how to use money?

I come from a long line of farmers and working class people. Hard work and struggle are in my genetics. Stewart's family definitely had access to more things because of living first in New York City and then on Long Island. I have told you that when he and I were first together, I was aghast at by what I considered his extravagances which to him were normal. He was aghast at my penny-pinching which to me was normal, for example, buying fresh bagels 1-2x a week from a bakery when you could be making them. To me, that seemed like an extravagance until I realized that buying bagels meant you got more for less money with less work. These types of revelations to me were revolutionary.

When I baked, his family told me that my baked goods were as good as the bakery. I was shocked because when I grew up, bakery items were frowned upon as less than. Once I wanted to knit an afghan for a gift for a relative. Stewart and his family were mortified that I would give something handmade for a gift. In my circle, giving something store-bought meant you hadn't put a lot of time and effort into what you were giving. Store-bought meant quick/easy/I-don't-really-care-enough-to-make-you-something.

Stewart and I experienced a lot of economic culture clashes for a variety of reasons. Sometimes he would even say, "I'm glad no one heard you say this/that so you don't embarrass your Self." He operated from the premise that "more is better" while I was trying to get "more for less". I have come a long way in letting go of my need to struggle, but not without a hefty price. I realize that all the people who have stolen money from me through the years played upon my need to struggle for whatever I had; my guilt whenever I had more so they made themselves appear to have less so I would continue to give more; my low Self-Value that said "I don't deserve"; my compassion for the world that says how can I have this when others don't even have food, water and shelter. No one can steal money from you unless your mind-pattern won't let you keep it.

My friend who always had her hand out to be paid immediately when she showed up at my door with my purchases came from a mind-pattern of wealth. She felt she deserved it now; not in 5 minutes, or tomorrow, but now. People who stole from me saw my vulnerability and used it against me; they did not rob me at gunpoint. They set the path and I simply walked down it and handed them my money. It was my own mind-pattern that gave up ownership because of low Self-Value. I literally said, "You deserve this more than I do. Here."

The masses are imprinted with honor in giving; shame in receiving. It is an honor to give to those who have less than. It is an honor to give to the poor; to give your time to those who need it; to give your life/limbs/sanity for your country. But it is a shame to take help when you need it. This mind-pattern separates us from our Source. If you can't take from others, you can't take from your Source which ultimately provides all.

- Are you imprinted with honor in giving; shame in receiving?
- How do people take money from you?
- Do you willingly or grudgingly give it?
- Is one mind-pattern better or worse than the other?

- Is willingly because of low Self-Value or because it is an honor to give?
- Is grudgingly because you can't hold onto it but you don't want them to have it either?

The more I examine my issues with receiving the more I realize how many issues I've had with giving. Giving sets you up to feel better than those to whom you give. You give to the less fortunate. You are imprinted with Selfless icons like Mother Theresa and even Princess Diana who even hugged AIDS patients which was scandalous at the time. You are so focused on helping those less fortunate than you that you certainly don't think about receiving. You do think, What if that would ever be me, God forbid, I would appreciate someone helping me. So part of you gives as a kind of insurance.

I never give to blood banks because I never wanted to be in the position of having to receive from there. In addition, what you freely give is sold globally, with American blood being one of the highest in demand worldwide. Sometimes when driving I let drivers into my lane in front of me when the lines are long. In return, when I need to get into a lane, there is a part of me that expects someone to let me in and eventually, they do. I give and I expect to receive.

Spending/buying is a form of giving. You give to the vendor/store/ organization. It is your money; it is rightfully your money and you choose to give it to someone hoping to get something of value. There is a difference between "hoping" and "knowing". Sometimes you think you know that you are getting something of value, but it isn't the value you had anticipated. I have given a lot of money away and gotten something of negative value. I obviously still had lessons to learn surrounding various factions of my life or the lessons would have been positive. I have had more negative spending lessons than I care to enumerate. When you look at it this way, you still have to thank your teachers. Otherwise, you would still continue giving your money away without fully understanding the ramifications of your actions. You need to reevaluate your giving.

- Why do you give?
- Do you give to make your Self feel better?
- Because every little bit helps?
- Do you know where your money is actually going and what it is doing?
- Or do you just think you know?
- Does giving to charity make you feel that you aren't so bad off because you are giving and not receiving?
- Does giving your castoffs to others make you feel good that you have castoffs to give?
- Does observing lower class people appreciate your castoffs enhance your feelings of economic superiority?
- If you like giving so much, why not buy new and give the new away?
- Why do you have to use it a few times and then give it away?
- What kind of negative spending lessons have you had?
- Who did you give your money to in ways you hadn't intended?
- Have you thanked these people as teachers about finances?
- If you had a few million dollars in the bank would you still have negative spending lessons?
- Who might you give money to that you shouldn't?
- Who might you give money to that isn't prepared for what you would want to give them?
- Who might you give castoffs to that shouldn't be getting your castoffs?
- When you get something, why do you feel the need to give?

- Why, when the global elite get something do they spend it on themselves rather than share?

## Why You Give

There are a lot of reasons why you give:

- Out of guilt

- Judgment of another's lifestyle and needs

- Giving to those who have less than points out how much you have

- Giving just in case you should ever be in that position, maybe someone will give to you (insurance)

- To feel good

- External validation that you are okay because now someone appreciates you or at least likes the things you gave them

- Low Self-Worth; I don't deserve this so I'm giving it to you, who obviously need this

- Can't hold onto things because you cannot accept what you manifest

- To feel needed

- Acknowledgment that you exist

- Feeling important

- Societal/mass imprinting

- Programming

I am working on giving in the most correct and beneficial manner for all concerned. This means not giving for any of those reasons above. Giving because it is the most correct and beneficial reason for all concerned. This gives you internal validation from your Oversoul. Many years ago my mother gave Christmas and birthday gifts to my

3 stepsons, $5.00 each. In New York, at the time, even to see a movie was $8.00. Every time they would open the card they would chuckle about what could they even do with $5.00, which was true. After a few times of this, I thanked my mom for remembering my stepsons, but I said if she could make it $10, then they could at least see a movie. She chose to stop giving to them.

When my sons were 10 and 13, she was giving them rubber bathtub toys and sponges that when soaked in water turned into some animal. My youngest could deal with it, but my older one just looked at me. I had to tell her that they were getting too old for these kinds of toys so maybe she should consider giving them something else, or even cash. She chose to stop giving to them. Her other grandson never wrote her thank you notes, so she stopped giving to them.

- How many people do you know who have had similar issues with giving?
- How many people don't get the response they are hoping for?
- How many people give to get something back?
- Should you expect something back when you give?
- Do you ask your Oversoul before you give?
- Have you had to not give even when you wanted to because you were shown that it was not for the most correct and beneficial reasons?
- Do you think the global elite remove their emotions when it comes to giving?
- How do they live with themselves, knowing the suffering that is going on in the world?
- How would you react if you had billions of dollars but your Oversoul told you the masses had to suffer, so you could not help them?

Giving is an interesting teacher when you realize that you are insidiously programmed to give but you are distracted from the receiving end. A few years ago, I thought that if I suddenly found my Self with tons of money, I had a gigantic list of people who I would help. I would pay off my home, cars, credit cards and then start moving out to help everyone I knew with enough left over to have a savings account. A really easy plan! In my ***Decoding Your Life*** book I wrote about how if you had the power to heal people, would that give you the right to heal them. You would have to ask your Oversoul if you could start with one hospital, go through all the rooms and then go on to the next hospital and the next.

In the same way, you have to ask what is most correct and beneficial when it comes to finances. You have to ask your Oversoul what is most correct and beneficial rather than automatically assume that you have the right to indiscriminately start handing out money. I have given a lot of money to a lot of people for a variety of reasons. At the time, and for the level I was on, it seemed quite correct. But as I've grown, in retrospect I can see the error of my ways. You cannot take away the struggle of others simply because you can. When my brother was ill, I knew that if I had the power to heal him, I could not. He would not learn his lesson if I, or anyone miraculously healed him; his healing had to come from within. I, and many, many other people did everything we could to pave the pathway for him to find it within him Self to accept healing But, it did not happen that way. In the same way, when you give money or things, you have to be circumspect about the why and make tough choices about whether what you are doing is correct or not.

- Why do people have lessons about money in the first place?
- What is money about?
- What does not having money teach you?
- If you don't have money for food, shelter, water, what does this mean?

- If you lose your home or your cars, what does this mean?

- Why the tough money lessons?

- Are these as tough as health lessons?

- Are you willing to put in your time so that when you do have access to unlimited funds that you would not play God, solving the financial issues of those whom you deem worthy and judging those whom you deem not?

- What would this attitude do to you?

- Would it make you a more balanced person or turn you into a dictator?

- With unlimited funds, how many people would ask for help and how would they react if you did not?

- How would you cope with your opulence while being directed to not help specific people?

- If the masses and the global elite are each out of balance, does this create financial balance within the God-Mind?

- Can you have financial illness in the same way you have a physical illness?

I never told my boys that they could not have something because we couldn't afford it. I didn't want that in their mind-patterns. I wanted them to have the mind-pattern that they could have whatever they wanted. So, they learned discrimination and I am impressed by their discernment to this day Even before you give, you usually ask your Self if you can afford to give. My mother used to arrange events at the Unity Church in Seattle for world famous authors. She told me how people who didn't have the money, but wanted to attend, got the money. Once she told me about a woman who sold her washer and dryer so she could go to an event. At the time, I thought that was awful. But, via life experience, I am learning not to judge. This person did not ask, "Can I afford it?" Instead she said, "How can I make this happen?" and she did! It is not my place to judge how she made that happen.

Instead of asking "Can I afford this?" ask "What is most correct and beneficial for all concerned?" This is saying "God's way, not my way." You may want to give for one or more of the reasons on the why you give list. But if you ask if it is correct and beneficial, then you will know what do to for the correct reason. Sometimes, no matter how small of an amount, it is not correct to give. Sometimes, you are asked to spend a lot of money on something you may not want to do at all. Or, if you are told that this is the most correct and beneficial path for all concerned, and you take that leap of faith, the money comes to you in unexpected ways.

Someone who worked at a casino told me that a customer won $500,000.00 and spent it all in one year. And then was right back to the beginning. Another time, someone stole a lighter from the gift shop for $1. He was seen taking it and exiting the casino. Apparently he was known there, and had entered his name in a drawing for a car. You had to be present to win. Because he had exited with the lighter, he was not present when his name was drawn and he did not get the car. He never knew, yet he was probably thrilled with his $1 lighter. In the same way, you may be set up to receive a lot of money, but because you wouldn't handle it correctly, it is best that you wait to receive it. If you are happy with taking a $1 lighter, then you aren't ready for the big prizes in life, either. Often there is a lot going on behind the scenes that is simply waiting to happen.

Sometimes, we have people attend our events that don't have money, but they know that they have to be here. They make payment plans and do what is necessary to get themselves here. And their lives change. And their income streams open because they didn't think about the cost first. They asked, "Is it most correct and beneficial for me to be there?" Sometimes, there are people with tons of money who cannot part with it even if it is most correct and beneficial for them to be here. Every day, you are faced with monetary choices. Maybe you think, It's only $5.00 so I can part with it. But maybe that sandwich you want to buy could give you food poisoning. Maybe you think, It's $5,000.00; I can't afford it. But if you spent that $5,000.00 your whole life would open up and bloom.

- Is the first question that you ask before spending money, "Can I afford it"?
- Is it better to ask, "What is most correct and beneficial for everyone involved"?
- Would you sort your answers in a different way?
- Would this stop the lack mind-pattern and replace it with "I can have what I want, when my Oversoul tells me that I can have it?"
- Would this stop mindless giving?
- Would this stop people taking/stealing from you?
- Would you be able to obey Source vs. what you want to do at the moment?
- Would you be able to let go of your current reasons for giving?
- Would you learn to stop the mindless outflow of all resources by asking this one question?
- Could this one question change the incoming income as well as stop the incorrect outflow?
- Could this be the question that balances your income stream?

Every time you say, "Can I afford it?" or "How much can I afford?" you remind your Self that you are limited. Your focus is on what you can or cannot do financially. When you change that question to What is the most correct and beneficial thing to do? the frequency changes enough to put you in a better alignment. It takes the focus off of your Earth-based seemingly finite reality and puts your mind up into unlimited resources of Source.

Can I afford it? keeps you in the programming loop of limitation. You always think, If I had x amount of money, I could do this or that. This mind-pattern is similar to hope. Hope means that you can do it one day, but not now. "If I had the money, I would" also takes you away from the Eternal now. Later may never come, because you continually affirm someday vs. now.

Sometimes, news stories focus on a poor person giving when that person has very little. For example, a person gives a $5 donation, that person barely has enough money for food, but still he/she shared. This is to encourage everyone to share because every little bit helps. The bottom line is $5 is $5 and purchase power of that $5 does not change depending upon who gave it. If that person only had $5 to give, then maybe the charity ought to say, Here's your $5 back with another few hundred so you can pay some bills and eat. Instead, the person gets his/her picture in the paper or in the news. No one mentions the billionaires taking from people like this.

**Receiving**

When it is in your mind-pattern to receive, there is nothing that can stop that money from getting to you. I love the story of the brothers in Bulgaria who were so poor they lived in a cave but somehow they managed to inherit billions from their grandmother. At the end of this article, it says:

> Normally people of modest means only come into a sudden fortune is through the lottery. This a nail in the coffin of dreams and hopes of every modest living person.
>
> http://www.telegraph.co.uk/news/worldnews/europe/ hungary/6704685/Brothers-living-in-cave-to-inherit-billions- from-lost-grandmother.html

People with metal detectors find troves of coins and jewelry; deep sea divers find shipwrecks laden with precious metals; farmers plowing their fields dig up ancient artifacts. My oldest son used to find money everywhere. If he sat down on a park bench, there would be coins in the boards. Once, when we took our Siberian Husky Natascha to the lake she wandered into the beach grass and came back with a mouth full of paper bills. Both of my sons have more job offers at their university than they can accept. They both have fantastic scholarships, far exceeding any amount they could have saved if they worked while attending high school classes. I told them at the time that their jobs were to get A's. This is what they did and this is how they can afford to go to university. Money comes to them because no one ever told them that it wouldn't/couldn't.

- Can you name something that you give on a regular/daily basis?
- With the correct mind-pattern, does money find you?
- Do you feel limited in life due to the amount of money you don't have?
- Do you feel like the only way to get money is like the article says, in a lottery?
- Do you think money could find you in unexpected ways?
- Is trying to reason out the possible unexpected ways fruitful?
- Are you committed to removing your Self-imposed/programmed limitations?
- Are you too invested in your poor me story that a part of you doesn't want to give up?
- Do you see why poverty mind-patterns are generational?
- Do you observe how one generation teaches the next one how to live in limitation?

When I was growing up, there were a lot of things that I wanted that we could not afford. I wanted candy bars, ice cream, fresh fruit, seafood, a brand new bicycle and brand new clothes, not hand-me-downs. I wanted burgers from the drive-ins. So, when I was on my own, I spent a lot of money on these kinds of things. I even bought my Self a brand new piano after my mother put a ridiculous price on her old used one that she wanted me to purchase.

I also detested housework because my mother made me spend hours every Saturday morning trying to get all the dust out from under my bed; washing dishes every day I couldn't get the tines of the forks clean enough for her; nothing I did was ever good enough. So I detested housework until the year I was sick with pneumonia and couldn't clean. That was when I let that attitude go so I could move forward. There were so many things that I did not like about my childhood that I set about balancing in my young adult years. I was in charge; I was in control; no one could tell me what to do or not to do; I liked being the boss of my life. I bought store-bought clothes, tons of them, just so I could look at them, even if I didn't have a place to wear them, since I lived out on my farm. I also liked to lay everything out all over the place where I could look at my things. I was never allowed to do that growing up. Sometimes, yes, I did like leaving my bed unmade for a whole day. I was a rebel!

There are a lot of things, at various stages in your life that you want because you did not have them in childhood. These are your unfulfilled needs that must be fulfilled.

- The issue is, are you still re-fulfilling them years later, or have you moved on?
- Are you able to let go of what you did or did not receive in childhood?
- Are you still trying to prove something to your child Self?
- How many childlike adults have you come across who are still re-enacting their childhood because there is no one to tell them, "No"?
- Is it healthy to be stuck in the past?

- Because you felt deprived of something in childhood, do you have to repeat it now?
- Do you make it a point now to prove that you can do whatever you want?
- Do you see how these old cycles and mind-patterns trap you in the past instead of allowing you to move forward?
- If this is your attitude, do you think you would use more money to move forward or to dig your Self in deeper?
- When you give to your Self, do you ask, "Is this the most correct and beneficial?"
- Does what you did or didn't have as a child influence what you do with your financial stream now?

As a child, you are expected to watch your parents grow old, fall apart, become helpless and then help to financially support them. You are supposed to leave home, make your way in the world, not leach off of your parents, serve others, serve your country, be independent and make it on your own so you can then come back full circle to take care of aging/ailing mom and dad. On the other hand, the global elite parents always take care of their children financially. You do not see the parents of the global elite falling apart, laden with disease and barely able to talk. This shows you how strong the mass imprinting is. The global elite show you how they do things, yet, you still fall into the imprinting of the masses.

Today, I was with my sons at a university event. Part of it was honoring a math professor who they both have had and I have conversed with on a few occasions. This professor is retiring and even though he loves his work, he wants to leave so he can travel while he still can. Every person I know talks about the inevitable falling apart the later years bring you, whether it is a joke or in seriousness. There is this fearful knowing that "my time is coming" and people lay down and simply accept their fate. You never see this attitude in the global elite. They don't talk about growing old, falling apart, having their children support them. President Trump is in his 70s, the Pope is in his 80s, the Queen of England is 91 and the Queen Mother was 101 when she passed away. These people are going strong, not discussing their ailments, but instead showing people how healthy they are and nothing stops them or their finances.

Their children are not taking care of them, but they are taking care of their children. Nepotism rules the world. But if you are of the masses and you inherit your family's business, you didn't earn it you were given it, thus a badge of shame. In the masses it is a shame to have parental help. And in case you didn't know that, everybody and their brother will tell you. Family fortunes are not amassed because the global handlers buy out the successful financial investments. The money from the sale gets wasted away by people who don't know how to handle that kind of money.

Maybe if your parents were not there for you when you were growing up, and you are back home with them now for whatever reason, this is their opportunity to make up for what they did not do when you were younger. Maybe instead of focusing on what you are getting from them, you need to focus on what they are getting from you. Maybe they were not financially generous or emotionally kind, and now they can be. Even though living with your parents may feel forced due to economic circumstances, there is a reason.

- How do you feel when people give to you?
- Are you good at receiving gifts from other people?
- Are you good at taking help or are you too busy being independent?
- Would you rather give than receive?
- Do you have to give to be able to receive?
- Is your ability to receive conditional upon your terms?

- Do you judge how your finances come to you?
- Do you feel guilty about how they come to you?
- When money comes to you too easily, do you feel like you didn't work hard enough/struggle so therefore you really shouldn't have what you were given?
- Did you receive an inheritance, so you feel guilty that someone had to pass away before you received something?
- Did your family share their money with you to make your life easier?
- Did they offer you money, did you have to ask, or could you even dare ask?
- Are you are a good receiver?

When I was first married, my step mother-in-law was very good to me, but I was not appreciative because no one liked her. I definitely felt my loyalties being torn between her and my mother-in-law, who hated the step mother-in-law. My step mother-in-law and father-in-law suggested that my first husband and I return from university to rent part of their farm to begin our dairy business. At the time, the government had a program to help young farmers get started. I was 19 when we borrowed $48,000.00 to begin our venture.

We actually paid more to my in-laws than other people would have and they did everything they could to sabotage us. We wound up in a lawsuit because I elected to withhold rent one month, so they took us to court. Monetary damages were clear since we had not paid rent. We were given 30 days to vacate the premises which meant our home, cows, young stock, machinery, everything. It was a tough lesson for me. Morally, I knew without a doubt that I was correct, but I broke the human law and it was easily provable by my in-laws in court. We did not speak to his dad and stepmom for about 5 years.

One day, the dad came to our farm, apologized and we all made up. Then, some years later, the dad wanted my ex and I to farm again, same promises. We foolishly went back and long story short, wound up in a similar position. In fact, my step mother-in-law actually told us that some children killed their parents for inheritance, suggesting that we had that in mind for them! Of course, this time we left in a different way, but it was a huge monetary set-back, again. Another breach of family trust and again, we did not speak to them.

When I first met Stewart, we lived with his parents for the first year we were together, in a tiny room. I made up my mind that I would get a long no matter what, and I did. I was extremely grateful for their financial support because without it there was no way that Stewart and I could have been together. They did not have a lot, but they shared generously with us. His relatives gave generously to the older 3 boys and the 2 little ones when they arrived, always remembering birthdays and holidays as well as passing along hand-me-downs of all kinds. Stewart and I managed financially, managed to grow our business until the situation came up in the *Blue Blood* book. We were forced to move as we could not afford living in New York. I had to ask for financial help from my dad, and I cried. I felt like a total fool and failure.

Fast forward ahead when my webmaster stole my website and my business crashed. Again, I had to ask my dad for financial support. I was grateful he helped us, but resentful that I had to ask. I was resentful that my Oversoul had not provided for me, not realizing that my Oversoul was providing for me but not in the way I wanted to be provided for. Not everyone has a parent to turn to in case of financial crisis. I have had to go back and look at all of my financial crashes. I have to see how I was provided for, even at some of my worst times. It was not how I wanted to be provided for and I was resentful because it happened in God's way, not my way. I mislabeled it all. Instead of being appreciative, I was resentful and stuck in the past.

I have been overly generous to everyone but me. I have had to learn to give to my Self. That isn't always so easy when you are raising 5 boys and building a business. Sometimes, I have had to give to my Self and be late on a credit card payment. But without giving to me, too, my finances cannot grow, but I found out my resentment, low Self-Value and other such negative emotions can grow. I am excellent when it comes to telling you how to get money; telling me how to get it is a bigger challenge.

- How many times have you given to others when you needed it?
- How many times did others take from you unfairly because you can't hold onto it?
- How many times have others helped you, but you were resentful because the help didn't come in the ways you wanted?
- How many times did you have the opportunity to go back to correct something, but you didn't because parts of you weren't ready?
- How many times did the emotional child within throw a temper tantrum while the adult you went into the background and hid?
- In what ways do you still react as a child instead of as an adult?
- Can a huge financial stream come into a child sub-personality?
- What would your child within do incorrectly with a huge financial stream?
- How does a narrow financial stream focus your child within?
- How does a narrow financial stream focus your adult within?
- Does a narrow financial stream force your child and adult within to merge rather than to be at odds with each other?

# AFFIRMATIONS—RELEASING MIND-KNOTS

Your mind is purposely confused by the global handlers so that you do not have a clue as to who you are, where you came from and where you are going. When you untangle the knots within your mind, you are going to be amazed at how easily your life flows on all levels.

*I release the need for confusion.*

*My Self-conviction is strong.*

*I recognize that I AM more than I think I AM.*

*I keep my Ego in Balance at all times.*

*I objectively evaluate my positive attributes via the Oversoul level.*

*I release the need to inflate my positive attributes*

*I release the need to deflate my positive attributes.*

*I Self-Value.*

*I release the need to inflate my negative attributes.*

*I objectively evaluate my negative attributes via the Oversoul level.*

*I Self-determine from within, in conjunction with my Oversoul.*

*I hold my Self in balance at all times.*

*I stabilize my Self from the effects of the outer world.*

*I anchor deep within my Source.*


*I allow my outer world to untangle in the way that I can most easily handle.*

*I easily move through change.*


*I release all the energetic entanglements that I no longer need.*

*I experience the freedom of Self-expression.*


*I release the need to hold onto that which weakens me.*

*My inner strength grows.*


*I visualize all the energetic entanglements within my mind.*

*I let them go so I can grow.*


*I follow the frequency threads that comprise my life.*

*I diligently untangle every knot in every frequency.*


*I release the need to have mind-not/knots.*

*I now have mind can do frequencies.*


*I release my mind-patterns that say I cannot/knot.*

*I build the mind-pattern that says I can.*

*I stop mind-not/knots before they start.*

*I observe where I accept mind-not/knots in my life.*

*I release the programming that says, "I can't".*

*I allow my Soul to function and flourish as it was intended.*

*I find and untangle all hidden mind-not/knots.*

*I accept that I AM in control of my life at all times.*

*I observe the mind-not/knots in others without judgment.*

*I rise above the masses.*

*Mind-not/knots represent safety for the masses.*

*I rely on my Source to protect and keep me safe.*

*I utilize all that I AM for positive growth.*

*I release the need to match the mind-not/knots of others.*

*I have compassion for those with mind-not/knots.*

*I have compassion for Self as I release what I know for something better.*

*I accept responsibility for Self-change as my mind-not/knots unravel.*

*I accept the challenge that change for the better brings.*

*My mind-not/knots unravel in the least uncomfortable way.*

*I accept a life that easily flows in alignment with my mission and purpose in this reality.*

*I accept the way of my Oversoul and God-Mind vs. my way.*

*I recognize the Higher Power of my Source that is ultimately in charge of my life.*

*I release the need to Self-sabotage as my mind-not/knots unravel.*

*I accept a life with less pain and suffering.*

*I release the programming that holds my mind-not/knots in place.*

*I allow comfort to be a greater part of my lifestyle.*

*I untangle my mind-not/knots without guilt.*

*Each person must find his/her own way.*

*I AM a beacon that shines a light for others to follow when they are ready.*

*I walk a balanced path of pride and dignity.*

*I know my audience.*

*I have compassion for those with malice of intent.*

*I release my need to judge the path of others who are laden
with mind-not/knots.*

*I have been there, done that, survived and surpassed;
"There but for the Grace of God, go I."*

# Gold Fortune

You are not damaged, but you are indeed a Divine Spark within the Mind of God. You have High Value and you function multidimensionally. There are a multitude of obstacles that challenge you to allow your Inner Light to Shine Brightly. And, instead of allowing the winds of change to blow your Light out, you use the movement to fan your Inner Flame, ever-strengthening the Light Within.

Your Inner Light is your "Gold Fortune". Gold represents God-Mind Wisdom. Your Fortune is to know that herein lies your True Value and your True Worth. The Obstacle Course of Earth is your trial by fire; your opportunity to connect to your Source and bring out the best by surpassing your trials. Exploring how you can personally connect to your inner Gold Fortune shows you how to manifest your outer Gold Fortune. When you feel damaged, it is easy to settle for less than.

When you connect to your Higher Spiritual Mind, you identify with your Divine Spark. This knowing allows you to choose to identify with Source First, and then compassionately understand your trials and tribulations as the strengthening tools that they are.

- Why is Gold metal so highly prized within all cultures?
- Why does Gold always hold its value and considered a good investment?
- Why did other cultures lavishly adorn their places of worship in Gold?
- Why does the global elite always decorate with gold and wear Gold?
- Why are so many Gold-plated trinkets produced?
- Why is Gold hoarded and protected?
- How would your life change if suddenly your living quarters were adorned with Gold?
- Do you feel like your life is one of good luck and good fortune?
- Are you committed to increasing your Self-Worth and Spiritual energies?

At one time, people carried coins made of precious metals. Even in my lifetime, I have watched coins made of precious metals be replaced with low-grade metal combinations. Each metal carries a specific frequency that affects you in one way or another. Gold is God-Mind wisdom. This is why it is held in high regard by everyone on the Earth and why you are hoodwinked into giving it up. In the same way, you are hoodwinked into giving up your inner Gold Fortune. I have had a rough day today for a variety of reasons. But the bottom line is, in spite of the viciousness and nastiness that happened, I wasn't hoodwinked into giving up my inner Gold Fortune.

*I AM not going to allow my Self to fall into the trap that takes me down.*

*I AM focusing on my inner Gold Fortune; my connection to my God-Mind Wisdom that feeds my Soul.*

*I AM trusting God-Mind Wisdom to take care of me and ferret out all that I no longer need, even when it is not pleasant.*

*I AM one with my inner Gold Fortune.*

Stay the course with Who You Are vs. what the world can sometimes try to force you to believe about your Self. You hold the precious frequency of Gold Fortune. Visualize the God-Mind Gold Fortune Wisdom frequency permeating each and every cell of your being; enveloping all aspects of every layer of who and what you are; imparting exactly what you need to know when you need to know it.

- Does the world try to hoodwink you into giving up your inner Gold Fortune?
- Do you too easily hand over what is rightfully yours?
- Can you withstand the attacks of the outer world, knowing that you are being challenged to prove to Self who you are?
- Do others attack you when they cannot deal with themselves?
- Does being a target make you stronger?
- When you are strong enough, do you stop being a target?
- Is being a target a function of this reality?
- Do you think there are other realities where being a target is no longer necessary?
- Can anyone take from you what you are not willing to give?
- Are you one with your inner Gold Fortune?

Today is the birthday of one of my best friends that I have known for almost 40 years. She is a beautiful Soul who is now in her 70s and still a magnificent potter. Yesterday, I was looking at 3 of her pots that sit on my kitchen windowsill. They are labeled, Joy, Peace, Love. I was thinking about how every home should have a set of these jars. Sometimes people see these jars in my home and ask me what is in them. I always answer, "Joy, Peace, Love". You should see the puzzled looks on their faces. I tell them to open them up and take some. Today is also the day that Stewart's sister got married 20 years ago. It is also the birthday of one of my brother's best friends. These people are all part of my Gold Fortune.

This morning, I received notice that one of our longtime supporters passed away yesterday. Christian Abrokwah. 38 years old. He was a rap musician and built much of his music around our work. We have known him for years and years. He has a young teenage daughter who he adored. Apparently, his heart just stopped at work and he was gone. His last post on social media was of our book, ***Healing Archetypes and Symbols*** and how much he was learning from it. His aunt has my birth date, but a different year. He has taught his daughter our techniques since she could talk. And now he has passed over. What a shock. Then I heard that author and researcher Jim Marrs also passed away yesterday from a heart stoppage. 73 years old. Stewart met him at a couple of conferences. He had been ill and now he is gone, too. Both Christian and Jim's ages add up to New Beginning numbers of 11 and 10 respectively. My brother was 65 when he passed this year, another 11. All men gone too soon from my linear perspective. Gold Fortune for these men is no longer in this reality.

My dad is 91, a 10 this year and heading toward 92, an 11 next year. God Bless him, because he is my Gold Fortune. His New Beginnings are in this reality. Life passes quickly. Being mean and nasty does not add to the quality of your life. Accepting meanness and nastiness does not add to the quality of your life. Don't be hoodwinked into giving up your Gold Fortune. Stop and appreciate the people who are your Gold Fortune. Let go of the aspects within you that attract meanness and nastiness. Without dealing with Self, another such person will pop up to take the place of the one you just dismissed.

- How challenging is it to acknowledge your responsibility in attracting people who try to make you feel bad about your Self?
- Do you accept their challenge and feel bad?

- Or do you stand in your own Gold Fortune and refuse to let them take from you?
- Do you give too much and too willingly to resource thieves?
- Why do others want your Gold Fortune instead of being satisfied with their own?
- Why do others want to make you feel bad?
- If this was your last day in this reality, can you say that you accomplished what you came here to accomplish?
- What would you regret not doing?
- How can you correct that regret now?

On the inner levels, we are All-One and we know everything. The All-One cannot fit into one physical body so It divided It Self so It could experience It Self. Stewart and I are "one Soul, 2 bodies". Well, continue that extrapolation into "All That Is" and you will see that everything in existence is the Divine Mind exploring It Self. This is why you already know everything, but not everything can fit into your physical container/body.

Many indigenous cultures practiced this 24/7. They knew the Souls coming in; they knew the frequencies; warrior; shaman; hunter; gatherer; clothing maker; weaver; scout. Each person came into this reality on a specific frequency and therefore was mentored in the specific frequency by someone already here working within that frequency. Each group of people operated as a conscious collective group mind.

If you were a chief, you fulfilled that mission. If you were a hunter, you did not covet the position of the chief because that was not your frequency. If you were a gatherer, you did not covet the position of the chief or the hunter because these were not your frequency. Like a well-oiled machine, many indigenous cultures thrived because everyone had a place/frequency and performed the functions therein.

This does not mean that life was easy; but, you knew your mission and purpose and you did it. If you are born an elephant you do not covet the role of a turtle. If you are born a monkey, you do not act like a deer. Without a place in a family or a home, most people have totally forgotten to acknowledge their inner Gold Fortune. You do not feel worthy of having anything valuable within, much less acknowledging it. Generation after generation now perpetuates the dysfunction and disconnection. It is up to you to bring back the memory; to know that your Soul is part of a larger Soul, the Ultimate All-One. You are not here to fight about who has what, when, why and how. When you fight against your brother or sister, you fight against your Self. Ultimately, we are all family; we are all related; we are from the same family tree. Recognize that cooperation is the key to your inner Gold Fortune.

If you are an elephant, then you need the monkey because the monkey can accomplish specific tasks that you cannot, and vice versa. With cooperation, you can each appreciate the skills of each other to build a community that works.

- Why would you want to be the same?
- Or get rid of the monkey so you can try to do his tasks, too?
- Or enslave the monkey so you can sit back and do nothing?

There are layers upon layers within layers; enough layers for everyone to explore; enough layers to know that learning from each other can strengthen the knowledge and the abilities of the collective group mind. Everyone has a place; there is order when you tap into your inner Gold Fortune rather than ignore what already exists to try to take from another.

- Why do people fight instead of cooperate?
- Why does an elephant want to be a monkey?
- Can you visualize One Soul with all the energy streams flowing down, forming into various life forms?

- Does cooperation mean survival on this planet?
- What would happen if they gave a war and nobody came?
- How challenging is it to let go of your own inner angers, resentments, bitterness, fears, anxieties, worries, concerns, nervousness?
- Is there a part of you that fears not having Gold Fortune within?
- Is there a part of you that fears outshining others?
- Do others want to take what you have instead of find their own inner Gold Fortune?
- Is there a part of you that is afraid of being a Gold Fortune example?
- Is it in your genetic structure to be subservient and victimized?
- Do you want to park a brand new, fancy vehicle in front of your home while your neighbors are barely making a living and paying their bills?
- Do you want to move to a new neighborhood where people start judging you by your new, fancy vehicle instead of by who you are?
- What are the positive and negative ramifications of consciously finding and accessing your inner Gold Fortune?

When you fail to see your own Gold Fortune, others who see it take advantage of you, become jealous and refuse to acknowledge anything positive about what is within you. When you really know who and what you are, you don't flaunt it. You are not looking for outer confirmation, in fact, just the opposite. You don't want to draw attention to your Self. When I first started my work, I wanted to share what I have with everyone. I wanted to change the world. At the time, I didn't look at it this way. It was a huge blow to realize that people weren't waiting for me, lining up to buy dozens of my books to give to all their friends and relatives.

Without understanding the world in the way I do now, it was crushing to see people with, in my opinion, practically worthless information selling thousands of books and on all the television shows while I, with methodologies that actually help people, was not getting any public recognition at all in comparison. In retrospect, I was looking for outer recognition but I did not have enough Self-Value. I had the correct information, but the reasons were not yet correct. I had not yet recognized my inner Gold Fortune. I was looking for an outer validation in a way that would never allow me to find what was already within.

When you are in the public eye, others tell you who you are, both positive and negative. Then, with the pressure, you become what they want you to be instead of who you are. My journey has forced me to find out who I AM, in spite of my own efforts to stop/slow the progress. The fight against Self to move and grow is quite insidious. After all these years, I feel like I AM finally getting it, but I feel like releasing the resistant parts of Self is like trying to unhinge heavy, thick glue. It takes a lot of energy and perseverance, much more than I ever could have imagined so many years ago. If I would have known then what I know now, I don't know that I would have had the courage to continue. I recognize that the theme to "change the world" is simply another box. We are not here to change the world. We are here so the world can change us. That is a huge eye-opener for me.

- Did you/do you have the desire to change the world?
- Are you recognizing that the world is what it is?
- Do you know that you are here to change you based upon the experiences the world gives you?
- Do you find the fight against Self more challenging than the fight against others?

- Do you fight against others, even if it is only in your own mind?

- Do you see people change to fit the expectations of others?

- Have you felt the need to change to fit the expectations of others?

- Does recognizing your inner Gold Fortune make you want to move deeper into the public eye or out of it?

## Another Box

It seems like there is an article for every, single uncomfortable situation that you can imagine, thereby imprinting you with uncomfortable is bad instead of just a part of life. Stress is always discussed with negative connotations, yet stress has a positive side. Plants, for example, grow under stress and so do you. I feel like my inner Gold Fortune increases every time I find another layer of the box. You are so used to the box that every time you step out of one, you don't realize that you step deeper into another one.

I read that NASA is looking for a planetary protection officer and that this position was sanctioned in 1967. The current person in this position has been there since 2014, so I question whether this means that the position was only recently filled or if it was always filled. In 1976 then President Gerald Ford passed an executive order saying that "noncitizens are not technically eligible". This makes me wonder what noncitizen and not technically eligible mean. You cannot dispute if these orders happened in 1967 or 1976. It is also interesting to note that 67/76 are mirroring each other. It is possible that the orders were inserted yesterday. I would have no way of knowing.

There is also a book circulating that was supposedly written 200 years ago about a youth named *Baron Trump* and his guide named *Don*. I cannot prove or disprove that this book was actually written 200 years ago, 2 years ago, or 2 days ago, or if the Trumps are a modern-day time-traveling family.

No matter where you turn, there is another box waiting for you; another stressor; something else to think about; contemplate, and perhaps take action. When you are out of your comfort zone, the box gets bigger and more challenging to extricate your Self. Then, Fear and Panic set in, defocusing and distracting you because you are imprinted with Stress is bad; stop stress; get away from stress; eliminate stress; if you experience stress it is because you are bad and do not know how to handle stress.

First of all, you always feel what you feel. Emotions have no linear logic. You cannot explain them away. You may be able to explain them, but you cannot explain them away. You have to delve into your inner Gold Fortune; God-Mind Wisdom, multidimensional-thinking to deal with your internal craziness much less the external craziness. God-Mind Wisdom explains that you are "okay as is". Rely on your inner Gold Fortune to instruct you step by step. One foot in front of the other and you will get to where you are going.

Stress is a part of life. Being uncomfortable is okay. "The Box" helps you define your boundaries when you cannot. Panic happens to everyone; you are not alone. Anxiety means that you feel out of control which means time to give control to your inner Gold Fortune God-Mind Wisdom for guidance and direction.

- Can you be okay being uncomfortable?
- Can you be comfortable in the midst of your discomfort?
- Can you turn to your inner Gold Fortune to help you deal with emotions-out-of-control?
- Can you agree to take the first step, knowing that your Gold Fortune within will then reveal the next step?
- Does the box give you boundaries so the entire world isn't overwhelming to you at once?
- Does the box make you stop, think and question?

- If you got out of the box all at once, would your world as you know it come crashing down upon you?
- Do you grow under Stress?

When you use your Gold Fortune, more becomes available. Using what I have is one of my most challenging lessons. I used to can fruit every year, but I was afraid to eat it because I was afraid that I would run out and not have enough. I used to buy beautiful new clothes that I never wore because I was afraid that I would wear them out and not be able to replace them. I had great examples of this recently from both of my sons. My oldest son purchased an engagement ring for his now fiancée. This meant emptying his savings account. I was slightly aghast at this. Okay, I was a lot aghast at this. But he simply said, "I will make more."

Then, my youngest son who is proving to be an amazing photographer decided to upgrade his current camera. He, too, emptied his savings account to do this which also left me wanting to say a lot. But, what was most interesting is that he said the exact same thing that my other son said, "I will make more."

And, they will. They both have jobs, they have scholarships, and they have a sense of their own Gold Fortune. They have always had what they wanted. Whether it is from my family, Stewart's family, their brothers, or friends they are using their Gold Fortunes and it continues to increase for them. They are building their resumes; they always have more job offers from the university than they can take; they do well in their classes that are preparing their future; they have mentors in their chosen professions. Their Gold Fortunes continue to increase as does their ability to accept what their positive mind-patterns attract.

They are grateful and appreciative; they have both worked diligently to get to where they are. They have invested their time in themselves and are already reaping the benefits. And because they are Self-invested, those who share their future with them will also benefit.

I still hang on too tightly for fear of what might not replace it. I AM still working on "*letting go and letting God.*" Even sharing my Gold Fortune is an issue because I have had the fear that others might not appreciate it or step all over me. Well, this has happened to me and I have still survived.

- What good is anything if you don't use it?
- If you sit on your Gold Fortune without utilizing it, how does it really benefit you?
- Are you afraid to spend money because where will more come from?
- Are you afraid to use outer representations of what you have, because where and/or how will you get more?
- Do you hoard because you might not get it again?
- Do you overeat because when will the food be available again?
- How much do stress, fear and panic drive your decisions?
- Whatever you use, do you know that you will make more?
- Do you know that you will make more of the negatives?
- Do you know that you will make more of the positives?
- Do you know that your Gold Fortune multiplies the more you use it?

Hoarding denotes stagnation. Hoarding old things represents holding old mental/emotional stuff that you fear letting go of. If you use or let go of it, you worry about what will replace it. When I was growing up, I had favorite television shows that were the highlight of my week. Every fall, old shows were cancelled and new ones announced. Every fall, I held my breath, praying that my favorite shows would continue. Sometimes, I had a favorite food given to me as a gift. I wouldn't eat it, because once I ate it I worried if I would get more. Sometimes, I held onto it so long that it went bad before I could eat it.

If you ask most people what they would do with any windfall, most often they say, "Give it away" to friends, family, poor, charity, organizations. Self-Worth determines what you keep/don't keep. Because you don't think you deserve it you don't hold onto it. The minute you get it, it is gone. You are imprinted to always focus on the less fortunate. This is a huge hoodwink. There is a saying, "If you give a poor man tons of money, he will soon be poor again. Take the money away from a rich man, and he will soon be rich again."

No matter how little you have, you are taught to focus on those that have less, so there is no reason to want more. Feel grateful that you are you and not that person. In balance, this is a great observation. Out of balance, you cannot accumulate too much or you feel guilty. To live with your internal feelings of low Self-Worth, you spend, spend, spend and low Self-Worth does not allow you to replenish your financial storehouse until you have suffered enough to finally say "I deserve the abundance of my Gold Fortune/God-Mind Wisdom within."

- What do you hoard?
- Do you know why?
- Can you trace your hoarding to an origin point in this lifeline?
- Did you do without as a child? or at some point in your life?
- Did you have more than others, so you hid what you had to fit in?
- Do you focus on the less fortunate in balance or out of balance?
- Do you understand why a poor man will always be poor and a rich man will always be rich?

- Do you feel you have to suffer before you deserve something positive?
- Have you heard the expression, "Do not cast your pearls before swine"?
- How does this apply to your own Gold Fortune?
- Is there a risk to exposing your Gold Fortune to others?
- Is there a risk to exposing your Gold Fortune to Self?

Today was an odd day. 8-9-10 is the date, the way we Americans write it. 8+9 is a 17 = 8. Add the year 8 + 10 = 9.

8 is Oversoul/energy/money.

9 is completion

89

Stewart realized that this was the date that his family purchased their Long Island Home. I realized that my brother had a stuffed toy rabbit, which I now have, named "8-9".

I left early to go to the Department of Motor Vehicles to renew my registration. Proof of insurance was required so I either had to mail it in or go in person. I was there 15 minutes early and there were already 30 people in line. I decided to wait, thinking they would put me in the fast line. There usually are about 5 employees, so it would move fast. No such luck/mind-pattern There was no triage line and only 2 employees at the counter. The first person in line took almost 30 minutes to complete her complicated transaction. Her issue was so rare, I heard the clerk say, that she had to look it up. I debated about leaving, but once I start something I like to complete my goal. I decided via the Oversoul level to brown-X out the people who were thinking about leaving to encourage them to do so to speed up where I was in line. As I mentally did the exercise, one person left. Well, that wasn't enough. I did it again and the brown-X was over me. I thought, I'm not leaving.

Then a young woman sat next to me with her baby. I tried to ignore her as I wasn't in the talking mood, but she decided to chat with me. Long story short, I did leave and I gave her my ticket which was 20 places ahead of the one she was holding. I did not complete my task. I thought perhaps I was there to hold a place for a new mother so she wouldn't have to wait so long with her baby.

I decided to make a quick stop for lightbulbs. Another long line at the checkout counter. There was a checkout counter with its light on, no line, but no clerk in sight. I finally found the clerk who replied that she was open when I asked. Great. I thought. But she wasn't nice, and when I tried to use my credit card it wanted a PIN number which I don't know because no machine has ever asked me for one. Finally, I realized I had my check book, so went that route. Lights got purchased!

Then I stopped for fuel. The car ahead of me was making a left turn on a busy street. I sat behind it for 15 minutes but at least I did fuel/energize my path in life. In total, I was gone about twice as long as I originally anticipated. I did my best to be calm not only on the outside, but on the inside. I would say I mildly succeeded, but definitely not totally. One of my favorite aunts received the test results of a cat scan saying she has to go for a biopsy next week. And, my dad phoned to say his longtime companion is in the hospital with congestive heart failure. I am still hoping to hear from my dad before the night is over to see how she is doing and of course how he is doing through it all. My father let me know that his companion is still in the hospital and we are still not sure what will happen. He says she is perking up, so that is positive and encouraging news.

It has been one thing after another today. It is a 9 day, a day of completion, but many of the things I wanted to complete were left undone. Other things I hadn't anticipated completing, got completed. I AM doing my best to tap into my inner Gold Fortune on an Oversoul/Silver day.

384 • HEIGHTS OF WEALTH

## You Are A Book

You are a book; a living repository/a storehouse of knowledge. At one time, each living repository had an apprentice to whom his/her knowledge was passed along. Even Waldensian barbs/pastors passed their knowledge from one person to another this way. Your book is part of your Gold Fortune. When I wrote my first book, it was to change the world, but as you know, my book changed me. Before I had my books, I used to go to Psychic Fairs, trying to find my place. But, because I did my Personal Consultations without things I was considered an enigma. People just could not understand how I could do this without the aid of things.

I can read anything and have taught classes in how to read sticks and stones to give you an idea of how this is done. It is easy once you know the tricks of the trade. Using something physical takes the onus off of you. This happens when people use something physical like Tarot Cards, for example. When the cards are laid out, you focus on the cards. This causes you to drop your guard allowing the reader to psychically gain access to you. The cards, whose origin is attributed to the Waldensians, are physical reflections of your inner world.

Writing a book tells you who you are. Writing a book puts you in touch with your inner Gold Fortune. Just like writing on this blog, I consistently hear, I didn't know that I knew all of that; the words just came tumbling out and everything came together. Books are like your business card. They are your Gold Fortune that you can share with others. Books are a thing that creates emotional distance from others. People feel less threatened to discuss ideas in a book. Whenever you participate in such discussions, you activate your own Gold Fortune. The more you use what you can access, the greater your access grows. There are a lot of people who know a lot of information, but without utilizing it, it is simply stagnant knowledge.

- If you were to write your own book what would you write about?
- Is writing a way to access your inner Gold Fortune?
- Is writing a form of communication that is less threatening than the spoken word?
- If you write a book and no one likes it, does it mean you are a failure or you need a new audience?
- Do you write for others or for Self?
- Is not writing your book because you do not know how to sell it an excuse not to start?
- If you do not have money to print the book you want to write, could writing it change you enough so the money manifests?
- Do you think of your Self as a living repository/storehouse of knowledge?
- Are you worth getting to know?
- Are you spending the time to get to know Self?
- Do you acknowledge your own inner Gold Fortune?
- Can writing a book activate what already exists within?

Many years ago, a person's word was binding. Now, everything has to be in such complicated writing that you have to have an attorney to read any contract that you sign. From my experience, even a written contract is only as good as the person behind it. I like the idea of a written contract to help clarify the intent of each party because often what you just said is not what I understood. A written contract clarifies your part and my part. However, even when you think you are both in agreement, there can still be misunderstandings. But again, the contract is only as good as the person behind it. Miscommunications are opportunities for clarifications.

The primary reason to put anything in writing is to anchor the nonphysical into the physical. This is why it is generally a positive for committed couples to marry rather than just live together. When you sign that paper, you anchor your nonphysical commitment into this reality. Living together says, "when the going gets tough, I can run away." Because your inner Gold Fortune is nonphysical, you must find a way to anchor that into physical reality. Writing is one way to do this, which is why I always suggest you write your affirmations.

Writing can bring clarity and confirmation to what you already know. You open the funnel to your inner tunnel of Gold Fortune/God-Mind Wisdom. You are literally learning how to mine your Gold Fortune. It is there; now you determine how to get it out without collapsing the funnel or the tunnel. You learn when to chip away; when to add support; when you have a vein of Gold Fortune; when one vein is depleted; what direction to go to find another vein; how to access the big veins, and how to ask the correct questions that give you the correct answers. All of this Self-teaches you to do what you need to do, as you need to do it, when you need to do it.

- Does writing help you anchor your nonphysical ideas into the physical?
- Have your spoken words been misunderstood?
- Have your written contracts been misunderstood?
- Would you prefer a world where a person's word is binding or do you like things in writing for clarification?
- Or is a balance of both verbal and written contracts important?
- Are written contracts only as good as the people behind them?
- Is there power in the Spoken Word?
- Does the Spoken Word Manifest?

- Can the Spoken Word Manifest?
- Is the Spoken Word part of your Gold Fortune?

Writing is part of my Gold Fortune. Writing is one of my creative outlets. I have always liked to do activities with my hands. Physical actions set new processes in motion. This is why the global handlers always have a physical ritual to bring the nonphysical into this reality. Indigenous people always gave something to the Earth when they took from the Earth. I was raised to bring something when I went to someone's home. In the country, if you brought someone food that you made, the container had to be washed and returned. An extra touch, but not required, was to put something in the clean dish when you returned it. The energy kept flowing back and forth; ebb and flow; in and out; open and close; help each other; give what you can, when you can; united we stand.

This is why there are labyrinths around the world; to set specific archetypes/mind-patterns when you walk them. There are books showing how city streets are laid out in geometric shapes/archetypes and buildings laid out in geometric shapes/archetypes. Ancient architecture was all about archetypes. Recently, this article was written about a popular restaurant:

> Outback Steakhouse is at the center of the latest internet conspiracy theory involving the Illuminati and Satan unveiling that in several cities, the home of the Bloomin' Onion has several locations that form a pentagram -- the five-pointed star that is often associated with organizations who worship or follow that guy you may have heard of... You know, the one who goes by SATAN!
>
> https://www.aol.com/article/finance/2017/07/31/outback-steakhouse-satanism-conspiracy-theory/23058456/

Your inner Gold Fortune helps you determine what actions to take to access and activate more of your inner Gold Fortune. This is a true conundrum because it is easy to get on the loop and stay on the loop. You can think a lot of fantastic thoughts and you can speak a lot of words, but to truly anchor into this reality, you need action.

- How can you get what you need if you are reluctant to access and activate something?
- After you think and speak about something, do you have good follow-through?
- If you are not a person of action, is it because you are afraid of your inner Gold Fortune?
- Do you think your inner Gold Fortune might bring changes that will frighten you?
- Are you willing to do what is most correct and beneficial to access and activate your inner Gold Fortune?
- When you get, do you give?
- When you give, do you get?
- Do you have daily rituals with specific actions that set the tone for your plans?
- Do you have a morning bathroom routine?
- A morning dressing routine?
- A morning eating routine?
- Is a routine the same as a ritual?
- What other regular actions/routines/rituals do you do?
- Do you have any regular actions/routines/rituals that bring your inner Gold Fortune into outer world manifestations?

**In The Beginning, Was The Word**

I found that if I had ideas and spoke about them to others, the energy behind the words dissipated. There is a saying which I have observed to be true, "All talk, no action." Technically, when you speak, you should instantaneously manifest. The challenge for most people is that they do not understand the frequency/tone/color/archetype of their own words. When asked if they like the tone of their voice, most people answer in the affirmative. What is interesting is that these same people have sharpness, fear, anger, bitterness and other negative frequencies embedded in their voice. Apparently, they like these qualities of their voice.

So let's say that you can manifest with your Spoken Word. You want a new car, but you do not realize that when you Speak the car into Being, your tone carries anger. You now have the car, but it attracts accidents. Or, your tone carries nervousness, so the car manifests, but breaks down consistently.

- Do you want the car enough to Speak it into existence knowing that it carries accidents and/or breakdowns? or maybe worse?
- Do you know the colors that your handwriting carries when you write/anchor nonphysical into the physical?
- Do you know anyone who is all talk, no action?
- When you do cleanup/clear up your words and writing, do you upgrade or create more of what you just released?
- Have you observed people who get rid of one partner only to get another one exactly like the one before?
- Have you ever left a job because of colleagues you don't like, only to get another job with more of the same type of colleague?
- Can you gossip something into manifestation?
- Do you know what colors flow out of your mouth when you speak?
- Can you hear the colors of others who speak?

- Do you know people who think they are impressing you with their Gold Fortune yet you can't hear/see/feel any Gold in his/her Spoken Word?

- Is your own Gold Fortune something to be protected or shared?

- How easy is it to give it away and then not be able to access more because you feel unworthy and undeserving?

- Do you allow your Self a little burst of Gold Fortune here and there?

- Do you use your inner Gold Fortune to rise above the crowd?

## Stop Judging

I was reading a story about a woman from Michigan who passed away as a result of a hippo attack in Tanzania. The story shows her happily sipping champagne as she leaves on her trip aboard an airplane. Maybe she thought this trip was part of her Gold Fortune. Yet, she was attacked by a hippo, according to this article, the most violent animal in Africa. She died in her son's arms. While this sounds tragic, maybe on the deeper levels, she had to go to Africa to complete whatever her Soul needed in this reality. It is easy to judge her passing as bad, but perhaps this is exactly what she needed so she could move on to something bigger and better. Perhaps this way of passing was her Gold Fortune, unbeknownst to those who she left behind. There are so many stories that are tragedies at first glance. But, because you know that you cannot judge the path of another, it is highly possible that what you consider a tragedy is that person's Gold Fortune.

- Have you heard stories about a personal tragedy that turned the person's life around for the better?

- Do you think people can be given a second chance or several chances to turn their lives in another direction?

- Can your Gold Fortune be a redirection?

- Does redirection mean easy?
- Have you had a tragedy that redirected your life?
- Does Gold Fortune/God-Mind Wisdom always come in ways that the outer world understand?
- Does reaching deep into your own Gold Fortune give you understanding of life in ways that others cannot yet comprehend?
- How challenging is it to not judge an experience as good or bad?

Understanding that every experience on this planet exists for a reason that is most correct and beneficial for all involved aids in your access to your own Gold Fortune. When you learn to stop judging the experiences of others, you can stop judging your Self. There are more experiences than you can count or read about involving the tragic lives of others. Yet, when you label the experience tragic, you are judging. This means every man, woman, child and beast has a part to play that must be played. The flesh is not the Soul. The flesh is the necessary costume to exist in this reality on this planet. Condoning an action does not make it most correct and beneficial. Condemning an action does not mean that it is not most correct and beneficial. Maybe you have something to complete in this reality in a specific way so you can move on to other realities to do something else. You can go the slow way or the quick way. It is possible that the quick way is more painful to the flesh but more liberating for the Soul.

My Ancient Waldensian ancestors chose to give up the flesh rather than the lessons of the Soul. They knew that the flesh would be tortured and returned to the Earth in horrible ways. No matter how many people tried to stop it, their persecution persisted for centuries. Someone had to play the role of tormentor.

- If the tormentors were removed, would the Ancient Waldensians have received the same Spiritual lessons?

- Would my genetics be different if my ancestors had not suffered in the same way?
- Would I have the same knowledge without their suffering?
- Would I have the same compassion for those who suffer?
- Would I have the strength to not stop the suffering if that is what someone needs?
- Is suffering a judgment?
- Do you have suffering in your family lineage?
- Do you think this suffering affects you?
- Do you have compassion for those who suffer?
- Do you think you inflict suffering on others?
- Do you have as much compassion for your Self-suffering as you do for the suffering of others?
- Is being nonjudgmental part of your Gold Fortune that you feel guilty for accessing?
- If others suffer, must you suffer, too, or feel guilty?
- Does Guilt equal Compassion and Understanding?
- Does Guilt prevent you from accessing your own inner Gold Fortune?

Accessing your inner Gold Fortune can make others jealous. This means that you are open to attack. People who are locked in their Animal Mind forget that they, too, have their own Gold Fortune, so they want yours. Of course, they do not understand that they already possess that which they seek. This is why they try to get yours. And this often comes out in a variety of unsavory ways. Even when you try to explain that they already have what you have, people do not want to listen. They want to listen to their own programming and Animal Minds because that is the job of the programming and the Animal Mind.

When you access the Higher Spiritual Mind, the programming and Animal Mind think that they will die, so they do what they can to trick you into allowing them to survive in their way. Programming and Animal Mind will even sit in the background for a while, allowing you to think that your Higher Spiritual Mind is in control. Then, when you are feeling happy and satisfied that you are winning, you let your guard down. As soon as this happens, programming and Animal Mind jump out to get you. This is their job, to show you how many ways that you are/can be a victim. Every time this happens, you have a deeper Self-understanding of what a victim is and can be.

You have a choice at this one moment to either give in and participate in your programming/Animal Mind, or to surpass. Under stress, most people fall back into what they know and with what they are most deeply imprinted. This means you get to try a multitude of times to get up and get going out of victim-mentality. This is your Gold Fortune, to understand what victim mentality is, in all of its formats. You always have a choice to participate or not participate. Your programming and Animal Mind are betting that you choose to participate.

You are fed by the constant media news stream about all victims; about how many ways you can be a victim; how innocent people just like you can be and are victims; why you should be enraged over the injustices of the world (God's world, so are you supposed to be judging God's world); day in and day out. You are constantly and consistently fed about what is wrong with the world.

- How do you hold onto what is right with the world?
- Can the world just be what it is without constant judgment?
- If you could fix the world, does this mean you are supposed to fix it?

- Is part of your own inner Gold Fortune to be able to define what a victim is and in how many ways victimization can happen?
- Is the explanation of what is a victim part of this reality?
- If you know what is a victim without judgment, then are you no longer a victim?
- If you are no longer a victim, do you need to experience this reality in the same way?
- Is part of your Gold Fortune to be here without judgment so you understand another aspect of God's World and therefore of your own?

Your inner Gold Fortune encompasses much more than you realize. You are the only one who can access it and actualize it. No one can do it for you and ultimately no one can be against you but you. When you are afraid, you manifest something to be afraid of. When you are angry, you manifest something to be angry at. When you are a victim, you manifest an oppressor. When you don't believe you have an inner Gold Fortune, you manifest something to confirm this belief.

You have to look at all the insidious ways that you give up access to your own Gold Fortune. You find a way to look everywhere but where you need to look. The first things most people give away is Self-Value and Self-Worth, closely followed by Self-Confidence. As much as I know, I am still challenged to fully encompass my own inner Gold Fortune. The best way to work on these inner issues is to help each other; to walk together; to unify; to see the inner Gold Fortune in others so you can see the same in Self. Become a Living Example of what you want to see in others and in the world. If you could change the world, you would have done it by now. If you could aid all the victims of the world, you would have that by now.

- Are you are here to change God's world and to aid all the victims?

- Can one person save/change God's world?
- Is the imprinting of "Jesus the one Savior" meant to imprint you that one person/you is meant to Save The World?
- Are you imprinted/programmed with guilt because you are not doing what you are supposed to be doing which is changing/saving God's World that even Jesus Christ, Our Lord and Savior couldn't do?
- How many people are affected by this imprinting?
- How many people have "Savior Programming"?
- How many people do not know that their inner Gold Fortune is within?
- How many people cannot access what they do not even realize exists?
- How many people can access pain, fear, anger and guilt without a problem?
- Is pain, fear, anger and guilt part of your inner Gold Fortune that needs to be embraced as part of the whole?
- Are you learning to value Self?
- What are your outer reflections to verify your inner work?
- Do you respect the inner Gold Fortune of others even more than they respect it?
- Does less judgment/criticism increase your inner Gold Fortune?

On a recent flight, there was an older woman having a lot of challenges. The aircraft was smaller, so all passengers with carry-on luggage with wheels were instructed to check their bags before boarding the craft. This woman brought her luggage on the plane and could not find a place to fit it. A flight attendant eventually came along to tell her she would have to check her bag. The woman protested, saying she only had 30 minutes between flights, so the flight attendant helped

396 • HEIGHTS OF WEALTH

her remove a couple of items from the bag that weren't supposed to be on the plane and shove it under another seat across from where the woman was sitting.

Upon landing, the woman struggled to get the bag out, struggled to get the items replaced, and could not even pull the bag down the aisle behind her. Now, the woman was complaining loudly to no one in particular that she only had 20 minutes to get to her next flight. Her helplessness and whining about the situation caused several people on the flight to help her upright her bag and prevent it from tipping over. She never said thank you, she never showed any gratitude and I observed that she definitely was a bitter person. She walked slowly up the middle of the jetway pulling her bag behind her so there was no way to get past her. In front of her was an even slower gentleman walking down the middle of the jetway with a bag in each hand held out to the side so no one could get past him either.

I was grateful that I wasn't in a hurry, but eventually had to kind of tuck and roll to get around both of them.

There would have been a time in my life when I would have gone out of my way to help people like this, but I have learned that they are not grateful and they feel entitled to be waited on. There is a lot that I can do, but I have to ask what is most correct and beneficial for the situation before acting/not acting. There is a saying that those who aren't smiling need a smile the most.

- But is it my job to give them a smile?
- Is it my job to take away their pain in the moment?
- Did I create their situation or did they?
- If I take away their learning by giving them my Gold Fortune does it diminish what I have?
- Have you been in these positions where you could do something, but felt what was most correct and beneficial was to let people be?

- When this happens, do you feel bad or guilty?
- Do you Self-Value enough to maintain Self rather than give Self away to others who may not Value what you give?
- Can you receive as well as you can give?
- Can you ask for what you need?
- And when it is your turn to receive, do you feel guilty?
- Do you need to be able to receive in order to build/access your own Gold Fortune?

One thing that I consistently observe is the need to do something physical to set the energy. Doing something physical helps anchor in the nonphysical. Be sure you know what it is that you want to anchor in. Not talking or doing is huge. You are imprinted and programmed to measure your worth by doing than by setting up your inner world so the outer falls into place. Setting the energy is different than your intent. I was laughing with my aunt, telling her how I am good at apologizing because my good intent has many times offended others in ways that I never consciously wanted. Not doing anything physical is extremely challenging. It is challenging to not waste your resource of inner Gold Fortune by not thinking of solutions to issues that haven't happened, but in your mind, might happen.

My conservative, Southern Baptist aunt is challenged by some of our discussions, but I admire the fact that she doesn't judge me and is doing her best to understand what I tell her. She even says that what I talk about goes way over her head; it goes against everything that she grew up with and was taught; she doesn't know how she could ever explain it to anyone; yet, she continues to ask questions and most importantly, not judge. I explained to her that what I have gone through has only strengthened my faith in God; that it is my deep faith in my Source that pulls me through and protects me. I must stay anchored in God to do what I do. When you don't have anyone or anything, you finally turn within. Basically, your choices are eliminated which forces you to focus on and reach into your own Gold Fortune/God-Mind Wisdom.

- What has forced you to reach deep inside?
- How many times have you tried to do something without success, so you finally turn within?
- Do you feel like you must do something physical to make something happen?
- Do you feel helpless if you are not performing a physical function?
- Have you spent time asking Source to guide you in setting the energy in a way that is most correct and beneficial?
- Or, do you simply wallow in fear and negative Self-talk that serves no purpose but to drag you deeper into your programming?
- Is it more challenging to do mental work than do something physical?
- Do most people do everything they can think of and then go to Source when all else fails?
- Should you be more diligent in going to Source First and then take what you know into the outer world?
- Do you need negative experiences to push you deeper inside?
- Do you run faster if there is someone chasing you?

Most people can recall almost every single major painful/stressful/ horrible event that happened in their lives. This is because these are your lessons. When you remember that you are not here to change the world, but the world is here to change you, you also know that you have a choice. You can choose to become a pained, stressed, horrible person or you can choose a more positive route.

Living in New York definitely changed me. I learned how to communicate in ways that I could be heard. Being nice meant pushover/

victim and this is what people did. I stood my ground, anchored in the strength of my Oversoul and God-Mind. Then I looked the person in the eye and said what needed to be said to hold my space. My goal was not to overcome them, make them my friend, or walk over them. I set my boundaries and held them there. In New York, this meant others respected me. This doesn't mean that they liked me, but it meant if you try to walk on me, I'm not letting it happen. I didn't defend my Self; I fortified my boundaries with the strength of my Oversoul and God-Mind. These were tough lessons, but ones that continue to help guide me today.

In my perfect world, I would always be nice but some people do not know nice. This means that you have to match their color, tone and archetype to get their attention. Then, under the direction of your Source, you know what to do and when to do. People like this have usually been used and abused, but I didn't make them this way. Unless I am specifically told to do otherwise, I do not have to help them get over it, nor is it my intention to give my inner Gold Fortune so they feel better for 2 seconds without doing their own inner work.

There is the saying that "the good die young" and I can tell you that I have encountered a lot of really nasty, mean older people. They are here because they haven't gotten it yet, but on some level they are still trying. It is not for me to judge their journey, only to observe it.

It is the manure that fertilizes the fields and gardens. This is exactly what you are learning to do. Instead of becoming old, nasty, bitter, mean and crotchety like so many people, you are learning to accept that the manure of life can either suck you in to make you like manure, or you can use that same manure to fertilize your garden to grow worthwhile plants that add to the beauty and meaning of your world.

As a former dairy farmer, I know a lot about manure. You cannot put green/fresh manure directly on your fields. Fresh manure is too strong and will burn up anything living and all plant life will die. The soil can also be ruined from the fresh manure. The manure needs to dry and age. After it has set for some time, depending upon the manure storage facility, the manure breaks down and then it can be spread on the fields Even when it is spread, you cannot put too much on or the overabundance will cause the plants to die and ruin the soil. Some dairies only spread every few weeks or even months. When the manure is aged/broken down, this is when you have beautiful fertilizer for your fields. The best crops I ever grew came from manure, never from artificial fertilizers.

There is an art to spreading your manure. There are even all kinds of classes and courses in waste management. You, too, are learning about your own waste. If your painful/stressful/horrible events still elicit negative feelings, then this means your inner manure is still green/fresh and needs to be broken down so it is usable. When you start feeling like manure, you know it is time to age/break it down so it is useable. This way you use it; it does not use you.

- Do you have experiences that you still cannot look at?
- Do you feel there are experiences that have buried your inner Gold Fortune in manure?
- Do you feel your waste management is done in a way that is most correct and beneficial for you?
- Have tried to deal with your inner manure only to find that it was too fresh to sort through, burning you rather than helping you?
- Is it okay to set some manure aside and look at it later?
- Does your inner manure break down on its own or do you have to help it along?
- Do you know people who want to keep their inner manure and maybe splash it all over you?
- Have you ever felt your Self slipping into the manure instead of managing your waste properly?

- Can proper waste management add to your inner Gold Fortune?

- Is proper waste management something that the global handlers don't want you to know about?

- Does correctly releasing your physical waste correlate to releasing your mental waste?

One reason my older relatives have bodies that are disintegrating is because they do not have the proper building materials to repair them. They are victims of the no fat/low fat campaign; not enough vitamin D; cholesterol lowering drugs that destroy the liver as well as its ability to make CoQ10 for the heart. So, they have frail bones, frayed nervous systems and poor cellular structure from lack of fats; heart issues; thyroid issues and even some dementia setting in. They have given away their inner Gold Fortune by listening to authority figures rather than to Self and Source. It is extremely challenging to go against the crowd. But the more years you are on this Earth, the easier it is to see that going with the crowd takes from your inner Gold Fortune; it does not add to it.

The more I allow everything to be as it was destined, the less it seems I need to participate within it. The key is understanding that nothing can hold onto you unless you hold onto it in some way. I think one of the biggest challenges ever is to let go.

- When you let go of something with what do you replace it?

- Do you use your inner Gold Fortune wisely?

- Is it too easy to give your Gold Fortune to people who do not appreciate it?

- Does your inner Gold Fortune outshine others?

- Is your physical body rebuilding or disintegrating?

- Do negative mind-patterns disintegrate the body until the Soul can no longer stay in the vessel/body?

- Do people understand that holding onto negativity destroys?
- Is it important to hold onto negativity until you get the lessons built into the negativity?
- Can negativity be part of your inner Gold Fortune?

When you don't match the color, tone and archetypes of other people, you may not be noticed. You may feel nonexistent and you may not fit in. Many, many people tell me they have had this issue. You have the basic human archetype because you are in a human body. You have other matching color, tone and archetypes that allow others to communicate with you. When you observe a group they have many matching color, tone and archetypes because this is what constitutes a group.

When you are moving out of group consciousness into individualized consciousness you have to release the matching color, tone and archetype of the group. The more you release, the more you are not seen, except for whatever is still within you that is also within them. Then, you have a choice to remain in the group consciousness with matching color, tone and archetype or leave the group consciousness by releasing matching color, tone and archetype. When game over actually happens, you choose not to match color, tone and archetype in any way, effectively becoming invisible to people who do not know what you know

You can now consciously match the group consciousness as appropriate. For example, perhaps Source tells you to bully the bully via matching color, tone and archetype to that of the bully. In this way, you control color, tone and archetype, rather than color, tone and archetype controlling you.

- Do you want others to notice your inner Gold Fortune?
- Did you go unnoticed as a child or as an adult, or both?
- Is this because you did not have matching color, tone, or archetypes?

- Do you know how to change your color, tone and archetypes at will?
- Have you observed how clothing colors emulate energy field colors?
- Have you used Gold as a clothing color to pull out your inner Gold Fortune?
- How does wearing Gold color affect you?
- What do you think when you see others wearing Gold?
- Can you be visible/invisible depending upon your mind-pattern?
- Can you consciously change your colors, tone and archetype to become more or less visible?
- Can you cloak your energy field based upon mind-pattern?

The more you understand color, tone and archetype, the more you understand and know your audience. You must always remember that the people cannot reach your level, so you must communicate at their level. This means that they are what they are. Most thoughts, words and actions are not really conscious for most people. The more you become conscious of what you do, when you do and why you do, the more choices you have.

Always ask your Oversoul to guide you. You no longer can unconsciously spew forth words and actions because you are not so deeply entwined into the group consciousness. You must learn how to interact with the group mind of human animals. The deeper you Self-explore, the deeper your inner connection becomes. You know that we are All-One. You accept Self and your place, therefore others and their place. By accepting Self you allow others to accept you and you accept others.

Because I know a lot about many things, I can speak with confidence about many subjects. Others often either look up to me as an expert, which I most likely am not, or as arrogant. They are judging from their perspective. Instead of feeling abandoned and rejected, I am learning how to speak to others in a way that they can understand without compromising my Self. This means I don't have to display everything I know and everything I AM because I know how. If I want to be seen and understood, I must first know with compassion that, "*There but for the Grace of God, go I.*" I must hold within my heart gentleness and kindness, regardless of what I am told to say or do via the Oversoul level. I have to be strong enough to take whatever comes back to me. The reactions of others teaches me to stand strong in my center; Self-validate, reaching deeper into Source.

- Can your Gold Fortune intimidate others?
- How can you maintain your Gold Fortune when others berate and belittle you?
- Have others thought negatively about you because of what you know instead of accepting what you know?
- Do others judge you because they don't have all the facts?
- Do you make an effort to go to the level of your audience knowing that they cannot come to your level?
- Do you control your color, tone and archetypes or do they control you?
- Why do companies put their employees in matching smocks with the logo/name/archetype plastered all over the person?
- Why do people break bread/eat together at any important business/social function?
- Have you been to events where you haven't really liked the food?
- When this happens, how do you feel about the event?

**Status Quo**

Sometimes, you may feel like you are damned if you do and damned if you don't. Remember that you are learning to find the balance of how much inner Gold Fortune to access; share; reveal; sometimes extremely challenging choices.

I loved discovering what I found within. I loved sharing it with my teachers in school and of course I loved being recognized for doing so. But, the older I got, instead of being praised for what I knew, I was rejected or ignored. Instead of moving deeper into the support system that I imagined, I moved deeper into chaos and isolation. It is extremely challenging for humans to move out of the status quo. It is extremely challenging for me, too. The way you learn is to do your best and then observe. Your observations will show you how to navigate the next twist or turn in the road. If you access too much, too fast, you can become overwhelmed. If you share too much, too fast you overwhelm others. If you reveal what you have, you may be judged by others. As a general rule, most people will never appreciate what you are because they really don't want to get to know you. They want to get to know Self, yet live in fear of doing so. The challenges faced here on this planet are all looped together. Untangling the Self-loop reveals your own inner Gold Fortune.

- Once your Gold Fortune is revealed to Self, what do you do with it?
- Do you sometimes feel that the more you know, the less you know?
- Does knowledge confuse you?
- As you grow stronger, does this highlight the weakness of others?
- Does viewing the weaknesses of others make them more challenging to deal with?
- Does your strength intimidate others?

- Is tough love, kindness and compassion appreciated by others?
- Is consciously accessing your inner Gold Fortune a blessing or a curse?
- Does more inner Gold Fortune complicate or simplify?

Accessing your inner Gold Fortune may mean that others can be afraid of you. This outer isolation is your opportunity to push deeper within. Source becomes your guide and companion first. Sometimes you wish that your inner Gold Fortune would manifest monetarily so you could accomplish your goals. This is where I have to say, "Be careful what you wish for, you may get it." Here in the US, a woman recently won the largest lotto in history of 758million dollars which she elected to take in one lump sum of 480million dollars before taxes.

My son commented that she would soon lose it, as most people don't know how to handle that much money. This is exactly what we have been discussing. Often, when people get something good in their lives, something goes bad. For example, you start a new business, it goes bankrupt. You get a new vehicle, you crash it. You get a new relationship; the relationship sours. There are so many things that you label good when you get it, but then when the bad side reveals it Self, you wish you hadn't gotten it. This can be rough because ultimately the bad serves a purpose.

When I got the Italian webmaster, I labeled it good. I was thrilled with the possibilities. Yet, 6 years later I was still being sued for criminal slander in the Italian courts because he stole my website and I told people about it. Yet, I have to label the experience a positive because I am still learning and he is still teaching. I could not have learned what I am learning without him. I remind my Self that if it wasn't him, it would have been someone else. I have to determine what is within me that I need to divest my Self of to stop attracting these kinds of issues with my webmasters. I always remember that *rejection is God's protection* so I do not become disappointed when I don't get what I think I really want.

- Is it possible to get what you want, turning good into better?
- When you first receive, have you thought it was good only to later realize it was bad?
- How many inner, or outer, hissy fits have you had when life let you down?
- Were you being protected in spite of your Self?
- What if you have plans on how to spend your physical Gold Fortune that are not most correct and beneficial?
- Would you rather have the experience of having it and losing it?
- Or waiting until you can hold onto it?
- Does impatience lock you into linear time line?
- Does patience put you into the Eternal Now?

Is dealing with time a challenge when you want the outer manifestation of your inner Gold Fortune now rather than later?

One of the most challenging issues you face is the outer manifestation of your inner Gold Fortune. There is fear of outshining others and then really not fitting in as well as not knowing how to manage too much.

I don't care who you are, from my years in business I have found out that regardless of how much money you say you don't have, if it is something you are determined to get, you find the necessary money. People will say they don't have money to come to our events, then the next time they see us they say they went to India and spent months in an ashram. Or, they can't afford a consultation, but they find the money to give to a charlatan that messes with their head who took all their money so they can't afford to pay us when they need to be fixed from the trauma.

Through the years, regardless of what Stewart and I had or did not have, we always made his monthly child support payments and he is still obligated to pay for his adult children's college loans because of his divorce agreement. Regardless of what other bills have had to wait, these obligations were and are always met. The same with the house payment, phone and Internet bills, gas and electric bills, car payments, property taxes, home and car insurance. These bills are always paid. I have thought about how I would feel without having to financially juggle this to pay that, or this to make that happen. I use a lot of my creative resources to keep home, family and business running.

- What if all your bills were suddenly paid?
- Would that leave an empty place inside of you?
- After you run around buying what you have done without, then, what next?
- Does lack fulfill a need to create?
- Would you be lonely and isolated with physical manifestations of your inner Gold Fortune?
- Who would you trust?
- How many people take advantage of you now or have taken advantage of your generous nature in the past?
- Would the money that you seek be a blessing or a curse?
- Or a blessing that turns into a curse, something that you label good that turns bad?
- Do you want to dictate how much of your inner Gold Fortune outwardly manifests?
- Do you trust Source to know how much and when?

Today, I was looking at my son's savings account. There was a note from the bank congratulating him for his latest interest earnings of three cents. And another congratulatory note right under that because to celebrate his past year with the bank he is earning an additional three cents. When I was visiting my family, we spent some time at a local museum where I learned there used to be a US token called a mill which was 1/10 of one penny.

Interestingly that at one point, the President of the US said that no US citizen could own more than $100 worth of gold at a time. So, for people who think investing in gold is wise, think again. Remember, if you don't have the inner Gold Fortune to hold onto the outer displays, you aren't going to keep anything physical. It is amazing how quickly your material possessions can turn to trash.

We also have a truth in lending law here in the US that means with the amount owed on any credit card, you have to be told how much interest you are paying. This means that whenever I phone in a credit card payment, I am told at least three times how much I owe and then how much I have to pay. On the statement, you are told the amount you owe and if you pay only the minimum it will take you 28 years to pay it off and you will pay thousands of USD's in interest, but if you pay 2-3 times the minimum you can pay it off in only 3-5 years. All of these things are designed to make you feel worthless. Most people get angry, fearful, nervous, anxious, uptight, stressed out and everything else in between.

I am doing my best to not give these statements power over me. There was a time when I was very anxious about not having my credit cards paid off. I used to stress and lose sleep over being in debt. The more I relax and let it go, the more opportunity for funds to come in to pay them off. Even throwing away coupons used to make me feel guilty. Yet, when a loaf of bread costs $3-5 and I get a coupon for a discount of ten cents. I am damned if I do and damned if I don't. To me, throwing away a coupon is like throwing away money. If I use the coupon, I ponder if I am saying that I am so in need of money that I'm grateful for ten cents so I can get a loaf of bread. Even seeing the coupon is supposed to remind you that you are not worth much. The store is insulting me by only offering me ten cents off a loaf of bread in the same way the bank insults by only offering three cents on a bank account.

- Are these subtle reminders that no matter what you do, you are worthless?
- If you get a coupon, is it most correct and beneficial to use it, save it, or throw it away?
- Did you realize that the US government can limit the amount of gold you have in your home?
- Have you known poor people that always stay poor, no matter what they are given and wealthy people who lose, only to get wealthy again?
- Does limited outer manifestations of Gold Fortune push you deeper into creativity?
- Does limited outer manifestations of Gold Fortune help you refine what you want vs. what you need?
- Do you worry about losing what material manifestations that you already have?
- Or do you know, that if something happens, you can always get more?

Most people are so busy trying to earn a living that they think the answer to everything is more money. But more money means different things to different people. And more money is the outer manifestation of what you have within. More money doesn't have anything to do with anything other than following Universal Law. You manifest more money so you can trade it in for something that you can use in this reality.

- What if you did not need the instant manifestation of more money?

- What if your home stayed warm or cool based upon your mind-pattern?
- What if your home instantaneously formed around you because of your mind-pattern?
- What if food appeared on your table because you can think it into existence?
- Is converting energy to money another way to protect you from your Self?
- Or develop your creativity?
- What if you are on your way to instant manifestations but you need time to make the most correct and beneficial choices?
- Does the need for money buy you time to wade through the options available in this reality?
- Are there too many options?
- If your inner Gold Fortune instantaneously manifested as Gold, how would your life change?
- Who would be after it?
- How would you protect it?
- Where would you go?
- Where would you live?
- Would this be condemning you to a life of isolation?
- Would you trade outer manifestations for the companionship of others?

I have often said that because those of us who study Hyperspace/Oversoul Methodologies create a group mind, we do move together and grow together in similar ways. If one person stands out too easily, it is too easy for global handlers to squash you like a bug. But because we are all growing together, there is strength in our numbers. Joined together, our mind-patterns strengthen the whole.

Your learning is my learning; my learning is your learning. Our outer manifestation of Gold Fortune is truly each other. Balance is a huge key. I think I never realized how out-of-balance I was until about 10 years ago. And as you are discovering, balance changes depending upon what you are studying. Another conundrum. United We Stand.

- Does it take all of us to consciously bring true Gold Fortune to this reality?
- Do you think there have been others before us doing the same thing?
- Are we here to wake up the world or to help anchor mind-patterns for brave Souls?
- If this world is meant to change us, does that mean we move on into another reality?
- Could outer manifestation of Gold Fortune without stability of your inner Gold Fortune mean taking short-term pleasure instead of long-term gains?
- Is it possible to bring your inner Gold Fortune out without stress?
- Is it your stress that forges your Soul Growth, turning your inner Gold Fortune into something usable?
- With all that you know, are you still too hard on your Self?

## AFFIRMATIONS—OBSTACLE COURSE: EARTH

You choose to be upon this Earth in this moment in time and space for your Personal and Unique Soul-Growth opportunities. Develop new coping mind-patterns that allow you to move beyond simply tolerating your life, to accelerate and take advantage of your ever-present classroom. Earth is your friend and teacher.

*I AM well-rested.*

*My Source provides all the energy that I need.*

*I AM well-nourished.*

*My Source provides all the nourishment that my Soul needs.*

*My physical body is a reflection of my Soul.*

*My physical body is maintained by my Source.*

*I take care of my physical body, under the direction of my Oversoul and God-Mind.*

*My physical body is happy, healthy and flexible.*

*I take care of my mind.*

*I make the choices that are most correct and beneficial for every situation, under the direction of my Oversoul and God-Mind.*

*I mentally and emotionally ingest only that which elevates and uplifts me.*

*I AM mindful of my choices and options.*

*I only participate in elevating thoughts, words and actions.*
*I do my best to stay clear and clean in all circumstances.*

*I release the need to judge others.*
*I release the need to judge my Self.*

*I observe with compassion and understanding.*
*"There but for the Grace of God, go I."*

*I focus on what I need to learn.*
*I thank all who interact with me.*

*Everyone and every circumstance teaches me.*
*I AM grateful.*

*Every perceived block is a stepping stone to strength and balance.*
*I AM strong, yet flexible.*

*The strength of my Soul is reflected in my physical body.*
*My physical body is strong and supportive.*

*The strength of my Soul increases in every moment.*
*The strength of my physical body increases in every moment.*

*The strength of my Soul-energy coursing through my physical body increases in every moment.*

*My physical body strengthens to support the strength of my Soul-energy.*


*I observe my Earth obstacles, without judgment.*

*I understand my Earth obstacles.*


*My Soul-Personality strengthens.*

*I accept my purpose and mission on this Earth.*


*I utilize the opportunities on Earth for Soul-strengthening.*

*I have compassion for my journey.*


*My support system is my Self and Source.*

*The strength of my outer world supports reflects my faith in my inner world support.*


*I stand in alignment with my Source.*

*I allow my Source to direct my process.*


*I greet each day knowing that my Source guides me.*

*I AM safe and protected.*

*Every obstacle is an opportunity to more closely align with my Source.*

*I listen with my inner ears.*

*I pay attention to the instructions of my Source.*

*I trust the process before me.*

*All tasks are surmountable.*

*I follow Source instructions one step at a time.*

*I release the need to control and manipulate the outcome of my opportunities.*

*Source guides me.*

*My Source knows the big picture of my Soul-Personality.*

*One step leads me to my next step.*

*I choose long-term success.*

*I stay the obstacle course.*

*I chose to be here.*

*I choose to do the best that I can.*

*There is no obstacle too lowly.*

*I AM humble.*

*There is no task too great.*

*I AM courageous and brave.*


*Obstacle Course Earth exists for my benefit.*

*I give thanks to the Earth for agreeing to provide my personal Obstacle Course.*

# Money! What It Is & How To Get It!

Money is an emotionally-charged topic, especially amongst those people who don't have any. Many people think that they can buy Self-Worth/Self-Value. So, they surround the physical body with things from the material world. Some people think the more things they have, the more the Soul is worth.

This is what surprises people who are not used to money when they finally get money. They get a high from the initial purchase because being able to get what you want makes you feel powerful. But because this is an external boost, it eventually goes from a high to non-existent. Then, you have to buy again and again and again. The high doesn't last. People come into your life because of your money and not because of you. They, just like you, are looking for a high from things. If you don't have money and can't buy things, then they don't want you because it isn't you that brought them into your life in the first place.

This leaves a lot of empty people who keep searching. This is one reason why many people want money. They want things to fill the empty spaces within the Soul. The Soul is energy. It does not hold things. The Animal Mind needs things because things come from the Earth, just like the physical body is a product of Earth.

- Do you know people who have things but are still never happy?
- Have you ever thought a thing was going to bring you happiness only to discover that it did not?
- How do you distinguish between Self-Value, value that others place on you, and the value that things give you?
- Have others placed values on you that you felt you did not deserve?
- What does Self-Value have to do with Money?
- If you always put your Self second, do others learn that you always come last?

People get angry at the government, politicians, pesticide companies, pharmaceutical companies, terrorists, whomever/ whatever, because they think these people/organizations are taking away their Self-Value. No one can take away your Self-Value. They put out the illusion that you are powerless to see if you will grab the bait. The majority of people do. They are flunking their own Self-tests. These organizations only exist because of the mind-pattern of the populace. These organizations build their very existence with the collective psychic energy generated by the mind-pattern energy of the masses. The lessons become increasingly intense the more you fail the Self-tests. Most people continue to get angrier as the lessons grow. This feeds the energy of the lesson so the cycles Self-perpetuates, thus continually feeding the same organizations that the people despise.

The global handlers know this and use this universal law to their benefit while the masses perceive this to be to their detriment. On the Oversoul level, you understand that the reason the global handlers do this is because the people have lessons to learn. As long as the people fail to learn the lesson, the global handlers appear to become increasingly powerful, viewed as oppressors that have to be stopped. The reality is that the mass mind-pattern is creating this perceived enemy. The bitter is the cure only when people embrace the bitter instead of running from it.

You are learning to recognize the bait and then reject it in favor of the bigger picture. You are learning to have Unconditional Love, Compassion, and Acceptance for those who accept the bait because they are not ready to grow. You are learning to withstand the attacks of those who take the bait and now see you as the enemy. The further you remove your personal energetic involvement from the entangled mind-pattern of the masses, the less you have to participate in the lessons of the masses. This is one of the first steps in helping your income grow.

- How do you feel about the control organizations of the world?
- How have you transitioned from taking the bait to ignoring the bait?

Some kind of money in some form exists in all cultures. When people start talking about how materialistic and terrible societies are, realize that all cultures assign value to something and then that something is used as a medium of exchange. People act like money just popped up and it is bad. Period. The Pope and the Queen of England both have unlimited resources yet few people talk about why they are not spreading their wealth. Instead, the masses are mesmerized by the Pope and the royal family. But when it comes to you or I having money we are brutally attacked and called evil. Ultimately, people are not so upset about the concept of money but the distribution of wealth. They are angry that enough is not distributed to them. Thus begins and continues this Self-perpetuating cycle of lack/poverty consciousness.

- Why isn't money distributed to everyone?
- If you had the gates of money open up and pour out an unlimited supply, what would you do with it?

- Would you be like the Queen of England or the Pope?
- What dilemmas would resolve and what new ones would be created?
- What Universal Laws do the Global Handlers follow that you do not?
- If all the money was equally distributed throughout the world, would the rich still get richer while the poor get poorer?
- Is mind-pattern still the difference between rich and poor people?

Changing the mind-pattern does not happen overnight. Many times I have heard people say that they have had our Expansions' books for many years and never looking at it until now. They say that they had some issues, remembered the books and now after all these years, they are doing their inner level work. In the same way, you can have all the answers that you need right in front of you but until you actually use them having tools is inconsequential. Even when you are consciously trying to change, you cannot see Self all at once or you would explode. From fear of your own magnificence and internal power to fear of all the negative buried within. You simply do not change overnight. When someone appears to change overnight, the process to put them in this position was ongoing for a long time prior.

- Why do the truly wealthy not associate with those of a lower economic status?
- Why do wealthy people believe that staff has a shelf life?
- Do the truly wealthy flaunt their wealth?
- Are the truly wealthy examples for others?

The majority of wealth is held by approximately 1% of the population. This top echelon practices Universal Law because they do not have any sense of lack in their mind-pattern. They do not Self-Value by their things because they do not have a thought in their mind that they might not ever have whatever they want, when they want. There are always articles on social media about the newest yacht being built for millions and billions of dollars; for opulent private jumbo jets and apartments and condos worth millions and billions decorated with solid gold fixtures. Universal Law.

They value Self without one shred of doubt. And, they give to each other; to their children; spouses; associates; top employees and top house staff. They take care of and support each other. They share homes, staff, yachts, airplanes, inside tips, businesses. Another Universal Law. They get back what they give out.

They do not take from others; others give it to them. If you get your Self in a financial bind, it is ultimately your responsibility. And, if it wasn't this situation, it would be something else. Someone receives what you give up. These people position themselves so that if you throw something away, they are ready to receive. Universal Law. They only take what they are given.

They do not give money to the masses because the masses cannot handle money. Universal Law. They do not interfere with the lessons of others.

They do not try to mitigate the experiences of others. Universal Law They do not take away the lessons of others.

They lay everything out in black and white. Even if you don't understand it, your lack of education is not their issue, it is yours. Universal Law. They tell you upfront what they are doing. These are just a few examples of the truly wealthy using Universal Law in their favor.

**Breaking Through Programming**

The first time I read that Christopher Columbus did not discover America. I could not believe it. I was incensed that I had been lied to in school all those years. In the same way, the masses have so much programming surrounding money that it almost hurts your brain when you recognize what is really going on. All your defenses go up to say the truth is incorrect because this is your indoctrination.

The us vs. them mentality keeps you angry and fighting in such a way that you never stop to think that you should not be fighting with them. They are actually your teachers rather than your adversaries. They taunt you to get you angry and too often people take the bait. They dare you at every turn to reach inside and pull out your most vile thoughts. They goad you into even more vile deeds, provoking your Animal Mind to gain control of you. Instead of looking at the block as a stepping stone to something bigger and better, too often people simply stop whenever they perceive a block. They want you to feel boxed in, closed off, isolated, hopeless, helpless, incapacitated, and like you will never get ahead financially. This means you continually Self-justify why you do not have enough money.

Sometimes you have to help people even when they do not want help. For example, I knew my children had to have a coat on when it was snowing outside. If my children refused to put their coat on, I was going to make sure the coat got on, and they knew it. No discussion. I told them to put on their coats and the coats went on. I have had parents tell me that their children wouldn't put their coats on and the parent didn't know what to do. I made my children put on their coats because this was what they needed even if the child could not see beyond the warm room they were currently in.

Now, I have parents tell me they don't even begin potty training their children until they are between 2-3 years old. Both my boys were dry even through the night by the time they were one. My boys sat on the potty after every meal or snack and learned what it was like to be clean and dry. We read while they were on the potty and it generally was a pleasant time. If they did anything they got one chocolate chip. When I was at my mother-in-laws house, same thing. After a meal, the boys went on the potty. But because there was lots of activity, my child started to fuss. But you know what, my child still went on the potty. My mother-in-law thought I was terrible for forcing them. I was a tough teacher by forcing my boys to put on coats and use the potty. I could have just let them run around and do whatever they want. But I set the rules and I enforced them. The boys knew they better do what mom said.

In the same way, the Illuminati are meting out lessons and forcing you to learn; forcing you to say, "Hey, wait a minute, I'm better than this"; forcing you to take a look at your life, what you have and compare to what you could have. Your lessons are forced upon you, putting you in a reactive position.

- Keeping in mind that your Soul is ageless, where did you come from and why are you in this position in the first place?
- Which lessons do you remember the most, the tough ones or the easy ones?
- Which lessons make you grow the most, the tough ones or the easy ones?
- Who are the biggest teachers, the tough ones or the easy ones?
- When do you try the hardest, when life is tough or when it is easy?
- Do you consider your Self a reactive person or a proactive person?
- Does reactive force you to grow more than proactive?

Money is a medium of exchange that keeps the balance. You took this book, you give money in exchange. You take food from a store, you give money in exchange. Indigenous people all over the globe give to Mother Earth whenever they take something from her. They took, they give to create balance. When I have been criticized for asking for money for my products/services, I have satirically replied:

I sent my electric company a smile; my gas company some hugs; my mortgage company a good thought for the day; my insurance company a lovely picture of a sunny day.

A smile and a compliment are always wonderful because these feed the Soul. But to maintain the human animal, you need some form of currency so when you take food, clothing and shelter you have something to give to maintain balance. Currency is called currency for a reason. Currency is energy. If you expend your energy working for me, I give you currency for balance. Then you take this currency so you can take care of your animal body. You need that Earth-based exchange to fulfill Earth-based need. You live on the Earth yet you are programmed to feel guilty for fulfilling Earth-based needs.

- Why do you accept this?
- Are you here for your body to starve?
- Are you here for your body to be ill?
- Are here you here for your body to be cold or hot or uncomfortable?
- Do you feel guilty when you take care of the animal body?
- Do you feel guilty when you take care of your Soul?

The global handlers try to make you feel guilty about what have by constantly showing you people who have less than you. And, you should always give to the needy. Huge campaigns are organized to entice you via guilt, to give to the needy. It costs a lot of money to run these huge campaigns. The global handlers have enough money to take care of everyone financially with tons left over. But they don't. Instead, they entice you to do this. They want you to interfere with the mass mind-pattern. They manipulate you to give more while the global handlers get more.

Giving to the needy feeds into Savior Programming. Saving others does not leave you time to save Self. This also allows you to feel/be superior to someone so you forget about those who are superior to you, at least for a few minutes. Your conscience tells you to help others, because "what if this was me?" However, this is why you have to go to the Oversoul level to determine who to help, when, and how. This is extremely challenging because some people need their lessons. Universal Law says you are not allowed to interfere without Oversoul permission.

- Have you had these kinds of conundrums?
- Why do the global handlers entice you to help while they sit back with plates of abundance running over?

The global handlers do their best to keep you out of balance. All the charities and organizations that you give to, appeal to your emotions. The emotions are tied into your Animal Mind which includes your Reptilian brainstem where programming occurs. This means fight or flight are also activated, so when others do not go along with your emotional response, you want to either flee/avoid or fight/argue/rampage. This is also why brain-balancing techniques are so important. T-Bar balancing at the pineal gland as well as the breathing technique I teach you in *Decoding Your Life* are paramount to beginning to get a handle on what is really going on. Walking is good for this, as is any exercise in moderation that alternates left, right, left, right. This helps both hemispheres of the brain work together. This begins to take you out of the Reptilian brainstem, Animal Mind, fight or flight response mode.

However, others may not like your new attitude. "Misery loves company" always seems to be true. This is because animals operate as a group mind. Whatever one person feels, instinct says that you, too, must feel. If you don't feel as the pack does, there must be something

428 • HEIGHTS OF WEALTH

wrong with you. When I was in Suriname, I was told by the locals about an uprising instigated by one of their leaders. I was told that they didn't know what it was about, just that their leader called upon them, and they went.

When you get into your Higher Spiritual Mind, you begin to deviate from the pack. The pack, or Animal Mind, is threatened. To survive as a species in the status quo, certain behaviors are expected. Therefore, instinct says you are either brought back into the pack or are attacked until death. This is the way of the animal world. This is why emotional attacks are so vicious. They are truly animalistic, brutal and ugly. You cannot reason with emotion.

- Have you seen others emotionally attack others?
- Have you been the recipient of these kinds of ugly and brutal attacks?
- Do you do brain balancing techniques?

Societal classes are further divided via education and money. In the US, anyone can do anything, if you have enough money. Those without money don't always want education. Schools in poor areas only teach basic reading, writing and math. Goals are not high because expectations are not high.

The spellcheck dictionary on my website is very limited. If I type in a word that I know is correct, there are times when the spellcheck will say it is incorrect. This makes me wonder if it is even a word. Then I go to the Internet and the word is there. My elementary school kept a huge dictionary in the library laying open on a stand. It was at least 12 inches thick with huge oversized pages that were very thin. When we couldn't find a word in the dictionary we kept in our desks, we were sent to the library to look in the big dictionary. Eliminating words from our everyday vocabulary is another way to downsize and divide the masses from the scholars/elite.

Every school has a basic agenda, but curriculums taught in a private school that charges $100,000 per year is definitely different than curriculums taught in a public school supported by taxes. Medical care is different for those with money than those without. The global elite view the masses as nothing more than expendable animals that exist to support their luxuries. Because the masses are treated like animals, most respond as animals. As the classes further divide, the middle class is shrinking out of existence. The lower classes attack the middle classes who they perceive as wealthy compared to them. This cycle continues to perpetuate it Self until one of these days the middle class will cease to exist. These are all ways that the global handlers get you to attack each other. The global handlers set the stage and the people willingly step into character and carry forth the play. When you use your energy to attack others, even if you view it as a justifiable attack, you are still attacking.

Whatever you give out, returns to you.

### *Divided we fall; united we stand.*

### *Anger is an acid that can do more harm to the vessel in which it is stored than to anything on which it is poured.*

#### *Mark Twain*

- What can you do to change the division within the masses?
- Are the masses ready for higher education, better healthcare and more wealth?

When you are divided within your Self, the outer world reflects this back. Illusions split you into many pieces. For example, sometimes you argue with Self about what you should or should not do, buy or not buy, give or not give. You are not sure of where to focus; goals are elusive and constantly changing; distractions are everywhere; choices feel overwhelming. These are all divisions within Self.

- What aspects within Self cause division?
- When you Self-Value, do you have this kind of inner division?
- Do the global handlers know what they want and just do it?
- Do they take risks?
- Do they make excuses why this or that didn't work?
- Do the global handlers overwhelm you with choices it distracts you from accomplishing anything major?

Leaders must make quick and often unpopular decisions. Let's say you are a village chief and you know each one of your people. You suddenly become aware that an attack on your village is imminent. You know that some of your people are doing to die. You know that they are going to have to fight. You know that some have to be on the front lines and these will be the first to die. You know that this is your only chance to save those who are at the back of the line. You know that you are the best leader. If you go to the front of the line, you are going to die. If you go to the back of the line and are protected, there is a chance that you can lead those who survive.

- Does putting the people front line out there make you less compassionate?
- Here is another example. You are a parent who wants your child to grow into a responsible adult.
- Do you shelter your child from the bitterness of the world?
- Do you educate him/her about what to expect and how to handle the possibilities?
- Have you seen parents who tie the children to the parents into adulthood?
- What happens to the child?
- What happens to the adult child when the parent is no longer around?

- Does the child grow from bitter experiences?
- Who has the tougher job, those who must discipline or those who hand out treats and rewards?

Many people make assumptions. Remember, when you assume you make an "ass" out of "u" and "me". This is why you are learning to go to the Oversoul level. When you go to the Oversoul level, this does not just apply to your everyday life. This applies to everything you do. You are learning that the outer reflects the inner. This includes all people, places, and things with which you interact on a daily basis.

It is challenging for most people to apply these same Universal Laws when it comes to the global handlers. It is almost as if you forget that the outer reflects the inner. The global handlers cannot exist unless they reflect something about you, personally. To understand the reflection, you have to understand what they are. This very small group has most of the world's assets, the best that this reality has to offer in all things from gold to relationships to support to family ties to secret knowledge to anything else you want to name. You must go to the Oversoul level to see what is behind/within/motivating these Soul-personalities. Because as long as they evoke any negative feelings, this exists within you and they reflect it back. And, when they evoke negative emotion from within you, this hurts you, not them.

These are tough lessons, but ones that you must look at if you want to get through your own blocks and barriers to bringing in wealth and prosperity to your daily living. It is easy to kick something that seems far away and irrelevant; but this group is a direct reflection of you and what you choose to express in this very moment, right now. People often assume that these people have qualities that you do not have. But, because you don't see these qualities does not mean that they do not have them.

- If your Soul-Personality needs to go to war, do you need someone to put you in that war?

- If your Soul-Personality needs to go without food, do you need someone to make sure you don't get it?

- If your Soul-Personality needs to experience lack and limitation, do you need someone to create this experience for you?

- If you see the possibilities, does this make you want more?

- If you never see the possibilities, would you instead settle for what you have without striving to improve?

- Does a runner's speed increase when he/she races against another runner?

People often see our large home and automatically make many assumptions that are ultimately none of their business. They don't stop to think that maybe we got a good deal on the home, or that we worked hard to get the money for the down payment. Or that we have suffered and we deserve a nice home. You can actually go on the public records to see what we paid for our home and when we paid it, as well as the taxes that we pay on it. They don't think about the many people who we have let stay with us under a variety of circumstances; the cost of upkeep and what we must do to maintain it; that we have 5 children and need a home that accommodates them and that my father has his own apartment on the 3rd floor. We have written about our humble beginnings in **Alien Connection**, and it seems that this is where some people want us to stay. We do our best to practice what we preach. Our large home is a result of our mind-pattern and inner efforts to grow and expand. We want to be an example that you, too can follow. I sometimes wonder if they would prefer that someone who is trying to teach wealth and prosperity consciousness live in a small home with small vehicles and thus small mind-patterns. Stewart and I have many people angry at us. It is easier for them to be angry at us than to take Self-responsibility.

- Do we do anything to make them angry?
- Or do we simply exist?
- Or do they look at us and then react with what is already active within themselves?
- Do the global handlers keep you angry at them, or do you keep your Self angry at them?
- Do they set up outer distractions so that you only see Self but you think you see them?
- Who keeps you in the loop, you or them?

People attack. The group mind is to attack. Anytime you are different than the pack, you are attacked. If you have anything from supportive relationships or career advancement to having a nice home, there has to be a reason why you got it that most likely isn't flattering. Sometimes, from a distance, people will wish you well. But most likely, they attack. When you go to the Oversoul level, you know that it is always the mind-pattern of the Soul-Personality in its current expression that attracts whatever he/she has in this reality. Whatever you have, you earn regardless if you view it as a positive or a negative.

If I have a negative experience in my life, I have earned it some way or another. If people attack me, then somewhere along the way I am attacking my Self. If I don't have supportive relationships then somewhere along the way I have earned this by not supporting my Self. If I have wealth and prosperity then I have earned that regardless if you see it or not. Perhaps the wealthy had the most despicable jobs ever such as sending people to war, devising tortures, upholding faith, who-knows-what, either-positive or negative. Thus, they have earned their positions of power, wealth and prosperity in ways that we cannot even begin to imagine.

- If you can't imagine why they should have ostentatious wealth and not you, should be angry or make assumptions?
- Should you instead observe and learn?

- Is it your Animal Mind that wants to attack the global handlers?
- Does the world need global handlers?
- Can the masses handle wealth and prosperity?
- Even with equal distribution of wealth, would there still be some people who have more and some who would lose it all?
- Should those that pull ahead give to those that fall behind?
- Are those that fall behind entitled to the wealth of those who pull ahead?
- What is fair and equitable?
- Who determines this?

Even with the same initial wealth, some people will quickly go through whatever they have and others will turn whatever they have into more while others will maintain the status quo. Think of how some people chow down without even tasting, others savor every bite while others only eat to sustain their bodies. Every person is unique in his/her own way. This is because the mind-patterns of the individuals are so varied.

When you see poor people with little or no food, clothing, or shelter you must to go the Oversoul level to determine why. Because you are kind and caring, you want to help them. If you had no emotions, you would not care what happens to them as long as you are okay. Your Oversoul can explain that these people are exactly where they need to be for now. Perhaps one of the reasons you are here is to learn that everyone has a place and a purpose. Because you don't understand it at the moment does not make it wrong. Maybe it is most correct for some people to be in poverty. Maybe it is most correct for some people to be in ostentatious wealth. You cannot fix all the impoverished people of the world. Nor can anything you say or do make the ostentatiously wealthy lose their wealth.

- What can you learn about you by observing these opposite examples of wealth?
- Why are you somewhere in between on the scale of wealth?

Global handlers exist first as a projection of the mind-pattern of the masses and second, because most people need to be handled. Ghandi led his people to freedom from British rule. But once the people were free, his supporters started infighting and it was his own supporters that eventually assassinated him.

- Were Ghandi's people better off under British rule?
- Was Ghandi better off under British rule?
- Did his people need handlers?
- Did he lead his people to freedom or to different oppressors?
- Who has oppressed you in your life?
- When you got rid of the oppressor did you just get a new one?
- Why did you even need an oppressor in the first place?
- Do you still need oppressors in your life?
- Are you ready to be Self-responsible?
- Do you need an oppressor so you have something to fight against?
- Does the fight make you stronger?
- Without the fight would you even think about change?

## Credit Cards

When credit cards first appeared I can remember sitting in the back seat of my parents' car while they were discussing them. It seems that credit cards were mailed out all over the place to everyone, and my parents only talked about how awful they were. I guess this must have been the general sentiment at the time, as eventually a law was passed where you could only be sent a credit card if you requested one. Then my parents were bombarded with letters wanting them to request credit cards.

My parents refused to get them, continuing to say that they were no good and you should only buy what you could pay for, unless it was something major like a house. My parents even saved up for their automobiles so they could pay cash. I remember their discussions on how they rotated their expenses. One year they painted the outside of the house; one year they painted the inside of the house; one year we went to the Midwest to visit family; one year we took a local vacation; one year they bought a new car. Every pay check my parents put something into one of the above funds until the designated year when they used that fund for its designated purpose. Then, they started over.

No one forced anyone to accept the credit cards; but gradually, people started using them, no longer saving but buying now to satisfy the Animal Mind. I first got a credit card to collect the points so I could get something with the points. But, I paid it off every month. At that time usury rates were in effect, meaning that the interest charged had a limit. At that time the highest interest rate that could be charged was 12% in my state. I knew of other states where it was 18%, which I thought was awful. Today, I know some credit card companies charge as much as 35%, and the worse your credit score, or if you are late with a payment, the higher your rate. You agree to the terms on the credit card willingly. No one forces you. Now, there are some places that won't even accept cash. You definitely cannot check into a hotel without a credit card, or even make a reservation.

You agree to constantly be in debt when you accept these cards. On one hand, if you accept the debt there has to be a part of you that is capable of paying it off. Some people can't even get a credit card. Sometimes I think these people are better off. Immigrants who are used to working hard and saving don't use credit cards often pull ahead financially because they do not incur debt. Someone with a small home and older car might actually be worth more on paper than someone with a huge home and fancy cars. The first person has no debt; the latter owes more than he/she owns.

- Does accepting a credit card build a mind-pattern of debt within you?
- Who do you owe?
- Would you rather have life with or without a credit card?
- Do debit cards promote a mind-pattern of having whatever you need readily available?
- Are people better without credit cards?
- Did you pay off your first credit card or use it to go further into debt?

Credit cards continue to imprint you with a variety of emotions. For the most part, they are a negative, making you feel embarrassed, overwhelmed like you don't have and you never will; addictive mind-patterns; false sense of security; giving you a sense of power when you spend and then something else when you get the bill. There are declarations on your statement that say, if you only make the monthly minimum payment, it will take you 12 years to pay this off and you will spend $15,000 in interest, but if you pay more it will only take you 9 years and you will only spend $11,000 in interest. These kinds of statements are uplifting and elevating. However, if you control the credit card rather than the credit card controlling you, then credit cards can serve a useful purpose. I have experienced all of these emotions from the credit card. What is important is that you be aware of both positive and negative aspects so that whatever you do, you do in awareness.

Once you have a credit card, you cannot just get rid of it without it hurting your credit score. This seems totally incorrect to me, but that is the way it is. It is better to have inactive cards, so I have a place where I put these cards. Because once you have a card, your credit limits keep increasing until you could buy an entire city yet never pay off the card. If you find your Self in credit card debt, you can phone the company and ask them what you can do to work it out. Some are hostile and some will work with you. Sometimes you can close the account and pay the principle without the interest and without affecting your credit. The next thing that you can do is choose the card with the lowest balance, and pay extra on it every month. This sets the mind-pattern that you can pay more.

Pay only the minimum on the other cards until you get the one with the lowest balance paid off. then, go to the next card with the lowest balance. This might take some time, but you will make progress. You really only need 3 or 4 credit cards. I have been places where my credit card won't go through and I can't phone the bank to find out why. Sometimes they just don't work. But, you still have to watch that you don't allow the balances to creep up because you forgot that you used it 3 weeks ago.

Another trick I use when paying my bills in general, is to pay an amount that adds up to the number 8 as 8 is the Oversoul/energy/money number. If my electric bill is $250 I pay $260. Or if my insurance bill is $120 I pay $125. When I pay my hairdresser or my bill at a restaurant including tip, I do my best to make the total add up to an 8. The more 8's you can get in your life, the more your Oversoul/energy/money grows and strengthens.

- Do you have a plan on how to pay off your credit cards?
- Do you know not to close your accounts but to put them away and not use them?
- Do you realize that the companies keep raising your credit limits?
- And also the interest rate and penalties for late payments, too?
- Are you able to keep your mind out of the debt mentality and into the "I can use this to my benefit" mentality?

• Do debit cards encourage people to overspend?

## Found Money

Here is an interesting article published by CNN in 2013:

**Millions of Americans are missing out on billions in forgotten cash.**

Currently, states, federal agencies and other organizations collectively hold more than $58 billion in unclaimed cash and benefits. That's roughly $186 for every U.S. resident. The unclaimed property comes from a variety of sources, including abandoned bank accounts and stock holdings, unclaimed life insurance payouts and forgotten pension benefits.

Some people are owed serious cash. Last year, a Connecticut resident claimed $32.8 million, proceeds from the sale of nearly 1.3 million shares of stock. The recipient of the funds requested to remain anonymous and no further details were provided. More than $300 million in pension benefits is currently owed to some 38,000 people, according to the Pension Benefit Guaranty Corp. The unclaimed benefits currently range from 12 cents to a whopping $704,621, with an average benefit of $9,100. Benefits may go unclaimed because an employee is unaware they had accrued retirement benefits at a previous employer, the agency said. However, the majority of the forgotten funds -- roughly $41.7 billion -- are held by the states, according to the National Association of Unclaimed Property Administrators.

Under varying state laws, financial institutions and other companies are required to turn over any funds considered "abandoned," including uncashed paychecks, forgotten bank account balances, unclaimed refunds, insurance payouts and contents of safe deposit boxes. They have found some pretty unusual items like diamonds, bottles of liquor and sardines. Property is usually considered abandoned after the holder of the account or property has had no activity or contact with the owner for several years.

"The money belongs to the owner in perpetuity. Even if the owner dies, then their heirs could come back and claim it," said Carolyn Atkinson, West Virginia's deputy treasurer for unclaimed property and a past president of the National Association of Unclaimed Property Administrators.

Florida's chief financial officer announced this month that the state had received 61,271 new unclaimed property accounts worth more than $25 million as part of a settlement with insurance company AIG (AIG). The settlement is one of several reached last year with major insurers, including MetLife (MET), Prudential (PRU) and Nationwide after regulators in 20 states audited the methods they used to locate life insurance beneficiaries after a policyholder's death.

http://money.cnn.com/2013/01/24/pf/unclaimed-money/

So, the masses are crying that they don't have money, yet this article proves that the masses have plenty of money that they don't even know about. This is why I keep telling you that lack is a function of mind-pattern.

Here is a website that I regularly share:

http://unclaimed.org/

In the US, you look up any state you have ever lived in to see if you have any unclaimed funds. Every year, people I know use this website to find money that they didn't know they had. Share this website with others, even though many people think it isn't real. I have found people I know on these lists as well as relatives. The lists are being continually updated so it is always a good idea to look here every once in a while. Also, look for relatives that have passed on because if you can prove that you are heir you may be able to claim.

## Coins

Frequencies/energy/currency/money used to be in coin. Gold/God-Mind/Wisdom, Silver/Oversoul/Energy, Nickel as defined by

Wikipedia/ silvery-white lustrous metal with a slight golden tinge, and Copper/strength. You can see how and why carrying these frequencies/ energy/currency/money can empower you.

A system was devised to make you think that you are at risk if you have these precious metals on you or in your home. Once you can see the risk, you are given a solution: paper as a representation of what you had in the bank as well as coins, with decreasingly fewer amounts of precious metals in them. Then, the bills became not what you had in the bank, but what the government had/has in the bank.

This reminds me of the tale of Hansel and Gretel, who followed a trail of crumbs until they got to a house made of candy. Once they ate the candy/frequency, they are lured inside by someone who turns out to be a wicked witch that wants to eat them. What the global handlers do to you is really about the same thing. Always remember that while they set the scenario, it is you who decide to participate. And just because you forgot that you agreed to participate and now you are trapped does not forgive your part in the entrapment.

Now, most people carry little currency. Many stores refuse to take $50 and $100 bills. I used to carry a $100 bill at all times to give me the feeling of being wealthy. I liked that for a while. But when you try to spend it and the clerks hold it up to the light to see if it is counterfeit, or call a store manager over to verify that basically, you are not a criminal by looking you up and down and all over, the joy of having a $100 bill passes. Now, if you have a $100 bill you are more seen as a criminal than a working person.

- Have you thought about what currency once was compared to what it is now?
- Where do you think the precious metals that were used for coins are now?
- How do you feel if you have a $100 bill in your pocket?
- Do you carry any cash now?

Paper currency used to be in denominations of $500, $1000, $5,000 and $10,000 bills. I only know this because my grandfather was a coin collector. When I was very little I remember him showing me a $500 and $1000 bill. I don't remember if he had any bills higher than these. I researched this to be sure memory wasn't deceiving me, and this is what I found:

> On July 14, 1969, **David M. Kennedy,** the 60th Secretary of the Treasury, and officials at the Federal Reserve Board announced that they would immediately stop distributing currency in denominations of $500, $1,000, $5,000 and $10,000. Production of these denominations stopped during World War II. Their main purpose was for bank transfer payments. With the arrival of more secure transfer technologies, however, they were no longer needed for that purpose. While these notes are legal tender and may still be found in circulation today, the Federal Reserve Banks remove them from circulation and destroy them as they are received.
>
> http://www.treasury.gov/resource-center/faqs/Currency/Pages/denominations.aspx

Some people think they should buy gold as an investment. The issue is in time of crisis gold isn't going to do you any good. There is no way to value the gold. And, to sell gold, it has to be assayed, which means having a plug drilled in the gold to make sure that it isn't gold on the outside with something else on the inside.

I have traveled to other countries, such as Iceland where USD100 equals as of this writing, almost 13,000 Icelandic dollars (ISK). This means that a USD3 cup of coffee is almost ISK400 in Icelandic money. This must be reverse psychology because the first time I had Icelandic money I thought that I would feel like I really had a lot of money. But when I had to pay ISK400 for a cup of coffee, I thought about how expensive the coffee was and after a while, everything seemed expensive. The huge amount of money I had seemed like very little.

When considering historical currencies as well as currencies in foreign countries, you see what happens with your mind. When all you know is $5, $10, and $20 bills, credit/debit cards, coins with little to almost zero valuable metals, you don't understand the full picture and what is being done to you as an individual. Currency is fake. Currency is energy.

- If your currency is fake, what does this say about you and your life?
- How can you maintain your Self-Value when the physical representation you carry is fake?
- Why buy gold if you can't easily sell it if you need to?
- Why invest in gold when you can get gold-plated and imitation gold for so much less money?
- Should you buy higher quality and have less?
- Or buy higher quality to open you up to more?

Thinking that you own anything is truly a scam. Because if the people at the top want it, they will take it. During times of war, they can take your home and money in the bank. If you have a skill that they think is valuable to the war effort, they can conscript you. They can even take your pets, German Shepherds here in the US; Norwegian Elkhounds in Norway. Of course, they prefer if you give willingly, because this absolves them of any Universal Law retribution. They want you to think you have a choice, and you do. When my children were small, I always wanted them to have a choice:

- Do you want to eat dinner at 5 pm or 5:05 pm?
- Do you want beef with or without sauce?

- Do you want to play indoors without a coat or outdoors with a coat?

They always had a choice. I never dictated to them what to do or not do. While the choices are narrow, they are still choices. When all you ever have is narrow choices, you don't even realize that they are narrow choices. When my stepsons stayed with us they loved boxed macaroni and cheese for lunch. That was all they wanted. When our younger boys figured it out, then they wanted it too. I didn't want them to have it, but I never told them no. Instead, I made them a lovely burger and then set a big bowl of macaroni and cheese behind their burger. I told them when they finished their meat, they could have the macaroni. Well, guess what, by the time they finished their meat, they didn't have a lot of room for macaroni and cheese. I never told them no. They never felt deprived. They never figured it out. I was still in control and they did not have a clue.

So, while money is handy to have so you can function in everyday life, you still need the mind-pattern to have whatever you have and then to keep it. You also have to be able to see the narrow choices that you are offered, and realize that you make the choices, no one makes them for you. You may feel like you have no choice, but you always do.

You can choose to follow the law or to break it. If you break it, you choose negative consequences for your actions. You may even choose life or death situations. But ultimately, you choose. You chose to be born here. You chose to live in a society that has a monetary system. You chose to have global handlers because you still need someone to help narrow your choices. Your life lessons, when you choose to learn from them, prepare you for more.

- Do you realize all that you have chosen?
- Do you realize that you choose your specific monetary system?

- Do you realize that you choose to have global handlers?
- Do you know why you chose what you chose?

I remember when potato chips used to come 3 bags to a box. Then, the number of chips in each bag slowly began to decrease. Then we went from 1 box with 3 bags to only 1 bag. Then the 1 bag was 16 ounces, then 14 ounces, then 12 ounces, and so forth with the missing product being replaced with air, which is free. One can of tuna fish used to make 4 nice sandwiches. Then the can began to shrink and tuna was replaced with more oil or water, another choice. Now I'm not sure if you can get only 1 sandwich out of a can or 2 small ones. You are always told what they are doing. Packages are frequently labeled with notices telling you that the product is sold by weight not volume and some settling will occur during shipping.

Real fabrics are replaced with synthetics. Real building materials such as wood and stone are replaced with synthetics. Bit by bit the synthetics are made to look attractive with a lower price. Instead of saving for the real thing/real frequency, the Animal Mind chooses to save money/energy by buying an artificial product now, thus instant gratification.

You no longer carry the frequency of gold, silver, nickel and copper. You carry monopoly money. Frequency is being diverted and diluted so you are further and further away from your Source. You are increasingly forgetting who and what you are; where you came from and why you are here. You are forgetting your Source. You are depending upon the global handlers to be your Source. You want them to feed you, shelter you, clothe you, tell you who to have relationships with and define you. You trust them to keep you safe and to take care of you in sickness and health as well as in old age. When you turn away from Source Energy you have to turn toward something. When Stewart and I talk about the power of you, the power of mind, someone inevitably says, "But they have machines."

- Well, who is greater, them with their machines or Source?
- How much do you depend on the System to be your god?
- What are you, and society, turning toward?
- Are you blaming God?
- Do you trust God to take care of you?
- Do you trust that your Source is greater than the global handlers?
- If the global handlers can take away everything you have and are, including your identity, why do you trust them?
- Do you trust Source to take care of you with as much faith as you now have in the System?

***Ultimately there is only One Source with everything you need, always.***

I proudly saved enough cash to buy my first car. I thought I would have better leverage because I had cash. The car salesman said they could give me a better deal if I put it on a payment plan because then the dealership would get interest, too. My son recently upgraded his phone and instead of paying for the phone, I was told that this was no longer an option. I had to put the phone on monthly payments. It was the only way I could get the phone.

We are being entrained to have payments, payments, payments for the rest of our lives. You pay one bill and another one comes in. I always have a stack of bills on my desk. There is never a time when they are all paid. I have thought that one day I would like enough money to pay one time per year instead of every month. Then I would not have this constant stream of never-ending bills. These are the mind-games that the global handlers play with you so that you always feel impoverished. It is up to you to move through and past these mind-games. These are the tests to show you where you are in your mind-pattern.

When you always live in fear of losing what you do have, you stop the energy/money flow before it even begins. Only by Valuing Self can you be a money magnet. This is why you study and observe the global elite so you understand what they are doing correctly to know what you can learn from them. They focus the masses on what they know will be perceived as their wrong-doings because they know that this will keep the masses in poverty. Therefore, you are growing by acknowledging what they are doing correctly. They hold up mirrors so that the masses infight with each other. This prevents the masses from fighting with them. They focus you on being angry at the system which defocuses you from them. They focus you on being angry. Period. Because they know that:

***Anger is an acid that can do more harm to the vessel in which it is stored than to anything on which it is poured. ~Mark Twain***

To the global handlers, the world is their oyster. They hold a mind-pattern of limitlessness. They can eat what they want when they want; go where they want when they want; they do whatever whenever with whomever.

- Where is your consciousness when it comes to limitlessness?
- What does your cup of limitlessness hold?
- Is it full of doom and despair?
- Or do you know that it holds everything you need for whatever you want?
- Are you saying/writing/living your daily affirmations that Self-reprogram into what you do want/need in your life?
- How do you demonstrate your Self-Value?

Staying on the same income level as your peers makes you safe, but when you rise above the pack you are no longer liked as much. The following article is a perfect demonstration of what happens as your wealth increases:

As part of the series, the presenting couple got to sample what it is like to be super-wealthy as they travelled all over the world meeting billionaires who own £2 million watches, fly via private jet at a cost of £10,000 a trip and will pay £100,000 just to secure a table at the most exclusive clubs in Ibiza.

"We genuinely thought we were embarking on a mission to meet a series of snobs," said Holmes, of meeting wealthy oligarchs from all over the world.

"You just thought they would be flash, bling, stupid, undeserving - whatever. And just time after time after time, people just won us over with their charm and their respect and their dedication."

On his own spending habits, he revealed he has "a big conscience" about his own money and that because both he and Langsford are from "a working-class family", they "can't get away with too much bling".

"As your earnings go up, you run out of friends," he said. "Because you run out of people to share it with. It's alright saying 'We can afford a weekend here', but so few people around you can.

"I went through a stage where I used to pay for everybody: 'Come on, come with us - I'll pay for it'.

"Then I realised people really didn't admire you for that, they actually resented you a bit for it. And you sort of find your own level and you realise the more wealth you get is a difficult thing to balance."

http://www.belfasttelegraph.co.uk/breakingnews/offbeat/eamonn-holmes-thrown-out-after-fancy-food-taste-test-goes-wrong-34123618.html

When I was farming and without children, I paid my Self a monthly salary of $200.00. This was my money to do whatever I wanted with it. I went to a lot of art shows and had a lot of friends who were artists.

So, when I came across something really unique I often bought gifts for my friends who had children and therefore no disposable income of their own. I loved buying and giving things to my friends, but I realized that as much as they liked receiving they also were disturbed that they could not reciprocate. This didn't bother me, but I didn't like to see them disturbed, so I had to stop doing this, to their relief.

I had other friends who were doing better than other farmers. They bought a condo in Hawaii and invested in the stock market. Originally his father had taken the farm out of sagebrush and they had lived through some really tough times. These friends were genuinely thrilled with how far they had come, but other people truly hated hearing about how well off they were. Misery loves company. As long as you want to sit around and complain, you will have plenty of company. You are learning to not to judge others and not to focus on the misery. You are learning to rise above the pack. You are learning the consequences of doing this. When your income stream changes, so do your friends as a consequence of growth. You must have matching color, tone, and archetype to even say hello to someone. When your income level changes, you must be prepared to accept what comes with it. This is why many people Self-sabotage. Self-sabotage is a huge issue when it comes to finances.

- How many reasons can you list why you Self-sabotage?
- Do you Self-sabotage more or less with awareness that you have a choice to move out of poverty consciousness?
- Does it upset you to think that as your income stream grows that most likely your friends will change?

### Success

Some people creatively succeed where others only see lack. On social media, I saw a man in Africa who had access to tires, so he made sandals from them, children in India who made classical musical instruments from garbage, a young man who made a bicycle including wheels, from wood. I have seen people without cars carrying entire families, including pets and livestock, on motorcycles. These people are creatively surpassing. Rather than sit at home and complain, they are actively engaged in creative pursuits. Many people are losing their desire, and thus their abilities, to create.

You often see pictures of a cat sitting in a box beside tons of cat toys. In the same way, children used to create with sticks and stones but now they are so inundated with so many premade toys that they have no need to create. When I was a child, I remember playing in the front of my house. I built houses out of rocks along the side of the street; gathered grass and flower petals to make food for the inhabitants of the rock houses; sewed clothes for my dolls and even learned to embroider and crochet when I was about 8. As long as I can remember, I have been creating. I have always had hobbies. I have painted, made pottery, hiked, bicycled, done photography, sewn, done handwork, canned, took voice lessons, had pets, and studied French, Spanish and Italian. I've always kept my Self entertained. I have always enjoyed my own company. Even as busy as I am, I take time to exercise, read, cook and spend quality time with my family, even if I have to give up sleep some nights to do it. Money is energy; energy is what you need to create.

- Do you have energy?
- Do you get up every morning excited about life and what your day holds?
- Are you creating every day?
- Do you have hobbies and interests?
- If you are without anything, can you figure out a way to be "with"?
- Do you have joy in your life?
- Do you know how to create joy?

- Are you responsible enough to have more energy?
- Does more energy mean more Self-responsibility?
- Do you use your energy wisely?
- Are you demonstrating to your Oversoul and to God-Mind that you are capable of more than what you have?
- If your cup is already full how can you expect more to come to you?
- How do you view your Self?
- What do you do to attract money?
- What do you do to repel money?
- How do you think the global handlers keep you down?
- How do you buy into the schemes of the global handlers?
- How do you objectively observe and learn?
- How do you stop being distracted and focus on your goals?

You are pushing through your comfort zone, allowing Self to be uncomfortable enough to explore to find out if there is something to explore. You are learning to stop the judgment so that you can find the trees within the forest.

## AFFIRMATIONS—SELF-VALUE

"If you always put your Self second, others learn that you always come last. "You may think this quote extreme, but it is your own mind-pattern that determines how life reflects back to you. Do you value what you do? Do you find value within Self? Do others value you? Explore Self-Value to Value Self.

*I always value all aspects of my Self.*
*I keep my physical body healthy and active.*

*No one makes me react.*
*I Self-Value by choosing my actions/reactions wisely.*

*I Self-Value by releasing all unhealthy emotions up to my Oversoul.*
*I consciously choose the emotions I carry within.*

*I Self-Value my healthy emotions.*
*I only allow healthy into my space.*

*I Self-Value by allowing others to own their own emotions.*
*I Self-Value by keeping clear boundaries of where I start and where I stop.*

*I Self-Value by allowing those who challenge me to be in their space.*
*I Self-Value by passing all Self-tests reflected back to me by others.*

*I Self-Value by anchoring deep into my Source.*
*My Source confirms my Self-Value.*

*Every experience has value.*
*I find Self-Value within all experience.*

*I release the need to judge and/or criticize the experiences of others.*
*I value the experiences of others.*

*I only share my time with those who value me.*
*I value my time.*

*I value my bitter experiences.*
*I value the richness of all experience.*

*I value the process that creates me.*
*I value all aspects of my life experience.*

*I Self-Value my "good, my bad and my ugly."*
*I Self-Value the totality that is me.*

*I value my physical possessions.*
*I value all that I have with grace, dignity, and gratitude.*

*I value the power of my thoughts.*
*I value my ability to change.*

*I value the power of my actions.*
*I value my inner creative force.*

*I value my inner spiritual connection.*
*I value my internal, eternal Source connection.*

*I value my own intuition.*
*I value my ability to know by knowing at all times.*

*I value my own Soul-Personality.*
*I value my unique position within the overall scheme of Creation.*

*I value the equality of all, on the Soul level.*
*I value the beauty of my Soul that emanates in this reality.*

*I value the importance of my contributions in this plane of existence.*
*I value whatever part my Oversoul assigns me to play.*

*I value all that exists.*
*I value the right of all that exists to play his/her/its unique role.*

*I value my impact on the collective unconscious.*

*I value my output on all levels.*

*I value the unique role of each individual without judgment or criticism.*

*I value my own vessel and the thoughts/frequencies contained herein.*

*I build my vessel with thoughts/frequencies that I value.*

*I value the vessel that holds my Soul-Personality.*

*Because I Self-Value, value comes to me.*

*Relationships of value come to me.*

*Because I Self-Value, value comes to me.*

*Financial value comes to me.*

*Because I Self-Value, value comes to me.*

*Opportunities of value come to me.*

*Because I Self-Value, value comes to me.*

*Spiritual value comes to me.*

*Because I Self-Value, value comes to me.*

*Valuable hidden information reveals it Self to me.*

*I value my own Soul-Personality.*

*I AM valuable within the Totality of the God-Mind; Source values me.*

# Spiritual Connections, Energy & Money

A t first glance, you may wonder what these three topics have to do with one another. Many people think you have to give up money to be spiritual but everything comes from One Source. There is only One Creator and in this reality, Money anchors in the Energy that you allow to flow from your One Source Highway down to you.

This planet is a place where people struggle. Part of its higher purpose is to provide an experiential journey for you so that you have the opportunity to overcome whatever holds you back.

- Is Planet Earth designed to keep you in a struggle loop?
- When you are off that struggle loop, will you stay here or move on?
- Does the physical body have to die if your mind-pattern no longer matches here?
- Did you come here to hold the energy for those who are able to attach to a higher path?
- Does wanting this planet to be a Paradise make it so?
- Have you asked the One Creator what It wants for this planet?

- Do you only listen to what the outside world tells you this planet should be?

- Is it possible that this planet exists to provide lessons for victim-mentality mind-patterns?

- Can you decide what is the best path for this planet?

- Have you ever communicated with this planet?

- Are you swayed by media reports that tell you how the planet should be?

- Do media reports degrade humanity for supposedly harming the Earth?

- Does this planet have its own consciousness?

- Could this planet rebel against the humans if it wanted to?

- Is humanity so powerful that it could actually destroy this Planet?

## Energy

When you lack energy you cannot do what you came here to do. You forget that you are always connected to your Oversoul which means you do not even realize that conscious connection is possible. For this reason, many people feel depressed, lethargic, isolated and lack motivation. When you accept and outpicture these feelings, you sink deeper into despair and further away from the part of Self that uplifts and elevates. This is why you must make conscious efforts to do the opposite of what you feel when these feelings find their way into your conscious mind. When this happens, this is the time to fortify your protection; check your T-Bar Archetype for balance; make sure all your chakras are spinning in the same direction and the correct color is in the correct location; get that Self-Integration/Merger Archetype in the correct color at the pineal gland; and say/write your affirmations.

- If this Planet is designed to pull you down, do you think you came here to succumb to this pull?

- Do you think you came here to overcome the downward pull?

- Is it possible that Earth is a testing ground for Souls who think that they are ready to move on?

- Is it possible that temptations exist so you can determine where you are still weak?

- Does finding weaknesses within make you feel bad or does this give you a progress report?

- Can bad get worse?

- How do you uplift Self when this happens?

- Is Earth a Prison Planet, too?

- Can this planet serve many purposes at the same time?

- Why does it seem easier to succumb to the negatives then elevate with the positives?

- Is Programming an excuse or an explanation?

You may not realize how isolated and compartmentalized you are within your own Self in this reality. You are not consciously connected with you, much less with your Source. When I fast, the evenings are the most challenging. I am tired and I want to eat. Eating is a reason to sit, relax and not work. Eating is my distraction and my entertainment. Without that distraction and entertainment, I have to work on the thoughts, feelings, and issues that bother me. Writing helps me sort my own feelings about me. I used to think about what other people would say when they read my work. I had a lot of conversations with my Self about my own Self-doubts. I have realized over the years that I write more for me than for you. This is all part of this process of spiritual connections because you have to be consciously connected to you to get that next level of conscious connection coming in.

Fasting forces me to consciously connect with me; to consciously ask what is bothering me and upsetting me as well as actually answer those questions, and then think what I can do to fix the unpleasantness I feel. You must recognize that whatever you do, you do for you. This is a prime secret that pulls you through the other side of struggle, depression, lethargy, isolation and lack of motivation. First, you realize that you are not alone with these feelings. Second, you realize you don't have to stay there. You may not know the exact path out, but you have a direction. Honest, conscious Self-connection.

- Is your conscious connection to Self is increasing?
- Are you more aware of what you do, why you do, and when you do?
- If you fast, do you recognize how much of a distraction and entertainment food is and how much of life revolves around eating?
- Does fasting force you to stay more focused on Self?
- Do you do what you do for Self, first?
- If so, does this alleviate some of your inner stresses?
- Are you okay with you?
- Are you working on releasing the need to judge and criticize Self?
- Are you at peace with Self and your day when you go to sleep at night?

The more you try, the more help you get. Writing anchors your energy/frequency into this reality. This is why living together is not enough to hold a marriage together. You do need that piece of paper because you create a commitment that is anchored into this reality. This is why it is more challenging to leave a marriage than it is for 2 people who only choose to live together. The energy is not as strongly into this reality. Marriage is a commitment; a joining of 2 lives. In the same way, your presence in this physical reality is a commitment.

- What are you doing to anchor in that commitment to this reality?
- Do you say, "I AM committed to my Being"?

Some people do not want their pictures taken because they think it captures their Soul. Well, they are correct. Photographing your frequency does capture a portion of your Soul. Photos do have the potential to capture and anchor in your frequency. My ***Decoding Your Life*** book tells you how to reclaim your psychic energy that is spread all over the planet, universe and everywhere in between. The more you pull in via the Oversoul level, the stronger the Soul-Personality.

- Did you make a contract to be in this reality?
- Is your birth certificate a contract with Self and/or your parents?
- Are your handprints/footprints on your birth certificate your signature?
- Do your handprints/footprints supersede your birth name?
- Why are births always recorded in some way?
- Why are birth weights, dates and times important?
- Do you go to the Oversoul level to pull your psychic energy back?
- Are you committed to Being in this reality or do you play at being committed?
- Is every moment of your life a prayer?
- Do you feel the greater power that moves your Soul?
- Do you feel abandoned by your Source?
- Are you proud to be a part of Source exploring Source?

- Are you pulling your weight when it comes to Self-exploration?
- Do you complain about Being here?
- Do you care more about what you think of you or what others think of you?

When you set your experiences in motion, you have to clean up the results whatever they may be. For example, if there is a barrel sitting at the top of the hill and you push on it ever so slightly, it will roll down. If you don't push on it at all, it doesn't go anywhere. But give it just that little touch and off it goes. Then, when you try to stop the barrel, it takes a lot more energy to stop it than if you had never started it in the first place. This is where most people are. They have touched the barrel and it is rolling down the hill. Now, you have to stop it. And if you don't stop it correctly it will run you over, keep on going and perhaps veer off onto an unexpected course. Conscious Source connection gives you the direction and guidance that you need to most easily, least uncomfortably, get that barrel back where it belongs. This is the situation where most people find themselves. The barrel is rolling and they don't know how it happened. Well, somewhere, somehow, you set that barrel rolling and now you have the responsibility to stop it.

Self-responsibility is huge. Sometimes it is easy to admit to things and sometimes not so easy. But ultimately, your world is about you and what you did to bring you to this point. You have to trace back to what you know and then go back even further into the tangled frequencies that somehow began what is happening today. This does not make you a bad person. This makes you a normal person. This happens to everyone. Now that you know there is nothing wrong with you, you can make the conscious choice to correct what needs to be corrected in the most correct way. This is why you need your Oversoul to guide you. You are already connected and now you have to know that you are connected. You have to feel that knowing inside when something is correct vs. incorrect.

- How many times have you done something that you knew was incorrect because you wanted to do it?
- Are you the most important person that you know?
- How do you feel when you veer off of your plan?
- How do you feel when you stay on your plan?
- Can you feel when you are in your center vs. out of your center?
- Can you feel when your energetic boundaries are in place?
- Can you feel when others violate your energetic boundaries?
- Do you give thanks for the violation so you can make your energetic boundaries stronger?

As you declutter your mind, your body declutters, allowing for your psychic energy to flow more freely through your physical body. As the debris comes out of your body it is important that you feed your body to consciously make it stronger. If you have a better vehicle, you have to put better fuel into it. It always amazes me what people put into their bodies and then wonder why they have health crises. It is also amazing to me how much the physical body can take and still bounce back.

I did not have a healthy body growing up. I did not like the food my mother gave me. I preferred to starve. The one thing I did like was sweets and she taught me how to bake from the time that I could walk. I remember standing on a chair at the kitchen counters chopping, stirring, measuring and basically making whatever I wanted. And the beauty of this was that while I was baking I could eat as much as I wanted. I practically lived on sugar and white flour. There wasn't much else that I liked, other than peanut butter and some fruit when we had it. I liked meat when it was prepared simply and not diced up in a casserole of some kind. I had a lot of health issues growing up and this only exacerbated once I was on my own at 17, continuing to eat the only way that I knew. All of this started changing when I was about 20 and began realizing the down side of all the sugar I was consuming.

My big change began when I was about 25 and had a pneumonia crisis. After being ill for over a year, I started fasting in a desperate attempt to get off my prescription medications and get my energy back again. As my body got stronger, I studied the process of my psychic energy flow. I consciously decided to build a body with a stronger cellular structure to hold more psychic energy. I would say that since this time period, with some exceptions, cellular upgrade is a strong motivating force for me. I want more psychic energy coursing through my body so I can do what I need to do when I need to do it. I don't want to be dependent on anyone or anything other than my Source.

- Do you have the energy that you want to have?
- Do you think about upgrading your cellular structure so you can hold more?
- Do you do the *Green Psychic Flush* visualization that I developed from this time period in my life?
- If so, do you feel the psychic energy flowing through your system?
- Do you feel the psychic knots?
- Are you able to push the energy through to untangle the knots?
- Can you improve your health, strength and energy as you move through life?
- How do you define strong?
- What does a strong body mean?
- Do you have a strong body or is it stronger than it was before?
- Can you have a strong body but not have a lot of energy?

You need strong muscles and strong internal organs to have a strong body. When all of this is in order then you allow more energy from your Oversoul to power through the physical body, thus giving you tons of energy. Think of body builders as an example. They built their body to lift huge weights but this does not automatically mean that they have a lot of energy. It takes a lot of energy to walk around with all those muscles on your body, so after they have lifted their weights, they may not have a lot of energy left for other activities. Sometimes, people look physically fit and lead active lifestyles but all of a sudden drop dead or get deathly ill.

- Were their bodies strong or did they just look strong?
- Did they push their bodies via body-abuse?
- Did they only have energy to be athletic but the body wasn't strong?
- Can muscles be strong but internal organs, such as heart, lungs, kidney, liver digestive system be weak?
- When you think of a strong body, do you think of external body parts that you see and internal organs?
- A child has lots of energy, but is a child strong?
- Do most people have equally strong external body parts as internal body parts?

Fasting used to be looked down upon by the medical community, but recently it is gaining more mainstream attention. Here are two articles that are of interest to you:

### Fasting triggers stem cell regeneration of damaged, old immune system

Protection from chemotherapy immunosuppression indicates effect could be conserved in humans the first evidence of a natural intervention triggering stem cell-based regeneration of an organ or system, a study in the June 5 issue of the Cell Stem Cell shows that cycles of prolonged fasting not only protect against immune system damage — a major side effect of chemotherapy — but also induce immune system regeneration, shifting stem cells from a dormant state to a state of Self-renewal. Prolonged fasting forces the body to use stores of glucose, fat and ketones, but it also breaks down a significant portion of white blood cells. Longo likens the effect to lightening a plane of excess cargo.

During each cycle of fasting, this depletion of white blood cells induces changes that trigger stem cell-based regeneration of new immune system cells. In particular, prolonged fasting reduced the enzyme PKA, an effect previously discovered by the Longo team to extend longevity in simple organisms and which has been linked in other research to the regulation of stem cell Self-renewal and pluripotency — that is, the potential for one cell to develop into many different cell types. Prolonged fasting also lowered levels of IGF-1, a growth-factor hormone that Longo and others have linked to aging, tumor progression and cancer risk.

"PKA is the key gene that needs to shut down in order for these stem cells to switch into regenerative mode. It gives the OK for stem cells to go ahead and begin proliferating and rebuild the entire system," explained Longo, noting the potential of clinical applications that mimic the effects of prolonged fasting to rejuvenate the immune system. "And the good news is that the body got rid of the parts of the system that might be damaged or old, the inefficient parts, during the fasting. Now, if you start with a system heavily damaged by chemotherapy or aging, fasting cycles can generate, literally, a new immune system."

Prolonged fasting also protected against toxicity in a pilot clinical trial in which a small group of patients fasted for a 72-hour period prior to chemotherapy, extending Longo's influential past research.

"While chemotherapy saves lives, it causes significant collateral damage to the immune system. The results of this study suggest that fasting may mitigate some of the harmful effects of chemotherapy," said co-author Tanya Dorff, assistant professor of clinical medicine at the USC Norris Comprehensive Cancer Center and Hospital. "More clinical studies are needed, and any such dietary intervention should be undertaken only under the guidance of a physician."

"We are investigating the possibility that these effects are applicable to many different systems and organs, not just the immune system," said Longo, whose lab is in the process of conducting further research on controlled dietary interventions and stem cell regeneration in both animal and clinical studies. https://news.usc.edu/63669/fasting-triggers-stem-cell-regeneration-of-damaged-old-immune-system/

### Diet that mimics fasting appears to slow aging

Benefits demonstrated in mice and yeast; three cycles of a similar diet given to humans

https://news.usc.edu/82959/diet-that-mimics-fasting-appears-to-slow-aging/

These articles are really talking about regeneration. This means healing and building up the internal organs. When the body fails, it fails from within. The body's natural survival instinct is to protect the most valuable organs. Therefore, available psychic energy flows to the heart and lungs before the skin. It is the psychic energy that keeps the body functioning and this is the reason for the "Green Psychic Flush" visualization. You can mentally direct the psychic flow of energy through your body and through the internal organs. You effectively become your own acupuncturist. Instead of using needles to force open the knots on your energy lines, you are mentally doing this. You can feel the flow; the tingling on the bottom of your feet; the tingling into the marrow of your bones; the movement up through your digestive tract; lungs; heart; blood veins; muscles; neck; through your head and so forth. You feel it and you direct it, opening up your own energy lines so that all body organs have equal access to the psychic energy grid around which the physical body is built.

You cannot have true health and energy unless you address the internal organs first. My massage therapist does visceral massage. This means that your internal organs, when not functioning correctly, get knotted up and pull on the rest of your body, thus creating misalignment. She works on unknotting the visceral organs so that the rest of the body can align. When your body is misaligned, nothing can flow and nothing can heal, except on a hit and miss basis.

Fasting gives your body a chance to rest and relax. You are giving the visceral organs a chance to unwind which in turn allows for the psychic energy flow to move through and heal them. These articles may begin to give you the scientific explanation; I am giving you the energetic explanations.

- Will fasting become a trend?
- Will it be used as another way to control people?
- Have you done the *Green Psychic Flush*?
- Do you feel the tingling of energy in the bottom of your feet?
- Are you able to bring it up through your legs and into your torso and through your head?
- Do you feel the knots in your internal organs?
- Does this exercise make you think about your internal organs where before you had not?
- Do you think the body has to heal from the inside out?
- Can your body be strong with high energy if your internal organs are failing?
- Can your body gain strength and energy if your internal organs are fit?
- How can you heal your internal organs besides fasting?
- Was your digestive system the first system to get knotted up when you are a child?

Not too long ago, I worked in my stepson's house for 20 hours a day for 4 days and about 16 hours on the last day. I tell my Oversoul to supply the energy that I need to do what I need to do. And it does. Along with your Oversoul, you set the energy and then you live the experience. I have been pulling in a ton of Oversoul energy, releasing on all levels what I don't need and building my mind and my body. From an energy standpoint, I have a ton of energy available that I know my physical body can withstand.

- Do you have all the energy you need available to you?
- Can your body withstand all the energy that could be poured into it?
- Do you overuse your body?
- Does your body repair and regenerate?
- Do you consider where your energy Source originates?
- Can sleep be an escapism?

Setting the energy is asking your Oversoul to cast forth the energy for you to use as you need it. For example, when I asked that the energy be set for the home clearing/cleaning/rearranging, the energy was cast by the involved Oversouls and home to use that energy template to elevate all to their highest potential. The first night, the oldest boy age 7 came to me and asked if I could work on his room. I took one look at his face and went with him. We went into his room and proceeded to work together for about 4 hours. Cleaning, dumping, hauling garbage bags out. He performed the task of an adult easily and effortlessly. Without him I could literally have only accomplished half of what we accomplished together. The energy had been set for the clearing and he chose to use it, with the help of all the Oversouls involved. He was focused, never complained and never quit. That is quite a task for anyone, much less a 7 year old child. It was amazing how everything and everyone fell into place. No one got upset, no one cried or whined, everyone performed their functions and the task was completed within the time necessary. Energy is Source. Strength is an expression of energy stored and available for use. This is different than setting an intention. "I intend to do this or that" is not the same as actually doing it.

When you ask via the Oversoul level for the energy to be set for something specific, then your Oversoul casts into physical reality an energetic template. To set the energy for my New York cleaning marathon, via the Oversoul level I actually worked with the home, Earth and family. I worked for two weeks at night, every night doing the mental work via the Oversoul level to get everything in alignment before I even left. I was awake more than I was asleep, and when I was sleeping I was still working. It took a lot of time and focus to set the energy.

This way, when I arrived, I didn't wonder what to do and how to do it. It was already done in the Eternal Now. I had to fill in the energy grid that was in place. This is why everything went so smoothly once I arrived. Everything was already done except the physical part. This is beyond setting your intention.

In the same way, the physical body has an energy grid that emanates from your mind-pattern. Then the food that you ingest builds around this energetic grid. This is why the Green Psychic Flush visualization is so important. I developed this work when I was a young teen with health issues. Even then I could see focusing on what was bad did not help the physical body. It made more sense to strengthen the entire physical body so the strongest parts elevated the weakest parts.

If you want a conscious spiritual connection, you have to do the work. If you want energy, you have to do that work. But you do need an idea of what this means. The better your definition, the purer the frequency is that is available to you. You have to hear the frequencies so you begin to recognize pure ones vs. those that are tainted. Then, you have to hear what taints it. This means you have to become increasingly discerning and ask even more questions. That is why I continue to give you all these questions at the end of various sections. This pushes you to not only think, but to recognize that these questions make you ask Self even more questions. Your goal is not to continue to ask the same questions but to develop new questions that lead to new answers that lead to new questions. As you get going with this, you are really off and running as a teacher of Self.

- What does energy mean to you?
- Do you have to be healthy to have energy?
- Do you have to be strong for energy to flow in and through you?
- Does the weakest link in the chain mean that you can be strong in one area, but the weak link doesn't allow you to optimally function?
- Can a weak link make you physically ill?
- Are you learning to hear frequencies?
- Are you asking more questions?

Energy is Source. Strength is an expression of energy stored and available for use. Take me, for example. I am not a large person. Yet, I consider my Self strong. However, when I was cleaning the house in New York, I did not move the heavy furniture like dressers and cabinets. My stepson did this for me and he did this easily. After 2-3 days, he told me that he couldn't keep up with me, that I could outwork him. He had the physical strength but I surpassed him on endurance. On the last day I was there, he said, "I just don't know how you do it. What's your secret?"

I looked at him, hooked into my Source and said with a lot of expression and arm-waving, "I've found Jesus! and by the grace of the Lord, he works in and through me." I had him and his wife rolling on the floor laughing. But this was the truth, only in a humorous way. I could not say, My Oversoul supplies me with whatever I need. But I managed to put the Source into the conversation without being overly preachy. Enough said.

- If energy is Source, how do you plug into that and make it work for you?
- Can you plug into Source and make that energy available with the strength of your mind-pattern?
- What if you used that energy in a way that was not correct and beneficial?
- Would you/could you misuse this?
- Could this energy use you?
- Are you being protected by having limited energy and/or limited strength?
- Does using the energy correctly have to do with wisdom?
- What if you have wisdom but you can't control your Animal Mind?
- Do you have control over your inherent Animal Mind fight or flight instinct?

I have an article called *Creating Your Ark* that explains how everything in and around you has a frequency. Together, these frequencies create a sound. Think of being out in the middle of the woods, on top of a mountain, in a meadow, by the ocean. Think of all the sounds, each sound is frequency and frequency is energy that vibrates. When all is in order, it is a harmonious sound. Even destructive weather has a sound. Fire has a sound. Everything is frequency. Everything has a place. Everything has an order. If you walk around picking things up and moving them around, you are disturbing the natural order of the universe.

- Do you have objects in your space that don't even belong there?

- Does your environment have a harmonious sound?
- Is it as pleasant to be in your home as it is to be in the middle of a meadow?
- What sound do you want in your personal environment?
- Did you put the objects in your environment against their will?
- Did you consciously ask your Oversoul for permission to touch the objects before you thought about bringing the objects into your home?
- Did you consciously ask via the Oversoul level if the object would be in harmony with the rest of the objects in your home?
- If you have the correct objects, are they in the correct place?
- Does your environment have energy?
- If so, what determines the energy of your environment?

If you want energy to flow in and through you, you must also consider your environment as part of the conduit that allows this to happen easily and smoothly. You must continue to expand your awareness to determine all the influences on what you need to do. If you need to block your finances so you can narrow your focus, you will set your environmental energy up in a specific way. If you need to narrow your focus so your energy flows through your physical body in a specific way, you will have blocks here, too.

Having too much energy and too much strength could set you up to make choices that are not for your benefit. The more power you are able to express, the more responsibility you have to express that power correctly. Without control of the Animal Mind, you could dig your Self deeper into this reality in negative ways rather than dig your way out of it. You are exploring extremely foundational mind-patterns in such a way that you are looking for every single loophole where negativity could enter and gain control. This happens every day via fear, anger, frustration, and other negative emotions. It still happens to me. I am certainly much better than I was, but every time something happens I definitely can see where I still have more work to do.

Fasting is one way to gain control over your life. The beginning point is only 12 hours. This is like a long night; that is why I always suggest you start at night, after dinner. In the morning, you have another choice which many people already make, which is to skip breakfast. And if you are busy, you may even skip lunch. This takes you to dinner time. Many people don't eat until 7pm or later, so you could have a meal at this time which takes you to a 24 hour fast. But, if you want to stretch your Self, then even if you have to go to bed early, take a warm bath or shower, grab a good book, snuggle into bed and sleep through the night to get your last 12 hours in. 3 sets of 12 hours imprints your mind that you are in control. The Animal Mind wants to gain control. The idea is to determine what controls you so you can break the mind-pattern of letting something else control you. If a thing can control you, then certainly a person can. The most effective fast is a water fast where you eat nothing and the only thing you drink is steam-distilled water. You must determine:

- What is the person/place/thing that controls you the most?
- What is the emotion that controls you the most?
- What is the habit that controls you the most?

You can choose to fast from anything to get your Self going. Fasting is not about Self-abuse. It is about gaining control over Self without giving power away. Some people with chronic health issues definitely should not be doing a strict water fast. If a person/place/thing, emotion, and/or habit controls you, then you will not have correct Self-control over more energy in your life. In the same way, you will not have correct Self-control over the physical representation of energy in your life which is money. And you must have the correct Spiritual

Connections so you can determine how to bring in more energy, more money, and more positive experiences in a way that you can handle.

## Positive Changes

Positive changes bring challenges. Any time you step out of the status quo, whether positive or negative, things change. And when things change you are challenged., even when the change is positive. You are working on opening up your energy flow. You are opening up the Spiritual Flow for the Soul and the psychic energy flow for the physical body. Each has challenges. The more Spiritual Flow, the more responsibility you have. More psychic energy flow, the more responsibility you have. The more financial flow, the more responsibility you have. You are learning to bring all this in balance, which means you have to give up some of your imbalance.

It is the imbalance to which you are attached. And generally, the imbalance is caused by the Animal Mind. Fight or Flight. Survival of the fittest. Fear. Giving up these imbalances is a challenge. So, you keep your environment messed up to reflect the imbalance. You keep your physical body messed up to reflect the imbalance. You keep your Spiritual connections messed up to reflect the imbalance. And, you keep your finances messed up to reflect the imbalance. I know, for example, that I feel better when my desk is in order. But when I get tense and disturbed because my finances are not flowing the way I want them to flow, the first thing that goes is my desk. It gets messier and messier and messier. I could stop and straighten it around which is easy enough to do. It is interesting how much people hold onto what they know in favor of what they do not know.

- Is your financial center/desk/checkbook/pile of unpaid bills in order?
- Do you hold onto your food/exercising imbalances?
- Do you hold onto your Spiritual imbalances?

- Do you only want conscious Spiritual connections on your terms?

- Do you listen when your Oversoul tells you to not do or say something that you really want to do or say?

- How many times does your Animal Mind try to grab control of your life?

- Do you fear you won't have enough shelter, food, supportive relationships, answers to puzzling questions?

- Do you get those fight or flight feelings?

- How challenging is it to give up your imbalances in favor of creating balance?

- How attached are you to that which pulls you down instead of that which pulls you up?

## Trusting Source

Parkour is a military training exercise turned in to a sport that involves free-running. This means the person goes from one point to another by jumping, climbing, rolling, vaulting, swinging or whatever possible to avoid the obstacles in his/her way. These people definitely are going into the unknown. At every second they risk permanent bodily injury and death. These people either have a death wish or they are breaking out of their box in the best way they know. Perhaps they do not care if they live or die. Maybe they trust their Source connection enough to allow Source to make that call for them. I wonder if the global elite get up every morning grateful for what they have or wonder if someday they won't have. You may want to trust Source in your decision-making, but this is easier said than done.

- Is the reason you don't have what you want because you do not trust Source and Self enough to have it?

- Do you worry about keeping what you have or might get?

- What do you think about these people who perform daredevil stunts such as Parkour?
- Do you wish that you could do that?
- Do you admire them or think they are foolish?
- Do you think the truly wealthy ever think about not having their wealth?
- Do you think the truly wealthy have Soul Satisfaction?
- What level of trust in Source do these people have to create their lifestyles?

It is definitely much easier to trust in Source and Self when all is going well. It is much easier for Source-doubt and Self-doubt to creep in when all is not going well. Trusting in Self and Source to provide what you need, when you need is huge. What is extremely frustrating is when you are doing everything that you know and you still have holes in your income stream. Most importantly do not overlook the beginning point of fixing those income stream holes. There is a way to accomplish your goal, but you do have to begin.

Some people are so overwhelmed that they never begin. I have seen success stories of people who have accomplished huge goals over the course of many months. These people basically realized that if they never begin, they will always be in the same place. They reason at least being there is a chance that they will be somewhere else. I have seen this with massive weight loss and educational goals; I have seen this with people with physical disabilities as well as people with financial goals and dreams. You can't accomplish anything if you don't begin. Rather than say you can't or you do not know how, you have to begin.

This is what fasting does. The imprinting says that you have some kind of issue, you do not know what the issue is, but you are going to being to resolve it, and this is the route you choose to see if it can help. Success opens the frequency for you to begin in other areas of your life. If you can begin fasting then you can begin other things, too. Your new imprinting says that you trust Self to follow through. You trust Source to support you. This imprinting extrapolates to other areas of your life to change as well.

- What are simple ways to begin opening up your income stream?
- Do you try to tell your Source how you want the funds to flow in?
- Do you allow Source to bring funds to you in Its way?
- Do you sometimes feel so overwhelmed that you don't begin?
- Do you have unfinished projects laying around?
- Do you have a habit of not finishing things?
- Or a habit of not starting something?
- Do you have a fear of success?

Never overlook the simplicity of the beginning point. This means that you have to begin. You may feel overwhelmed, so you don't begin. You are afraid of success or you are afraid of failure; so you don't begin. Or you think too hard about where to begin and how it is all going to happen. You get involved with controlling the process. You forget to release your thoughts and feelings up to your Oversoul. You focus on the ending and how you will get there. You forget that after you do step 1, that step 2 automatically reveals it Self. And then, step 3 shows it Self. You worry too much about step 2 and step 3 before you even begin. You may have a direction and you may have a goal, but you have to be flexible in how everything pulls together. You really don't know and won't know until you reach your destination.

- Can cleaning up where you take care of your finances in your home be the beginning point that changes your income stream?

- Do you have old wallets and purses that are broken, dirty, or ripped that need to go?
- Is the color of your wallet/purse/handbag conducive to pulling in and holding wealth?
- Is your wallet/purse/handbag organized or full of clutter?

**Energy Equal Funds**

Most people are always looking for ways to increase their income stream. This is all tied into your spiritual connection and the energy you have available to you. Without this connection, you do not know how to use nonphysical energy and its physical representation of money.

*As above, so below.*

You can have nonphysical energy line up and ready to flow in, but you block it. Poverty programming is an extremely deep and inherent mind-set. I am learning to do my best to be an example of how to surpass Poverty Programming. Flying business class, for example, has been a challenge for me to accept because you can ride in the back a lot cheaper. But in the back, you are treated like cattle. In the front, you are treated like a person. And of course, business class boards first. Then, after you are comfortably settled, all the cattle file in, look at you as they file by, wondering who you are, how you could afford to pay so much for a flight and why would you even want to when you can fly so much cheaper in the back.

I observe old, crippled people file through; young families with children; couples; people flying alone. I think about how much more comfortable they would be if they were in business class. I also observe their mind-patterns and what they think they deserve. And I recognize that I am caught between the two worlds. I want to be an example that they aspire to; an inspiration so that one day, there will be only business class and no back of the plane seats/experience. Someone has to break out and open up this frequency for others at the risk of being extremely uncomfortable, which I used to be. Now I am only mildly uncomfortable.

- When you see the inequities in the world, how can you justify having something when others have nothing?
- Do you have guilt?
- Are you willing to be uncomfortable to open up new frequencies for others to follow?
- When you feel desperate do you feel less guilty when you finally get the funds that you need?
- Do you think the more empty you are, the more easily you accept what you get?
- Does a drowning person care whose hand he/she grabs?
- Is a drowning person grateful that there is a hand to grab?
- Does a desperate person have guilt about accepting what he/she needs?
- Does desperation and suffering justify receiving money?
- Is suffering a way to divest your Self of guilt?

The 13 families who rule the world do not follow the same rules that they lay out for you. For example, they keep their families together; they keep their businesses in the family; they intermarry; when everyone else is selling their stock they are buying. Even their servants have a status; families are employed by the elite for generations.

- Does wealth mean something different to these families than to you?
- If wealth is rejected by you, does it make sense that these families are there to scoop it up?
- If you willingly hand your money over, is it their responsibility to give it back to you?

- Why do you think that you were not born into limitless wealth?
- Or were you and you don't accept it?
- Why don't old, sick or handicapped people have what they need?
- Why is worry and suffering important?

With all the ups and downs of my business, there have been times when I have seriously considered doing something else. I can do a lot of things and I'm not afraid to make changes. I don't mind working a 9-5 job and letting someone else have the stress, collecting a paycheck and walking out the door at the end of the day. I have been Self-employed since I was 19 years old, but I have supplemented my income with a variety of jobs and activities. I started babysitting full time in the summer when I was 14 and 15 years old. When I was 16, I worked after school and on the weekends in a fabric store. When I was 17 I was a maid in a nursing home, scrubbing toilets and floors. I have always worked both mentally and physically. One thing I have learned about my Self is that I thrive on hard work and mental challenges. This doesn't mean that I always like what is presented to me, but I am willing to do the work to get through them. When I have made it to the other side of the challenge, I am grateful to have survived once again.

During the more challenging times of this business, I have definitely questioned if I am in the correct profession for me. But when I get really honest with my Self, I know that there isn't anyone else out there doing the work that Stewart and I are doing in the way that we are doing it. I know in my heart that this is exactly what I am supposed to be doing. Finances, I think, are more challenging than the Spiritual Connection and more challenging than having enough energy. For me, finances have been my toughest challenge.

I've thought a lot about why I wasn't born into a wealthy family. Over the years I've decided that I most likely would not be a nice person. Money can give people a false sense of identity; they identify with the money instead of who they are as a person. Money can give you your identity. Everyone wants money, so if you have a ton of it, you may not know who are your friends or your support system. Throughout history, you read of family members destroying other family members to acquire their wealth. I even know people who have been unscrupulous when it comes to taking from other family members what they should not be taking.

Hitler and the Nazis were on a Spiritual Quest in their way. Knowledge is Power. This is why they wanted to invade Tibet and find Shambhala, amongst their other agendas. In this physical world, most people are challenged when they have things which you can generally only acquire with money. If you lived on a secluded mountaintop, it wouldn't be an issue. But you live here, amongst other people who may not be so fortunate. It has taken me a lot of years to be okay with watching people struggle. This doesn't mean that I like it, but I realize that without the struggle, they would fall off their path. I have seen it too many times. Take away the struggle; take away the pain; take away the lessons and the people quit learning. In fact, they can even go backwards.

- Do you work harder when you are backed into a corner?
- Do your creative forces heighten once you pull your Self together?
- Is Knowledge Power?
- Do you want a Spiritual Connection for the correct reasons?
- Do others appreciate it if you can outwork them on a consistent basis?

- Do others perceive you as a threat because of what you can do and they cannot?
- Do you have empathy when you see others struggle?

In the same way, as you work through your Spiritual Connections, understanding your own personal Energy Flow and how all of this connects to your Financial Flow, you begin to realize how much you block Self because of what you hold onto. Compare Self to the lady who needed the tarter to hold up her teeth. If the dental hygienist took off all the tarter, her teeth would fall out. She doesn't want to let that tarter go. Metaphorically speaking, you may be impatient to have the tarter off, but you don't want to lose your teeth in the process.

Discipline in this work is huge. You are proactively learning to be your own disciplinarian instead of waiting to react to negative experiences. You are allowing the negative experiences to challenge you to grow positively instead of becoming further entrapped. You are learning to consciously connect and allow your Source to teach you. You are learning how consciously connected you already are and have been. You are learning to observe and label your experiences so you progress forward in a more correct and beneficial manner for Self.

- Do you have inner level movement that ruffles the surface, even when you aren't sure what it is?
- Are you okay with letting the negative come to the surface so it can be released back to Source?
- How comfortable are you with allowing the positive to surface so good can get even better?
- Are you okay with having more than others, including more knowledge; more energy; more money?

While the energy from Universal Source is unlimited, your ability to attract it and hold it is another matter. You cannot have a weak mind and a weak will, and then expect to wield strong information, strong energy and a huge financial stream. Whether you like the global handlers or not, you have to admit that they have strong information, strong energy and a huge financial stream. What they do with this is their business, but clearly they have mastered strengths that most people have not. Conversely, you have mastered strengths that they have not. However, God-Mind must always be in balance. Decades ago, I said that Russia had limited freedom while the US had a lot of freedom. This was God-Mind in balance. I said that if the day ever comes when Russia has more freedom, the US will have less. And this is exactly what is happening today.

In the same way, as you find your own inner balance, you will have more; and more than enough. But if you aren't up to the game, then someone else will come along and take what could have been yours simply because it is there. If you see an abandoned apple tree by the side of the road, loaded with fruit, you very likely will stop to take the fruit. In the same way, this is why the global elite have what they have. I have mentioned that there was about 32 billion dollars in 2012 of unclaimed money. You can research this for your Self, but in the US, here is a legitimate website where you may find your name or a friend or relative's name.

https://www.usa.gov/unclaimed-money

- With all the poverty, why is there so much unclaimed money?
- Do the masses have the mind-pattern to hold onto money?
- Have you checked the unclaimed money site?

I have made many financial decisions that made perfect sense to me at the time, only to realize later that I was really, really stupid. I paid for those lessons in many ways. I do my best to not harbor grudges against my Self for my own stupidity. I continually do work on me to responsibly accept the positive limitless of the universe.

*Rejection is God's Protection.*

If my requests are denied I know that I have more work to do. If I am blocking my own acceptance, then I'm doing my best to remove my blocks.

Have you made financial decisions at the time that made sense only later to realize that they weren't what you thought they were?

Do you harbor grudges against your Self for what you would have/could have/should have done?

As you release the old ways, you make room for the new ways. When you are in between the old and the new, life can feel scary. Fear is huge in the Animal Mind. Fear is what protects you. When you control fear instead of letting the Animal Mind control fear, the Animal Mind perceives you as a threat to the body. This is another reason to fast. The human body says it will starve and die if you don't feed it. You have to prove to the body that you are in control and it will not die. The human body says only food from the Earth will sustain it, but you are learning to sustain the physical body with food from Source. The cleaner and clearer your physical body, the less food from the Earth it needs to function. And this means more room for your Soul-Personality. The physical body becomes subservient to you.

**Understanding Frequency**

One example I like to use is how I taught my children to understand the meaning of words. First, I taught them "big" and when they got this concept I taught them "bigger" and then "huge" and then "gigantic" and then "humongous" and so on. Big is the starting point. If you never get the concept of big I cannot teach you what bigger is. If you never get the concept of bigger I cannot teach you what huge is. And if you never even start understanding what big is, there is nothing at all I can teach you. Because you are unwilling to learn does not mean that I don't know anything or I can't teach.

When I start teaching you about frequency, as in my ***Decoding Your Life*** book, and you don't get it beyond the written words in the book, I can't take you any further. But if you get it, even in the most minute way, I can then teach you what bigger means. And once you have that concept, I can teach you what huge means. Many people get to understand big and they don't realize that they have just begun. There is so much more beyond that, but they think they are out of the box. They are so proud of this accomplishment that they don't realize that they are only at the beginning point. When you start to read the frequencies, the knowledge contained therein is amazing. But I can't teach you how to get that knowledge if you won't do the work and it is work. Knowledge is hidden in plain sight. It is the easiest place to keep it safe.

- Are you afraid to part with your fears?
- What do you fear the most about positive Self-growth?
- Are you patient with your own process or are you more frustrated?
- Do you see your own potential?
- Have you found Knowledge Hidden in plain sight?

You want to break the old ways because by doing so you have the opportunity to elevate Self. Some people feel that once things are broken, they are never the same. This is true, but I like to use the example of the Japanese art form of Kintsugi. This is a method for repairing broken ceramics with a special lacquer mixed with gold, silver, or platinum. I like this art form because it uses gold/God-Mind, silver/Oversoul and platinum/Silver-white/Oversoul purification. Breaking the old ways allows you the opportunity to upgrade. If you take the same pieces and tried to repair them with glue, you would not have the same effect. But with gold, silver and platinum, the pottery takes on new dimensions that would not otherwise have happened.

Mistakes, such as breaking something, are a part of life; of learning; growing; stretching. The only way there would not be mistakes is if you were on familiar ground which does not allow you the opportunity to elevate. I have made billions of mistakes in my life. I am learning not to tear my Self down over them; instead, to take a look at my learning curve. Sometimes I get it the first time; sometimes it takes dozens of times and some things I'm still working on and figuring out decades later.

This is the same with your conscious spiritual connections, your energy and your money. This entire world is designed to test you at every corner. So when you meet a new test, it is odd that you think you should immediately pass it the first time. You are really only Self-testing. When you finally do surpass, what a grand feeling of completion because of the trials and errors that put you here. You have your own process. While you may want to compare your process to others, ultimately, your journey is unique to you. You have exactly what you need for the lessons that you need.

- What lessons do you keep repeating that still frustrate you?
- Do you need to break your internal pottery bowl so you can put it together in a new, elevated form?
- Does your internal pottery bowl sometimes break at the drop of a hat and other times even when you pound it with a hammer it does not budge?
- When you finally have the old broken up, do you elevate it with gold, silver and platinum?
- Do you give the broken pieces of your life to Source, with an attitude of gratitude?
- Do old broken pots no longer have a place in your life because you are releasing old broken mind-patterns?
- Are you slowing down so you can understand your life rather than rushing so you can tick off your list and label it done?
- Are you giving your Self permission to make mistakes?
- Do you, like everyone else, have a learning curve?

- Are you kinder to Self, more accepting of who you are, where you came from and how much you have accomplished?

Indigenous people are coming together from all over the world at Standing Rock in unification over water. Some of these tribes were once fierce enemies of each other. There is an old saying that the enemy of my enemy is my friend. So now those who were once enemies are developing new bonds and friendships. Fierce Native warriors and ancestors of fierce native warriors are calling upon the Creator for protection. They are not relying on guns and weapons. They are relying on something more powerful than guns and weapons. They are not resisting arrests. They are going peacefully, knowing that their faith is in a higher power. They are making the heavily armed government armed forces look ridiculous. Unarmed men, women, children, and horses who are singing, dancing, praying. People who are putting Self above the material. The tribes have said that they have more resources now, much of it because of legalized gambling. They are transmuting a potential addiction into the physical, material world to help their people. Food, water, supplies.

- Are you relying on your own inner faith to bring you through your own internal battles?
- Are you relying on your internal prayers above external weapons of war, including your words and actions?
- Are you using your challenges to push you deeper into your own conscious spiritual connections?
- Are you thinking about the most correct and beneficial way to use your energy in any given situation?
- Are you thinking more before you react?
- Are you transmuting internal addictions of isolation, Self-abuse, anger, frustration, lack, abandonment into something positive for Self?
- Are you changing your own internal "whine" into "water"?

- How does Standing Rock reflect you?
- Why is it happening now?
- What fierce enemy do you have inside that has kept you from your conscious Spiritual Connections, your energy and your Money?
- Where are you making peace between your internal tribes?
- Do you have internal tribes that form bonds to take you down and prevent you from accomplishing your positive goals?
- Just like the Kintsugi pottery, what did you have to break apart so you could bond Self in new ways that are even more beautiful and stronger?

The Animal Mind never goes away as long as you have a physical body. The Animal Mind is master of the body. The Animal Mind is your survival instinct. It is located in the solar plexus, so when you can't get to your Higher Mind, go with what is in your gut. For the human species to survive in this physical reality, it has to have a body. The body must be maintained. It must eat, drink, sleep and procreate. This is why it is so easy for the global handlers to use it against you. You are not taught about this mind, but the global handlers know all about it. They set you up to give control to your Animal Mind. Then your Animal Mind does what it is designed to do. then you wonder how you got where you are. When the Animal Mind is in control, it is like the tail wagging the dog or the cart before the horse. You are the steward of the body, but you are not the body. As the steward of the body, its Animal Mind reports to you. Each cell has an intelligence and it is all governed by the Animal Mind. But you are still in charge.

The Animal Mind is in charge of most people. This is one thing that fasting does. It tells the Animal Mind that you are in control. When you don't eat, it is the Animal Mind that says you will starve to death and die. Look at all that food in your refrigerator, in your cupboards, in the stores, maybe even in your own hands as you give it to others. You are fortunate that you have food all around you. The Animal Mind is not supposed to go away or be repressed. It is to be tamed. Then you can work together as a team to accomplish your goals while you are here and in need of a body. If you have ever trained an animal, you know that you do not relate to them as you would a human. They have different rules. If you are going to train an animal, you have to treat it like an animal, not another human.

The Soul of a child is too vast to fit into his/her body. A child's body is more animal than human. As the Soul container/body grows there is more room for more of the Soul-Personality. If you don't control the animal body of your children, the Animal Mind of that animal body will control you. Humans do not get all of their bodies until they are 21. Children need adult supervision/mentors until they are 21 for a reason. Sending 18 year olds off to university sets 99% of them up for failure. Not giving a smack on the bottom to a 2 year old having a temper tantrum is setting the child up to have his/her Animal Mind in control his/her entire life. You have to get the animal's attention and then you can move on.

Children are separated from their parents practically at birth now because this way they can be trained according to the state vs. the care of loving parents. "Spare the rod and spoil the child" was at one time an acceptable way of raising children. A rod might be strict words or a stern look. The animal body must be contained and trained properly. As the Soul-Personality enters, the body is trained to respect its master vs. doing what it wants to do because it is an animal.

The global handlers play on the emotions of the people to let the child do whatever he/she wishes otherwise you are cruel and you infringe upon the rights of the child. The more terror the child is, the less you control the child, the less attachment you have for each other, and more control the state is then forced to exercise over the child. The child is attached to no one. An animal in a pack is attached to its leader, even after the leader beats it up. An animal is attached to whoever gives it food. This is basic survival instinct. An animal has sex whenever it can to procreate its species. When you study animals, you study your own Animal Mind. When you study the ways that humanity focuses on food, sex and shelter, you study your Self. Fasting puts you back in the driver's seat. This is why I have been teaching it more and more these past few years. I continue to see people successfully surpass other challenges when they get this Animal Mind in control. You learn what the Animal Mind is, how it got out of control in the first place and how to get it back in control. Then you are in control.

You are able to go to your Higher Mind and then right on up into your Oversoul and God-Mind. This is how you gain your conscious Spiritual Connection; this is how you begin to understand what energy from Source is. Source energy maintains you in ways that are more important than the food from the Earth. And from here, you understand the responsibility that comes with more conscious Spiritual Connections including its outpicturing in the form of money.

- When you weren't sure what to do, have you relied on your gut to tell you?
- Are you learning to distinguish between the body and you?
- Have you ever trained an animal?
- Have you observed how the ways of animals are different than the ways of human?
- Is a child basically an animal waiting to grow so more of the Soul-Personality can enter?
- Have you seen humans who you thought acted more like animals than humans?
- Have you observed animals who acted more human than most humans?
- When you fast do you pull in more Soul-Personality because you are not so full of food/energy from the Earth?

I have been eyeing my basement storage room for a number of weeks. Basement storage has to do with what I am storing in my foundation. When my mother passed away, I put the mementos that I received from her apartment in the middle of the storage room. Today, I made space and stacked the boxes in the shelving. I also noticed that I have a few years of paper tax records that I can toss now, so I pulled all those files off the shelves.

I threw out some old inventory and several boxes. I still have a ways to go. But I think about the foundational mind-patterns that affect my life today. My mother definitely has a place. Now her place is neatly organized. Even though I was making it better, I recognized that good can get better. This means that while I am making a pass through the foundation, there is still more to go. This is the way the whole house is. I clean and organize each area and then in another 1-2 years, I have to do it again. Each time I throw out more.

This is just like your life and all your release work that you are doing. You do great on one level, but once you have some order, you find out you have more to do. Well, once I clean out my basement, I can put more junk in it. Or, I can choose to keep it neat and organized and keep looking for what else is in my foundation that needs to go.

- Do you feel depressed that as much work and effort that you put into your process, there is still more to do?
- Do you realize how much you are digging around in your foundational mind-pattern?
- Do you choose to keep your foundation neat and organized or do you have a tendency to clutter it up again?
- Can you maintain a positive attitude as you declutter, organize and strengthen your foundational mind-patterns?

## AFFIRMATIONS—INCREASING MY VALUE

When you do not value you, others cannot value you. Increased income flow, energy flow and Oversoul conscious connection are all tied into your own Self-Value. Now is the perfect time to increase Your Self-Value mind-pattern.

*I release the need to judge and criticize my Self.*

*I value my Self at all times.*

*I release the need to settle for less than.*

*I deserve to have the best of everything that this reality offers.*

*I release the need to participate in the degradation of humanity.*

*I carefully choose the aspects of this reality in which I participate.*

*I easily decide my activities and agendas under the guidance of my Oversoul and God-Mind.*

*I choose to uplift and elevate my Self at all times.*

*I release the need to be afraid.*

*I build my mind-pattern of courage.*

*I release my need to compare my Self to others.*

*I AM a beautiful, unique flower in the Garden of Life.*

*I release my fear of the future.*

*I maintain my focus in the Eternal Now.*


*I release my fear of the unknown.*

*I AM always protected.*


*Anger covers fear.*

*I release my internal anger.*


*I allow my inner fears to rise to the surface.*

*I release my inner fears.*


*It is often darkest before the dawn.*

*I trust my Source at all times.*


*My Oversoul knows my plan for Me.*

*I take my life one step at a time, under the guidance of my Source.*


*Limited finances mean limited choices*

*I learn how to focus on what is most correct and beneficial for me.*


*I focus on creating a strong and healthy foundation.*

*The strength of my foundation supports all that is most correct and beneficial for me.*

*I AM never given more than I can handle.*
*I find my strength in all that I do and accomplish.*

*The stronger my mind, the stronger my body.*
*I AM consciously aware of my mind/body correlation.*

*My body follows my mind.*
*I have a strong mind, I have a strong body.*

*My energy stream follows the strength of my mind.*
*My finances follow the strength of my energy stream.*

*I always have everything I need.*
*I trust the decisions of my Source.*

*I align with my Source for conscious guidance and direction.*
*I trust that what I need comes to me when I need it.*

*I trust my Self.*
*I trust in my own Self-Value.*

*I AM Worthwhile.*
*I deserve the best that this Reality has to offer.*

*I AM Beautiful in my own unique way.*
*I AM Beautiful within the Mind of God.*

*I allow my inner light to shine.*
*I AM Magnificent.*

*I rise above the crowd.*
*I AM okay with who I AM, exactly as I AM.*

*No two Souls are exactly alike.*
*I Value my own special place within the God-Mind.*

*I contribute to the upliftment of this Reality and True Reality.*
*I Value my contributions to All That Is.*

*I AM an important aspect of All That Is.*
*I AM the most important person that I know.*

*I Value the vastness of all my experiences.*
*I Self-Value at all times.*

*I Value others; others value Me.*
*My Self-Value reflects back to me.*

*My Financial Flow, Energy Flow, and Oversoul Connection Flow increase exponentially in a way that is most correct and beneficial for Me.*

*I Self-Value because I Value All That Is.*

# When Money Isn't The Answer

You are always thinking about how to increase your financial stream so you can do more things in this reality. There are so many choices and options that any creative person has a plethora of ideas of what could be next on the to do list. There are so many possibilities sometimes I wonder where to even begin. Interestingly, I have realized that I like to buy items on sale not so much to save money but to narrow my focus.

- When to shop?

Wait for a sale.

- What to shop for?

Wait for a sale.

- Where do I want to shop?

Look for a sale.

Fewer choices make my life easier. I used to think I shopped sales only to save money. But, I have learned that yes, I like saving money but that is secondary to helping me make decisions. I am more challenged to make purchases when things are not on sale. I am now stretching my Self to buy things at regular pricing. Inevitably after I make a purchase, what I just bought at full price comes on sale. More tests for me. I have learned from experience that when this happens I can contact the merchant and ask for the sale price. Generally, they are very nice and give it to me. Now, when this happens, even though there is a good chance I can get a refund or credit, and even though it is challenging for me to not ask knowing I can get something, I am determined to position my Self to stop using money to narrow my focus. This all has to do with Self-Worth and Self-Value.

I have used sales to justify buying anything for my Self. It has always been easier for me to pay full price for anyone but my Self. There are so many layers to sales. Sales have been a stepping stone to something more; I am grateful for them and I still use them. But I am working toward spending my money when it is most correct and beneficial regardless of pricing. In the same way, I am working on spending my energy when it is most correct and beneficial regardless of what I want, when and where.

- Do you use money as a way to create Self-Worth and Self-Value?
- Is debt a stepping stone to Self-Value to create Self-Worth?
- Are sales a stepping stone to Self-Value to create Self-Worth?
- Do you use sales to justify spending money on your Self?
- Do you use money as an excuse to not buy for Self?
- Do you use money as an excuse to not buy for others?
- Does not having money confirm low Self-Worth?
- Do you use money to narrow your focus?
- Do you sometimes feel that there are so many things you want to do that you will not have the years to do it all?
- Do you have a to do list?

- Can there ever be too many options and choices?
- Can there be so many options and choices that you never do anything?

I know people who have money but are challenged to spend it on Self. My grandfather was very generous with my family, but he was challenged to buy him Self a candy bar. He loved fish so when he came to visit my parents wanted to take him out to a nice seafood dinner. He made lemonade from the lemon on his water glass and some sugar on the table. Then he got up and went for a walk rather than pay restaurant prices for his food. I have an uncle who would drive distances to save one cent per gallon when he fueled up his car.

I have seen the extreme when people have money yet refuse to turn the heat up in their homes, choosing to wear long underwear instead. Others insist they love the heat rather than install air conditioning in their homes. I know people who use toilet paper that is so thin you can read the newspaper through it. One person stuffs his pockets full of tissues when he uses public restrooms instead of buying his own. These people could all afford what they need but instead, they refuse to spend the money on what they need or would make life easier. If they didn't have the money then you could easier understand their choices. But when you have the money and you choose to live like this then you need to examine the mind-pattern. Obviously, money isn't the issue or the answer.

Low Self-Worth says you do not deserve; others do, but not you. I understand this because it is really easy for me to get for others what they need, regardless if it is on sale or not. While definitely better than I was, when it came to me, I was always last on the list. I would have to wait for the sale to justify buying what I needed. Some people are insistent on suffering even when they do not have to; or, trying to get something for nothing even if they get crap. I guess they think free crap is okay.

- Do you know people who would rather suffer and be miserable than pay for something that could make their life easier?
- Do you know people who are truly poor and have to live like this?
- Are you tempted to take something if it is free, whether you need it or not?
- What is it about free that gets a person's attention?
- Is there truly anything for free?
- Does free mean that there are hidden psychic hooks designed to reel you in?
- Can you justify getting something for someone else easier than you can justify getting something for your Self?
- Do you have to wait until an occasion to justify buying more expensive food, clothes or something special?
- How would you define a cheap person?
- What benefits does a person gain by being cheap?

**Free**

I used to love anything I could get for free. I lacked in so many areas of my life that anytime anyone gave anything I was right there; if I couldn't use it I tried to think of who could. When I stayed at a hotel I loved all their free soaps and shampoos. A long time ago in magazines, you could send away for free samples. I especially loved free food samples. When I lived in New York there was a Costco that was close by so I often took the boys and that became lunch. It was all a fun game to me. I eventually found all of these freebies piling up. I would gather them up and give them to places like the Salvation Army or Goodwill. The more I learned to value my Self the less and less I enjoyed free. I realized that I would most likely not use them, they would gather at home and eventually I would have to give them away. Instead of just taking anything that anyone gave me I became more discerning.

In fact, now whenever I see free I remember that there is always a price somewhere. Nothing is free; there must always be an exchange. A couple of winters ago a local restaurant advertised their burgers buy one get one free on certain days of the week. I could justify bringing burgers in for everyone at the price they offered. I placed my order, went to pick it up, and guess what, everything was regular prices. I asked about the ad and they said that was dine-in only. I showed them that it did not say this in the ad. Oops! So I asked to speak to a manager. They would not budge on their pricing. My choice was to pay full price or to leave the order and then have to deal with a last minute dinner at home. Of course, I begrudgingly paid full price but I was not happy and I told them so. Another lesson for me about sales and getting something for nothing. And, you get what you pay for.

I have had to learn to honor my Self by honoring others. Whatever you think your service or product is worth is now what I pay or I don't get it. I don't bargain, fight or throw a fit, which I have seen people do. I may get a bit of resentment such as what happened in the burger incident. But even then I made it my issue, not theirs. I took responsibility for trying to justify a purchase.

Recently I found a chocolate online store that I like. I placed an order and sure enough even before my chocolate arrived a holiday sale on everything was announced at 20% off. I elected not to say anything to the owners, but I did place a second order to take advantage of the sale. Guess what, about ½ of the chocolate bars I was interested in were now out of stock. I contacted the store to ask why so many were out of stock only to be told that there was an ingredient shortage. Okay, but then I was told that if I told them what I wanted they would honor the 20% off after the first of the year. Again, I elected to pass, thanking them very much for the offer. I am learning but ultimately it is about me honoring my own value. I saw this meme on social media:

*If I do a job in 30 minutes it's because I spent 10 years or more*
*learning how to do it in 30 minutes.*
*You owe me for the years, not the minutes.*

- Do you honor your own value?
- Do you give too much of Self away for free?
- Do you try to bargain with people for products or services?
- If you do, are you honoring these people?
- Do people set their products and services prices based upon what they feel they need as compensation?
- If you offer less than they feel they deserve do you think they will provide you with a less than service?
- Why do you think there is such a discrepancy in pay scales?
- How do you value the contributions of one person as being more than the contributions of another?
- Does the price of a product or service provide the opportunity for you to think carefully about your reasons for wanting that product or service?
- Will you buy something because it is cheap or on sale?
- Does making the most correct and beneficial choices lead to opening your income stream to more because you Self-Valued?

It always amazes me that poor people think they have to stay poor. This tells me that societal programming is working. There are so many ways that you can earn money. With the Internet, you can reach a global audience very easily. You may not make a huge amount of money but when you have nothing, even a very small amount can make the difference of whether you have any decent food to eat that day. When I was a child I babysat to buy what my parents would not or could not buy me. I spent an entire summer and then some babysitting for my first pair of contact lenses and another summer babysitting for money to buy a dog I wanted. I learned to sew and made my own clothes. And as a younger child, I even made many of my own toys. As soon as I was 16 and could get a real job, I was clerking in a fabric store after school and on weekends. I was not afraid of work, saving my money and waiting for what I really wanted. Yes, there were a lot of things I wanted and could not buy. Money helped me to decide what I really wanted.

One of my sons decided he wanted an air purifier when he was 8 years old. He saved his money for over one year and then he bought it. I thought he would give up, but he did not. I learned a lot and my son learned a lot, far beyond saving money. If someone would have given us the money, yes life would have been easier and the goal reached quicker, but what we both needed could not be bought with money.

I have known poor people to somehow procure money for alcohol and drugs, choosing these kinds of things over substantive food. This tells me that money is not the answer for them, either. I have learned through the years that people find money for what they really want/ need. If you can find money for drugs and alcohol you can find money for substantive food. Trying to fill empty holes with alcohol and drugs tells me the emotional holes of these people run deep. Giving them money is not the answer to fill emotional holes.

A person on our Youtube channel commented about her new T-shirts she bought with wonderful messages on them, but said she couldn't afford a monthly membership on our site. Really?

- What would happen to the membership if we gave her one?
- Do you think it would have had any value for her?
- Do you think she would have used it?
- Or did she value the T-shirt over her mental/emotional/ spiritual growth and physical healing?

It is a lot easier to complain about what you do not have and blame it on money. But money is not the answer for this person, either. Hard work can be extremely therapeutic whether you appreciate it at the time or not. Outer hard work means inner hard work is happening. Hard work comes in a variety of ways; it is not all physical. Even hard work starts in the mind before it can become physical. You have to think really, really hard to come up with inner solutions that you can implement in the outer world. As you can see, money is not the answer in any of these situations.

- Have you had periods in your life when you had to do hard work, physical, mental, emotional and/or spiritual?
- Did you learn more from the experience than if you had the money handed to you?
- Have you known poor people who, in your opinion, spent their money on foolish or even dangerous things?
- If so, do you think giving them more money would have helped them?
- Why does addiction treatment work for some people but not for others?
- If you put all such people in treatment would the money spent help all of them?
- Have you tried to spend money to fill your emotional holes?
- Are emotional holes always looking to be filled?
- Is it better to put something in an emotional hole than nothing?
- Do poor people have to stay poor?
- When people do not have the physical things they want do they consider themselves poor?
- Do even the poorest of the poor have what they need or they could not be here?

You may have experienced going hungry where there was no food in the house. There was always food in my home but my mother restricted what I could eat. When I did not like what she was making I was supposed to eat it anyway. Sometimes I sat at the table for hours, sometimes she got disgusted with me and sent me to bed, sometimes I would vomit and then she would put more of the same on my plate. Once she got so mad that she said all she had growing up to eat was fried cornbread and pinto beans so that is what we were going to get. I don't know how many days this went on for but I usually chose starvation over eating what I did not like or could not choke down.

For my mother, it was not about money; it was about control. Not eating was one area of my life where no one could force me to do what I did not want to do. Anything that was force-fed to me came right back up. Trying to force-feed my Self led to vomiting. I'm sure I tried every nerve in my mother's body as I refused to let her control my eating. In fact, I often passed out from low blood sugar, but that was so normal I did not realize this was abnormal. I called them blackouts. As soon as I felt one coming on I just leaned up against a wall or sat down if I could until it was over. Giving my mother more money would not have resolved the situation. I would have been happy with a peanut butter sandwich, but she would not give me that even when I requested it. It was her way or the highway and one of many reasons why I left at 17 years old. I had enough. You could not have paid me enough money to stay there.

- Have you been in situations where no one could have given you enough money to stay in a situation that was distressing to you?
- Have you tried to cope with situations because money was involved?
- When did you figure out that you were the common denominator and you had to change because your circumstances kept repeating?
- How easy is it to say that you have to stay because of money?

- How challenging is it to leave a situation with money to one filled with uncertainties?

- Are there times when the money is what keeps you exactly where you need to be?

- Do these types of situations force you to look at and change Self?

- Have you repeated the same scenario except with different people?

- Is this another level of Self-responsibility?

- Is it better to stay and face what you have rather than keep running from the same situation to the same situation?

- Can money soothe the pain of suffering?

- If so, is this a temporary or permanent fix?

- Does a financial settlement compensate for the loss of a loved one?

- Can you put a price on a person?

I had so many situations where I left because of the emotional strain, in the same way I left my mother. Money was never the issue. I could work; I could make money; I could support my Self. But I could not deal with interpersonal issues. I was challenged to deal with other people that I did not like or who did not like me. When I managed a fabric store the store owners hired a pretty young Christian woman who let me know that she was better than me because she went to church and I did not. She was nasty; mean and condescending; she quoted the Bible at me every chance she got. I think she might have been there 30 days when I told the owners that either they let her go or I was going because I could not deal with her. The owners belonged to an extreme evangelical sect, but I got along with them without any issues. They finally agreed that I could let her go. Another confrontation that I was not looking forward to, but I was looking forward to removing her from my space. So, either I got rid of these types of people or I left as soon as I could extricate my Self for one reason or another.

Until you really look at your Self on an extremely deep level it is challenging to realize that you are the common denominator. Money may be the reason you think you are at any job, but the real reason you are there is to learn about Self. You cannot pay a person enough to make them get along with people. I was so miserable you could not have paid me enough to work alongside these people. I kept leaving and running away from my Self just like I ran away from my mother. I have learned through the years that if I have to pick between a super intelligent person and a kind person, I will take the kind person. As much as I value intelligence I value a kind person even more. When you write a resume you put down everything that somehow justifies or verifies your intelligence, supposedly. But if you cannot get along with people then you are going to keep looping, just like I did.

- Which do you value more in a person, intelligence or kindness?
- How do you know if a person is kind?
- Do you have more patience for a kind person than a perceived intelligent snob?
- Is being with a rude, mean nasty person torture?
- Is peace of mind for sale?
- Does money buy a kind colleague?
- Have you ran away from people you did not like or you perceived did not like you?
- Are you learning to stay put, understand your lessons and be grateful for the process?
- When you are in these types of situations, how is your mental and emotional health?

- Can money buy a respite or do you have to take time off for a respite?
- What about people who take the money and never take a respite?
- What is the point of accumulating money and never spending it?

Your left brain contains your skills that you list on a resume; your right brain contains your emotions, morals and spirituality. Left brain skills are valued and paid for while the rest is shoved under the carpet and ignored. Thus the separation of church and state, or right brain and left brain. Extremely intelligent people can do some extremely evil things. This is why you need the balance of right brain with intelligence. When I went back to school for my master's in counseling, I decided after only a few short weeks that if I stayed the program it would take every bit of intuitiveness out of me. So, I chose to leave the program. I wanted the degree for the validity the diploma would give me, or so I thought. I had to sort out what I wanted and why. Maybe at a different stage in my life I would have pushed through for the degree. But at that stage, I decided that how I felt about me was more important than the paper. I chose right brain Self-Value over societal left brain value. Then I used my left brain intelligence to get a Reverend's paper so technically, I am a minister. This gives me the right to do spiritual counseling. And I also used my left brain intelligence to say what I do is a Personal Consultation based upon my years of expertise. Balance of left brain, right brain.

You need both hemispheres of your brain working together to get where you need to go. Societal programming forces you to pick and value the left brain. Jobs and careers that use the left brain are valued and financially rewarded over jobs and careers that focus more in the right brain. It is your mission to use both halves of your brain together to bring your life together. People who only value money are stuck in the left brain. They need something to hold and count. People who give no value to money are stuck in the right brain. These people are often quite poor while rich in spirit and ideals. This is why you must balance your brain; you were not designed to only use part of your brain, otherwise you would not have what you have.

Left brain thinkers use money to justify not taking care of the poor and needy of society. Right brain thinkers want to give them everything. When your brain is balanced you realize that simply giving people money is not the answer. Without your own training, it is challenging to bring together what people do need to truly help them in the left brain physical world as well as the right brain world of morals and integrity as well as emotions. Without brain balance, giving those in moral, integrity and emotional deficit money gives them the opportunity to exacerbate what is already going on within them.

- If money isn't the answer, how do you help people who are in a right brain deficit?
- Does society focus on either left brain or right brain?
- Does this make societal programming easier to install?
- Does programming shut off or exacerbate the emotions?
- Both, but not at the same time?
- Is this why people who consider themselves spiritual often disdain money?
- Do people who consider themselves spiritual often give away any money they get so they are continually in a financial deficit?
- Is splitting the brain purposeful beginning in school?
- Can morals be taught to children?
- At what age does a person become responsible for his/her own morals?
- Are morals already inherent within each person?

- Why do some children who are not taught morals somehow surpass their upbringing with tremendous integrity and depth of character?
- Why do some children whose parental figures try to install morals do the opposite of what they were taught?
- Do you do the breathing work in **Decoding Your Life** to help balance your brain?
- If you don't do this, would you if someone paid you to do it?
- Would you value the technique more if you had to pay thousands of dollars to learn it?
- Do you give more value to something when you pay more for it?

Once you have employment, which is usually based on left brain abilities, holding the position takes right brain skills. If you cannot get along with people or people cannot get along with you, you will either find a reason to leave or the employer will have a reason to dismiss you. You might be able to get a job but the next issue is if you can keep it. You can only get a job if you have matching color, tone and archetype. If you do not get the job you want, no matter how much you want it rather than bemoan what you didn't get, remember that *rejection is God's protection.* What you see as the ideal position may have other hidden pitfalls of which you are not consciously aware. This saying has kept me sane since I first heard it.

It is extremely easy to fall into Self-pity when you do not get what you want but when you realize that Source has your back it is easier to accept the perceived rejection when you realize it is Source protecting you. Most businesses that fail do so because of personality clashes, not money deficits. Most people get along just fine in the confines of their own home, but when they are with others life becomes more complicated. This is why you need to learn to center and balance so that no matter what happens you stay grounded in the most important way, Self, Oversoul, God-Mind. Everyone and everything will try to throw you out of balance and actually even out of your body. Like the expression "I was beside my Self with anger". Yes, if you are not appropriately buttoned into your body you can get thrown out of your body. No matter how many left brain skills you have, you must have the right brain skills to cope. No one can do it for you and no amount of money buys you the skills you need.

This is work that only you can do. All you need are 2 basic books *Decoding Your Life* and *Hyperspace Helper*. Many people have these books but have discounted their validity. So the books were never opened and read, or they were given away or thrown out. You cannot buy the information that you seek. When your mind-pattern is where it needs to be what you need automatically comes to you. Even these books are only icing your own cake that you created simply by existing. Self and Source is all you need, something that money can never buy.

- Do you often think about what you could do if you had money?
- Are you more challenged to creatively stretch when you do not have money?
- Can having money be a detriment to your creativity?
- Or help you be creative in ways that are not for your upliftment?
- If you think money is your only answer, are you more likely to fall deeper into the abyss without it?
- Do people value themselves based on how much money they have?
- Do people value others based upon how much money others have?
- Does information come to you one way or another when your mind-pattern is ready via a book, movie or even a stranger on the street?

- Does Hyperspace/Oversoul work teach you to rely only on Source and to not judge what Source provides?
- Have you ever been so angry or upset that you were "beside your Self"?
- If so, does it take a while to come back to center, even if you were not aware of what was happening?
- Have you had jobs where personality conflicts caused the business to not do well?
- Do personality conflicts in families cause dissension?
- If families are supposed to love and support each other why do these things happen?
- Are right brain coping skills challenging to implement?
- Is it easier to get a job than keep it?

When you have emotional holes (right brain), they cannot be filled by something physical (left brain). Money is physical. You can hold it and count it but you cannot ingest it as healing for emotional holes. Social scientists are people who try to take right brain emotions for quantifying and measuring. Social scientists are usually really kind people with wonderful intentions, but usually without left brain balance. Therefore these people often become the bleeding-heart-liberal-do-gooders who do their best to heal society, which is impossible. As you already know, society can only be healed from within, by each individual. And, I know many people who take issue with the scientist part of social science.

I have met so many people who try to heal their emotional holes with money. They are greedy, cheap and generally whatever you have, they want. They justify in their minds why they should have more. Gathering money in any way possible is practically addictive which is why so many of these types of people steal and embezzle. They are not bad people. They are damaged people making bad choices. This is why truly poor people can often be extremely kind. They do not have money they have no hope of ever having money, so money is not really on their radar. They often share resources amongst themselves or even strangers. I have seen numerous social media videos of homeless people being given something who turn around and give all or part to someone they perceive as even less fortunate.

- Have you been truly poor or been around truly poor people?
- Have you observed that they are extremely kind amongst each other?
- Are extremely poor people apt to observe others as rich whether that person is rich or not?
- Are poor people easy targets for predators?
- Do poor people have a different set of values?
- What does poor mean?
- Are Indigenous people poor?
- Have you witnessed people with emotional holes trying to fill those holes with money?
- Does money give some people comfort in a way that nothing else can?
- Can gathering money to fill emotional holes become addictive?
- Have you observed damaged people making bad choices?
- Is social science a valid science?
- Can you quantify and measure human emotions in an accepted scientific way?
- Do you know people who are super kind because they are centered in their right brain without much, if any, left brain balance?
- Why do people expect something physical like money to heal emotional holes?

- Can money heal some layer of emotional holes?
- Can money be used as a boost to the mind-pattern?

If you don't have any money you are not afraid of losing it. When I first started farming I had nothing. The government gave me a wonderful loan which I was able to pay off which meant I now had something. This also meant I had to protect it so I wouldn't lose it. People spend much time and money trying to protect what they have so they don't lose it. Taxation is the biggest game the government plays to keep you juggling your resources so you get to keep more and give them less. It is all legal, but you are always on your toes because you need to be a CPA and an attorney to really understand the laws. Even when you do your best to stay within the law you might make an error because you might misinterpret or not know about a specific law.

I was always taught that real estate is a good investment. That sounded good to me because as a farmer I had to own land to earn a living. Then I found out that the government can take your land any time they want for any reason under the law of eminent domain. In time of war they can claim any property you own, including your house. They can take your car and your dogs! Next, I was taught that precious metals are a good investment, especially gold and silver. That sounds good too, except to sell your gold it has to be assayed, meaning a small hole has to be drilled into the metal to prove that it is what it is claimed to be in case it is really something else. In time of crisis you cannot walk into a store with your gold coins and buy something. As much as I would like to believe you, if I have a product to sell at this point I'd rather take my chances on paper money. And, in time of crisis, the government can also take your precious metals as well as money in your bank account. The government can take what you have basically at any time.

As the years went by and I thought about what I had to protect I finally came to the conclusion that there was no point in trying to protect whatever I have. Because when it comes right down to it, I really own nothing. I am using certain properties and things but it isn't really mine because at any time anyone could theoretically take it. I have this insurance and that insurance and do my best to follow the legalities of taxation under the advice of my accountant, banker, attorneys and everyone else I have to pay so I can continue to do what I do. But ultimately, money isn't the answer.

In California recently, people were losing their fire insurance because of the wildfires; through the years I have seen California residents lose their mudslide insurance as well as earthquake insurance. So even though people may have paid for decades on their insurance policies, God forbid, they could lose their homes through fire, mudslides and/ or earthquakes and that would be the end of all their hard work. Food, shelter and memories wiped out in practically the blink of an eye. I have seen people who were let go months, weeks and even days before their retirement was to start. Companies with mandatory stock options have reduced the value of what employees own, again reducing what employees have for retirement purposes.

- Have you thought whatever you have was protected only to find that it wasn't?
- Has this made you question what you have and how to keep it?
- Have you been in the position of having nothing so you had no worries about how to keep anything?
- What is sentimental value?
- Why do people want to hold onto things to hold onto memories?
- Can you own anything?
- Do things own you?
- Or, are you in a partnership with whatever is in your space?
- If something leaves your space, or your space leaves you, do you trust the process or fight the process?

- Do you worry about losing what you have?
- Do you have what you have as a result of your mind-pattern or your money?
- Can anyone take your money?
- Can anyone take your mind?
- How do you protect what you have?
- Do insurance and taxation play games with your mind?
- If you are always focused on what is left, loss, paying taxes, obeying laws are you defocused on the positive part of what you do have?

As much as you are programmed to believe you need money, the more important thing you need is your mind to draw to you what you need when you need it. I have seen numerous stories of socialites, both male and female, who nobody really knows who they are, where they came from or how they got their money. Sooner or later these people are exposed as frauds, but somehow they had the mind-pattern to get what they wanted for a prolonged period of time. What they really are doing is playing a game of power with money being their prize but not the goal. Many people think that money buys power, but it does not. There is only One Power and it is not for sale. If all the money in the world was gathered up, no one could purchase or own that power.

Money gets you the illusions that say you are powerful. Other people look at the illusions and claim you must be powerful. All the feedback comes from the outer world which cannot stand without inner power. Then you have to think about how you are going to protect your physical assets. Remember that if something is yours no one can take it from you; if it isn't yours you cannot hold onto it. Stewart purchased an iron ring that he lost while cleaning out his lizard cage. He could not find it after a lengthy search. I asked my Oversoul where it was and found it within about 30 seconds. Then, he lost it again in his vegetable garden. After a lengthy search, he could not find it. I asked my Oversoul where it was and found it in the garden within about 30 seconds. The third time he lost it was while he was in New York. I wasn't there and I couldn't find it for him. Apparently, the ring was no longer his. When something is yours, no one can take it. Sometimes you release things because it is the most correct and beneficial thing to do, even when it is rightfully yours. However, when this happens then that thing or its equivalent, will find its way to you. Whatever is yours, even something physical, cannot be purchased or held onto unless there is matching color, tone and archetype. I think of my Self more as a guardian than an owner. I am the guardian of my animals, the guardian of my home as well as any and all physical items considered mine.

- Does it make sense to be a guardian rather than an owner?
- Does owner imbue a false sense of security?
- Does guardian imply stewardship vs do whatever you want because you own it?
- Does whatever you have in your care have a consciousness of some kind?
- Is it important to elevate rather than denigrate what is in your stewardship?
- Can anything be in your care without its consent?
- Does money give people the illusion that they are powerful?
- Can you buy real power?
- Can you use money to control others through fear?
- Is money the answer to power?

Many people want what they want now, taking the short term solution as their prize when ultimately the long term solution is your goal. You are not here to accumulate things, you are here to learn. Money focuses your attention and that is its main goal.

Money is never the answer to anything. In fact, money often is the downfall of many people. They have enough money that they hang themselves. So many negative incidents happen when people go on vacation, for example. People get sick, fall overboard on cruises, become the victims of violence. Without the money, these things could not have happened. As excited as these people were for their vacations, think of what might not have happened had they not gone on their vacation in the first place.

Most people want more money because they want more experiences. Many years ago I won a cruise that was given away to shoppers at a supermarket. I did not know that this contest was even happening. My mind-pattern pulled this cruise to me. However, I still had to pay for airfare to get there and back, as well as extra to take my 2 children. Without winning this contest I would not have made this trip. Consciously I had no intention of ever taking a cruise. But this is where my Oversoul wanted me, so this is where I went. This is only one example of the strength of your mind-pattern pulling something to you.

- Have you ever won something of value unexpectedly?
- Is this one proof that your mind-pattern pulls to you what you need, even if you do not have the money in your pocket?
- Do things and experiences come to you in unexpected ways, without you having to give money for them?
- With a strong enough mind-pattern could you get what you need without any money?
- Does money focus you on the short term prize rather than the long term goal?
- With all the choices available can you be grateful to money as a tool to help you focus?
- Do you sometimes purchase something only to find that your short term satisfaction is short-lived?

- Do you sometimes wish that you had kept your money so you could have spent it more wisely?
- When you want something now, does time play games with your head?
- Do you feel like saving for something you want is taking forever?
- Are you challenged to convince your Self when you do not get what you want that *rejection is God's protection*?
- Is the main goal of money to focus your attention?

### *I have what I have as a result of my mind, not my money.*

Too often people think that if they just had more money, all their problems would be resolved. When you do not have the money you want or feel you need, you look at people with money who seemingly have the comforts required by the Animal Mind. The Animal Mind tells you that money must be the answer. Those people with money have food, shelter and relationships for procreation/survival of the species. If you do not have money and struggle for food, shelter and maintenance of relationships then you look to the obvious answer of money.

"If I had more money, I would have food, shelter and relationships just like those people." The issue is those people have a different set of mind-patterns than you do or they would not have the money they have. And because you want money for the basics, you do not think beyond the basics. You do not think of the other complications that are in the lives of truly-moneyed people. People who are truly-moneyed are not in the public eye. They are smart enough to stay hidden. They do not flaunt their wealth in any way. You do not see their food, homes or families. They do not want you coming after them or coveting what they have. You cannot covet what you do not know about.

Those people who you see are programming icons placed in the public eye as a barrier and buffer. The truly moneyed people want you coveting such things that make the icons appear wealthy such as cars, plastic surgery, fancy vacations and jewelry as well as things that make you stupid, like injections, body fillers, tattoos, piercings, plant-based foods and anything that divides your family. Marriages, divorces, child custody, abortion, daycare. Whatever the truly-moneyed global elite want you to want, they tell you that you can't have it. Then you fight for the right until you win so you are happy and they are happier. People are so busy fighting for/against vaccines, for/against pesticides and herbicides, for/against climate change that they never accomplish anything of substance. The global handlers taunt the populace and off the people go; predictable and unsurprisingly. Everyone is programmed to believe that more money means a happier, healthier more peaceful world.

- Why is it so easy to buy this programming?
- Do you easily identify the latest trends that the global handlers use to distract the population?
- Is there something for everyone?
- Are there too many choices?
- Does all of this lead to chaos and confusion, regardless of country, race, religion?
- Do people fight amongst each other because they are overwhelmed without clear direction and/or focus?
- Do populations need leaders?
- Is the leader a result of the mind-pattern of the people, whether they are for or against the leader?
- Is so much attention given to the programming icons that people really do not even consider the truly moneyed?
- Do the truly moneyed give you people to love, hate, admire, despise, emulate, distract, anger and keep you entertained on all levels, one way or the other?

- Do people need to see and experience all of these emotions because they are within each person?
- Without the barriers/buffer of the programming icons would the people revolt against the truly moneyed?
- Do the barriers/buffer of the programming icons keep society and even the government that you see more stable?
- Are the truly moneyed the global power brokers?
- If the global power brokers gave people food, shelter and helped maintain families would the world become more peaceful?
- Is money a Pandora's Box?

People think the money system is bad/evil, but I think it is a brilliant way of being able to exchange energy for what you need or want. It is the intermediary that gives you faith that if you want/need something, you can have it. Without money, you would just depend on the strength of your mind-pattern to pull it to you. Perhaps then, you could simply materialize what you want/need out of the ethers. I have thought the same way about transportation and telecommunications.

- Without things and without the money to buy things, would you be forced to use your mind to transport you to various locations?
- Is money a buffer that slows you down so your choices are wiser/more correct and beneficial?
- Can too much money enhance a reckless mind-pattern?
- Or give you a false sense of security?
- Does not having money make you depend upon Source for protection instead of an alarm system?
- Can too much money make you think outer world confirmation of Self is more valuable than inner confirmation of Self?

- Can money make you lazy?
- Does not having money create more independence and stimulate inner creativity?
- Once your basic needs are met, can having money put you on a path to Self-destruction rather than Self-actualization?
- Is it challenging to know the pluses and the minuses of both sides of the coin until you have lived them?

When you do not have money you think about how much better your life would be with money. You are always focused on money, money, money. This is really a distraction from your real issues. Once you have money, you find this out. Then, money is not so important anymore. For example my aunt with cancer. She has great health insurance and enough income so that she can get the best conventional medical care available. If she did not have such great health insurance and access to the best conventional medical care, perhaps she would be more willing to try unconventional treatments. Right now, there is no amount of money that can buy her health. In my opinion, if she had less money she might take a different path. I have seen so many people, over the past few years pass on. There is no amount of money that can buy the health care that anyone needs.

The best health care is in your mind. It does not matter what food you eat, what supplements and vitamins you take, what medical care you get, conventional or nonconventional, if you do not fix what is in your mind none of it is a permanent cure. You may be able to boost your mind-pattern into a better space or depress your mind-pattern into a worse place. I have seen both situations happen. The only permanent cure is in your mind. Money can give you false hope. If you don't have money and need healthcare you can blame your ill health on the medical system.

- When you have the money to utilize the healthcare system and it still doesn't work, then who do you blame?

- Do people think that money buys health or healthcare?
- Does all healthcare come from the same Source?
- Does the path to healing really matter?
- Can you use anything to boost your mind-pattern into healing?
- When your mind-pattern is in the correct place can healing happen through conventional paths as easily as nonconventional paths?
- Can people be too trusting of nonconventional paths?
- Can people not trust conventional paths enough?
- Do you keep in mind that all healing paths originate with one Source?
- Is each healing path designed to heal your body or to help you find your mind so your body can follow your mind?
- Is your mind the best path that you can take to health?
- Do most people feel more comfortable paying money for healthcare rather than utilizing what is in their own minds?
- Have you read of people who were told their health issues were uncurable, only to prove differently?
- Is your mind the strongest healing tool you have?

Having money can give you what you think are easy answers. You have a health issue, you see some kind of medical professional, you are fixed and you get on with your life. But, there are tons of people who get caught up in the healthcare system who have long term issues. I have positive and negative experiences with both conventional and nonconventional practitioners. I am stubborn enough that I prefer to use the strength of my mind to heal whatever needs healing. I used to avoid conventional practitioners because I did not believe in the validity of their healing work. Once I started fasting I did not see a conventional doctor until my first pregnancy, so a span of about 15 years. I was determined to have a natural childbirth, but first I had pre-term labor at 5 months so I was on bed rest until the baby was born. Then, when I went for a checkup in my 37th week the baby was showing signs of distress, so labor was induced. When that failed to progress the doctor had to do an emergency C-section. If not for conventional medicine most likely one or both of us would not be here to talk about this.

Since that time I have used conventional medicine on an as needed basis while my preference is always nonconventional. But, I have met some truly unethical nonconventional practitioners as well as those who did not know what they were doing. I had no choice but to admit that all healing comes from one Source. So, depending upon what is most correct and beneficial is where I go when necessary. I used to do my best to vilify conventional medicine. But enough truly horrible experiences with nonconventional medicine forced my views to become more objective.

Even with money, your mind-pattern is going to draw the practitioner to you that matches what you need, whether you like it or not. Your money cannot buy expertise. Some people think that the more they pay, the more the person is an expert. Often, the more you pay the more arrogant the practitioner. Having money can make people arrogant, condescending, and imbue them with a holier-than-thou attitude. Not desirable qualities in my book.

- Have you paid a lot of money for someone you thought was an expert only to find that they had a ton of undesirable qualities?
- Was paying them the extra money worth having to deal with their negative attributes?
- Have you experienced people with money who were nasty and rude?

- Even with all their money, do you think about what makes them this way?
- Is money the answer to their life issues?
- Is not having money a distraction for most people so they do not have to face mental, emotional and spiritual issues?
- Does not having money force you to deal with mental, emotional and spiritual issues?
- Is there a perception that having money makes dealing with these issues easier?
- If this were the case, why do you see so many people with so much money commit suicide or even turn to criminal activity?
- Can having money be a curse or a blessing?
- Is it money that buys the correct practitioner for you or your mind-pattern that pulls the correct one?
- What is more important: whether the practitioner is conventional or nonconventional or your mind-pattern?

No matter how you look at it, money does not buy your health. The less money you have, the more narrow your choices. This means you have less opportunity to mess up. In a world where billions of choices exist, you may feel upset and left out. A young child needs his/her choices focused. Sometimes, 2 choices are 1 too many for a child. As a parent, you need to teach them to make the best choices at all times so when he/she is on his/her own, the child can function in a world that can easily overwhelm.

You need to be able to make the best choice and you need to learn discernment. When I read the stories of the celebrity icons, it seems the majority have some really sad stories that include drug, alcohol and/or sex addiction, multiple marriages and relationships, accidents, illnesses, death. They had a ton of money but that ton of money did not resolve their inner conflict. They had enough rope to hang themselves. They have enough money for plastic surgeries but that hasn't bought them health.

I always tell you that fasting is free. Fasting is one of the best ways to regain your health. Money isn't the answer to learn how to fast. I taught my Self through trial and error. This is why people who go vegetarian/vegan often get well when they are deathly ill. They give their bodies enough food so they do not die from detox, so the body has a respite which then allows it to heal. A vegetarian/vegan lifestyle is much cheaper than medical care. The issue is once the body reaches a certain level of healing you need to give it material to build it Self back up. Without this material, the body begins to deteriorate. Balance in all things. Balance does not cost money. Emotional/mental balance cannot be bought with money.

On an interesting side note, I buy chicken hindquarters in my supermarket that usually are priced from 60 to 80 cents per pound. Dark meat is better for you than white meat, but with the marketing, most people prefer white meat. I will eat white meat but my preference is always dark. I use dark chicken meat for the majority of my soup stocks. Chicken livers, as well as beef livers, are usually quite affordable and are great sources of iron. Eggs are great sources of iron. If you are short on money your food choices are narrowed down. You learn how inexpensive it is to feed your body well. You learn that your body does not require as much food as you are told. Sometimes, narrower choices are exactly what you need to teach you about what is important and what is not.

- Does not having money narrow your choices?
- Do narrow choices make you grateful or resentful?
- Do you focus on what you have or what you don't/can't have?
- Does limited money force you to focus on what is most important in life?

- Have you discovered that your body does not really require a lot of food to live?

- Do you focus on providing your body the proper building materials so it can regenerate and heal?

- Do you focus on your Oversoul and God-Mind to give you what you need, not what you want?

- Even in your darkest moments do you stop to think that you still have work to do here on this planet or you would not be here?

- Do you recognize that you have a purpose and you are doing something right or your Earthly opportunity would be taken away?

- Have you learned how to fast according to the needs of your physical body as well as your emotional, mental and Spiritual aspects of Self?

- Does not having money force you to depend on Source?

- Does depending on Source go beyond societal norms?

- Does not having money teach you discernment?

- Is it easy to get overwhelmed by billions of choices?

- As a child, were you allowed to choose or were all the choices made for you?

- Are all the choices in this world are designed to appeal to the child within especially one with a credit card?

- Do narrow choices teach you responsibility by forcing the child within to grow up?

There are many stories about people helping to provide housing for the homeless. I applaud these efforts but I wonder if there is any mental and emotional support for these people. Even with all the bills paid there is something within these people that put them in a homeless situation to start with. Some people may have attracted the housing because they corrected their mind-patterns. Others may have attracted it as tests to see if their mind-patterns are really corrected. Some may have attracted it to show them that they still have a lot of issues that need correcting. Every person has a unique experience even though the base experience is the same. As you already know, giving money does not fix anything. Money is a temporary solution to a much deeper issue. You can keep putting the band aid on, but until the wound is cleaned out there is only so much a band aid can do.

Wounds run deep in every person who walks this Earth. You are never alone in your suffering. But in your healing, you can feel very alone and sometimes be very alone amongst other people. All of this is to continue to push deeper into Source. Always remember that it is darkest before the dawn. You are here for a purpose, learning and growth. Keep asking why, knowing that somewhere within you already know. Use your energetic affirmations to pull out that which is already there, waiting for you to discover it.

- How do you explain this to people who think that money is the answer?

- Do you get frustrated knowing that the answer lies within yet you are challenged to bring that answer into your conscious mind?

- Do you use affirmations as energetic tools to dig around in your energy field to bring to the surface that which you already know?

- If your answers are buried deep within, are you going to bring up a myriad of other issues and answers before you get to the deeper answers?

- Is it easy to get discouraged?

- Do you do even more inner level work when you least feel like it?

- Do you use positive affirmations to help pull your answers to the surface?
- Do you know that in the Eternal Now you have your answers already?
- Do you stand in your center, anchored deep into Source no matter who/what is trying to disturb the calm peace of your Soul?
- Is giving housing to the homeless the first step in a long process of mental, emotional and spiritual rehabilitation to a wounded population?
- Can money heal mental, emotional and spiritual wounds?

Valuing the process more than the end result is a challenge for most people. Most people want what they want and they want it now. I used to be like that but I have learned that this only stresses me and usually doesn't change the process. To make life easier on me, I do my best to see the best parts of the process rather than the worst part. If the process is slower than I would like, I realize this means that God's timing is different than my timing; same as if I feel I can't keep up with the timing because it is going too fast. This means I have to adjust faster than I would prefer, but it is doable or the opportunity would not be there for me.

When you are suffering in any way, the process to get from here to there always takes way too long in your estimation; in God's timing, there is something to be learned so time is slowed down so you can get it. The rewards you get here and there are the carrots that keep you moving forward. Enjoy them while you have them because you never know what is around the bend. The only way you can truly understand the process is to spend some time focusing on the Eternal Now where time and space do not exist. The more inner work you do the more likely your world is to be thrown into what appears to be chaos. But, as you dig around in your inner world your outer world merely reflects this. Eventually, your digging process will slow down so you can take a good look at what you just dug up; you will need to reorder and reorganize all the inner stuff you just unearthed. As this happens your outer world will appear to come together for a time until the next inner excavation begins.

Thus the process continues in a way that no amount of money is going to slow down or speed up. You cannot buy God's timing. What happens behind the scenes is not for sale, no matter how much money you have. Your Soul growth is not dependent upon money. The more money you have, in fact, the more frustrated you are likely to become because you cannot buy what you want. Unless God happens to let you spend your money and get things done your way in your timing simply to show you why it is not a good idea to put your timing ahead of God's timing.

- Do you know people who think they can buy anything, including people and time?
- How does this work out for them?
- Have you ever tried to force something through with money, but it has not worked out no matter what you did?
- Is it frustrating when things do not go your way, especially when you have the money?
- Do people think money is a magic ticket to make everything happen their way?
- When things are not going according to your plans is it tempting to say that things would be different if you had more money?
- When you are in a physical world how challenging is it to follow nonphysical laws?
- When you are in a physical world how tempting is it to not follow nonphysical laws?

- Do you ever wish that you did not know as much as you know?
- Do you sometimes think that life might be easier if you were less aware rather than more aware?
- Does digging deeper usually mean your outer world becomes more chaotic?
- Are you challenged to see the best part of the process instead of the worst part?
- Do you keep the best attitude you can even when life feels unpleasant, unkind and even cruel?
- Do you value the process more because this is where the most learning occurs?
- Is the goal the moment when your learning actually slows down and maybe even stops?
- Is the goal your moment of respite before the next layer of learning starts up again?

You know by your diligence in your Hyperspace/Oversoul work that there is no amount of money that can be given to you to buy what you know. Reading the books, watching the videos and attending lectures, webinars and seminars are great ways to gather information but until you apply and use the information, you really do not know the material. When I wrote **Decoding Your Life**, I thought I was done. I gave people enough information to take them through a lifetime and beyond, just learning these simple Universal Laws and applying them.

When I met Stewart my work expanded his work and his work expanded my work. And we have both been digging deeper and exploring ever since. There is no way that anyone can ever monetarily compensate either of us for what we have been through and our knowledge gained. It takes a lot of time and effort to take what I know and put it out in a way that people can understand. I can tell you what an orange tastes like but if you have never tasted one we cannot really have a conversation about one. Money is not the answer to knowing what an orange tastes like. Only an orange is going to give you the experience you need.

In the same way, until you experience what I am telling you we cannot really have a conversation about it. We can discuss concepts and you can get an idea of what I am saying, but when you do the work with your own results then we can really talk. Money isn't the answer to giving you the experience you need. It is easy to say, "If only I had the money, then I could/would…" and life would be better. That is only an excuse for not doing your personal work. I have had many of those days when you really want to blame something. Money is a handy thing to blame to which most people can relate.

- Have you had days when you wanted to blame money and dream that money would be your all-encompassing problem-solver?
- Do you know people who think this way?
- Is it challenging to explain to others that money is not the problem-solver they think it is?
- Would people be more agreeable to thinking money is the answer instead of doing mental work?
- Why is it mind is the last place people look for change?
- Why do people think they need money for experience?
- Is this a Self-sabotaging mind-pattern that stifles your creativity?
- Do you value your own life experience and learning?
- How could you ever impart to another all that you know and the process that took you there?
- Can what you know be bought and paid for with money?
- In what do you consider your Self an expert?

I like to watch the superhero movies because I always think that this is the way I should be, always eager to face the evils of the world without fear as well as with supreme confidence that I will be the victor. You cannot buy courage or confidence. Some people think they can pay for a gun or a security system which in turn gives them courage and confidence, but I do not agree. No thing can ever protect you and no thing can give you confidence. Perhaps this is why we exist in a material world. The outer is the illusion that tricks you into thinking that it has power, but ultimately it only has the power that you give it.

My weapon of choice would be a martial arts type of physical training. Then I would apply superhero speed and strength to my techniques. At least this would be an extension of my mind. Of course, then you could become too reliant on the body as your weapon. Ultimately, I prefer my mind. I would like my thoughts alone to be enough to fight the evils of the world. That would definitely instill in me the supreme confidence that I am accomplishing what I came here to accomplish. Interestingly enough, this thought brings everything right back to the beginning point. I need to be eager to face whatever I find inside of my Self without fear as well as supreme confidence that I will be the victor.

- Can money buy the powers of your mind?
- Can you buy courage or confidence?
- Does money buy your safety and protection?
- Have you known people who thought they could buy confidence only to find that when the money is gone so is the confidence?
- Have you watched superhero movies and wondered what it would be like to have superhero powers?
- Have you seen these superheroes vilified when people do not understand them as well or glorify them when the superheroes accomplish what the people want?

- Are superheroes either loved or hated with little in between?
- Would you want to be in either of these positions?
- Are you a superhero to your Self because of what you do to face your own inner evils?
- Would you want outer weapons for security reasons?
- Is the strength of your mind-pattern enough to keep you safe?
- If you were a martial artist, would that make you safer or only make you feel safer?
- If you feel safer, is this a boost to the mind-pattern that can ultimately connect you deeper into Source?
- Is the outer an illusion that tries to trick you into believing that it has more strength than you do?
- Why do people want to imbue things with greater power than Source?
- If you cannot buy Source, is buying objects the next best thing to do?

Everyone believes that he/she needs money to survive. This thought directs your attention to the outer world to give you what you need instead of to Source to give you what you need. When you do not have what you perceive you need, it is easy to grasp at straws which generally furthers your downfall. You cannot hold onto straws and expect them to support you in any way. When you least feel like doing your Hyperspace/Oversoul work is when you need it the most. What you know cannot be bought or sold. Money can be a band aid but it is never the solution.

However, the band aid may be what you need to keep from completely going under, Even this small respite is a result of your mind-pattern. The band aid is a small window of opportunity to not sink further if there is any chance you can get your lesson wherever you stand now. If you don't get it, the band aid fades away and you sink a little deeper. I have certainly been in these types of situations and it is challenging. You have to be relaxed and deepen your connection and trust in Source while you feel like you are falling into a bottomless abyss. This is extremely challenging to do. Yet, you would not be in this position if you could not handle it. You are still here on this Earth because you are learning, you are willing to learn, there is something more for you to learn and do.

If you cannot determine the most correct move when you ask, it is always better to do something rather than nothing. Movement shows Source that you are trying. Movement allows Source to correct you. I always ask Source to correct me in the least uncomfortable way if what I am doing needs correction. Some days it feels like I am wading through quicksand but I keep moving. I keep telling Source that I am trying and I am doing my best. I pray and give thanks that each step reveals it Self in a way that I can handle. I trust this process even when I do not know the outcome. I trust that whatever happens, in the way it happens, is what is supposed to happen. And. I. Keep. Moving.

- Why is it important to keep moving?
- Is it better to loop than to do nothing at all?
- Is it better to try a solution even if you are unsure so Source can correct you?
- Is it easiest to live in the fear of the Animal Mind vs. trusting the process of Source?
- When you are afraid is it easier to fall back into what you know?
- How challenging is it to find the courage to keep moving?
- What color is courage?
- Do you allow the color of courage to permeate your Being on all levels?
- Do you ask that all your Simultaneous Existences where you are courageous merge into your current life stream as taught in *Hyperspace Plus*?

- Do you tell your Oversoul that you are doing your best, so please correct you in the least uncomfortable way possible?
- Do you tell your Oversoul to please guide and direct you to the most correct and beneficial door and you will walk through it?
- Do you give thanks that you now know your next step in the process?
- When you have felt like you are falling into the abyss have you been given band aids that slowed down the fall?
- Do band aids give you a breather so you can have a minute to go deeper into center?
- Do you recognize a band aid as a band aid or is it too easy to think a band aid is a permanent solution?
- Do your efforts make you a superhero to Self?

**Grateful**

I have learned that being grateful for what I have is one of the biggest keys to attaining whatever is most correct and beneficial for me. Like everyone else, I have wanted a variety of things to transpire in my life. I have had tons of disappointments and upheavals that were anything but pleasant. I have waded through these negatives, done my best to learn what I needed to learn from them and move along. I have learned to be grateful for the negatives as well as the positives. No matter how little or how much I have had, I have done my best to every day be grateful. Rather than focus on what I wish I had, I focus on what I have right now, in this moment. By appreciating this moment, the frequency opens for more.

When you have an issue that is overwhelming, find something that you can accomplish and do it. For example, washing your car represents cleaning your path in life. Accomplishing anything, no matter how seemingly small, sets the frequency to accomplish bigger and better.

### *Money cannot buy gratitude, appreciation or problem-solving.*

I've had an issue with my main phone line for over a month. At first, I thought it was my phone so I bought a new phone. It wasn't the phone so I called my phone company and after 4 hours they couldn't find the issue so they suggested I phone my alarm company. I had to wait for 2 weeks for someone to come. Today, the technician told me he couldn't find the answer but thinks maybe an animal chewed through my outside line, he can't fix it so I have to find someone to do this. No amount of money could speed up my appointment times and no amount of money can get any of the techs to solve the phone issue. I will have to look for another person to get this resolved. And still, pay for those who could not resolve the issue. I'm sure you have had these situations too. It does not matter if you have money or do not have money, you still have to sit, wait for someone to come and maybe or maybe not help you. I have to be grateful for the process, know that there is a reason that my communication is being changed and when the timing is correct the situation will be resolved. The situation has nothing to do with money; it has to do with some inner communication process that I am having to re-wire.

- Have you had situations that no amount of money could resolve the issue?
- Can paying money buy a solution or speed up your time waiting in line?
- Can you buy God's timing for your personal situation?
- Is it difficult to always have an attitude of gratitude?
- Are these Self-tests to see if you will allow the process to unfold in God's timing?
- When solutions do not come in your timing is it easy to become distraught?
- Is it easy to feel discouraged, disappointed and sometimes even fearful?

- Can you find something positive to focus on, regardless of how small, to demonstrate that regardless of adversity you are grateful?

There are so many situations where money isn't the answer. The Animal Mind is so focused on survival that it is easy to forget that there is more to life than food and shelter. The global handlers make it look like money will resolve all your issues, so if you don't have money it is best just to resign your Self to a horrible life. Or, you can drive your Self crazy trying to get more money to create a good life. Some people even turn to a life a crime or borderline crime to create a good life. Of course, the good life you strive for is the one that the global handlers paint for you. Their illusion becomes so real that your only focus is on the money that you Self-deceive will solve all of your problems and issues. This keeps you looping. For most people, the loop is easier to deal with than actually looking at Self.

Plus, there are so many things that money cannot buy. Like supply and demand. People fight each other for things on Black Friday. People come to the store with money in their pockets but because of scarcity, they start fighting each other over silly material possessions. There will be a lot of people who leave with their money because there is not enough product at the advertised price to meet the demand. Sometimes you read about wealthy people who shoplift. People who could well afford the items they stole but for them, money isn't the answer. They have plenty.

- Why do people like this shoplift?
- Are new products often introduced with low inventory to get people hyped up to buy the product before the product is all gone?
- Does scarcity focus you on money, even if that is not the real issue?

- Can you buy a ticket to an event after it is sold out, regardless of how much money you have?
- If you are on an overbooked airline flight on your way to a wedding, funeral, business meeting, or another important event, can the airlines give you enough money to give up your seat?
- Would you sell a beloved pet if someone offered you enough money?
- Or a family heirloom?
- How much money would it take for you to tattoo your forehead to advertise something for a company?
- What do you have that is not for sale?
- What would you not do for any amount of money?

There was a recent article about a lottery winner in the United Kingdom who shot his 5 and 11 year old sons and his wife. Then turned the gun on him Self. His wife survived, but the 2 boys and husband all died. Apparently, he spent all the money on drugs and prostitutes. There was another article about a couple who just won 102million pounds in a lottery win. They are celebrating while the surviving member in the first example is probably wishing they had never won the lottery in the first place. Money is never the answer. The family obviously had problems before they won the money. If you already have problems, more money means more problems. You have more money to do more of whatever it was you were doing in the first place that was not most correct and beneficial.

You may wonder what is in the mind-patterns that drew the money to them in the first place. Each person and family is unique, but in general, they have to know they deserve money to pull it to them. I have studied money so much for so many years that a part of me says more money could make my life a lot easier in so many ways, Yet, I also know that I do not want more than I can handle. In the same news service, there was also an article about an extremely popular South Korean musician aged 28 who killed her Self. Popularity and money was not the answer for her, so she extricated her Self from it all. So many people want both, but all you have to do is observe daily life to see that money is the distraction/temptation that is flaunted at you so you do not look deeper within.

There are a lot of things that on the surface would be nice to have or do. A grandfather who dropped his 3 year-old granddaughter from the balcony of a cruise ship and killed her is beside him Self with grief. If that family had not had the money to take the trip the specific incident would not have happened. Many people are killed when they try to take Selfies in dangerous, exotic places. Without the money to get there, perhaps they would have lived.

Money is not the answer. Money can be the problem rather than the answer you are programmed to believe. As much as you might want to do something or go somewhere or have a specific thing, it may be you are being protected from a hidden tragedy. I would rather not have any of it than have something that would cause me so much grief.

- How tempting is it to blame not having, doing, going on not having money?
- Do most people find the money for what they really want to do?
- Do most people accept the excuse that "I can't because I don't have the money" more than "I don't want to"?
- Do you accept that not having money can be a blessing?
- Does not having money focus you on mind-patterns that you would not otherwise see?
- Does having money give people an excuse to stop doing mental work?
- Do most people see having money as having arrived?

- Docs money solve your health, career and/or relationship issues?
- Could having money result in your living in a geographic location that does not suit your Soul needs?
- Could having money put you in all the wrong places, metaphorically speaking?
- Are you better to deal with what you do or do not have right now, in this moment than get money before you can handle what that means?
- Is the money you do or do not have teaching you more about Self?
- Do you keep in mind money is an outpicturing of personal energy?
- If money is the medium that your Oversoul chooses to force you to grow, are you willing to accept the medium without judgment?

**Purpose**

Everyone needs a purpose; some reason to live and feel Soul-satisfied. I have conversations with Solomon my Maine Coone cat all the time about this. He is really soft and fluffy and really seems to enjoy just laying on the stairs in the front hall watching the world go by. So I decided that his purpose is to be soft and fluffy. I told him that he fulfills his purpose really well and is doing a good job. When I had my two sons I really felt that I had a purpose. Now that they are grown that purpose has been fulfilled, so one of my purposes is being the guardian to our 4 pets. I used to have the purpose of thinking I was going to change the world. That changed and now my purpose is to get out all our books that are in the queue.

Money cannot buy you a purpose. It is something that you have to feel deep down inside and then act on it. Sometimes you do not realize your purpose until life presents it to you. I did not know that one of my purposes was to be a mother. Originally I thought it was, then I thought it wasn't. Then, surprise, it was! Without a purpose, life can feel like it has no meaning. I have felt this way when I have been in between conscious purposes. Whatever I have done at any given time has still kept me on a trajectory of some kind. I do know that I feel better when I have a purpose and when I feel like I am making headway.

- Do you feel you have a purpose?
- Do you have more than one purpose?
- Do purposes ebb and flow with your life?
- Are purposes always in a state of flux?
- Do you feel lost without a purpose?
- Do you feel better when you have a purpose?
- Can money buy a purpose?
- Do people wither away and die without a purpose?
- How is a purpose different than a goal?

My observation is that if people do not have a purpose they lose interest in life. You need a motivation to get up and get going every day. Without a purpose, health fails and people pass out of this reality. It happens with people who are retired without anything to do; people whose families move or pass on; even with animals. Your purpose may be to get out of bed and take care of a home or others; it may be to go to work to earn money so you can pay your bills. Your main purpose is to be here right now and learn to be grateful for whatever you do or do not have.

Maintaining my own small business is a challenge for me. I finally have a great bookkeeper and CPA; a fabulous customer support person who does a great job and is loyal; and I have 2 great webmasters and social media people who are loyal and trustworthy. But I have been through a ton of people to get to this point Stewart takes care of the home maintenance. We have found that it is challenging to find people who do what they say they are going to do. We still do not have great help for the gardening, lawn, and snow removal people. We have paid a lot and we have paid a little, but service is hit and miss. We have a big house and live in an upscale neighborhood in our area. For this reason, many people who we need immediately increase their pricing. For example, to cut one tree down in our ravine averages about $500.00. When we first moved here almost 20 years ago we had people quote us $1200-1500 per tree. I have looked online at huge mansions and thought a lot about what it would be like to own one. After the thrill of thinking how beautiful they all are, I thought about all the staff that would be necessary to take care of such a place. This is beyond the money. From my current experience I know paying a lot of money for help does not guarantee that the job will be done correctly. Many questions go through my mind.

- What if the housekeeping staff pilfer or steal?
- Or don't get along with each other?
- Or pilfer and steal from each other?
- What if they gossip about you behind your back, sneak into your closet, drawers and personal effects?
- Would you lose all of your privacy?
- Where could you find people who are loyal?
- What about groundskeepers and outdoor staff?
- Does money buy loyalty, a good attitude, honesty, or people who care?
- Does money mean others are jealous and want what you have?
- Does money buy privacy or true friendship?
- What is the downside of having money?
- Are you willing to accept the parameters of your Oversoul?

Money is energy. Energy is the most valuable commodity on this planet. Energy is what animates the body and gives it life. Without energy, you do not have a life force and therefore that is the end of your existence here. Because your home represents you it makes sense that you need energy to run your home. Because your car/transportation represents your path in life, it makes sense that it takes energy to run your mode of transportation. Energy is what moves your physical body; food fuels your body to create the energy to do this. Everything that exists on this planet comes down to energy. This is why money, as the physical representation of the nonphysical energy, is so coveted. This is why people cross boundaries for it and go to great lengths to take yours.

People do not want to deal with what they have created, including Self. They do not want to assume responsibility; they want to blame others and make whatever their life experiences are your fault and/or the fault of their perceived oppressors. When you get this concept and are willing to do something about it, the tide turns. But as I always tell you, turning the boat takes the most energy. You are turning the boat but you are also seeing how many people do not want to make the same effort that you are making. You can observe their journey but you cannot judge them for it. You do not have to participate in their journey. You can see where you were or where you might be if you were on a journey similar to theirs.

- What separates and makes you different from others?
- Why do you agree to take Self-responsibility when the majority refuse?
- Why did you come here?
- Is this your biggest Self-test yet?
- Is Energy is the most prized possession on the planet?
- Is Energy a possession?

## AFFIRMATIONS—VALUE YOUR PATH

If you don't value your own path then you cannot expect anyone else to value your path. Most people want outer recognition to give Self value; you are learning that value must first come within. This is the way you stand up for your Self in healthy ways to gain inner strength and Self-respect .

*Out with the old and in with the new.*
*I "let go and let God".*


*I agree to the constant motion of my life.*
*I release the need to fight for what was.*


*I agree to the ebb and flow of life.*
*I easily ride the ups and downs of the stormiest seas.*


*I AM able to re-balance and re-position as needed.*
*I greet my life changes as necessary for Soul-growth.*


*Soul-growth takes precedence over stagnation.*
*I consciously stretch all aspects of my Being.*


*I live in the Eternal Now.*
*Each moment of my life sets the stage for the next moment.*

*I give thanks for Source guidance.*

*I AM exactly where I AM supposed to be.*

*Every moment has value.*

*I AM in a perpetual state of learning.*

*Every person has value.*

*I AM always grateful.*

*I study my outer reflections.*

*I value all outer reflections.*

*I instigate inner movement as appropriate.*

*I value all experience.*

*I strive to attain what is most correct and beneficial.*

*I surpass what I want, to gain what I need.*

*I allow my Self to receive my rewards.*

*I Self-Value at all times.*

*I receive my rewards in the most correct and beneficial way.*

*I value the way of Source.*

*I value the uniqueness of my Path.*
*I AM okay with what my Soul needs.*

*I recognize the pitfalls of distractions and temptations.*
*I AM where I AM for a reason.*

*I value the strength of my inner light.*
*I AM placed where I AM needed.*

*I AM a reflection of something for others.*
*I value my knowledge and wisdom.*

*I value my process.*
*I AM a way show-er.*

*I value the light in the darkness.*
*I courageously go wherever I AM guided.*

*I AM patient with the process of Source.*
*I value the process of Source.*

*I objectively observe the values of society.*
*I value who I AM at all times.*

*I understand the value of the spiritual mind vs Animal Mind.*

*I value the appropriate places for both my spiritual mind and Animal Mind.*

*I understand the value of money.*

*I understand that money is rarely the answer.*

*I value Spiritual Law.*

*I value the higher road even when it is more challenging.*

*I value the strength and commitment it takes to walk my path.*

*I value the process that gave me strength and taught me commitment.*

*I value my ability to persevere when correct and beneficial.*

*I value my ability to walk away when correct and beneficial.*

*I value my courage.*

*I value my ability to make correct choices against the odds.*

*I value my ability to be flexible.*

*I value my ability to change directions whenever most correct and beneficial.*

*I value my ability to think multidimensionally.*

*I Self-Value in balance at all times.*

# God-Mind Wisdom

God-Mind Wisdom is more precious than Gold. Interestingly, many people have asked over the years the best way to invest their money to protect it. I have always said that anything you have can be taken away; the government can confiscate your land and even gold during a crisis. Then I went on to say that during a crisis that even toilet paper would be more valuable than gold, which has to be assayed and certified to actually be gold before anyone will take it. If you show up at the supermarket with a gold coin as currency, you are not going to get too far.

Guess what, the events of the Covid-19 Plannedemic definitely proved me correct. In fact, my son in Tennessee could not find any paper goods at all right from the start, so I loaded up here in Michigan and sent him some. I was more worried about the toilet paper getting to him than the books that I shipped out that day. And, when the price of oil plummeted to (-$35), a roll of toilet paper was more valuable than a barrel of oil!

These events continue to emphasize that you are your most valuable investment. Because when all else fails and everything is stripped away, you depend on Self, Oversoul and God-Mind. Everything you ever need is always within and always accessible. The issue for most people is thinking that someone else can do it, but not me. There are plenty of people out there who tell you that they are special and you are not. So, you listen to them, become dependent on them, and then in times of crisis, these are usually the first people to leave you high and dry. Cultivating your inner relationship with the God-Mind within means that you will always have access to what you need, when you need it, in the most correct and beneficial way and timing.

*Focus on how your needs are met vs. why you don't get what you want.*
*God-Mind Wisdom.*

- Is it easy to whine and complain about why you don't get what you want?
- Is it challenging to stay where you are to understand why your Oversoul put you where you are?
- Do you get frustrated trying to find the reason why you are still here when you feel like you are ready to be there?
- Do you sometimes feel abandoned by God?
- Do you get angry, frustrated and upset by situations that you want to be concluded?
- Have you thought that others had unique/special inner abilities but not you?
- Do you now realize that everyone is already connected to Source and you cannot ever be disconnected?
- Is it challenging to have the faith and courage to rely on Self?
- Is it easier to look for someone else to feed you the answers?
- When something doesn't go as planned, is it easy/convenient to blame someone else?
- Do you know that you are your most valuable asset?
- Are you making the correct investments in your Self?

- Do you miss opportunities to invest in Self because of low Self-Worth?
- Does investment in Self increase your Self-Worth?
- Do you need money to invest in Self?
- Did you ever think that you would see a time when a roll of toilet paper would be worth more than a barrel of oil?
- Are you using your Plannedemic time to invest in Self?
- Are your needs being met during this time period?
- Are your wants being met?

Often, when you have the least amount of money is when you invest the most in your Self. It is very easy to fall into the trap that with money, you could buy your way out of any situation that you are in. There are so many ways that no matter how much money you have, you cannot buy your way out of your predicament. In fact, money is often the very tool that can bury you instead of saving you. The less money you have, the more refined/narrow your choices. This goes back to needs vs. wants. When it comes to wants, the world is your oyster and you can go anywhere, do anything, be anyone. Discovering the needs of your Soul can actually be quite challenging when you have so many choices before you. Thus your Soul narrows your focus by restricting your financial flow until you are pointed in the correct direction. This is not a fun position to be in; I am definitely the voice of experience.

Today I had over 50 boxes of books delivered by FedEx. The driver knocked on my door to see where I wanted the books. I asked him to drive around to my garage and wait while I backed my car out of the garage. I had 3 titles, ***13-Cubed Squared***, ***Heights of Deprogramming*** and a reprint of ***Hyperspace Plus***. I needed each title stacked in its own area with the title facing out. Two guys were on the truck, one seemed to be in charge and the other young man was heavyset, wearing a mask, and appeared to be in training. It was a warm day in

Michigan and the heavyset guy was especially out of shape, seemed to have an attitude, and definitely was not enthused about the job. But I cheerfully directed the show, carrying one box at a time while the guy in charge carried 3 and the heavyset young man checked everything out of the truck on his handheld tracking device. In the end, it was discovered that I was missing a box although their records showed that it was on the truck.

I told them no problem, deliver it when they can, and then gave each of them a $20 tip, told them I appreciated their efforts, and thanked them for taking the time to knock on the door rather than just throwing the boxes all over the front porch, which has happened in the past. The guy in charge was appreciative, but the heavyset guy with the attitude immediately perked up. You could tell that what made the day wasn't so much even the tip, but the words of appreciation which were backed up by something that said he has value. That guy definitely did not want to be working on a hot day unloading boxes. But he obviously needed to be there or he would not have been. These delivery people who stay with it get in physical shape and are paid to do it. How great is that! Perhaps with time, if he stays with it, the heavyset guy will realize this is a blessing in disguise.

*Recognize your blessings in disguise.*
*God-Mind Wisdom.*

- How many times have you not wanted to do something only to later recognize that it was the best thing that could have happened to you?
- Have you found value in something where originally you thought none existed?
- Do you value your Self based on how much money you make?
- Or on a job well-done?
- Or, on unexpected acknowledgments of your efforts?

- Is an attitude driven only by money dependent only on outer appreciation vs. inner appreciation of Self?
- Who do you work for, your employer, Self, and/or Oversoul/God-Mind?
- Ultimately, does your Oversoul/God-Mind determine your employment and your rate of pay?
- Can limited funds be a blessing in disguise?
- Do you appreciate opportunity first and money second?
- Do you feel your opportunities are limited?
- Do limited opportunities narrow your focus on what your Soul needs?
- Can limited opportunities be blessings in disguise?

**You Reap What You Sow**

My dad and I were talking today about how fortunate he is to have his health and be financially stable. When he and my mother divorced about 35 years ago he lost almost everything. He said at the time, his colleagues told him to hide money so my mother would not get so much. My father said that he just could not do it; he had to be able to live with him Self so even though he didn't like it, he did what he felt was the correct thing under the circumstances. My mother, on the other hand, had a lot of health issues and spent most of her money on doctors, medications and a nursing home.

I always wanted her to move to Saint Joseph where we have a wonderful retirement home on the lake right downtown. My mother was very social and I was able to get her to spend a few weeks there every year, but I could not get her to take the leap of faith to actually more here. Then, she got to the point where her health did not permit her to travel. I often think that if she made different choices her health would have been better and she would have enjoyed many more years in good health.

I had an uncle who was very good to me, but he had some unethical business practices. He accumulated a lot of wealth, but wound up first with dementia and then practically unable to move so he spent his final years in a nursing home. He could not enjoy any of his accumulated wealth. You reap what you sow. One of Stewart's best friends accumulated a lot of wealth which really changed him, or maybe it brought out what was already within him. He eventually turned on Stewart and I; at 53 years old he had a heart attack and died alone in his car, waiting to pick up one of his 4 young children. He could not take his money with him. The money he left behind for his family meant they would be well taken care of financially, but all that money wasn't going to bring their dad and husband back.

Alexander Duncan Cameron, one of the kindest people you could ever know, helped everyone he could but could not accept help. He was finally forced to set up a Go Fund Me account to ask for help to pay for alternative medical treatments. Asking for help was devastating for him. Even though people lovingly gave, and he was moved by the generosity of so many, he was challenged to feel worthy of the help that was offered. He could sow love and kindness for others, but he could not sow it for him Self. He could not reap what he did not sow.

*You cannot reap what you do not sow.*
*God-Mind Wisdom.*

- Can you reap what you do not sow?
- When you think about what you want and what you think you are not getting, do you consider what you need to sow to make it happen?
- Do you know kind and loving people who can sow for others but cannot sow for themselves?
- Does it count if you do something that is against Spiritual Law and you do not get caught?

- Do the ramifications of breaking Spiritual Law eventually catch up to you?
- Are the ramifications more severe if you knowingly break Spiritual Law?
- Do you live your life so you can sleep at night, even if you do not always like the process even when you know it is correct?
- Have you observed people who get away with things until one day they don't?
- Is the temptation to take the money and run too great for some people?
- Can you ever run away from Self, Oversoul and God-Mind?
- If, in retrospect, you know that you have broken Spiritual Law, do you do forgiveness and release work on Self as well as anyone else involved, both known and unknown to you?
- Can you unknowingly harm others?
- If you unknowingly harm others, are there ramifications?
- Does one always reap what one consciously and/or unconsciously sows?

When something happens that you feel is morally inept and perhaps even downright evil, you can be challenged to not want to take revenge on some level. You want to see the person get what you feel they deserve in the most negative way imaginable. I have been in these positions where people have attacked Stewart and I, our family, our business with the intent to ruin us one way or the other. That definitely brings out my anger. Of course, of course, this is exactly the response they want. Your negative reactions mean they are successful. I have learned from these various attacks that there is nothing that I can do to ever damage them in the way that they damaged me. They have no feelings and no morals; their mission and purpose in life is to destroy. I have yelled and screamed at them via the Oversoul level as well as ripped them to shreds. Nothing hurts them; this behavior only feeds their demonic nature and possessions.

I finally asked my Oversoul what to do with my feelings because feeling angry, hurt, upset, despondent and depressed was the response they wanted. These negative reactions/feelings harm your body, mind and therefore your Soul. There can be so much inside that even giving it to your Oversoul only continues to unleash a well of animosity within. My Oversoul showed me that they cannot deal with the higher frequency colors. Via the Oversoul level I was instructed to send them Pale Pink for Unconditional Love, Medium Green for emotional healing; Silver for Oversoul Connections and Gold for God-Mind Wisdom. Any color that uplifts and elevates. That is when I saw these demonic-natured and possessed people finally wince in the throes of pain, death and destruction. It was like throwing a bucket of water on the Wicked Witch of the West in the *Wizard of Oz*, who then just melted into nothingness. And, what I give out comes back to me; definitely a win/win!

***Sometimes you may be extremely challenged to do the correct thing but 2 wrongs do not make a right.***

### *God-Mind Wisdom.*

- Are you sometimes challenged to not seek retribution when someone has clearly done something wrong and/or evil against you?
- Does the Animal Mind want to attack?
- Does the injured part of you want to injure the other parties in the same way you were injured, or even worse?
- Is it challenging to remember that 2 wrongs do not make a right?
- Is it challenging to get into your center, become the observer and then send positive experiences to the perpetrators of evil?

- What do you do when you feel that political leaders, or others in positions of power abuse you, loved ones and/or even the populace in general?
- Do you want to seek retribution?
- Is there such a thing as righteous anger?
- Does anger destroy you as much, or more, than anyone else, regardless of what kind of anger it is?
- Is anger always anger?
- Have you ever been up against anyone or anything that you felt was truly evil?
- Is it easy to forget that not everyone thinks in the same way that you do?
- Do your negative reactions feed the very thing that you are trying to disburse?
- Have you tried changing your tactic to flooding the evil/negative with higher frequency colors?

**Suffering**

Many years ago one of my friends suggested that I read *The Crusaders Trilogy*, a series that he highly recommended.

The Crusades trilogy is a series of novels about the fictional character of Arn Magnusson. The series is written by Swedish author and journalist Jan Guillou.

After finishing the Coq Rouge series, Guillou wrote a trilogy about Arn Magnusson, a 12th century Folkung who was forced to become a Knight Templar. The series is an account of the life of Arn, a person who becomes witness as well as catalyst to many important historical events, both in his homeland of Götaland, Sweden and in the crusader states.[1]

The trilogy consists of the following novels:

The Road to Jerusalem, originally Vägen till Jerusalem (1998)

The Knight Templar, originally Tempelriddaren (1999)

The Kingdom at the End of the Road, originally Riket vid vägens slut (2000), also called Birth of a Kingdom

Guillou also wrote a follow-up novel, The Heritage of Arn (2001). In Guillou's story Birger Jarl, the founder of Stockholm and the protagonist in the book, is the grandson of Arn Magnusson.

https://en.wikipedia.org/wiki/Crusades_trilogy

I bought the series and tried several times to read it but just could not get interested in the books. So, the books sat on my bookshelves until a few months ago when I decided to try again, for some unknown reason. This time, I could not put the series down and absolutely loved them. There were so many great life lessons interwoven throughout the trilogy, but two in particular stand out to me. Arn, the main character, is followed from birth to the end of his life. All of the twists and turns that seemed like negatives positioned him well for the latter part of his life. When he went into battle, he prayed for the Souls of those whom he knew were going to die by his sword. He was separated from his wife-to-be for 20 years. During their separation each grew stronger so that when their lives came together they each brought tremendous skills and ingenuity that would not have happened any other way. The trilogy teaches timing, suffering and trusting the Higher Plan. It is so easy to look at your life and feel sorry for your Self because you do not get what you want in the way you want.

*There is always a Higher Purpose and a Higher Plan.*
*God-Mind Wisdom.*

- When you suffer, do you look for the Higher Plan?
- Does suffering always denote a negative experience?
- What is the positive aspect of suffering?
- Do you think the more years you live, the more you understand why your life went the way that it did?

- In the beginning phase of your life do your experiences feel more haphazard than purposeful?
- Does life seem to come together, only to fall apart, then come together again, to fall apart again, with this continual repetitive pattern?
- Have you ever had something in your possession that was not meaningful until time passed and then it became meaningful, like the book series mentioned above as an example?
- Is there always a correct timing for everything?
- Do you sometimes wish you had done something sooner?
- If sooner was the correct timing, do you think you would have?
- Is it easy to beat your Self up for not doing something sooner?
- Should your goal always be to find the God-Mind Wisdom in all that happens?

When my son changed middle schools, he was behind in math. But, he had a great math teacher who gave the students the opportunity to come in every single day after school to correct any problem on any math homework and exam. When they corrected their homework, their grades were increased. They had to retake the math problems on their exams, but if they passed then the grade was changed to reflect the improvement. I told my son that if he stayed behind in math he would always be behind because one math concept builds upon another. This teacher provided the opportunity to change that if he wanted to take advantage of the offer. So, every single day after school, Monday through Friday at the end of an already long school day, my son spent another hour working on math because he chose to succeed. My youngest son had to go to afterschool care while my older son stayed to work on his math. Neither son complained, both did what they needed to do. We pulled together as a family to help each other.

Some parents would have begged, pleaded, cajoled and even bribed their children to work on math and attend afterschool care when they were tired, had plenty of homework from other classes and just wanted to come home at the end of a long day. Instead, my oldest son took pride in his slow, day by day accomplishments of improving his math skills. My youngest one knew his brother needed help so he uncomplainingly went to afterschool care even though he was tired and would rather have been home.

Conventionally, you could say that both of my sons suffered. Suffering is not bad; suffering is about pushing your boundaries so far that you are uncomfortable, but the ultimate goal is growth. You can proactively suffer, as athletes, musicians, artists and military personnel do, or you can reactively suffer because you are unwilling to grow without a kick in the pants. Most people want to pick and choose how they suffer. I proactively suffered when I taught my Self to cook and sew by stretching my boundaries. I had plenty of failures but I did not stop. I still reactively suffer when it comes to technical skills. I don't want to learn them until absolutely forced. I did not like the farm machinery although I was proud of my accomplishments as I learned to operate each piece. I do not like the technical aspects of my computer and I am grateful for my son who helps me.

*Suffering helps you stretch your abilities and capabilities beyond your current set of Self-imposed boundaries.*

*God-Mind Wisdom.*

- How challenged are you to think of suffering as something that you consciously choose to do?
- Do you like the concept of proactively suffering?
- What proactive suffering have you chosen in your life?
- Is the purpose of suffering is to help you stretch your abilities and capabilities beyond your current set of Self-imposed boundaries?

- Is it okay to suffer or should suffering be avoided at all costs?
- Is there correct and beneficial suffering?
- Does suffering always create forward growth?
- Can suffering leave people bitter, angry and resentful?
- Are you now, or have you been, bitter, angry and resentful as a result of your suffering?
- Have you been ecstatic because you suffered, survived and grew beyond what you thought was possible?
- Does suffering generally conjure up a negative connotation in the minds of most people?

One thing I definitely learned is that one layer of suffering usually leads to another layer of suffering. Whenever you accomplish and complete anything, another door opens for you to walk through. You go from being on top to being on the bottom, once again. For example, when you leave elementary school, you are on top. When you enter middle school you are on the bottom again. When you leave middle school you are on top. But when you enter high school you are on the bottom again. The more growth you experience, the more the doors open for even more new experiences. Each new experience, even when wanted, holds layers of suffering. A new job is fantastic but wondering about all the unknowns can keep you up late at night.

I was very excited when I booked my tickets for Italy and Iceland this summer. Now I'm doing my best not to be disturbed knowing that the trip is only a few weeks away and I still do not know if I'm going due to the Plannedemic. I love bringing people with me, but I cannot promote the trips because I do not know if they will happen. Or, what I will do if I can't get to Italy but I can get to Iceland. No matter how excited you are about any new opportunity, there is always this layer of hidden suffering that may never be addressed, but there it is. You move out of one layer of suffering and the next layer of suffering opens up.

*Suffering is okay, part of life, and when you accept that this is normal, you know that you are always okay.*

### *God-Mind Wisdom*

- Have new opportunities opened up that initially thrilled you, but after further thought you wondered what you got your Self into?
- For some odd reason, do new opportunities often make you think that everything will be easy and smooth?
- Is easy and smooth usually a holding pattern that takes you nowhere?
- Is it the suffering that stretches and molds you into something more than you were?
- Is smooth and easy a boring story to tell someone?
- Do others prefer to listen to stories full of suffering and unknowns?
- Once you realize that suffering is okay, can you easily and smoothly get through it?
- Or, is suffering always destined to be bumpy?
- Can you accept the bumps as necessary suffering that entertains you rather than holds you back?
- Do successful people only take the easy smooth route?
- Or do they prefer experiences that push them to their limits?
- Do you like smooth ice cream or ice cream filled with interesting food items?
- What does preferring your ice cream one way or the other say about your life?

A worthy opponent can make you suffer tremendously, but will definitely help you ferret out your weaknesses as well as your strengths. You remember your worthy opponents because of the wealth of information contained within your experience. Underestimating your opponent can also cause you to suffer.

*Whether you do or do not survive a worthy opponent, you thrive.*
*Perhaps not in the ways you expect, perhaps not in what you consider*
*pleasant ways, but in the way that is most correct and beneficial for you.*

### God-Mind Wisdom.

- What constitutes a worthy opponent?
- Does a worthy opponent have to be a person?
- If not, what else can a worthy opponent be?
- Can you name your top worthy opponents in your life?
- Does a worthy opponent make you suffer?
- Do you get stronger and wiser regardless of the outcome?
- Have you ever underestimated your opponent?
- Were there consequences as a result?
- Is a consequence a negative or another point of personal instruction?
- Can a worthy opponent be one of your most valuable assets?
- Does a worthy opponent always bring you immeasurable wealth, even if you do not immediately recognize this?

Anything that has control over you is a worthy opponent. You have something to learn or it would not be in the middle of your path, seemingly blocking your progress. My past is filled with internal temper tantrums when my path was blocked; I usually wound up sick in one way or another. Instead of putting my energy into delving into the situation I panicked and wanted to run away when running away was not an option. I know people who thrive off of worthy opponents. They live to be challenged and even enjoy the suffering within their challenges. All of my worthy opponents were people exactly like this. They loved to see me dance. Even when I didn't think I was dancing in hindsight I was. Or course, I have learned to dance less through the years but you do learn to be on guard because you never know where/when the worthy opponent will strike.

It is important to know that no matter how high you are, you can fall. With all that I know, I do know that I can fall. I pray that I am never so arrogant to think that I am infallible. And if there are Soul lessons in my falling, then my Oversoul will make sure the fall happens no matter what I do. The *Crusades Trilogy* is full of these kinds of lessons. During war, the worthy opponents could attack at any time, in any way. You had to be prepared due to the constant threat of war, no matter where you lived. You could never underestimate your enemy no matter how prepared you were. When the main character, Arn, fell metaphorically speaking, his Soul put him exactly where he was supposed to be. He lives his life constantly questioning why his Soul put him where it did, when it did. In his later years, understanding of his earlier life comes to him. As long as you are learning, or striving to learn, your Oversoul keeps you here. It is when you are done that your Oversoul removes you from this reality.

### *If you are here, there is a reason.*
### *God-Mind Wisdom.*

- Have you ever looked at someone and wondered why they are still here?
- Have you wondered what the person could possibly be learning where he/she is in life?
- Does learning have to be consciously acknowledged?
- Have you ever thought that you were so well-positioned in some aspect of your life that you could never fall, and then you did?
- Have you had worthy opponents who loved to make you dance, and you did?

- Do your worthy opponents enjoy your suffering?
- Does it feel like worthy opponents are blocking your progress?
- Are your emotions worthy opponents? Animal Mind? programming? food/drink addictions? drugs?
- Knowing what you know, is falling still a bruising?
- Do you sometimes feel like life is out of your control?
- If so, do you acknowledge the Source behind it?
- Do you ever wonder why you are still here?
- Are you learning and/or striving to learn?
- Does your effort to be better than you were keep you here, utilizing this physical reality opportunity to its fullest?

I do my best when I first meet someone to not decide if I like/do not like him/her. This is an easy trap to fall into. Instead, I do my best to understand and appreciate the Soul-Personality as it is expressing in this reality. Like usually means someone who makes your life easy without controversy. Do not like usually means someone who causes you such feelings as aggravation, grief and discomfort. I want to know the person as he/she relates to me, both positive and negative. If you only see positive, the person is hiding something; if you only see negative the person is hiding something. No one is only positive; no one is only negative. It is important not to judge the person but to understand whatever you need to understand in accordance with the involved Oversouls. I have learned through the years that if someone shows negative behavior toward others, but not me, eventually that person will also display that same negative behavior toward me.

I find human behavior extremely fascinating which is why I am in this field. I used to talk a lot about other people before I realized that I was gossiping. Once, I had one person say to my face that if this is what I was saying about others, she wondered what I was saying to others about her. I hadn't looked at my discussions in quite this light before, so from that day forward, I made it a point to do my best not to speak about specific people. I have learned through my own Self-acceptance of my positive and negative qualities that this combination is what creates the identity of the Soul-Personality as it expresses in this reality. It is not up to me to like or not like a person.

I do my best to leave it up to my Oversoul who is most correct and beneficial to have in my life. I may know or not know the reason. I have stopped focusing on like/dislike and instead focus on asking my Oversoul why the person is in my life; what are the reflections; what am I supposed to learn; what can I do for this person and what can this person do for me; can we create a win/win/balanced type of relationship between all of our positives and negatives, and finally what matching colors, tones and archetypes brought us together in the first place. You see that this is another step beyond like/dislike and even positive and negative. This is about the best combination of frequencies for what is needed for the growth of the Soul-Personality. You may like certain aspects while disliking certain aspects, yet it is most correct and beneficial for you to have this person in your life.

*Every person is a package of multiple aspects of Soul-Personality.*

*God-Mind Wisdom.*

- Is it easy to fall into the like/dislike trap when you meet someone?
- Is it more challenging to ask questions until you determine why the person is in your life?
- Can you dislike a person, yet it is most correct and beneficial for that person to be in your life?
- Is it okay to dislike someone?
- When you come to terms with people, does dislike become an obsolete term?
- Can you like another person even when you dislike some of his/her aspects?

- Sometimes, when your dislikes outweigh your likes, do you have to release people out of your life?
- If so, do you first ask your Oversoul if this is the most correct and beneficial timing?
- Have you met people who you liked, only to find out later that you disliked them?
- Or disliked them only to find out later that you liked them?
- Have you watched the behavior of someone else, thinking that he/she would never do it to you, and then he/she does?
- Does it make sense to focus on why the person is in your life instead of like/dislike?
- Does every person in your life have a purpose and a function that somehow relates to you?
- Sometimes, are you puzzled by the color, tone and archetype reflections of others?
- Does it make sense to see others as a package and then ask your Oversoul if this is the correct package for your life at this time?

When you do not like and;/or appreciate all parts of Self, you are not going to like and/or appreciate all parts of others. When you do not have compassion for your own process, others can drive you crazy as you watch them with theirs.

*Wherever you go, there you are.*

*God-Mind Wisdom.*

If you think "I like my Self", you probably are only focusing on what you call the positive qualities. When something negative pops up then you may decide you do not like your Self. Back and forth, the pendulum swings without finding any balance. If you do not like your Self, you probably are only focusing on the negative qualities. You may not give your Self enough credit for the positive because the negative, to you, glaringly overshadows the positive. When you realize that all parts of Self are important, you move beyond like/not liking Self, because liking/not liking Self is really based on judgment of Self. What you consider a positive trait may be considered a negative trait by someone else.

For example, if you speak up for your Self you may think you are establishing boundaries and Self-Worth. Another person may label you loud and obnoxious, thus not liking you, which is a judgment. If you are quiet and respectful, someone may label you unintelligent and uncommunicative. Again, this is a judgment. You may be kind and helpful, but someone else labels you controlling and interfering. A judgment.

*You always have to go up higher, into the Oversoul level to surpass the judgments to determine True Reality vs. your perceptions.*

*God-Mind Wisdom.*

- Have you thought of like/not like as a judgment?
- Do you base how you feel about your Self on a like/not like basis?
- Do you like your Self when you do what you consider something positive?
- Do you dislike your Self when you do something that you consider negative?
- Do you like others only when they show what you judge as positive attributes?
- Do you dislike others when they show what you judge to be negative attributes?
- Can you like all parts of Self, even those that you judge negative?
- Is negative bad?

- Is it challenging to rise above your own Self judgments into True Reality to understand why you have the attributes that you have?
- Do all parts of Self serve a purpose?
- Can you have compassion for all aspects of Self?
- Can you like all parts of Self?
- Can you accept that all parts of Self are correct and beneficial?
- Does correct and beneficial change for every situation?
- Is it up to you to manage your positive and negative attributes without them managing you?

**Manure is Valuable**

It is the manure that fertilizes the gardens and makes them grow. When I was a dairy farmer, cow manure was the primary fertilizer for the fields. Sometimes there wasn't enough for all the fields, depending upon the year. Purchased fertilizer was used as a supplement but the most productive and verdant fields were the ones that received the most manure. In the same way, what you may consider the manure in your life is often what produces the richest internal fields. Generally, you are not taught to value anything which is uncomfortable. You are programmed to ignore it and move on. You don't talk about it. Often it is the manure in your life that makes you feel the deepest shame and sometimes guilt, amongst other Self-deprecating emotions.

This is why you continually play the same scenarios repeatedly in your life. The manure doesn't go away; it lies buried within, trying to percolate up to the surface while your programming keeps pushing it down. When you dig around in the manure you are going to get dirty. You have to know that getting dirty is okay. But, it can make you uncomfortable and sometimes even physically ill because you are emotionally ill. It is these emotions that create the physical illnesses which is why you want to dig them out before you get physically ill. This is challenging to do when logically you want to get it over with but the emotions do not care about logic. They are what they are. They need to be acknowledged, observed as most correct and beneficial for the time, released, and then, most importantly the empty emotional holes need to filled with emotional healing from your Oversoul.

### *Avoidance prolongs the pain.*
### *God-Mind Wisdom.*

- Do you avoid looking at the painful parts of your life?
- Logically, do you just want to get it over with and move on?
- Do you like breaking open old wounds and scars?
- Can a physical scar ever truly heal?
- Can an emotional scar ever truly heal?
- What painful parts of your life do you avoid?
- What emotional scars do you not want to open up?
- Do you think your emotional scars can be permanently healed?
- Do you need the manure of your life to fertilize your internal fields?
- Is it human nature to turn away from that which makes people uncomfortable?
- Can you thrive by embracing your pain?
- Can you use the manure of your life to turn your pain into something beautiful and worthwhile?
- Are you programmed to carry shame and guilt?
- Would you feel empty without these Self-deprecating emotions?
- When you ask your Oversoul, what colors, tones and archetypes does it send you to fill and heal the emotional holes within?

**Deep State**

Deep State could actually be a programming trigger for many people. When you want to hypnotize people, you need them in a deep state of relaxation. Perhaps this numbing of people to ignore all of their pain, trials and tribulations is about getting them into such a deep state of relaxation that they do nothing, care about nothing and no one, including Self. Disneyland 24/7, the happiest place on Earth, as it is known. While you may not be truly happy ignoring your pain, when you are numb at least you can cope. I have been here many times my Self; when the pain is overwhelming, that puts you in a nonfunctioning state of Being. You have to function; get up; get dressed; eat; go to work; carry on.

Last night, I saw the home of my aunt who passed away less than 2 months ago listed for sale. That was a bit devastating, even though I expected it. But, what devastated me even more, was the fact that it has only been listed 4 days and there is already an offer on the house. Of course, I was never offered any of her possessions as memorabilia of her, I hadn't been allowed to even see her for over 2 years, and a whole host of memories from childhood came flooding to the surface along with tears running out of my eyes like a river. There was no stopping feeling the deep state of my internal hurts once they were unleashed. One memory led to another. I finally pulled up social media and started scrolling through the Maine Coon cat and Yakutian Laika dog posts. They distracted me long enough so the tears could stop flowing and I could smile to my Self.

This all means, of course, I must revisit my past but I needed to put it on hold, at least so I could get some sleep so today would be better. I got up this morning, felt better, then talked to Stewart and the tears started again. But, when all was said and done, at least in this moment, I know that my relationship with her means more than her things; her house is now in my past so I need to let it go and be grateful for what was. Maybe I will feel differently in a few days, but for now, I am in kind of a bittersweet state of feeling. Which ultimately is better than numb. Sometimes, though, numb is where I not only want to be but need to be. But, I want to be the one controlling how deep I go into my emotions and how fast.

***Work with your Oversoul and God-Mind about your own Deep State rather than have it be artificially induced by outer sources.***

***God-Mind Wisdom.***

- Do you think the words "Deep State" can be triggering for many people?
- Do you think these words are intended to put people in a deep hypnotic state?
- Do you think Deep State can activate programming and alters?
- Is it important to keep your Self especially well protected with Violet, Ultimate Protection, Lion Frequency, The Name and more?
- Do you think you are especially vulnerable right now?
- Or especially strong?
- Does the Deep State push you to proactively look deeper at all aspects of your Soul-Personality?
- Do you sometimes need to take a rest from your mental work?
- Do you know how to numb your emotions without Self-harming?
- Are you in control of your own life, under the guidance of your Oversoul and God-Mind?
- Do you know when to drive into your own Deep State and when to take your foot off of the accelerator?
- Does an eternal state of happiness truly exist?
- Would you want to only be happy?

- Does "happy" limit your other emotions?
- Is societal programming directing you to be numb and not feel?
- Does the goal of a Deep State of relaxation mean that you are hypnotized rather than truly present?
- Do you want to be artificially numbed to your emotions?

If people go too deep, they get too uncomfortable so this can trigger alters as a form of protection. This is why people often do not have memories under the age of five; there is some trauma with which they cannot cope, so the memory is blacked out from the conscious mind. When I went through vision therapy, my therapist proved to me that I was blind in one eye with it open. It was truly a scary event! Then I was given a series of exercises to do to correct this. I do not even know how they diagnosed this. I was so stunned and frightened that I cannot tell you much about what they did with me to correct the issue. Once this changed I was exhausted and relieved that this never happened again.

This is also why you need to take your inner work slow and methodical, layering your knowledge with your experience at a pace that keeps you moving but does not overwhelm. Only you can do this. No one else can do it for you. As you unpack what you have stuffed inside, long-forgotten memories rise to the surface. When this happens, regardless of the memory, there is something for you to look at. Place whatever you see at the pineal gland and then keep going with your questions as I wrote about in *Decoding Your Life*. You have to ask questions until there are no more questions. Too often people ask a question or two, think they have arrived and that is the end of the digging.

The deeper you go the more physical symptoms you may experience, including shortness of breath, feeling smothered, panicky, queasiness, vomiting, dizziness and more. You are breaking through the body's protective mechanisms that keep the trauma from your conscious mind. When these symptoms happen, you may try to push through. Or, you may decide that you have had enough and will work on it again another day.

*Only you can decide what you can and cannot handle.*

*God-Mind Wisdom.*

- Have you had these kinds of physical symptoms during a Deep State of mental work?
- If so, did you push on or did you stop?
- Do you have blocked memories?
- Have you had old, long-forgotten memories rise to the surface during Deep State work?
- Have you done Deep State work seemingly without results only to have memories come up when you least expected them?
- When you do your mental work, do you ask enough questions?
- Have you ever tried to push your mental work too fast?
- Do you put whatever comes up at your pineal gland and then keep going?
- Have you ever had alters pop up during Deep State work?
- Do you have childhood memories under the age of 5?
- What is your earliest memory and how old were you?
- Do you think most people do not have a clear memory of childhood?

Going into a Deep State of any kind can be a trigger for an alter to come forward and/or activate. This is why before you do any mental work do your preliminary work to make sure that you are balanced and grounded into your Source, have your Brown Merger/Self-Integration Archetypes at the pineal and Reptilian brain stem as well as all your protection in place. The deeper your conscious internal work, the more likely you are going to run into zones of discomfort. When you are too uncomfortable, flush everything with Violet, flood your energy field with Brown and conclude whatever you are doing. If you keep going, you may find your Self agitated and out of sorts. The deeper you push and the more uncomfortable you are, the more likely you are to trigger the programming that you know can remove the pain. And yes, you can also trigger demonic attachments that can trick you into thinking they can take away your pain and discomfort. The Deep State of your mind is a mine field of its own. Proceed with caution so that you know that you are anchored deep within Source.

In the same way, something could inadvertently put you in a Deep State without your conscious realization. Review the back cover of *13-Cubed* which lists a host of symptoms of mind-control and programming coming to the surface. When you maintain the preliminaries 24/7 there is much less chance of anything triggering or activating you. Currently, Now, the buzzwords are "new normal". Watch for repetitive phrases pushed by social media. These repetitive phrases did not just come out of nowhere.

*Be mindful of repetitive words and phrases because they are carefully thought out agendas to hook onto some part of your frequency wherever and whenever possible.*

*God-Mind Wisdom.*

- Why does "normal" have to be new?
- Could this be a programming trigger for people to accept whatever is put in front of them as normal?
- Why is the entire world on lockdown; not just one country or area of the world?
- Does the new normal involve wearing face masks so your identity is hidden, just like a Muslim woman?
- Or to show that you are silent and obedient?

- Does the new normal mean that you accept it as okay to snitch on your neighbors, live in fear and not be physically close to anyone?
- What kind of programming does social distancing involve?
- Can these words trigger panic?
- Can panic push you into programming, alters and even into accepting demonic attachments as your friends and protectors?
- When people are frightened, do they care who/what is attached on the other end of the hand that they perceive is helping them?
- If the hand looks familiar, can programming activate to tell you that the hand is okay, even when it may not be?
- Do you think there could be programming already within people that is triggered by the words "new normal"?
- Might you already be programmed with a "new normal"?
- Could "new normal" mean a life with demonic attachments unleashed?
- Could social distancing be trigger words already programmed within people to isolate?
- How deep is the Deep State programming?

The tendency to fight the Deep State might be the first thing that some want to do. But as you know, what you give out comes back to you. And when you fight, you actually strengthen the adversary. If you push against a door and nothing pushes back you fall through, flat on your face. A runner always runs fastest when he/she has an opponent. Your fight allows your opponent to discover his/her/its weaknesses and strengthen them. If it is most correct and beneficial to fight, then fight smart. Do not show all your cards; only do what you must do. For example, when my Italian attorneys tried to extort more money from me I told them that the bank would not lend me money to pay them until they told me exactly their cost. In Italy, unlike the US, they have to tell you their fee upfront and then that cannot change. Only then did they stop harassing me for more money. When I was ordered to pay a fine by the Italian judge, these same attorneys told me to not pay from my bank account because the other party would know too much about me, but to send a money order from Western Union or MoneyGram.

If the opponent wants to push on your door, step aside when you can so that he/she falls flat on his/her face. If you push back, you expend more energy than necessary which then tells your opponent exactly how strong you are or are not. When it is most correct and beneficial, then that is what you do. However, when there is another way, then you must discover what it is. If you want to slay outer demons ala Deep State then this means that you have inner demons to slay, most likely metaphorically as well as actual attachments. Demonic forces cannot enter into this reality unless they are entered into those who inhabit it.

*You do what you need to do; you fight when you have to fight; you expend the least amount of energy required to accomplish what needs to be done.*

### *God-Mind Wisdom.*

- Is it wise to fight when you are angry?
- Does anger give you strength?
- Is anger powerful?
- Is there such a thing as righteous anger?
- Can you use anger as a weapon without anger using you?
- Do you have inner demons to slay?
- If so, are they physically attached, metaphorical or both?
- When you fight, do you show your opponents your weaknesses?

- Do you think the Deep State knows the weaknesses of the population?
- Does the Deep State also know the strengths of the populace?
- If you know your own weaknesses and strengths is an outside Deep State less inclined to affect you?
- Have you been in positions where you have no choice but to fight?
- Does fighting make you stronger?
- When your opponent pushes, do you know when to step aside?

When you are in a Deep State of pain it is normal to want it to go away. When you do not have any other tool, you numb it. You do everything you can to stop the pain. This is why some people cut themselves. It is an outer expression of what they feel inside. Instead of hurting others, they hurt themselves. Sometimes the inner pain is so deep that you do not even realize that you have pain. You are so accustomed to living with it that it embeds so deeply into who and what you are that you are not consciously cognizant of its existence.

I once knew a grandmother of a severely neglected young child. When she gained custody of him, she took him to a dentist who said his teeth were riddled with cavities. The dentist said that he was surprised the child was not crying with pain every time he ate. Apparently, the pain was normal to the child so he did not know that he was in pain. When it came time for the dental work, the dentist did not even have to use any deadening agent because the child was so accustomed to pain the procedures did not bother him. In addition, the child did not know if he was hot or cold. No one had been there to cover or uncover him. He did not feel hot or cold. He simply existed in whatever temperature he found him Self.

The issue with this kind of pain is that the emotions are buried so deep that they cause physical damage as well as emotional and mental damage. As you can guess, the child was fraught with behavioral issues. And the child then turns into a young adult and then into an adult with those same behavioral issues deeply embedded in mind and body. Even with Deep State work, the child is destined to a deeply challenging life. Interestingly enough, the grandmother had thrown her shoulder out of place some years back. When she went to the hospital she was given a drug to make her forget the pain that putting her shoulder back in would cause her. Like so many people, at the time, she didn't question this. She took the drug as she was told and has no memory of what she went through at the hospital, yet the pain still lives within her.

The genetics of numbing pain does pass down through family lineages. So while there is much that you may be able to look at in your family lineage by observing family members, there is also much that is buried and hidden away. This is why it is imperative that you unlock your own Deep State in a way that you can handle before someone/something does it for you such as via your programming. You can use your Deep State of emotions as a stepping stone to healing. But if someone else taps into it via programming, then your Deep State of emotions can and will be used against you. Tread carefully and wisely, but pledge to your Self that you are master of your ship. Look at your own Deep State under the guidance of your Oversoul and God-Mind. Do not let anyone else be in charge of your "new normal".

*What is normal for you is between you and your Oversoul.*
*God-Mind Wisdom.*

- Is normal always changing?
- Why does society need to be focused on a "new normal"?
- If balance changes, does it make sense that normal also changes on a personal basis for everyone?
- Have you ever been swimming in a cold pool or sea when you were in so long that you did not feel the cold?

- If so, what happens when you step out and then step back in again?
- Can you compare the cold water swimming experience to stepping in and out of the Deep State of your inner feelings?
- Can the ability to numb pain have a genetic origin?
- Do emotional situations sometimes pop up that you feel you cannot handle?
- Are you challenged to get your brain balanced enough to know that when something comes up, this means you can handle it?
- Does getting pushed further than you can consciously bear push you into your own Deep State?
- If so, is this a chance to Self-explore or Self-implode?
- Is your Deep State of emotions always a stepping stone to healing, whether you choose to use them this way or not?
- Is there ever any opportunity that is lost?

## Perceived Failure

Many people get lost in Self-perceived failures. You feel like you knew better, but you did something that you shouldn't have, anyway. Or you think you should have done better. Or known better. Regardless of what you did, there is a part of you that labels what you did and/or how you did a failure. This usually happens when logically you know something but emotionally you are not capable of doing what the logical part of you tells you to do. Left brain logic tells you that you failed while in reality, it is generally right brain emotions that do what they want when they want.

Logically, even when you know the rules, emotionally you may not be able to follow them. When my sons were little if they got tired of sitting at the table, which is understandable, I let them stand up by the table. Whenever something interesting captured their attention they were well-positioned to dart after it. Logically they knew the rule, but emotionally they could not follow it. So I realized that I had given them too much freedom. I could argue or chase after them as I have seen some parents do. Instead, I narrowed their parameters and changed the rule until we came up with a rule that set them up for success. The new rule was you could stand by the table when you were done eating, but you had to have one hand on your chair at all times. That hand on the chair was their reminder of the rule. If they let go of the chair, they lost their privilege of standing, which rarely happened. I gave them a rule that the left brain remembered and with which the right brain could deal with. I do not consider the first rule of standing by the table a failure. It was more than they could emotionally handle. Period. We had to redirect our thoughts until we could find a new rule with which they could be successful.

I have learned that if you could have done better, you would have. You did the best you could with what you had in that moment. And, the most important thing is always that you learned. No attempt is wasted.

***Every attempt helps you define and refine your focus on your personal roadmap to success.***

***God-Mind Wisdom.***

- How many times have you labeled your actions/reactions failure?
- Have you considered the role of left brain logic vs. right brain emotion in the equation?
- Is it possible that even though you know the rule you are not emotionally mature enough to actually implement what you know?
- Rather than judge what you perceive you did not do, can you observe what you did do?

- When you observe what you did without judgment, can you then define how to narrow your focus to set your Self up for success?
- Are you sometimes forced to emotionally grow up so you can succeed?
- Does emotional immaturity hold you back?
- Should you be held back if you are emotionally immature?
- Does programming encourage emotional immaturity?
- Does programming always attempt to keep left brain, right brain in a state of imbalance?
- Do you need left brain, right brain in balance for success?
- Is any attempt ever a failure and/or wasted?

When I decided to remodel my kitchen I had some ideas but decided to use a local designer. I was in her shop getting a painting framed and admired a mock-up kitchen that she had on display. I told her some of my ideas as well as my budget. I met with her several times over the course of a few weeks. Each time she made suggestions, I countered with what I wanted vs. what she was proposing. One idea she had was to make my current kitchen window more centered on the wall, so she wanted to move it 3 inches. One of my doorways she wanted to cut in half to give me more counter space. Both ideas sounded rather expensive for what I wanted. I do have 5 doorways in my kitchen which even in my opinion is a bit excessive, but it is what it is.

I told her right from the beginning that I wanted a laminate floor and not tile, but she kept telling me why I wanted tile. I finally gave up telling her I wanted laminate. Her final design only had seating for 3 people when I had told her that normally we have 4 people and on occasion 6. On and on. The last straw was when she presented her final design well over twice the low end of my budget range. The positive part of this was I didn't think twice. I told her I didn't want to do it. I did not tell her I couldn't afford it. I just did not want to do it. For her proposal, I could have purchased another home. When I told her my original budget she could have just said no way, it isn't happening for what you want to spend. But she didn't; she took my money for the design and then tried to sell me something that I didn't want. And in the process used up a lot of my valuable time.

At that point I gave up, thinking the kitchen was never going to happen. Then, Stewart came up with some ideas. We spoke to our handyman who said he could do it for us. And thus the kitchen actually began; not at all what I initially thought I wanted and/or envisioned in the way I envisioned in the timing I envisioned. But in the end, it is truly perfect for this home. I do not consider my time with the original designer wasted nor the money I gave her a bad investment. I realized that I needed that experience to truly define what I did not want. This made me much more open to Stewart's proposal. And the handyman who eventually did the work put his heart and Soul into the project. Plus, he found and corrected many things in our home as we went along. The project was slower and had some glitches, but most contractors would have done the job and called it a day. Our guy took pride in his work, fixed inconsistencies with our home as he found them, and truly helped us clean up the outer representations of our minds. He was a blessing.

### *God's timing, God's way; flexibility. Nothing wasted.*
### *God-Mind Wisdom.*

- Have you been in the position of determining what you do want when faced with what you do not want?
- How many times have you gotten something only to realize you did not want it?
- Is this wasted time, energy and/or money?
- Is it easy to say you wasted time, money and/or effort?

- Do these types of experiences lead you from what you thought you wanted into something you really want?
- How important is it to be flexible when you have your mind and/or heart set on something?
- If you are too rigid is it too easy to miss opportunity?
- Is it easier to blame outer circumstances than take a look at your own mind-pattern?
- Can you blame not having money for not getting what you want?
- Can you thank money for not being there so you are on the most perfect path for you?
- Is it sometimes challenging to accept God's timing and God's way?
- When you feel downtrodden, is it challenging to know without a doubt that you are being refocused to the most correct and beneficial path?
- When you finally give up, is this often when what you most want/need can find its way to you?

I once read that an expert is someone who has made all the mistakes. I keep this statement in mind because I feel like my mistakes/failures/ redirections are what make me so good at what I do. At various stages in my life, I thought I was doing really well and was feeling quite good about my accomplishments. These peaks of feeling like I was doing the correct thing usually were followed by something that felt like a massive failure. Usually, everything has to fall apart before everything can be put together again. What might appear like a mistake or failure most likely is a reward because you did so well at your current level, that your path was cleared for a redirection.

Sometimes redirection can take years by the time you clean up the mess, absorb the lessons and then get up and going again. Of course, the more years you have, the more patience you have for this process because you really have no choice but to keep going. The more years you have, the more mistakes/failures/redirections you have. Every year I have less confidence that I am done with anything; it seems there are always more layers waiting for me to discover. The reward of doing my work is more layers to dig into. I look at people younger than me who think they have so many answers. I was like that, too. With so many mistakes/failures/redirections under my belt, I realize that there never seems to be a final answer to anything. Even if the characters and scenery change, it is only to help me work on all of my mind-patterns that keep splitting open so I can go deeper into them.

My dad is 30 years older than I am; I think about how much more I will know when I am his age; how many more redirections I will have been through, and how I will view this time period in my life. I definitely have less confidence that I have all the answers but I AM more confident that I am developing the tools that guide me through whatever my mind-pattern brings me.

*Your inner level tools are priceless.*

*God-Mind Wisdom.*

- Did you ever have a time period in your life when you felt confident that you had the answers?
- Has your confidence since been shattered?
- Is shattering your confidence a step to going deeper into Self?
- Does shattering your confidence provide the opportunity for growth?
- Do you keep repeating the same life scenarios except with different people in different locations?
- How deep is each mind-pattern that you are exploring?
- Is the reward for doing your inner work more inner work that becomes increasingly more challenging?
- Do the challenges make you strong?

- Do the challenges force you to develop and hone your inner level tools and techniques?
- Does your inner level work build your Self-confidence to know that you can handle whatever comes your way?
- How important is it to keep your Self-confidence in balance?
- Do you see your Self in those who are younger than you who think they have the answers?
- Do your mistakes/failures/redirections make you an expert?
- As an expert, can you become an even better expert?
- Can a mistake or failure actually be a reward for a job well done to allow you to move deeper into Self?
- Is having your path cleared for redirection ever enjoyable when you feel that you are in a reactive position?
- Even when you are proactively clearing your path, do unexpected issues still put you in that reactive position?
- Are your inner level tools priceless?

## Feeling Useful

Everyone needs to feel useful. Just giving money to people does not encourage them to get up and get going. In fact, with the current plannedemic, some people who are on unemployment say that they are not going back to work. I have been one of those people who worked jobs that I did not like out of necessity. Without the necessity to work, it would have been very easy to stay home and do nothing. I am quite good at keeping my Self entertained. Bored is not in my vocabulary. Sometimes the very jobs that you despised so much at the time are ones that gave you the foundation for moving up into something better. Needing money is the impetus to get out and get uncomfortable.

When my children were little, they always worked here at home at something that made them feel useful, needed and a part of the family.

Before computers were so sophisticated, they alphabetized and filed all my paperwork; they pulled the inventory from the order receipts to ready them for shipping. If they ever complained, I would say things like, "Okay, I'll go do that and you make the dinner" which made them realize that everyone had a job and we all did what we could. They never received an allowance. If they wanted something we discussed their options. When they became old enough to work outside of our home, neither one ever had a bad job. They had jobs that were boring to them, but I explained these were their proving grounds to moving up the ladder. Their employers were testing them for timeliness, ability to follow directions and get along with others, dependability, attitude, and so forth. Sure enough, both boys always moved up the ladder into very nice positions, but first they had to prove themselves on the basic, boring fundamental and foundational requirements of having a job.

Such it is with life. The fundamental and foundational requirements for moving up the Hyperspace/Oversoul ladder can be quite boring, tedious and repetitive. But like everything, you have to do the time to prove your Self worthy to Self, Oversoul and God-Mind. Without these beneath your feet, you get into dangerous territory that can pull you under rather than elevate. The need for money often puts you in positions that force you to face the foundational mind-patterns that you need to move forward in all areas of your life. Without God-Mind Wisdom, it is too easy to throw in the towel, run away and be grateful for handouts.

*There is a greater plan to which you will be privy when you are ready.*
*God-Mind Wisdom.*

- Do you feel best when you feel useful?
- How often do you feel like giving up?
- Is there a difference between taking a helping hand when you need it and living on handouts?

- How easy would it be to walk away from boring, tedious and repetitive work if you didn't have to do it?
- Does boring, tedious and repetitive work give your life stability?
- Is money a major factor in staying at a job you do not like?
- Are there parts of Hyperspace/Oversoul work that you do not like, but you know you need to stay with it?
- What if someone said they would pay you to do boring, tedious and repetitive Hyperspace/Oversoul work?
- After a while, would the money be worth it if you felt you were going nowhere fast?
- Does needing to feel useful surpass your feelings of wanting money?
- While earning money is your motivation for staying at a job you do not like, is it better than doing nothing at all?
- Do you feel like there is a greater plan for which you are preparing?

One of my challenges is that I never lack for ideas and/or motivation to carry them out. This means I have a tendency to be too busy and spread my Self too thin. Sometimes I get depressed because I feel that everything I produce does not always reach the people who need it, when they need it. However, when I discussed this with my Oversoul, I was told to take all my blogs, divide them into subjects and put them into book form to reach more people. As you know, three are now out: *Heights of Health; Heights of Spirituality;* and *Heights of Deprogramming.* Stewart came up with the first title and I carried the theme forward. And my youngest son has produced the most amazing photos in the Cottian Alps along the paths of our Ancient Waldensian ancestors. I am currently working on editing *Heights of Relationships* and the final one this year is *Heights of Wealth.*

I will tell you that the editing is quite tedious, as each volume is around 600 pages. After that, I will take a reprieve, unless directed otherwise. Even when these 5 volumes are complete I will still have enough material for another 4-5 books. I have neglected a lot of other work around the house that needs to be done. My closet, shelves and storage areas have become messy, so they need sorting and organizing. I'm sure I'll be dumping things along the way. Since my Italy and Iceland tours have been postponed to next year due to the plannedemic, I will have "extra" time. Yes, the postponement of these trips put me into a minor depression.

This is the only time of year where I truly put everything aside; no computer, email, outer work, only inner work always with a beautiful group of tour participants doing the same thing. I like being removed from my comfort zone and walking the Ancient Paths filled with Ancient Wisdom. The frequencies there are protected and beyond words. But there is always a higher plan and reason so I trust my Oversoul to put me exactly where I need to be, when I need to be. I guess this summer, I need to be here finishing my books and getting my life in order.

*If you were there you wouldn't be here, doing what needs to be done.*
*God-Mind Wisdom.*

- Are you okay with wherever life puts you?
- Do you get disappointed and even depressed when you are not where you want to be?
- Has anything you wanted to do or places you wanted to go ever been postponed?
- If so, did you utilize your time well or did you mope around?
- Have you ever wanted to do more inner work, but you were directed to do more outer work?
- Does outer work help ground your inner work?

- Can you do too much Hyperspace/Oversoul work and not enough outer level work?
- Do you ever lack for ideas?
- Do you have motivation to carry your ideas forward?
- If you carry your ideas forward are you able to bring your ideas to fruition/completion?
- Is the startup phase exciting and the ending phase exciting while the middle phase can get tedious?
- Do you have patience with tedious outer work?
- How about tedious inner work?
- Is it always important to remember that if you were supposed to be "there" you would be?
- Are you "here" for a reason?

Too often it seems, you find your Self under the tyranny of someone who thinks they know better than you about almost everything. You can be exceedingly challenged to not say what you want to say, but instead, do as the person commands. This is a repetition of parental control. If you never worked this aspect out of your mind-pattern, you are going to draw people to you who are going to act as your parents. Many people resent the real, or perceived, tyrannical control their parents held over them, so your mind-pattern creates others with whom you can work this out. One way or another, you have to move beyond anyone who acts this way. Think of the world on lockdown now, in the middle of this plannedemic.

*When you do not like wherever you are in life, you may be angry at your Soul parent who put you in the position. When these situations happen, you must always correct the inner to change the outer.*

*God-Mind Wisdom.*

- What is in the mind-pattern of anyone who attracts a tyrannical control system?
- Why are people in an enforced lockdown?
- Is their own mind-pattern locked down?
- Is this lockdown another step in Isolation Programming?
- Do the governors who put their states on lockdown play the role of parental control?
- Have you had tyrannical bosses?
- Is this a reflection of parental control?
- Is your Oversoul tyrannical when it puts and keeps you in a situation that you would like to escape?
- Is it challenging to look at a tyrant as a teacher?
- Is it challenging to look at your parents as teachers?
- Is it challenging to look at anyone or anything as a teacher when you feel oppressed in any way?
- Is it easier to blame outer circumstances than spend the diligence required to understand your own inner Deep State that brought about the situation?

### Ownership

Blaming others is always the easy way out of any situation, at least on the surface level. Whatever situation you have attracted, still contains something that you need to learn or you wouldn't be where you are. Even in the current plannedemic lockdown; think about how people have locked down their Spiritual Minds in favor of their Animal Minds. There could not be an outer lockdown without an inner one. Personally, I intend to use my time at home to unlock whatever is hidden/buried within. This is an excellent reminder that somewhere, no matter how large or small, I have inner lockdowns that restrict my outer movement. And also, what I need is "here" otherwise I would be "there".

Taking ownership in this way gives you power. For example, even though I planned the overseas tours, my Oversoul is telling me that what is most correct and beneficial is for me to be home. Technically the situation is beyond my control. I cannot have regrets or be upset about lost time/opportunities. As emotionally disappointed as I was when I postponed the tour, logically I know there is a higher reason. I am determined to take advantage of this new opportunity rather than bemoan what I wanted vs. what I got. Taking responsibility for what you have done throughout your entire life gives you ownership.

*Ownership always gives you power. With that power, you can redirect into effective change.*

*God-Mind Wisdom.*

- Does taking ownership of every life experience give you power?
- If you claim responsibility for your life, does this set you up for proactive, effective change?
- How many times have you wanted to be "there" instead of "here"?
- Is this a form of escapism?
- If you keep escaping from your responsibilities, do you only get continually boxed in until there is no escape at all, ever, until you stay put and learn?
- Do you have any regrets about what you perceive as lost time/opportunities?
- Does taking ownership always mean that wherever you are is the most correct and beneficial place for you to be?
- Can you use the plannedemic lockdown to your benefit instead of your detriment?

- What have you locked down inside of you that restricts your outer movement?
- Is it always possible to use what you got vs. what you wanted, as a catalyst for change?
- If so, do you have to like the situation?
- Or, is liking the situation irrelevant and you only need to proactively use the situation as a stepping stone instead of a block?

Doing this work can bring out the worst in you. Nothing on the surface can truly heal if you have a deep infection feeding it. You have to open up the surface area and start digging. Once you open the infection it can spread as you focus on cleaning it out. If you can't clean it up in time it can consume you; if you are diligent you can eventually eradicate the infection and final healing can commence. So many times people label truly great inner work wrong/bad because negatives pop up along the way. Remember that "negative" does not equal "bad". It may not be pleasant but this doesn't make the experience bad. For example, as you clean out the infection, it may leak out, causing you to become ill. While the illness may be labeled negative it is important to get the infection out. Even though it is unpleasant in the short term, getting ill now is much more desirable than having a long term illness later on down the road.

While you are doing your work, you may think that you should not become ill. Yet, if this is what needs to happen to get the deep infection out, so be it. Being ill at this point is in its own way a badge of honor, not a badge of shame. It is a testament to the deep level work that you are doing. Whenever you get into troubling pockets of any kind within, you may want to judge what you find. Always remember that you feel what you feel, but do your best to pass everything up so that these troubling pockets do not grow and consume you. While this can happen, you have the tools to ensure that they do not.

It is often at this point when people are doing their deepest level work that they often become consumed with whatever it is they are cleaning out. Programming can kick in to tell you that you are "there" so you have no more need of Hyperspace/Oversoul work. Instead of releasing what you are working on, you lose control and it controls you. I have seen numerous clients take this route. This is why you need inner strength and your foundational work in place.

*No matter what tempts you to stop what you are doing, understand the game, and keep moving on the upward elevating spiral of your personal evolution.*

*God-Mind Wisdom.*

- Do you need the balance of positive and negative to reach an objective understanding of whatever you are studying?
- When others see you having a negative experience or reaction, do they label you in unflattering ways?
- Are you supposed to only be/feel positive?
- If God-Mind contains all things and you are a microcosm of the macrocosm, does it make sense that you will have all kinds of experiences?
- Does societal programming say you should only have positive experiences?
- Does societal programming indicate that negative experiences happen if you are a bad person in some way?
- When you are working on balance, does it make sense that you will have negative experiences to balance out the positive and vice versa?
- Do you judge and beat your Self up when you have negative experiences?
- If so, would a better route be to ask why so you can discover the objective reason behind the experience?

- Do negative experiences lead to growth?
- Can negative experiences push you into exponential positive growth?
- Can negative experiences push you into a downward spiral from which it can be challenging to recover?
- Do you always have a choice?

Giving order to your life is essential to your wellbeing. Chaos is only order not yet understood. This means that everything in your life that appears chaotic is not yet understood by you. The best way to understand chaos is to begin to organize it in some way that makes sense to you. The best way to make this happen is to begin with your living quarters. It does not matter how large or small your space is, when it is in chaos you cannot find the forest for the trees. Organizing the chaos creates energetic pathways for your experiences to reach you easier and faster. Of course, it is important to realize that this means the negative as well as the positive. This also means another reason to do your inner level work so as you organize the frequencies you are prepared for whatever comes your way.

This is another example of hidden growth. You have chaos, so you organize. You think you are doing something positive, but something negative happens. Instead of beating your Self up, recognize that creating order out of chaos loosens everything that was in the tangled web. The positive is that you unloosened things. The perceived negative may happen as part of the fallout. This is still a positive because now that this is unleashed you can make choices about how to handle the situation. If you do not know that something exists, you cannot correct it. Knowing that this negative has been hiding within is a huge growth opportunity.

Another example may have to do with your finances. If your frequencies are tied in knots, then it is highly possible that your financial frequency is tied in knots. Money cannot get to you until you organize your frequencies. Organizing your frequencies is extremely challenging for most people because they say they really want to see what is going on, but knowledge can actually be overwhelming. Sometimes it may feel better to have limited choices so you can complain about what you do not have. Remove those limitations and you have no excuses for not doing whatever it is that you think you want to do.

## Positive can be just as scary as negative
## God-Mind Wisdom.

- Is it easy to keep your world in chaos so you do not have to face your own frequencies?
- Does chaos knot your energetic frequencies so you do not have to deal with life?
- Do you think the energetic knots of chaos keep your finances from flowing?
- Does having money open up your choices?
- Can more financial flow create issues?
- Does your financial flow represent your own energetic flow?
- Does straightening out your financial picture straighten out your energetic flow?
- Why do people always think that life should only be positive?
- When something negative happens, are you learning to take it in stride as a part of life rather than use it to beat your Self up?

If you are short on energy, you are going to be short on finances because finances are currency/energy. Anything that depletes your energy depletes your finances. It can be easy to fall into a downward spiral that takes away your motivation for living. While I never lack for ideas, I do have days when I lack motivation. Sometimes I get depressed thinking about what needs to be accomplished vs. the hours in my day. I still press forward on these days, but it seems without the proper motivation I do not have as much energy and I do not get as much accomplished.

Fear takes away people's motivation. Fear of not succeeding; fear of what others will say; fear of not being where you think you should be; fear of not having enough hours in the day. Any negative emotion can put you in a downward spiral that takes away your energy and thus your finances. You are the only one that can infuse you with energy. Exercising infuses me with energy. Even when I do not feel like it, once I get my body moving my whole physical system feels better This then helps to pick up my mood which in turn gives me more energy for my day.

Cleaning always makes me feel better, thus another infusion of energy. Especially cleaning something that I have been avoiding or only thinking about. Anything that you can do to infuse your Self with energy opens the frequency for the outer world to infuse you with energy/currency/finances. You do not need a specific long term plan; all you need is to motivate your Self to take the first step; then the next step; and the next step. Every step you take reveals the next one; every step you take sets the mind-pattern that you are forward moving; you are motivated and you have increasing energy. Energy is nonphysical; currency/money/finances is the physical representation.

*Do what you need to do to anchor the nonphysical into the physical to bring about the results that are most correct and beneficial for you.*

### *God-Mind Wisdom.*

- Is it coincidental that currency is another name for money?
- As money becomes less physical, is the term currency less used?
- If currency becomes an outdated word, does this decrease the financial flow mind-pattern?
- Do you equate your personal energy with financial flow?

- Do negative mind-patterns decrease your energy flow?
- When your energy level decreases what do you do to boost your energy flow?
- Do you have more energy when you have more financial flow?

Financial lack affirms negative mind-patterns, especially low Self-Worth and Self-Punishment. Your low Self-Worth determines that you need to be punished, so you Self-punish by not allowing financial abundance. "Not having" enforces your suffering and pain. Intellectually you know you need financial abundance but your emotions will not allow you to receive what is rightfully yours. Wanting financial abundance is not enough to allow it in. You have to know that you deserve without guilt.

Trace back to the first time you received something when you felt undeserving and/or guilt. Perhaps you begged your parents for a toy, finally wore them down and got what you wanted thrown at you with some unkind words. Maybe as a teen you wanted certain clothes or to go somewhere with friends. You finally got your parents to give in, but you felt undeserving and guilty. Think about other similar events. This means that you associate getting what you want with not deserving it and/or guilt.

When I was quite small I begged my mother to put my hair in braids. She told me it would look ugly. I begged and cried so much that she finally relented, told me how ugly it looked and locked me in our attached garage. I remember banging on the door, begging and pleading for her to let me in and take the braids out. I got what I wanted, but the price was too high to bear. There are other similar events. It has taken me a long time to not look at anything and think "the price is too high". I could not ask for it because the emotional consequences might give me the same feelings of getting what I wanted and then getting locked in the garage.

My mother would not give me the food I wanted. No matter what she fixed, I had to eat it exactly as she fixed it. For example, she made tuna sandwiches with slices of onion and tomato which she then baked. I asked her to please take off the onion and tomato, but she would not. I could not understand this at the time because I thought leaving something off would make her work easier. So, incidents like these imprint you with you do not get what you want; you are not deserving or worthy.

You must search out these types of incidents to determine where the imprinting of low Self-Worth and Self-Punishment began. When the imprinter leaves your life, you take over where he/she left off. You may even pull in someone else to punish you in the same way your parents punished you in addition to your own Self-Punishment.

***Parental dynamics keep repeating in your life until you put a stop to them.***

***God-Mind Wisdom.***

- How do parental dynamics keep repeating in your life?
- Have significant others made you feel undeserving and/or guilty?
- Or in some way punished you at their discretion?
- Did your parents give you something and then make you feel undeserving and/or guilty?
- Did they imprint you to not get what you want?
- Did not getting what you wanted as a child make you feel helpless?
- When you do not get what you want as an adult do you feel helpless?
- How often do you think "the price is too high" when shopping for something?

- When you were a child, was the metaphorical price too high to pay if you got what you wanted?
- Can you remember the first time you received something when you felt undeserving and/or guilty?
- Is not allowing financial abundance a Self-Punishment?
- Do you know how to suffer?
- Do you deserve to suffer?
- Can you open up your financial stream but still not allow Self to receive it?

Regardless of what you say, letting go of your negative space holders is the most challenging thing that you do. You may be upset, uncomfortable and frustrated, but you hold onto your badge of honor with a vengeance. When your entire identity revolves around pain, misery and suffering, you do not know who you are without them. If you let go of what you know, you do not know what will replace it. Most people would rather have what they know than risk not having anything at all. This is why people stay in abusive relationships; it is what they know and for them, it is better than being alone. I have seen more people stay in unhappy relationships because they do not want to be alone. In their case, someone is better than no one. I have seen individuals crying and on the brink of suicide because he/she could not find a partner. Then, they grabbed onto anyone who came along.

People hold onto all kinds of relationships because they do not want to be alone. They hold onto bad jobs because they do not feel they deserve better. They hold onto all kinds of uncomfortable life circumstances because when they let go they are afraid that they will fall. Something is better than nothing in the eyes of most people.

When I was a child I wanted a bicycle for my birthday. I envisioned the perfect one in my mind. I was so disappointed when my parents presented me with an old used, outdated bicycle, but it was better than nothing even though I was embarrassed to be seen on it. My mother used to force me to wear hand-me-down clothes from her friends' daughters. Again, I detested the clothes but obviously, they were better than no clothes at all. Sometimes my mother made clothes out of material that I did not like in designs I did not like. But, I wore them. I think I protested one time and after that, I learned never to open my mouth again about my clothes. I had to make do with the negative because whatever positive I envisioned never happened. I learned to make do, hold on tight to what I did not want even it if was only barely better than nothing. These types of experiences set the imprinting for the rest of your life.

The child within cannot envision beyond what is in front of him/her in this moment. The child within can only see the present moment and is fearful of the unknown. The adult has faith and trusts the process, knowing that anything is possible when timing and circumstances are correct. As you grow up your child within so that he/she merges with the mature Soul-Personality, you can begin letting go with one hand to grab onto something better coming your way. This all may sound very simple and in the beginning, casting aside what you do not want can be relatively easy. But the deeper you go, the more you find that you are not willing to divest your Self of; you find areas of Self that served you well, it is what you know so you hold onto it for dear life.

*Now is the time to trust the process.*

*God-Mind Wisdom.*

- Are some things easy to let go of and some are not?
- Are some people easy to let go of while others are not?
- When you do not know what the future holds, have you fought against change?
- Would you rather have a broken relationship than no relationship at all?

- Do you need Self-Confidence and Self-Worth to let go of the old to create an energetic pathway for something new/different?

- Were you given what you perceived as negatives as a child and were forced to hold onto your negatives?

- Do you realize how never getting what you want as a child follows you into adulthood?

- Or always having to adjust to a negative puts you in this holding pattern for finances, jobs and relationships?

- Are you challenged to let go of what you have because of Deep State buried fear says something is better than nothing?

- Do you fear having nothing?

- How challenging is it to trust the process that brings you what you need when you need it?

- Is it okay to tell your Oversoul and God-Mind that if they want you to have nothing, then that is what you will have?

- Can you tell your Oversoul and God-Mind that you will let go of what you no longer need knowing that what you do need will fill the empty space?

- Can you let go and trust the process of Source at all times?

As you release what you no longer need, it is imperative that you fill the empty spaces with what you do need. Otherwise, you pull the old back simply because this is what you know. This is like the person who breaks off a relationship with a significant other. The void is too great for the person to handle, so he/she makes up with his/her partner and the toxic cycle starts up once again. However, if you break up with your partner and then fill the void with new activities, you are less likely to go back to the old, toxic relationship.

As you release to your Oversoul what you no longer need, do your best to mentally reset your mind-pattern to create the positives that you want. Whatever it is, dream it, feel it, be it, luxuriate within wealth and prosperity. Allow every cell to vibrate with the Limitless Positive Abundance of the God-Mind. Always end your visualizations with "its equivalent or something better" and/or "Thy will be done". If you try to push your own ideals through, it is possible that you are not ready for them. It is also possible that there might be something better waiting, but if you are set on what you want you can pull in something lesser rather than allow something greater to find its way to you. If you can visualize it, it already exists somewhere.

*Allow your Oversoul and God-Mind to filter your mind-pattern so you receive what is most correct and beneficial in the most correct and beneficial way/timing.*

### God-Mind Wisdom.

- Are you always mindful to be careful what you wish for, because you may get it?

- Do you allow your Oversoul and God-Mind to filter whatever it is that you want?

- Is it challenging to realize that there could be something even better than you can visualize waiting to come to you?

- Do you give Source the final say when it comes to getting what you want?

Remembering to fill the void left by your release work is something that seems to be easy for people to forget to do. This is often due to programming kicking in as well as Self-sabotage that sets you up to go backward instead of forward. For most people, the greater the positive reward the scarier the reward might seem. When I was offered a job at Boise State University I was depressed to the point of being suicidal. My ex-husband practically forced me to take the job or I would not have even applied. Yet, it was this job that gave me the courage and Self-confidence to finally leave that relationship. I was well-positioned to leave that relationship or I would not have received the job offer. I so dreaded what was coming I was challenged not to kill my Self;

the first time I had felt so suicidal in many years. If I would have committed suicide, that would have been the end of the road for me. I cannot tell you how tempted I was to get it all over with.

I begrudgingly took the job and I absolutely loved it. However, the job highlighted the difference between how I was treated at work vs. how I was treated at home. I could no longer live with such a strong dichotomy so I began plotting my escape. Within a year, my mind-pattern pulled Stewart into my life and I managed to escape. You can be extremely challenged to see a different linear future for your Self. Even when it presents it Self, programming and Self-sabotage are extremely strongly imprinted. You can have tons of opportunities waiting, even ones you may see, but actually allowing what you have created to come in to your life can be emotionally overwhelming. As you know, positive emotions can overwhelm you to the point of tears as easily as negative emotions. The pendulum swings from one extreme to the other, catching you off guard without words, only emotion. You are great at creating.

*Be great at accepting your magnificent creations.*

*God-Mind Wisdom.*

- Is thinking about what you would like the same as the actual experience?
- Can you create in your mind, but somehow cannot transfer the nonphysical creations into physical reality?
- Have you been so overwhelmed with positive emotions that you have cried?
- Are happy tears emotionally confusing?
- Are programming and Self-sabotage excuses for not moving forward?
- How tempting is it to go back to the known vs. stretch into the unknown?

- Is it easier to talk about seeing the magnificence of your Soul vs. actually seeing it?
- Are you positioning your Self to allow your Oversoul and God-Mind to fill the voids for you?
- Can you be richly rewarded by opportunities that may practically scare the life out of you?
- Do you deserve positive rich rewards?
- Are you great at accepting your magnificent creations?

## AFFIRMATIONS—SOURCE IS WEALTH

Yes, money is a wonderful tool to have in this reality. However, there is much that you cannot buy, regardless of the money you have. And, in times of crisis, there are commodities much more valuable than money. Expand your definition of Wealth to always have what you need, when you need it.

*Source provides all that I need.*

*Being provided for is Wealth.*


*Source determines struggle.*

*Struggle is Wealth.*


*Source directs me.*

*Direction is Wealth.*


*Source knows my capabilities.*

*My capabilities are Wealth.*


*Source knows my proclivities.*

*Awareness of my proclivities is Wealth.*


*Source gives me a variety of experiences.*

*My experiences are Wealth.*

*Source provides negative lessons.*
*Negative lessons are Wealth.*

*Source provides positive lessons.*
*Positive lessons are Wealth.*

*Source puts me exactly where I need to be.*
*Being where I AM is Wealth.*

*Source provides the opportunity to gain knowledge.*
*Knowledge is Wealth.*

*Source provides the opportunity to choose correctly.*
*Correct choices are Wealth.*

*Source demonstrates wisdom.*
*Wisdom is Wealth.*

*Source is Intangible Wealth.*
*Source is my Intangible Wealth.*

*Source turns Intangible Wealth into Tangible Wealth.*
*Wealth is Tangible.*

*Source is ever-present.*

*My Wealth is ever-present.*

*Source protects.*

*Protection is Wealth.*

*Source is safety.*

*Safety is Wealth.*

*Source is health.*

*Health is Wealth.*

*Source supports me.*

*Support is Wealth.*

*Source gives questions.*

*Questions are Wealth.*

*Source gives answers.*

*Answers are Wealth.*

*Source gives me guidance.*

*Guidance is Wealth.*

*Source provides balance.*
*Balance is Wealth.*

*Source provides ingenuity.*
*Ingenuity is Wealth.*

*Source provides courage.*
*Courage is Wealth.*

*Source provides Solace.*
*Solace is Wealth.*

*Source funds my life.*
*Source funding is Wealth.*

*Source feeds my Soul.*
*Soul-food is Wealth.*

*Source strengthens every aspect of my Being.*
*Strength is Wealth.*

*Source is expansion.*
*Expansion is Wealth.*

# Addendums

# Creating Your Arke

Most people are familiar with the "*Ark of the Covenant*" referred to in the Bible, as well as know about the extensive global search that has kept explorers busy for decades. By focusing world attention on this specific ark, no one stops to realize that every person is an ark unto his/herSelf. An ark simply anchors in energetic energy streams to create a battery of energy built for a specific purpose. The physical body of a person anchors in a specific energy stream into this physical reality. Think of a free-flowing river flowing through this reality. Wherever there is a person, this free-flowing river passes through in a specific order to allow the physical body to exist.

Things also anchor energy streams into this reality. Conventional education teaches of animate and inanimate objects. However, when you look at anything, it has an energy field. Looking beyond the energy field, you see that objects, too, have energy streams that pass through them. In reality, there is no such thing as an inanimate object. This false teaching leads you away from the true purpose of things. In fact, many people believe that to possess things is not a spiritual way of life. Conventional churches lead people away from earthly possessions, directing their attention to heavenly/spiritual pursuits.

Most people who are taught this way follow this imprinting, not recognizing what is in front of their noses—the very fact that the churches themselves are exceptionally wealthy with many things, the likes of which are beyond the comprehension of most people. People believe that the church should have these things but they should not. In fact, many people donate a large share of their income and time to build their church. They look at what the church has with pride while denying themselves and often their families the same material possessions that the church has. Unbeknownst to the majority of people, the churches collect these things to create their own ark of power. If the people give to the churches, museums, and other areas considered to be in the public domain, then the wealth is taken out of the hands of the lower classes and continually kept in the hands of the global elite.

When these public organizations are in need of funding, they often put part of their collections up for sale. Only the very wealthy have the funds to purchase these things. So, bit by bit, step by step, all that anchors valuable energy streams are removed from the public, falling into the hands of a self-selected few, while the public increasingly settles for owning cheap imitations.

By realizing that things are not inanimate objects, you begin to understand the true, intrinsic value of what is considered material possessions. Each material possession has its own frequency, or energy stream, that passes through it. When you take specific energy streams and arrange them in a specific way, you create a new energy stream that allows specific events to occur.

This is exactly what the Illuminati does when it creates rituals. There is a specific goal that needs to be accomplished so specific energy streams to bring the goal into fruition are combined. There is a recipe to follow to make this happen. This includes mixing the energy streams of specific people, geographic locations, and things. This is done in conscious awareness.

You create your own energy ark every day, except most people do not do this in conscious awareness. Every piece of clothing you wear has an energy stream flowing through it. How you arrange your clothing on your body creates a specific ark of energy. Every piece of food has an energy stream running through it. Every object in your house has an energy stream.

Your home is one giant ark that if properly put together, creates an extremely powerful energy ark. And, if you create your home in a geographic location that is in alignment with your frequency, the boost of this battery pack is even more powerful. Once you extend your concepts beyond the body, beyond your energy field, and start exploring energy streams, you realize how much more there is to the overall force of Creation. You also understand why it is important that everything you do is done with purpose, intent, understanding and awareness. As you learn to gain this knowledge through experiential learning, rather than through linear learning, the process is fantastically enhanced. Modalities such as feng shui begin to teach you about creating arks, but again, your actions are led by what the book says. This leads your attention outward instead of inward.

- What if you like your desk in a specific position but the book says this is not good?
- What if you are correct and the book is incorrect?

Learn about your own energy stream, and study the energy streams of everything that is around you. Pay attention to how you feel, and study under the direction of your Oversoul. Your Self-confidence in your own answers is often undermined by the imprinting of linear learning. Release that imprinting to open up to your true method of learning. Recognize the distractions that pull you outward. Walk away from them. Regardless of how tempting they look, they serve you only in the moment. Go for what pulls you up into your natural and unique evolutionary state. Be purposeful and conscious in all that you do. Create your own energy ark that pulls to you absolutely everything that you need to comfortably exist in this reality, from mind-patterns to people, places, and things. Ignore the imprinting that would have you do otherwise. When you finally do this, the power of that imprinting loses its hold. You are finally free to express who you came here to be and to experience what this reality holds for you.

# Wealth

*By Stewart A. Swerdlow*

Everything is a frequency and a formula. That is how The Absolute created All That Exists. Thought energy has a vibration and resonance called frequency. In humans, there are 1.4 million frequencies that constitute the body, mind and soul. Missing or weak frequencies create either physical or nonphysical issues. This means that your mind-pattern is not in proper order. What you think is projected onto the physical world that then reflects it back to you. Use the analogy that thoughts are like the film in a movie, the brain is the projector, and physical reality is the screen. If you do not like the movie playing, you need to change the film, meaning the way you think.

The mind-pattern of wealth develops within each Soul-Personality from the moment of creation. It is built up and knocked down with each incarnation and experience. It ultimately reflects issues of Self-Worth, Self-punishment, and Self-sabotage. When you are raised to believe that you are worthless, you will not attract finances. If you have lifetimes where you perceived lack and did not correct that mind-pattern, you will experience poverty or a need for more income. The best way to release a mind-pattern of lack and low Self-Worth is to do the *Golden Altar* release work exercise as outlined in **Hyperspace Helper**:

> Balance your T-Bar archetype and take a few cleansing breaths. Center the consciousness in Royal Blue and the rest of the body goes into a Gold color. Visualize a golden altar in front of you—it can look like anything you need an altar to look like. On the altar you place a person that you need to forgive and release; start with the father figure. From your heart chakra to the heart chakra of that person, you connect with a golden energy line between the two of you. Then say the following:

*I forgive you and release you, from all negative experiences between us, now and in the past, whether real or imagined. I forgive you and release you.*

> As you say the last line, visualize the person fading off of the altar in a flash of Violet. Then you can put the next person on and repeat the exercise. You might do your mother next. But, no matter how many people you place on the altar, you always put your Self on last and forgive and release your Self. When you fade your Self off of the altar, put your Self in Brown.

You will probably need to do this exercise several times with the same people. One day, weeks, or months from now, you will do the exercise, but will not be able to see the person on the altar anymore. They will not materialize. When this happens, you will know that you have released the image from the mind-pattern. Then, everyone in your life right now who is reflecting that mind-pattern for you will either change the way they deal with you, or they will not be in your life anymore.

Over the weeks and months that you do this work, you will see certain people leaving your life, and others coming in. Those who come in will be more accepting of you unconditionally, and more permanent.

Do The *Child Within* exercise and Oversoul release work from **Hyperspace Helper** and **Decoding Your Life**. This is like physical exercise, the more you do the better the results. Be consistent and persistent. You are the only one who can control this work. Learn and do Clear Energy work and incorporate that into your release work, as well as with the merger with all alternative selves in every universe where you exist, where you have the most perfect and unconditionally loving relationships in all categories of life.

There are many issues related to financial blockages. You already know about emotional abandonment issues that cause you to attract conditions that perpetuate the mind-pattern of not deserving what is abundant and prosperous in life. These are related to low Self-Worth, Self-punishment and Self-sabotage. Of course, you need to do Golden Altar release work, grow up the Child Within and Oversoul Communication on a daily basis to correct the mind-patterns. In addition, Brown X out the words that prevent you from achieving financial goals.

Most people entered into this incarnation with the purpose of completing what they know and creating based upon that. The triangle is a perfect symbol for you to use to manifest your financial goals. You are to tie up loose ends in this incarnation and finish what you have started. In Humanity, there is a tendency to do things too quickly. You are always looking for more choices, which scatter your ability to concentrate on one goal. Do one major project at a time, complete it, then move on to the next one. Humans are very creative and spiritual. Enhance those energies in any new career. There is a healing energy inherent in your DNA, so perhaps consider a career in alternative healing techniques or some related business to that category. This will increase income. Most humans have a frequency that shows unstable tendencies so they do not remain consistent in goals or pathways to achieve them. You need to stay focused on what you want to accomplish and not deviate from that goal.

Deprogramming is important because activations can block progress and keep you stuck and down. Outpicture your perfect financial situation mentally, then place the image in Brown, then your Self in Brown. Release it to your Oversoul. Balance your T-Bar Archetype and center at your pineal gland in Royal Blue. Visualize the Silver Infinity Archetype above your Crown Chakra and the Golden Aleph above that. Next, place a Brown Merger/Self-Integration Archetype through each of the 7 Chakra Bands as well as through the legs. Then say the following:

*I merge with all of my alternate selves in every universe where I exist where I AM financially secure and have abundance and prosperity at all times.*

Do the above exercise three times per day. Go to Brown after each session.

### Kabbalah Methodology

You can also use the 72 Names of God, which are energetic Holy formulas that increase a particular frequency. Name Frequency #45 is connected to the Power of Prosperity.

Hebrew letters, right to left: Samech, Aleph, Lamed

Say this Name Frequency as Sah, Ahl, Lah

Meaning: The Power of Prosperity. (Control ego to summon the forces of prosperity.)

Meditation: I acknowledge that the Light of the creator is the ultimate source of all prosperity and well-being. With this Name, I summon the forces of prosperity and sustenance and ask for the strength to keep my ego in check when the other checks start rolling in. https://freemindparadigm.wordpress.com/2015/01/23/kabbalistic-72-names-of-god-45/

Another way to utilize this Name Frequency is to sit quietly, then hold this Name Frequency at your pineal gland in White Hebrew letters. Simply hold this image for 20 or more minutes, at least once per day. You may see the image change or other images appear. You might even receive memories and experiences that need to be released that have been holding back your prosperity.

You can also invoke Ofriel, the Angel of Wealth and Prosperity. As you do your daily prayers, which should be at least 3 times daily, ask Ofriel in the Name of YHVH to provide you with better finances which in turn you will share with those in need as directed by your Oversoul and God-Mind. Selfless attitudes open financial flows, but you must always give as is most correct and beneficial for all involved.

An ancient Kabbalistic method to promote income is to visualize the Hebrew letter Gimmel at your right ear in White:

**Frequency Activator Numbers**

You can use Frequency Activator Numbers to renew, rebuild, or add to the frequencies that you may be missing in your mind-pattern. Say the following Frequency Activator Numbers out loud 7 times each day, 3 times per day. They will resonate with your energy and your DNA instructions, putting back and/ or activating the instructions for what you wish to have in your life.

If you stumble verbally on a number, stop, then start over again until you say the number properly for the correct amount of times. After a couple of weeks, you may feel that the number is now set. When that occurs, you can either stop saying it or say it less frequently. Once the frequencies are set into your energy field, you may feel the need for a new set of frequency numbers.

| | |
|---|---|
| Financial Abundance | 229578589 |
| Earning Money | 374685812 |
| Prosperity | 346325845 |
| Confident of Prosperity | 87467894 |
| Greater Financial Success | 48573847399 |
| Increase Self-Worth | 42688843678 |
| Open Up Future Finances | 36466878387 |

These numbers were determined by a nuclear physicist, assisted by an engineer who has tested and verified the frequencies on the human body. There are many more numbers related to wealth and prosperity, but these should keep you motivated and wealthy! Give them time as you need to change your mind-patterns and maintain a high Self-Worth at all times. As a Child of God, you deserve all the positive abundance and prosperity of the universe.

# Glossary

## A

**ACTIVATION:** When a program is brought to full function.

**AFFIRMATION:** A statement that defines a course of action, or a state of inner being; repeating words many times by thinking, speaking, or writing it to bring new avenues of action into your conscious mind.

**ANIMAL MIND:** Located at the solar plexus and controlled by the Reptilian brainstem; controls the physical body; in charge of fight or flight.

**AURA:** Your personal energy field.

**ALIEN:** A physical being from another planet.

**ALTER:** Section or compartmentalized personality within a programming matrix.

**ANDROGYNOUS:** Male and female combined without sexual distinction.

**ARCHETYPE:** Symbol or glyph from hyperspace or mind-patterns.

**ASTRAL PLANE:** The border zone between physical reality and hyperspace.

# B

**BEAR FREQUENCY ARCHETYPE:** Increases protective nature; enhances introversion for self-study; best for males.

**BISEXUAL:** Sexually desiring both males and females.

**BREASTS ARCHETYPE:** Enhances healthy breasts for Men and Women.

# C

**CANCELLATION ARCHETYPE:** Removes anything unwanted.

**CENTER:** Your center is aligned along your spine, providing a safe space from which to work; you pull yourself into it by willing yourself into it.

**CEREMONY:** Gathering to celebrate or honor an entity or Illuminati holiday.

**CHAKRA BAND:** Energy center of the body and encompassing area.

**CHAKRAS:** Along the human spinal column there are main nerve bundles called ganglions, which are esoterically called "chakras," a word that means "wheels" in Sanskrit. They form along the "S" curve of the spine, which looks like a snake. For this reason the chakra system is referred to as "Kundalini," the Sanskrit word for snake.

**COLLECTIVE CONSCIOUS MIND:** The body of space that contains the accumulated known knowledge of humankind.

**COLLECTIVE UNCONSCIOUS:** The body of space that contains the accumulated thoughts of humankind; these established thought patterns directly affect what you move through today.

**COMMUNICATION ARCHETYPE:** Speaking up as appropriate.

**CONSCIOUS MIND:** Contains your present.

**CONSTRUCT:** Similar to a physical object created in the programming matrix to work with the alter in a specific function.

# D

**DEPROGRAMMING:** Techniques to block and/or remove mind-control/programming.

**DIRECT AWARENESS:** To know by experiencing the knowledge.

**DNA SEQUENCES:** This refers to the DNA sequences opening up in the body, which is a form of Kundalini activation. DNA codes are the instructions that tell your body what to do and be. Some instructions you are running at birth. These dictate that you will have blue eyes, two legs, two arms, etc. Others activate later in life, such as health conditions, ability to play music, sing, etc.

**DOLPHIN FREQUENCY ARCHETYPE:** Eases mental shifting into hyperspace.

# E

**EMOTIONAL BALANCE ARCHETYPE:** Obtains healthy emotional balance by balancing left and right hemispheres of the brain.

**ENERGY:** A physical substance consisting of shape, weight, consistency, and color.

**ELF:** Extra low frequency generally related to microwaves for mindcontrol purposes; energy.

**ET (EXTRATERRESTRIAL):** Borderline physical/non-physical beings not bound to our reality.

**EXPANSION ARCHETYPE:** Increases and expands goals and desires.

# F

**FEMALE ORGASM ARCHETYPE:** Removes female frigidity; increase sexual responsiveness.

**FREQUENCY:** A rate of vibration that distinguishes one flow of energy from all other flows.

# G

**God-Mind:** Neutral energy; All That Is.

**Golem:** Human animal created from mud; animated by a controller.

**Group-Mind:** Formed when vibrations band together.

# H

**Habit Response:** An established pattern of behavior that allows you to react to any given situation without thinking, whether physical or mental. It can be positive, negative, or neutral.

**Happiness Archetype:** Establishes happiness.

**Horizontal Experience:** Pulls you out into similar growth.

**Hyperspace:** A region of consciousness that exists outside of linear space and time.

# I

**Illuminati:** Member or associate of one of the 13 ruling families on Earth.

**Illusion:** The way you perceive things to be.

**Individualized Consciousness Archetype:** Helps you rise out of the Group-Mind into Your Own connection with Mind and Personal your Oversoul and God-Mind.

# K

**Know by Knowing:** To understand through direct awareness; to understand the feeling of an experience.

**Knowledge:** Information.

# L

**Language of Hyperspace:** The Original Language that emanates from the Mind of God consisting of color, tone, and archetype (symbol).

**LEADERSHIP ARCHETYPE:** Installs Self-Leadership.

**LION FREQUENCY ARCHETYPE:** Increases your direct awareness to God-Mind power.

**LOGOS CHRISTOS ARCHETYPE:** Healing generator on specific body locations.

**LOVE:** Neutral energy that emanates from God-Mind that does not discriminate.

**LYRAE:** Star system in the Milky Way Galaxy that is the origin point for all humans.

## M

**MACROCOSM:** God-Mind; All That Is; the larger picture of everything.

**MALE ORGASM ARCHETYPE:** Removes impotence; increases virility.

**MATRIX PROGRAMMING:** The structure in the mind that facilitates mind-control; 13 x 13 x 13, which equals 2,197 compartments.

**MEDITATION:** A process that moves you beyond words and connects you with silence, the level of feeling; the listening from which information is gathered; centered in the right brain.

**MENTAL BALANCE ARCHETYPE:** Creates mental balance in all areas.

**MERGING WITH ASPECTS OF ALTERNATIVE SELVES ARCHETYPE:** Bring current goals to fruition by merging with your Self in the Eternal Now.

**MICROCOSM:** You; a world in miniature.

**MIND-PATTERN:** Blueprint of a persons' thoughts.

## N

**NEGATIVE:** Negative is not "bad," but merely a condition that exists; the opposite of positive, which explains another part of the same experience.

**NEW BEGINNINGS ARCHETYPE:** Start new projects, relationships, health, finances.

**NEW WORLD RELIGION:** Global religion.

**NEW WORLD ORDER (NWO):** Global government dictatorship being created by the Illuminati.

# O

**OBJECTIVE LISTENING:** Listening and evaluating without judgment or criticism.

**OBJECTIVE OBSERVING:** Watching and evaluating without judgment or criticism.

**OVERALL HEALING ARCHETYPE:** Heals body, mind, and soul.

**OVERSOUL:** Neutral energy that comes out of God-Mind; your Oversoul is to you what your Earth parents are to your body. Your Oversoul is your point of origin out of God-Mind.

**OVERSOUL ARCHETYPE:** Your Point of Origin out of the God-Mind.

# P

**PINEAL GLAND:** Organ at the center of the head.

**POSITIVE:** Positive is not better than negative, but is merely a condition that exists; the opposite of negative, which explains another part of the same experience.

**POWER ARCHETYPE:** Increases personal power via your mental abilities.

**PRAYER:** Request that affects the results of meditation; centered in the left-brain.

**PREGNANCY ARCHETYPE:** Increases fertility; maintain healthy pregnancy.

**PREGNANCY PREVENTION ARCHETYPE:** Cancels your fertility.

**PROACTIVE LEARNING:** Active learning; gathering knowledge before an experience occurs.

**PSYCHIC ENERGY:** Your personal energy; it flows back and forth, and is horizontal.

# R

**REACTIVE LEARNING:** Passive learning; gathering knowledge after an experience occurs.

**REALITY:** The way things really are; it may vary considerably from your perception of the way you think things are.

**REJUVENATION ARCHETYPE:** Enhances physical, mental, emotional, spiritual rejuvenation.

**RELEASE & RESOLVE PAST ISSUES ARCHETYPE:** Cleans out what you no longer need.

**RELATIONSHIPS ARCHETYPE:** Improves and enhances people connection.

**REPTILIAN:** A being with lizard-like characteristics from either the inner Earth or Draco star system; colonized Lemuria.

# S

**SELF-INTEGRATION ARCHETYPE:** Brown Merger Archetype; merges all parts of Self into one; great deprogramming aid.

**SHAPESHIFTER:** A person who physically changes from one species to another.

**SILENCE:** The deepest level of inner awareness; the level of feeling; you connect with your Oversoul and God-Mind within silence.

**SIMULTANEOUS EXISTENCE:** All lifelines occurring at the same moment in the Eternal Now.

**SPIRITUALITY:** A state of inner being.

**SPIRITUAL & INTUITION CONNECTION ARCHETYPE:** Improves conscious connection with your Oversoul and God-Mind.

**SOUL-PERSONALITY:** Individual strand of an Oversoul.

**SUBCONSCIOUS MIND:** Contains your memories, moment-by-moment, lifeline-by-lifeline.

**SUB-PERSONALITY:** A group of similar emotions that becomes strong enough to develop its own consciousness; a sub-personality is not you, but it is a part of you.

**SUPERCONSCIOUS MIND:** Provides the direct link to your Oversoul and God-Mind.

## T

**T-BAR:** Archetype emanating from the pineal gland relating to balance

**TRIGGER:** Sensory input that opens a program.

## U

**ULTIMATE PROTECTION ARCHETYPE:** Protects whatever you desire.

**UNIVERSAL ENERGY:** Energy that is available to everyone; using it allows you to keep your psychic energy; it flows up and down, and is vertical.

**UNIVERSAL LAW:** Rules and regulations that pervade all creation; emanates from God-Mind.

## V

**VERTICAL EXPERIENCE:** Pulls you up into new growth.

**VIBRATION:** Frequency rate of an energy.

**VIBRATORY IMPRINT:** Accumulated feelings of like experiences; they cause you to react to your experiences of today through your accumulated feelings of yesterday.

**VISUALIZATION:** Creating a mental scenario that can be manifested either mentally or physically; centered at the pineal gland.

## W

**WEALTH & PROSPERITY ARCHETYPE:** Increases finances.

**WISDOM:** Knowledge applied.

**WISDOM ARCHETYPE:** Enhances your correct use of knowledge.

**WOLF FREQUENCY ARCHETYPE:** Enhances family relationships.

# Y

**YOU:** Individualized neutral energy.

# Index

Suriname  27, 241, 274, 428

## T

T-Bar  172, 219, 427, 458
T-Bar Archetype  172, 458, 622
The system  160, 339
Toxic people  101, 103, 104
Travel Lies  23
True Reality  4, 72, 84, 131, 496, 570, 571
True World History  4, 162

## U

Ultimate healing  59
Unconditional Love  16, 191, 192, 193, 421,
    558
Universal Income  242
Universal Law  93, 94, 169, 216, 410, 422,
    423, 427, 443
Universal Source  483

## V

Victim-mentality  79, 393, 458
Victims  30, 100, 195, 393, 394, 401, 520
Violet  574, 577, 620
Visualize  54, 56, 134, 199, 316, 364, 374,
    605

## W

Waldensians  162, 163, 384, 391
Warrior Programming  85
Wealth  150, 151, 152, 156, 159, 160, 218,
    236, 241, 247, 262, 284, 286, 294, 298,
    305, 306, 307, 316, 317, 326, 346, 421,
    422, 429, 431, 432, 433, 434, 435, 447,
    477, 479, 480, 482, 521, 556, 564, 604
Wisdom  110, 134, 143, 147, 246, 260, 370,
    472, 549, 609